LATIN ALIVE

In *Latin Alive,* Joseph B. Solodow tells the story of how Latin developed into modern French, Spanish, and Italian, and deeply affected English as well. Offering a gripping narrative of language change, Solodow charts Latin's course from classical times to the modern era, with a focus on the first millennium of the Common Era. Although the Romance languages evolved directly from Latin, Solodow shows how every important feature of Latin's nature and development is also reflected in English. His story includes scores of intriguing etymologies, along with many concrete examples of texts and studies, scholars, anecdotes and historical events, observations on language, and more. Written with crystalline clarity, this is the first book to tell the story of the Romance languages for the general reader and to illustrate so amply Latin's many-sided survival in English as well.

Joseph B. Solodow is Professor of Foreign Languages at Southern Connecticut State University and Lecturer in Classics at Yale University. He is the author of *The Latin Particle Quidem* and *The World of Ovid's "Metamorphoses,"* and he received the Modern Language Association's Scaglione Translation Prize for his rendering of G. B. Conte's history of Latin literature into English, *Latin Literature: A History.*

LATIN ALIVE

THE SURVIVAL OF LATIN IN ENGLISH AND THE ROMANCE LANGUAGES

JOSEPH B. SOLODOW

Southern Connecticut State University
Yale University

CAMBRIDGE
UNIVERSITY PRESS

CAMBRIDGE UNIVERSITY PRESS
Cambridge, New York, Melbourne, Madrid, Cape Town, Singapore,
São Paulo, Delhi, Dubai, Tokyo

Cambridge University Press
32 Avenue of the Americas, New York, NY 10013-2473, USA

www.cambridge.org
Information on this title: www.cambridge.org/9780521734189

First published 2010

Printed in the United States of America

A catalog record for this publication is available from the British Library.

Library of Congress Cataloging in Publication data
Solodow, Joseph B.
Latin alive : the survival of Latin in English and the Romance languages / Joseph B. Solodow.
p.   cm.
Includes bibliographical references and index.
ISBN 978-0-521-51575-7 (hardback) – ISBN 978-0-521-73418-9 (pbk.)
1. Latin language – History.   2. Latin language – Influence on Romance.   3. Latin language –
Influence on English.   4. Romance languages – History.   I. Title.
PA2057.S65   2009
470.9–dc22   2009022592

ISBN 978-0-521-51575-7 Hardback
ISBN 978-0-521-73418-9 Paperback

This book is dedicated to those teachers who earliest and most deeply fomented in me the love of languages and literature.

To the men: my father, Philip Solodow, who in the course of migrating from his native Russia to the United States became acquainted with Yiddish, Russian, Hebrew, Polish, German, and English; Aaron Krumbein, Brooklyn Jewish Center, Brooklyn, New York; Jack Weiss, Public School 61, Brooklyn; George Bartelt and Wayne E. Mytty, Erasmus Hall High School, Brooklyn.

And to the women: my mother, Yetta D. Solodow, born in New York City, who loved studying French, German, and Latin, and was always observant of the niceties of language; her cousin, Rose Klepper, a font of learning and encouragement, and of books early treasured; Miss Einsidler, Lefferts Junior High School, Brooklyn; Harriet K. Felder and Grace Denman, Erasmus Hall High School; and, both last and first, my wife, Graziella Patrucco de Solodow, who was born in Argentina and later learned Italian in Peru and then English in the United States, and who is the true *fons atque origo* of this book.

CONTENTS

Contents

PART FOUR: EARLIEST TEXTS AND FUTURE
DIRECTIONS, OR WHERE THE LANGUAGES
DIVERGE

LIST OF MAPS

ACKNOWLEDGMENTS

The amount of the goodwill and assistance from which I benefited while writing this book may not be matched by the quality of the results, but it is still an exceptionally pleasant duty to record my unstinted gratitude to all the friends who helped. Ann Christmann, Henry Gates, Martha German, Erik Urdang, Marshall Clough, Henry Perry, and Ronald Quirk, reviewing early versions of some chapters, encouraged the embryonic project and offered valuable guidance. At a later stage, Elliott Urdang and Michael Maas strongly urged me to take corrective actions, the latter trying to liberate me from out-of-date historical notions, the former helping to direct the presentation toward those for whom I really intended it. Then, when the work was substantially complete, three generous souls were willing to devote their precious, much-appreciated time and effort to reading through the material: Joanne Martin, Marshall Clough (for the second time), and Molly Keller, by obliging me in this way, have effected important changes, making the book far better than it would have been otherwise; Molly in particular gave the entire manuscript the benefit of her most careful and skillful editorial scrutiny. To all of them I extend heartfelt thanks.

The maps were designed and executed by my nephew and god-son, Sergio Patrucco, to whom I am especially grateful: the book would certainly be poorer without these handsome and helpful aids.

Throughout the years I have been engaged in this project, I have been sustained by the confidence, the savvy, and the humor of my agent, Don Gastwirth, and also by the assistance, in the form of time and money, provided by Southern Connecticut State University, and in particular by the Dean of Arts and Sciences, DonnaJean Fredeen. Much is owed to them too.

Acknowledgments

Were it not for the toil of all these folks, the following pages would be more obscure, more unfocused, more inaccurate, more indigestible. Were it not, however, for my wife, Graziella Patrucco de Solodow, these pages would not exist at all. Through her, I first came to know Spanish and Italian; with her help, I created the course in which this work had its origin; as the result of her encouragement, not to say insistence, I undertook to make a book out of that material; and at every stage of its composition she has, with love and toughness bestowed in equal measure, helped it along. Rooted deeply in our past, it is a memorial to the lives and the interests we have shared for nearly forty-five years.

Woodbridge, Connecticut
January 2009

CHAPTER ONE

INTRODUCTION

English Is Not a Cousin to the Romance Languages, But...

This book recounts the fascinating story of how Latin became the modern Romance languages, and it does so for readers who know no language other than English. Such readers, perhaps to their surprise, will be able to follow the story easily, in part because each mention of another language is explained or translated, but chiefly because so much of the story is reflected in English itself.

Latin, the tongue of the ancient Romans, is the direct ancestor and, so to speak, sole parent of a host of languages spoken around the world today. Far from being a dead language, it lives on in them (and in English too) as substantially as our forebears, whose genetic material shapes us, live on in us. The two thousand years that separate the one language from the others have witnessed both remarkable persistence and dramatic, even revolutionary, changes, which raises the question: how is it that the current languages are so similar to Latin and yet so different from it? The notable variations among the current languages are another source of interest: how did it happen that, starting out from the same place, they – French, Italian, and Spanish, in particular – have arrived at such separate destinies? This tale is an entrancing saga, played out against the background of western European history and culture: which historical and linguistic forces, we may wonder, have shaped and driven it?

English is, in fact, only distantly related to Latin and her daughter languages. It belongs to an altogether different language family, the Germanic, which also includes German and Dutch, Danish and Icelandic. It is not a sister to Latin, nor even a second cousin. Nevertheless, the story of English is intimately bound up with that of Latin and the other languages.

After French-speaking Normans invaded England, in the eleventh century, French (and therewith Latin) got blended with the local, Germanic language, Anglo-Saxon (also called "Old English"), creating the mixture that led to

1

English as we know it. Ever since then, Latin, French, and the others have continually affected our language. To French–Latin influence, for instance, is due the basic rule that in English the plurals of nouns are made with -*s*. Myriads of words, half our vocabulary, come from the same sources, and these pages abound in etymologies. An intriguing special case occurs when a single word has entered English twice, once passed along through French, once taken directly from Latin; this results in pairs of words co-existing in the language that are identical in origin but often unrecognizably different in appearance and meaning. Such pairs are *loyal* and *legal*, and *forge* and *fabric* – who would guess that they are related? And who would suspect that behind *reverend*, *agenda*, and *laundry* lurks a common type of Latin adjective? Words like those, in fact, come from Latin adjectives that have the peculiar function of indicating that something needs to be done: a *reverend* is a person who "needs to be revered," an *agenda* is a list of "things that need to be done," and *laundry* comes from a word meaning "what needs to be washed."

English is present everywhere in the book. When recounting, in summary fashion, some necessary historical background, I associate certain crucial events with terms familiar to us, like *rostrum*, *vandal*, *frank*, and *sherry*. *Rostrum*, for instance, earlier "ship's beak," emerged with its current meaning from a decisive naval victory of the Romans over their neighbors in 338 B.C.E. When describing how Latin works, I illustrate key features with examples drawn from the English vocabulary: particular uses of the noun, with *bus* and *subpoena*; various forms of the verb, with *veto*, *habitat*, *debenture*, and *fiat*; participles, with *president*, *script*, and *adventure*; a notorious construction called the "ablative absolute," with *during* and *vice versa*. These are not merely lexical items derived from Latin; they embody and exemplify some feature of Latin grammar. Similarly, *mesa*, *casino*, *sauté*, *cinder*, and the names of the movie *La Strada* and of the painter Hieronymus Bosch encapsulate later developments in the story. Moreover, Latin is still vigorously supplying words to English and the other languages even today. The steady reliance on English is helpful in both directions: I disclose the etymologies of a certain number of familiar English words that are derived from or influenced by Latin, and, at the same time, I use those words to illustrate and render memorable various elements of the story I'm telling.

General qualities of English also emerge from the narrative, highlighted through comparison with the other languages, as points of revealing similarity or difference. A very marked parallel between the history of English and the evolution of Latin into the Romance languages, and still a fundamental characteristic of each today, is the loss of the many separate forms an individual noun might take: nowadays there are just two, singular and plural (*window* and *windows*, for instance), whereas formerly there were far more. English contrasts with the other languages, however, in the rich variety of its verb tenses, its hospitableness towards monosyllabic words, and the relative unavailability of diminutives: words like *cigarette* and *darling* are few. At almost every point, therefore, the story illuminates English and is illuminated by it. I invite readers to recognize unfamiliar aspects of their own language and to view familiar things in a new light – in short, to perceive the distinctive contours of their own language.

Visitors to Rome, the Eternal City, the capital of the Roman Empire, who in addition to all else are drawn there by the excitement of history, experience a unique double pleasure. They are aware that the city, as the stage on which many crucial events have been enacted over more than two and a half millennia, is of unmatched historical significance. But at the same time, they see with their own eyes pieces of that past preserved, monuments representing every phase of the city's history, from Romulus's hut atop the Palatine Hill and the basilica built by Julius Caesar in the Forum, through the early Christian church of St. Mary in Trastevere and the medieval fortress of the Orsini family that had once been a theater, on to the Baroque cupola of the church of St. Ivo and the national pride symbolized by the Tomb of Victor Emmanuel II, united Italy's first king. This book is, in a way, like Rome itself: it displays a grand history in perspicuous monuments that are still to be seen and heard around us – the features of our own language.

The study of words can also illuminate the societies they inhabited. That the Romans did not use native Latin words for "wolf" and "wagon" but imported them from neighboring peoples points to the fact that they were a sedentary, agricultural people, not given to herding or roving. One series of words, from antiquity and the Middle Ages (including *pecuniary* and *chattel*), when properly understood, reminds us of the great worth of cattle in earlier societies; another series, of late ancient and medieval words (including *constable, marshal, henchman,* and *chivalry*), reminds us of the high value formerly attached to those who rode or looked after horses. Such observations are like picturesque postcards of an older world.

In line with my aim of presenting as much of my material as possible through English, I bring the languages and the changes that took place in them right before the reader's eyes in a head-on, hands-on encounter. The languages themselves are not relegated to an appendix, as in other studies of the subject, but are the substance, the very stuff of this one. By no means does the book treat all the developments between Latin, on the one hand, and English, French, Italian, and Spanish, on the other, but those representative topics that are selected for treatment are explained fully and clearly. The reader will be able to follow the story every step of the way.

What I hope will also create a sense of immediacy is the inclusion of evidence. The reader will meet here not only assertions about what happened in this long tale of language change, but also at least some of the proof for those assertions. I explain how ancient Latin was pronounced – and also what enables us to know that. Toward that end, I often cite inscriptions, texts such as tombstones carved in durable material and thus preserved unchanged from antiquity, which through their uncorrected misspellings and other mistakes reveal features of the language in their day. I also draw on literary texts for evidence. A passage from the historian Tacitus, a debate he reports between two German brothers in 16 C.E., handily illustrates one important process by which local elites took up the Latin of the conquering Romans. Augustine in a sermon delivered to his north African congregation around the turn of the fifth century C.E. provides clear evidence that, despite the Roman conquest and the widespread acceptance of Latin, some part of the local population continued to speak the native Phoenician language. Glossaries, which explain a difficult term through a familiar one – primitive dictionaries, in effect – teach us which words were unintelligible to readers or speakers at a certain time and place, and which were current and comprehensible. All these documents arose from recognizable situations of actual people, our fellow-men, which lends human interest to each one.

The book begins, as it must, with Latin. It sets forth its prehistoric origins as an Indo-European language and how, as Roman power expanded, it spread from the area around Rome to the entire Mediterranean basin and beyond; it also explains how the language works. (It does not teach Latin, nor any of the other languages either.) Next, it gives a substantial account of the Romance vocabulary. Then it describes the deeply altered variety of ancient Latin that is the genuine ancestor of the modern languages. The book concludes with a few samples of the earliest texts in each one, ranging in date from the ninth to the thirteenth century.

Although many languages and dialects that exist today are descended from Latin, I deal only with French, Italian, and Spanish. They are the ones most studied and most familiar in the English-speaking world; in the United States, Spanish is an all but official second language. (Although the book assumes no knowledge of any of them, readers who happen to know something about one or another should enjoy it all the more.) Moreover, those languages have made the most substantial contributions to English. French, as already indicated, became an essential component of English nearly a thousand years ago, and its cultural attainments and prestige have assured its continuing influence: think of the *avant garde, lingerie,* and *faux pas.* Italian has given us many items having to do with the arts in particular: *spaghetti, piano, chiaroscuro, balcony.* The Spanish language too is the source of quite a few words (*algebra, stevedore,* and *peccadillo*), a certain number having entered American English from the western part of the country, where Spanish has long been the native speech of many: examples are *mesa* and *Colorado.*

This is not a history of English. The basic structures of the language and its core vocabulary remain true to the Germanic family. This book, though it aims to impart engaging, unfamiliar information about the language, leaves whole areas untouched. It is a very partial account of English, dealing only with those features affected by Latin – which, to be sure, are very numerous. It may even be said that some of Modern English's most pronounced and most characteristic features are untouched by, or liberated from, the influence of Latin. The drastic reduction in the number of a noun's forms has already been mentioned. A remarkable and potent characteristic is the ease with which English words move around from one function to another: adjectives are readily converted into nouns, like *sharps* (implements for drawing blood, or musical notes), or nouns into verbs, like *eyeball* ("you don't need to measure – just eyeball it") and *doctor* ("Hamlet doctored the cocktails"); it appears that just about any noun in the language can be verbed. Those possibilities were limited in Latin, and even today such conversions would be difficult for the Romance languages.

Familiarity with English, however, is all that is needed to follow the journey of Latin into the modern languages. I assume no acquaintance either with the other languages or with the terms of linguistics. Everything foreign I translate and explain, and the few technical terms used I define as the need arises and, ordinarily, through clear English examples. I employ no abbreviations. My hope is that, by these means, I will remove all obstacles to your enjoyment of a story about language change that is of unsurpassed fascination.

Though this book carries no footnotes, it should be understood that virtually everything here, except the presentation, depends on the work of other scholars; some suggestions for further reading will be found at the end. All translations are my own.

PART ONE

LATIN

CHAPTER TWO

THE CAREER OF LATIN, I

From Earliest Times to the Height of Empire

THE PREHISTORY OF LATIN: INDO-EUROPEAN

The subtitle of a recent book identifies Latin as "the world's most successful language," a claim it substantiates admirably (the book is Tore Janson's *A Natural History of Latin*, from 2004). The explanation for Latin's success lies partly in the nature of the language itself, to be sure, but far more in the achievements of those who spoke it – their conscious shaping of the language, the uses they made of it, and especially their success in imposing it upon vast numbers of people. The story of Latin is inextricably bound up with the history of the Romans, who spread their language from a small coastal region in central Italy to the greater part of the world that was known to them. It is the story of how a world empire was created and how, in the end, that empire broke apart, its fragmentation foreshadowing and furthering the process by which Latin dissolved into the variety of modern Romance languages we find today.

Roman history begins with the city's founding, in the eighth century B.C.E. For later periods of that history much of our information comes from written sources. For the earliest periods, before writing, we have to rely heavily on archaeology, the science that uses material remains to reconstruct the lives of societies. Our interest here being language, we may wonder whether something similar is possible for the earliest phases of an immaterial matter like language. The answer, surprising perhaps, is yes. The prehistoric period of Latin's life *can* be reconstructed – and in remarkable detail.

Curious Coincidences?

In Latin the word for "mother" is *mater*. Across the Adriatic and Ionian Seas from Italy, the Greek word for "mother," recorded as early as about 720 B.C.E., is *mater*. Moving still farther east and much farther back in time, to around 1500 B.C.E., we find that in Sanskrit, an ancient language of India, the word is *matar-* (the hyphen indicates that this is the stem of the word, not the word in full). In Old Church Slavonic, a language used by Slavic peoples and attested in the ninth century C.E., the word is *mati*. In Old Irish it is *mathir*. Thus, over a vast area, extending from India to Ireland, and over a period of three and a half millennia, the words for "mother" in a number of languages appear quite similar to one another. Coincidence?

Let us consider now a pair of nouns referring to agricultural life, the yoke that makes it possible for the oxen to draw the plow – and thus for the farmer to till his field – and the mouse that is the farmer's enemy, forever nibbling away at his store of grain. (Though I don't describe how the words were pronounced, the ways they are written are an indication of their similarity sufficient for our purposes. The table should be read across.)

English	Sanskrit	Greek	Latin	Old Church Slavonic
yoke	*yuga-*	*zugon*	*iugum*	*igo*
mouse	*mus-*	*mus*	*mus*	*mysi*

Very much alike, aren't they?

Here next are two common numbers, another fixture of human life. The Welsh language, still spoken on the western edge of Britain, is added to the table; Gothic is also added, the language of a Germanic tribe that entered the Roman Empire during the third and fourth centuries C.E.

English	Gothic	Sanskrit	Greek	Latin	Old Church Slavonic	Welsh
two	*twa*	*dva(u)*	*duo*	*duo*	*dva*	*dau*
three	*threis*	*trayas*	*treis*	*tres*	*tri*	*tri*

The resemblances are strong and striking. As we accumulate examples, the similarities look more convincing, and it becomes more likely that the words do not resemble one another by chance.

Continuing the search for similar-looking words in widely scattered languages, we may turn to a pair of verbs.

English	Gothic	Sanskrit	Greek	Latin	Old Church Slavonic
lick	*-laigon*	*lih*	*leikho*	*lingo*	*lizati*
mix	*(blandan)*	*miks*	*meignumi*	*misceo*	*-mesiti*

(The hyphen before *-laigon* and *-mesiti* signals that they are found only in compounds, just as one might write *-whelm* to indicate that in Modern English the verb in question is found only in a compound like *overwhelm*, not by itself.) With the addition of these examples, which could readily be multiplied, the evidence becomes... overwhelming, and our notion that the similarities among the languages are not accidental seems confirmed.

To the proof given by the vocabulary, another, still more potent proof can be added. This has to do with the morphology of the languages, that is to say, the different forms that a single word can take, for instance, the differing forms of the English verb *to play* seen in *I play*, *she plays*, and *they played*. Here now are two forms of the verb "to bear," which in all these languages means both "to carry" and (from the specialized sense "to carry a child") "to give birth to." Not only is the stem of the word similar from one language to another, but so too are the endings of the verb, the final sounds, which serve to indicate who performs the action of the verb. In this point the other languages differ from ours. Whereas Modern English needs to state the subject of the verb with a pronoun (*you* and *we* in the following example), the other languages do not. That information is included in the verb itself, at the end. To take the Latin forms as examples, the ending *-s* indicates that "you (singular) bear," whereas *-mus* indicates that "we bear." It's as if the words were "bear-you" and "bear-we."

English	Sanskrit	Doric Greek	Latin	Old Church Slavonic	Gothic
you bear	*bhara-si*	*pherei-s*	*fer-s*	*bere-si*	*bairi-s*
we bear	*bhara-mas*	*phero-mes*	*feri-mus*	*bere-mu*	*baira-m*

In this feature too, the similarity is striking, even though English happens not to share it.

And finally, here is the complete present tense of the verb *to be*, which is astonishingly similar from one language family to another. Observe again how the endings identify the subject of the verb.

English	Sanskrit	Doric Greek	Latin	Old Church Slavonic	Gothic
I am	asmi	eimi	sum	esm	im
you are	asi	essi	es	esi	is
he, she is	asti	esti	est	est	ist
we are	smas	eimes	sumus	esm	sijum
you are	stha	este	estis	este	sijuth
they are	santi	enti	sunt	sont	sind

That languages spoken by peoples so widely separated in time and space have such elements in common is altogether extraordinary. What can explain such extensive resemblances of vocabulary, stems, and verb endings?

The Reconstruction of Indo-European

When we pose such a question, we are entering a field called "comparative philology" (or "comparative linguistics"), which is the study of languages in relation to one another – French to Italian, English to German, or Norwegian to Icelandic and Danish. The study of Latin in relation to English and the Romance languages obviously belongs to this field as well.

Comparative philology, it has been said, is based on just one fact and one hypothesis. The fact is that "certain languages present similarities among themselves which are so numerous and so precise that they cannot be attributed to chance and which are such that they cannot be explained as borrowings or as universal features" (Calvert Watkins, *The American Heritage Dictionary of Indo-European Roots*, 2nd ed., 2000, pp. vii–viii). The hypothesis is that such languages are related genetically, that they descend from a single earlier language, a common ancestor. This was fairly obvious, of course, for French and Italian, since the original language, Latin, was well known.

The similarities shared by Latin, Greek, Sanskrit, Old Church Slavonic, Gothic, English, and Welsh, however, escaped notice for a long time. Towards the end of the eighteenth century, as Sanskrit became known to Europeans, it was proposed that those languages were derived from an earlier one of which all direct evidence had been lost. The prodigious linguistic scholarship of the nineteenth century, drawing on the known languages, did much to reconstruct the lost prehistoric original, which has come to be known as Indo-European. The twentieth century sharpened the picture in many significant ways, correcting, refining, and amplifying, and it also identified several previously unknown languages as belonging to the Indo-European group. For about two centuries, therefore, Latin has been recognized as a member of this far-flung family, and its prehistory begins with its origins therein.

Nowadays "Indo-European" is the dominant term for the lost ancestral language. It defines the eastern and western boundaries of the home territory over which the vast family of descendant languages is spoken. (Not that *all* the languages spoken across this territory are Indo-European: Basque, Estonian, Finnish, and Hungarian – just to confine the examples to Europe – do not belong to the family.) The term was coined in the early nineteenth century. Others formerly in use have been discarded over the years. "Aryan" was once a common name for the family, but now is restricted to a set of languages spoken in India and on the Iranian plateau. It came into general discredit through its employment by the Nazis, whom it pleased to trace German ancestry back to Aryan tribes, warlike invaders of the second millennium B.C.E. "Indo-Germanic," although generally abandoned on the grounds of giving undue prominence to the Germanic languages, nonetheless remains the name regularly used by German-speaking scholars.

To know something about Indo-European is especially valuable for the history of Latin, English, and the Romance languages. Indo-European is the starting point of Latin's history, and it bequeathed to Latin its salient features, including much of its vocabulary. There is nothing remarkable in this: language is by nature an extremely conservative arena of human life.

The philologists' reconstruction of Indo-European is no less brilliant an intellectual triumph than the archaeologists' reconstruction of, say, Celtic society in early western Europe. The English jurist and expert in eastern languages, Sir William Jones (1746–1794), was the first to assert the kinship of the Indo-European languages. In 1786, addressing the Asiatic Society of Bengal, in Calcutta, he declared:

> The Sanscrit language, whatever be its antiquity, is of a wonderful structure; more perfect than the Greek, more copious than the Latin, and more exquisitely refined than either, yet bearing to both of them a stronger affinity, both in the roots of verbs and in the forms of grammar, than could possibly have been produced by accident; so strong, indeed, that no philologer could examine them all three without believing them to have sprung from some common source, which, perhaps, no longer exists. There is a similar reason, though not quite so forcible, for supposing that both the Gothic and the

Celtic ... had the same origin with the Sanscrit; and the old Persian might
be added to the same family.

In these words, conveying Jones's remarkable perception, lies the beginning of
the discovery and reconstruction of Indo-European.

How is it that this man – and no one before him – discovered this deep yet
hidden linguistic kinship? Doubtless, his own brilliance and industry played a
large role. By the time Jones graduated from Oxford, he had learned Arabic,
Hebrew, and Persian (not to mention Latin, Greek, French, Spanish, Italian,
and Portuguese), and for some years afterwards he published translations and
studies of eastern languages and literatures. And yet the momentous discovery
would not have been made without the convergence of two other forces: the
need Jones felt to seek more remunerative work, and Britain's drive to fashion
a colonial empire. Jones turned from languages to law and soon distinguished
himself in that field as well: he wrote a treatise on bail that was long a standard,
and was appointed a bankruptcy commissioner. Recommended by his two
fields of expertise, in 1783 he was sent to Calcutta as a judge of the supreme
court. In this capacity he first came into contact with Sanskrit, for he regarded
it as vital to consult the Hindu legal authorities in the original language.
Such were the circumstances that led to his linking of the various languages.
Occupied with studies of Hindu and Muslim law, translations, and other
scholarly enterprises, he remained in India until his untimely death, at the age of
forty-seven. Jones's works, in particular his translations, with their philological
and anthropological appeal, became a major inspiration of a certain orientalist
strain discernible in Romantic poetry – one thinks of Coleridge's "Kubla Khan"
or Fitzgerald's "Rubáiyát of Omar Khayyám."

Jones, as it happened, neither elaborated nor pursued the remarkable insight
he had had. The next important contribution was made by a Danish scholar,
Rasmus Rask (1787–1832). In 1818, Rask published an essay on the origin of
Old Norse, in the course of which he produced a comparative grammar of
Germanic, Slavic, Lithuanian, Greek, and Latin, all kindred with one another
in his view. He indicated many lexical correspondences among the languages,
moreover, and hinted that Persian and Indian might also be related. Unaware
of Jones, who had come at the question from the side of the eastern languages,
Rask reached his conclusions starting from the Germanic. Had he published
the essay when he finished writing it, in 1814, he would be regarded as the
founder of comparative philology.

As it is, though, this honor is traditionally bestowed upon Franz Bopp (1791–1867), a German scholar who became a professor at the University of Berlin. A language prodigy, like both Jones and Rask, Bopp in 1816 at the age of twenty-five published his epoch-making book, *On the Conjugational System of the Sanskrit Language, in Comparison with Those of the Greek, Latin, Persian, and Germanic Languages*, the very title of which makes clear its fundamental insight. Bopp later brought out a comparative grammar of the Indo-European languages, which took account also of Armenian, Lithuanian, and Slavic. The work laid down a solid foundation for both comparative philology and the study of Indo-European, which flourish to this day.

Everything we know about Indo-European is based on reconstruction. As Jones suspected, the original language is lost; not one direct trace of it is to be found – no poem, no law, no proverb, not even a fragment of an inscription. Nonetheless, by careful comparison of the surviving languages, scholars have worked their way back towards the preliterary, prehistoric source and developed a picture of Indo-European, both detailed and extensive, that has won wide acceptance. The sounds of the language (phonology) are well established, on the whole, as are the different forms that a word can take (morphology), and the rules of grammar by which words are combined to produce meaning (syntax). Similarly, Germanic and Slavic, the parent languages of their subfamilies, are not directly attested, but have been reconstructed by scholars; in the case of Latin, this was not necessary.

The Indo-European vocabulary has been thoroughly described too, and this has made it possible to draw reliable inferences about the culture of the earliest Indo-European speakers. If a word is found in many of the derived languages, we can conclude that what it denotes was familiar to the speakers of the original language. By this criterion, we infer that the Indo-Europeans knew the bee and the salmon (but not the sea), birch and apple trees (but not pear), horses and copper, perhaps bronze (but not iron). They had advanced beyond nomadic pastoralism to settled agriculture. Their patriarchal society was ruled by a king. They associated their gods with the bright sky and brought them both prayers and sacrifices.

The Speakers of Indo-European

What historical reality lies behind these languages' kinship, so profound in nature and sweeping in range, established so painstakingly, so powerfully impressive when demonstrated? What human history explains the linguistic data? The comparative philologist's hypothesis is that the languages described all derive from a single ancestral language. That language, Indo-European, must have been spoken by a people living at a certain time and place. The best guess is that the original Indo-European speakers lived in the middle of the fifth millennium B.C.E. (It should be borne in mind that "Indo-Europeans" is here shorthand for "speakers of Indo-European." It does not imply a distinct race or people. Many millions speak English without being English.)

Where they lived is a fascinating and much-debated question. The usual approach is to examine the evidence offered by the lexicon, and identify a region where those natural features are found for which there are shared words in the various subfamilies. Using only the words just mentioned, one would conclude that the Indo-European homeland contained bees and salmon, apple and birch trees, and that it was neither warm enough for pear trees to grow nor near the sea. That limits the field. Now the archaeologist comes to the linguist's aid, indicating which regions were inhabited by people who knew the use of copper and the horse, worshipped gods of the sky, and were ruled by kings. This too serves to limit the field. On the basis of such linguistic and archaeological considerations – of course, much more material than this is put into play – scholars have tried to decide where the original Indo-European people lived. Unfortunately, the evidence is not always clear and sometimes is contradictory, and therefore many sites have been proposed, ranging between the north of Europe and southern Russia. In recent decades a people known to archaeologists as Kurgans, who lived north of the Caspian Sea, have emerged as strong candidates for being the original Indo-Europeans.

Whatever the true identity and homeland of the Indo-Europeans, we have to picture them as breaking up in time into separate groups, which moved out from their original territory and migrated, perhaps often coming as invaders, to other parts of the Eurasian land mass. They took their speech with them wherever they went, and over the millennia the speeches of the different groups, no longer in contact with one another, developed each in its own direction – for languages never stand still – to the point that they became separate and mutually unintelligible, despite their common origin. Had the Indo-Europeans stayed in one place or been under the rule of a strong central government, their language probably would not have split into so many different ones. But in fact, they did wander widely as independent groups.

The group, for example, that eventually occupied southern Scandinavia and the northern edge of Europe east of the Rhine spoke Germanic. As time went by, it in turn broke up into groups whose languages, as the people settled in distinct areas and lost touch with one another, developed in different ways. Another Indo-European group, speaking Italic, settled through the center of the Italian peninsula; out of Italic, Latin would develop, as well as other languages. And so on. Just as the period of common Indo-European explains the similarities among the various language subfamilies (Germanic, Italic, Slavic, Celtic, etc.), so the period of common Germanic explains the similarities among the various languages, including English, that are descended from it. And in just the same way, of course, the common period of Latin explains why the Romance languages resemble one another. The same processes of successive separation and individuation got repeated throughout the Indo-European domain.

Inflection, the Defining Trait

To this vast and varied family of languages, then, Latin belongs. Most of its sounds, forms, syntax, and vocabulary it inherited from Indo-European. Now the cardinal feature of Indo-European, marking it off from most other language families of the world, is that it was an inflected language. Inflection plays a central role in the story of Latin. Latin retained inflection as one of its distinguishing features, but then, to a large extent, shed it as it evolved into the modern Romance languages.

What are inflections? Inflection, when used with reference to grammar, has nothing to do with tone or modulation of the voice. Rather, it refers to a change in a word that indicates its grammatical relationships; the change is usually made at the end of the word. (The term derives from Latin *flectere flexus* "to turn, bend," hence "to change." Sometimes I cite a Latin verb with two words, like *flectere flexus*, in order to show its two slightly different-looking stems – what the two words represent will be more exactly explained later.) Each different form of the word is implicitly contrasted with one or more others. English, despite the fact that like the Romance languages it has many fewer inflections than Latin, can still provide some illustrative examples. The -*s* at the end of *boys* shows that it is the plural of *boy*, that the speaker is referring to more than one boy. *They* and *them* are two forms of the same pronoun, one used for the subject of a sentence (as in "they love the cat"), the other for the

17

object ("and the cat loves them"). We say *she plays* but *I play*: here -*s* is the inflection used (in the present tense) when the subject of the verb is third person singular. In the pair *they laugh* : *they laughed*, the ending (or inflection) -*ed* locates the action in the past. These are a few examples of such inflections as English possesses.

Indo-European used inflection to show these contrasts, between singular and plural, subject and object, first person and third, present and past. But all these sets of inflected forms were far larger in Indo-European than they are in Modern English. For example, in English only the third person singular of the present indicative has a distinctive ending (*he, she, it plays*); the other forms of the present are identical to one another (*I play, you play, we play, they play*), as are all forms of the past (*I played, you played, he, she, it played*, etc.). Indo-European had distinctive forms for each and every one of these, as with the present tense of the verb *to be*. Furthermore, Indo-European used inflection to show still other contrasts, such as cannot be illustrated through English. The language was characterized by a very large number of inflected forms (and for nouns, pronouns, and adjectives, as well as verbs), and this would remain true for Latin also. Other language families function by different means.

An intriguing but unanswerable question suggests itself: if it is self-evident that language must have begun simple and with time become more complex, how is it that an early language like Indo-European, spoken perhaps more than six thousand years ago, operated with such complexity of forms and grammar?

Bridges Across Time and Space

Indo-European was able to be reconstructed because sounds were discovered to correspond regularly between languages. A certain sound in one language either was the same in another language (Greek *mater* : Old Irish *mathir* "mother") or turned up regularly as a different sound in the other (Sanskrit *bharamas, bharatar-* : Greek *pheromes, phrater* "we bear, brother"). Regularity is the key. Sounds do change over time, and, as is easily proved for languages of which we do have direct knowledge, they tend to do so with some uniformity. Let's consider three sets of sound correspondences that illustrate this regularity.

Greek and Latin, though usually studied together for historical and cultural reasons, are not especially close to one another linguistically. And yet Greek words beginning with *h*- correspond regularly to Latin words beginning with *s*-. (*S*- was the original Indo-European sound, which was altered in Greek.)

This can be handily illustrated from English, which to its native stock has often added words derived from both languages:

- Greek *hemi-* "half" (as in *hemisphere*) : Latin *semi-* (as in *semicircular, semiannual*);
- Greek *hepta* "seven" (*heptagon*) : Latin *septem* (*septet* and *September*, which was only the seventh month in the early Roman calendar, where the year began with March);
- Greek *hals* "salt" (*halite*, otherwise known as "rock salt," *halogen*, an element, such as chlorine, that, when combined with a metal, produces a salt): Latin *sal* (*saline, salad* and *salami*, both dishes prepared with salt, *salary*, originally the salt allowance granted to Roman soldiers, then any regular payment for service – the word *salt* itself, however, comes into English from Germanic);
- Greek *helios* "sun" (*heliotropic*, said of a flower that turns toward the sun, *heliocentric*, said of a theory by Copernicus) : Latin *sol* (*solar, solstice, solarium*);
- Greek *hypnos* "sleep" (*hypnotic*) : Latin *somnus* (*somnolent, somnambulist* "sleepwalker");
- Greek *hypo* "below" (*hypodermic* "below the skin") : Latin *sub* (*subcutaneous, submarine, submerge*);
- Greek *hyper* "above" (*hypertension, hyperbole*) : Latin *super* (*superficial, supernatural, supersede*).

English, it is worth repeating, belongs to the Germanic family of languages, not to the Latin. But we find many native English words whose first sound corresponds regularly to the first sound of a Latinate word that was added later to the vocabulary. (Initial sounds tend to be less subject to change than others.) English *h-* often corresponds to Latin *c-*, the original Indo-European sound. By grasping the correspondence, we are able to see the resemblances between words that used to look unrelated:

- English *hundred* : Latin *centum* (*century, centipede, centigrade*);
- English *hound* : Latin *canis* (*canine, kennel*);
- English *horn* : Latin *cornu* (*corn* in the sense "hardening of the skin" – *corn* meaning "grain" or "maize" is unconnected – also *cornucopia* "horn of plenty," *cornet*, the musical instrument either resembling or once made

from horn, and *corner*, which developed its meaning from the notion of "point, tip, end" in *cornu*);

- English *heart* : Latin *cord-* (*cordial* "of the heart, hearty"; the noun meaning "liqueur" comes from the use of certain alcoholic drinks to stimulate the heart);
- English *hall* : Latin *cella* (*cell, cellar*; the earliest meaning was "place of concealment," then "a roofed space");
- English *hide* in the sense "animal skin": Latin *cutis* "skin" (*cuticle, subcutaneous*);
- English *harvest* : Latin *carpere* "to pluck" (*excerpt*, a passage plucked out from its original context, and *carpet*, originally cloth made from shreds that had been plucked apart; *carp* in the sense of "criticize, complain" and *carp* the fish are unrelated).

Similarly, a series of native words starting with *b-* correspond to Latin words with *f-* that have also entered the English lexicon. (In this case the original Indo-European sound was *bh-*, that is to say, *b* followed by a brief exhalation of breath, as in Nob Hill.) We have already met the pair *to bear* and *ferre*. Here are a few further examples:

- English *brother* : Latin *frater* (*fraternal, fraternity*);
- English *break* : Latin *frangere fractus* (*fragile, fragment, fraction*);
- English *bore* (as in "bore a hole") : Latin *forare foratus* (*perforate*);
- English *blow* (as in "blow a balloon") : Latin *flare flatus* (*inflate, deflate, flatulent*);
- English *bottom* : Latin *fundus* (*fundament, foundation, profound, fund*);
- English *ban*, originally "summon; curse, denounce," from an Indo-European root meaning "speak" : Latin stem *fa-*, as seen in *fama* "fame," *fabula* "story, fable," *fatum* "that which has been spoken, fate";
- English *barley* and *barn* : Latin *farina* "flour" (*farina*; a barn was at first evidently a structure for storing barley, then for other foods and livestock);
- English *bed* : Latin *fodere fossus* "to dig" (*fossil*, something ancient found by digging; the original meaning of the Germanic word was "a place dug up," as in "flower bed").

The last pair of cognates, that is, kindred words, is not only surprising but also instructive. It warns us to beware mistaking the commonest meaning of a word for the original. Most of us probably think of the *bed* in "flower bed" as an extension of its ordinary use, a somewhat whimsical, attractive application. In fact, the story runs the other way: the use of *bed* for an item of furniture came along only later. A similar phrase is "tax farming," which appears to mean the "cultivating" of a certain sort of revenue. That too would be mistaken. "Tax farming," which is a government's letting of contracts for the collection of taxes by a third party – the usual Roman system, by the way – is closer etymologically to the original meaning of *farm* than is, say, "dairy farm." *Farm* originally meant "fixed payment" (< Latin *firmare* "to fix, settle" – arrows like the one before "Latin" indicate that the word on the pointed side derives from the one on the open side); only in the fourteenth century did it begin to refer to the land that was leased in exchange for a fixed payment. The phrase "to farm out," that is, to subcontract, still shows the earlier meaning, and *firm* in the sense "business organization" has the same origin. A final example: today the word *quick* is a synonym of *rapid* or *swift*. In the beginning, however, it meant "alive" – it is cognate with *vivid* – as can still be seen from its use in "the quick and the dead" and "cut to the quick" and from *quicksand* and *quicksilver*, an old and apt name for mercury. Earlier meanings are often overshadowed by later, but they sometimes leave traces here and there, which it is the etymologist's delight to discover.

As an illustration of how widely Indo-European stems have diverged, and also as an appreciation of the range of sources of the English vocabulary, let me spring two lexical surprises on you. All these English words or stems originated in a single Indo-European root meaning "water" but followed divergent paths thereafter: *water, winter* ("the wet season"), and *otter* (all three from Germanic), *hydro-* (as in *hydrant* and *hydroelectric*, from Greek), *redundant* (originally "overflowing," from Latin *unda* "wave"), *whiskey* (from Irish), *vodka* (from Russian). From a separate Indo-European root meaning "water" come all the following: *aqua-* (as in *aquatic, aquarium*), *ewer, gouache*, and *island*.

THE CREATION OF THE ROMAN EMPIRE

The Conquest of Italy

By about 1000 B.C.E. an Indo-European-speaking people had come to settle in central Italy. The territory they occupied became known as Latium, their language as Latin. With archaeological finds and various accounts of the early traditions about the Latin people and with the first documents written in their language, Latin enters history. The story of the language from this point on is bound up with the story of how one branch of the Latin people, the Romans, dominated and conquered first their Latin kinsmen, then the rest of the Italian peninsula, and finally the Mediterranean basin along with many lands beyond. With the Romans, the Latin language spread from a small coastal plain on the western side of Italy to a world empire that extended from Britain to Mesopotamia, from the Rhine to the middle reaches of the Nile. The following account is no more than a rapid chronicle of Roman expansion, attending only to the successive stages of Roman territorial aggrandizement.

According to tradition, the city of Rome was founded by Romulus in 753 B.C.E. and was ruled at first by a series of seven kings. By around 500, Rome, a republic now, had established military primacy among the other Latin cities. Her Latin cousins rebelled against her and were soundly defeated at the battle of Lake Regillus (499 or 496). The alliance that was then formed between Rome and the Latins lasted more than a century and a half. Later, the Latins, in combination with other local peoples, rose up for a second time against Rome. Utter defeat at the battle of Antium (modern Anzio) in 338 marked the end of Latin resistance. The Romans were now undisputed masters of Latium.

For us today this signal victory is commemorated in a familiar word. The battle of Antium was a naval engagement, after which the Romans detached from the vanquished enemy ships the prows, or beaks (in Latin, *rostra*, from the verb *rodere* "to gnaw" – compare *rodent*), which were used for ramming other ships in battle, and with these trophies they adorned the speaker's platform at the western end of the Forum. Hence by association the speaker's platform itself came to be known as the *rostra*. The word is still with us, sometimes in the singular form *rostrum*.

Even before they crushed the Latins, the Romans had been militarily active in Campania and Samnium, two regions to the south of Latium. (Campania lies along the coast and includes the plain inland from the Bay of Naples. Samnium is the segment of the Apennine mountains that runs alongside Campania.) During the fourth century they fought a series of wars against the Samnites, climaxing in the battle of Sentinum (295), where they defeated a force composed of Samnites, Umbrians, Gauls, and Etruscans. The Romans were now the greatest power in Italy.

They were not yet, however, the masters of the whole peninsula. Their most powerful remaining opponents were the Greek cities of southern Italy (starting in the eighth century, many cities of the overpopulated Greek homeland had sent out colonies to southern Italy and Sicily). Fearing Rome's imperial ambitions, those colonies approached a Greek king, Pyrrhus of Epirus (Epirus corresponds to what is today northwestern Greece and southern Albania), and asked for his help against the Romans. He crossed the Adriatic with a large, well-equipped army, but, despite several victories, was decisively defeated in 275. With the victory over Pyrrhus and the Greek cities allied with him, the Romans extended their dominion all the way to the southern shores of Italy. In the following century they extended it to the peninsula's natural northern border by conquering the Po Valley, Liguria (the land at the head of the Tyrrhenian Sea), and Istria (the land east of the head of the Adriatic). Now the Romans were indeed masters of all Italy.

The close to Rome's conquest of southern Italy is also marked for us by a familiar phrase. Pyrrhus won two notable early victories, at Heraclea (280 B.C.E.) and Ausculum (279), although in both battles his own losses were

high. He is reported to have said, "If we defeat the Romans in one more battle, we will be utterly ruined" (Plutarch, *Life of Pyrrhus* 21). Hence the phrase
"Pyrrhic victory" for a military success so costly it might as well be a defeat.

The Conquest of Italy's Other Languages

The Romans' completed conquest of Italy is an appropriate point at which to
pause and survey the linguistic situation there. Eventually Latin would become
the sole language of the peninsula. Indeed, the propagation of it was one key to
Roman success in maintaining an empire. (Another, more important, was the
Roman strategy of incorporating the conquered, in some measure, into their
state.) A variety of other languages were spoken in Italy, however, and they
did not by any means disappear as soon as the speakers became subject to
Roman rule. A striking consequence of their contact with Latin is that, despite
the passage of the centuries, traces of them remain in the modern languages,
including English.

The Sabines were a people who lived near Rome and were quickly absorbed
by it: an early amalgamation is reflected in the legend of the rape of the Sabine
women. The language of the Sabines, which was closely enough related to
Latin to be classed with it as an "Italic dialect," affected its vocabulary. The
Latin verb meaning "smell" (in the sense "emit a smell") was *olere*, from which
come English *olfactory* and *redolent*. The Latin noun that corresponds to *olere*,
however, is *odor*, with *d* taking the place of *l* in the stem. It is likely that the
latter word, seen in English *odor*, entered Latin from Sabine. The two versions
of the stem co-existed in Latin, as they still do in English.

Two other Italic dialects were Oscan and Umbrian. Umbrian was spoken in
what is still called Umbria, the region to the north of Latium and Rome. Oscan
was spoken in Campania, Samnium, and other parts of southern Italy. Though
related, these languages were yet sufficiently different from Latin to be mutually
unintelligible. What we know about them we owe chiefly to inscriptions, most
of which date no later than the early first century B.C.E. Presumably, the
languages ceased to be used for official purposes around that time – which,
let us note, was a couple of centuries after the Romans gained military and
political control of their areas. Since some Oscan graffiti found in Pompeii
appear to have been scratched not long before that city was destroyed by the
eruption of Mount Vesuvius, in 79 C.E., it appears likely that that language
continued to be spoken for a while after it was dropped for official use.

Oscan and Umbrian were eventually suppressed by Latin, but not before they too had contributed to its vocabulary. Though it seems to defy belief, unmistakable traces of such borrowings have survived from Latin even into English and the Romance languages.

The names of two familiar animals, the domestic *bos* (stem *bov-*) "ox, cow" and the wild *lupus* "wolf," show that they passed from Indo-European into Latin, not directly, but through Oscan or Umbrian (which for our purpose can now be treated as one). With the changes expected in Latin they would have been **vos* and **luquos*. (Words preceded by an asterisk, like **vos*, are unattested; they are hypothetical forms, ordinarily posited by reconstruction, but sometimes imaginary.) The Romans, perhaps because they themselves were farmers rather than herders, adopted names that originated with neighboring, kindred peoples. So today when we hear words spoken like Italian *bove* and *bue*, French *boeuf* (source of English *beef*), and Spanish *buey* (not to mention English *bovine*), and like Italian *lupo*, French *loup*, and Spanish *lobo*, we are, without realizing it, hearing words that originated in Italic dialects rather than Latin itself.

Other doublets like *olere* and *odor* that existed in Latin and have persisted into modern times also show the influence of Italic dialects. To Latin words with a *b* in the middle there corresponded Oscan-Umbrian words with *f*. Three such pairs are *bubulus* (from the same stem as *bos* "ox") : *bufalus* "antelope; wild ox"; *sibilare* : *sifilare* "to hiss, whistle"; and *rubeus* : *rufus* "red." Each member of these pairs claims its own offspring in the modern languages:

- Italian *bove*, etc. (as above) : Italian *bufalo*, Spanish *búfalo*, French *buffle*, English *buffalo* (not connected, by the way, with the city in New York State, the etymology of which is obscure);
- English *sibilant* (a sound produced with a kind of hiss, like the sound of *s* or *sh* in English), Spanish *silbar* "to whistle" : French *siffler* "to hiss, whistle," Italian *zufolare* "to whistle," Spanish *chiflar* "to whistle at, boo";
- English *ruby*, *rubicund*, *rubric* (originally a title or heading written in red ink), Spanish *rubio* "blond" : English *rufous* "reddish," as in the *rufous hummingbird*, and *Rufus*, used as a cognomen among the Romans (Lucius Varius Rufus was one of Virgil's literary executors), in later ages as a surname for men of reddish appearance (William II, King of England 1087–1100, was nicknamed Rufus for his ruddy complexion), and as a given name in the last two centuries (Rufus T. Firefly).

In each case the forms with -*b*- (native to Latin) and -*f*- (from Oscan-Umbrian) co-existed in Latin.

North and west of Rome, roughly in the area of modern Tuscany (also called Etruria), lived the Etruscans, a people who exerted strong political and cultural influence over early Rome. The Romans received their alphabet from the Etruscans, who had received it in turn from the Greek colonies in southern Italy. Etruscan appears to be an isolated language (that is, it has no relatives: the same is true for Basque) and is certainly not Indo-European. The thousands of inscriptions that preserve almost all of what remains of it date from the seventh to the late first century B.C.E.

Etruscan too, though it succumbed in the end, contributed vocabulary to Latin. From it Latin received, and then transmitted, several lexical items that are familiar to us: *satelles* (stem *satellit-*) "bodyguard, attendant, follower" (applying the word to a small planet that revolves around a larger one was a stroke of imagination by the German astronomer Johannes Kepler, 1571–1630); *atrium*, the reception room of a Roman house (now also one of the upper chambers of the heart, which receive blood – another imaginative extension); and *histrio* (stem *histrion-*) "actor" (in the modern languages generally with some pejorative connotation).

Etruria was bordered by an area of Indo-European speech not only to the south (by Latin) but also to the north – by Celtic. The Celts, who were spread over much of western Europe, occupied the Po Valley and most of the rest of northern Italy; those Celtic peoples found in Italy, France, and the Low Countries were known as Gauls. In the year 390 B.C.E. a group of invading Gauls penetrated to Rome itself, which they captured and briefly held. Celtic inscriptions are found in Italy from the last two centuries B.C.E. A number of words were furnished to Latin by the language of the Gauls. Hostile relations evidently were not a bar to linguistic interchange.

Among the words that Latin adopted from Gaulish, the most remarkable are names for wagons, two of which have had particularly fruitful and interesting careers. *Carrus*, a Gaulish name for a wagon, was taken into Latin and is now continued in Spanish, Italian *carro*, French *char* (whence English *car*). From this word *chariot* is derived and probably *cart* also (but not *caravan*, which comes from Persian). Other derivatives in English, with cognates in the Romance languages, are *carry* (along with *carriage* and *carrier*) and *charge*, which at first meant "to load (as a wagon)" and then "burden; entrust; command; accuse," etc.; *charge* in turn led to *discharge*. *Cargo*, from Spanish, is a further derivative.

So too is *career*: it originated in the phrase (*via*) *carraria* "carriage(-way)," from which further meanings developed one after another: "race course; race; course of action; occupation practiced in the course of one's life." Another Gaulish word for "wagon" was *carpentum*. The man who built such a vehicle was a *carpentarius*, a term that, given the material of the wagon, came to designate any worker in wood; hence French *charpentier* and English *carpenter*.

Carrus is already found in Latin in the first century B.C.E., *carpentum* even earlier, in the third. This leads us to wonder why the Romans almost lacked native words for wagons and borrowed so many from the Gauls (not only *carrus* and *carpentum*, but others as well). The answer probably lies in the contrast between the Romans, cultivators of their land, a sedentary folk, and the Gauls, restless invaders who traveled about carrying their baggage on wagons.

The last non-Latin language of the peninsula that concerns us is Greek. The coasts of southern Italy and Sicily were populated by Greek-speaking colonists. Many a city in the west became wealthier, more splendid, and mightier than its mother city (or metropolis) – rather like America and Europe at a later date. A few of the more well-known are Sybaris (whose notoriously luxurious style of life gave us the adjective *sybaritic*), Neapolis (Greek for "new city" – "Newton," as it were – Italian Napoli, English Naples), and Panormus (Greek for "always fit for mooring," today Palermo, which does have a splendid harbor).

The Greek language also contributed words to Latin – at every stage of Latin's history, even the earliest, and in vastly greater numbers than the other languages of Italy. Because it continued to influence Latin over the course of the centuries, very markedly when Christianity became the dominant religion of the Roman Empire, and because later on it was influential upon the Romance languages and English directly, the Greek element in the European lexicon requires separate treatment, later.

Latin's conquest and absorption of the peninsula's languages has left clear traces in our modern vocabulary. The only language among them, however, that survived in use into the Common Era was Greek; all the others were given up in favor of Latin. The whys and the hows of this momentous linguistic transformation will concern us shortly.

The Roman Empire at Its Height

With Italy subdued, the Romans looked to expand their territory beyond its frontiers. Barely a decade after defeating King Pyrrhus, they were engaged in a war with the city of Carthage. Carthage, which was established as a Phoenician commercial station on the shore of north Africa, had by then become the greatest trading power in the western Mediterranean. The First Punic War was long (264–241 B.C.E.) and hard fought. (It is called "Punic" because the Romans waged it against people who by descent were Phoenicians, for whom the Latin word is *Punici*.) By defeating the Carthaginians, the Romans acquired their first overseas province, Sicily. In 238 they seized another large island, Sardinia, from the Carthaginians.

The Second Punic War (218–201) brought Rome as close to destruction as she ever came during the republican period. The Carthaginians, under their general Hannibal, invaded Italy and campaigned there for many years, winning a number of signal victories over the Romans. Eventually, though, Hannibal's allies and reinforcements were checked or routed, his troops worn down, and he himself was obliged to return to Africa in defense of the homeland. He was defeated in the battle of Zama in 202. As a result, Rome acquired the former Carthaginian possessions along the Mediterranean coast of Spain.

Macedonia (northern Greece – references to modern countries are approximations) had allied itself with Hannibal, and once the Second Punic War had ended, the Romans became more involved in the eastern Mediterranean and waged a series of wars against Macedonia. A turning point was the battle of Pydna (168), at which the Romans defeated King Perseus. By 146, they had made both Macedonia and Greece provinces. In the same year, at the end of the Third Punic War, they destroyed Carthage and turned its north African territory into another province. The year 133 was no less eventful. The Romans virtually completed their conquest of Spain, adding all the interior except the northwest to their empire, when they finally captured the city of Numantia by siege. (The fall of Numantia has been a popular subject in Spanish literature: Cervantes, for one, wrote a tragedy on the theme.) The northwest was not subdued until the time of Augustus. In the same year, the Romans received the Kingdom of Pergamum in Asia Minor (Turkey) as a bequest. It too became a Roman province, and within half a century the rest of that land mass passed into Roman control. By 121 the Romans had conquered southeastern Gaul (France), the part that today is called Provence (from Latin *provincia* "province").

Even during the period of the Roman revolution – those long decades of the first century B.C.E. when powerful individuals in command of virtually private armies fought one another for supremacy – new lands continued to be brought under Roman sway. In the 60's, Pompey the Great added Syria and Judaea.

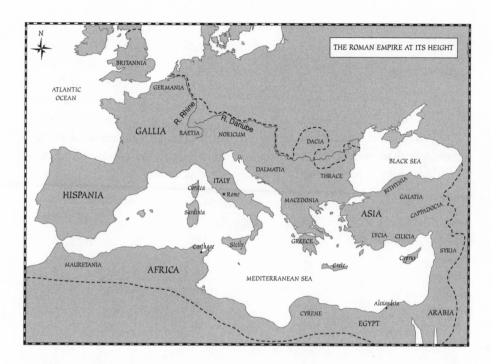

During the decade following, Julius Caesar, in the famous campaigns he himself chronicled, added the rest of Gaul, the Low Countries, and Germany west of the Rhine. After defeating Mark Antony, the young Octavian annexed Egypt (30). Octavian, later known as Augustus, by vanquishing all his rivals brought the civil wars to an end, and, while pretending to restore the republican form of government, moved Rome in the direction of autocracy. He is considered the first emperor.

The first century of the Roman Empire saw continued, but irregular, increase in the lands Rome controlled. Under Augustus, who ruled from 27 B.C.E. to 14 C.E., most of the Balkan peninsula south of the Danube was conquered (Bulgaria, Yugoslavia, Bosnia and Herzegovina, Croatia, Slovenia, Austria), as were the remaining Alpine regions. Most of Augustus's successors heeded his advice not to expand the Empire any further. Some lands that had been client-states were converted to provinces: Mauretania (northern Morocco), Thrace (Bulgaria), and parts of Asia Minor (Turkey). Still, during Claudius's years on the throne (41–54 C.E.) southern England was added to the empire; Wales and the rest of England were conquered by the year 71. The wedge of southwestern Germany between the Rhine and the Danube Rivers, known as the Agri Decumates, became Roman under Domitian (81–96). The last great conquering emperor was Trajan (98–117), who expanded the Empire both at the northern frontier, adding the province of Dacia (Romania, which lies beyond the Danube), and very much on the eastern frontier, where he added Arabia (southern and eastern Israel and western Jordan), Mesopotamia and Assyria (northern and central Iraq), and Armenia (which included much more territory than present-day Armenia). At Trajan's death the Empire – and the Latin language – had reached as great an extent as it ever would.

CHAPTER THREE

THE CAREER OF LATIN, II

The Empire Succeeded by Barbarian Kingdoms

THE DISSOLUTION OF THE ROMAN EMPIRE

Barbarians and the Division of the Empire

In view of the Roman Empire's vast size and exceptionally lengthy frontiers, it is astonishing that it maintained itself for as long as it did. A few further attempts to expand the Empire failed, and emperors and armies needed to fight hard just to retain the territories Rome possessed at the time of Trajan's death. For a century and a half the borders remained virtually unchanged. But beginning around the middle of the third century, and then, despite an intervening period of sturdy frontiers and renewed stability, increasingly from the mid-fourth through the fifth century c.e., the Empire was invaded, broken up, reduced, and replaced. At the end of that period of upheaval, the borders of Romance speech in Europe were set, and they have remained substantially the same for the succeeding 1,500 years. Since our reason for charting the changes of Roman territory is to explain why certain areas continued with Romance speech while others did not, it is necessary to trace out the fates of the western provinces. These borders were drawn in part by geography, but chiefly by the invasions of the barbarian tribes and by the Empire's own split into two halves, events which had linguistic as well as political consequences.

In this necessarily brief account, I will be using some terminological short-hand that needs explaining. I rely on the term "barbarian," for example, which represents the Roman view of those foreign peoples – and not always even that, because the Romans ceased calling them barbarians once they had entered Roman service, as many did. Indeed, the barbarians were often eager to participate in and support their civilization. Similarly, "invasion" inadequately represents the variety of relationships in which they stood to the Romans. Some were plundering attackers, to be sure (the Vandals, for instance), but many were not. Most tribes were invited by Rome to settle within the frontiers of the Empire, with the hope that they themselves would be content and cause no trouble, and that they would act as a buffer against their more hostile cousins still on the other side. Finally, terms like "tribe" and "people" may suggest groups more homogeneous and more stable than they actually were.

Whatever internal factors contributed to the collapse of Roman power – loss of leadership or manpower or will, political difficulties, economic or financial crisis, breakdown of the social order, changes in religious attitude – the chief external factor was the barbarian invasions, which had immense influence in determining the boundaries of Romance speech we find today. The invaders were nearly all Germanic tribes living beyond the Rhine and the Danube.

Even before the central regions of the Roman Empire were invaded and occupied by barbarian tribes, the emperors were obliged to give up some of the outlying territories. Money and manpower could not be spared for their continued defense but were needed elsewhere. Under Aurelian (270–275 C.E.) two provinces had to be abandoned. Roman legions were withdrawn from both Dacia (Rumania) and the Agri Decumates (in southwestern Germany), and so the Empire's northern frontier was pulled back again to the Danube and the Rhine. (It was a further sign of the troubled times under Aurelian that massive defensive walls were constructed for Rome, which still encircle much of it today.) Then, in the early years of the fifth century, the Romans withdrew their arms and administration from Britain, and let the English Channel replace Hadrian's Wall as their northwestern frontier. Large bodies of water again separated the Romans from menacing outsiders.

A curious discrepancy exists between the subsequent careers of Latin in Dacia and in Britain. Although Dacia had been a Roman province for only 170 years, the language of the modern country of Rumania is a Romance language. (How exactly this came about is a notorious historical puzzle.) Britain, by contrast, had been a province for 350 years, twice as long, and yet, with the departure of the Romans, nearly every trace of the Latin language on the island was wiped out – at least for a while.

By the middle of the fifth century, the inhabitants of Britain were already being attacked by Angles, Saxons, and other Germanic tribes from the continent, who brought with them their language, which soon dominated the island. Unlike in Gaul and Spain, Latin in Britain gave way almost completely to Germanic. That success is due partly to Germans who had earlier settled on the island, partly to an epidemic in the sixth century, which may have wiped out many Latin speakers. The Celtic people who were conquered by the Germans contributed little from their own language to what would become English, and passed along only a few of the Latin words they had acquired during three and a half centuries of Roman rule.

Here are several among the oldest Latin words surviving on English soil (they are cited in their modern form): the element *-caster, -chester, -cester* in place names (such as *Lancaster, Manchester, Worcester*) < Latin *castrum* "military camp"; the element *-wick* or *-wich* in place names (such as *Warwick, Norwich*) < *vicus* "village"; *port* < *portus* "harbor"; *street* < *(via) strata* "paved (road)" (compare Italian *strada*, as in the Fellini movie, *La Strada* "The Street"); *wall* < *vallum* "rampart"; *wine* < *vinum; mint* "place where coins are made" < *moneta; pound* < *pondus* "weight."

Ultimately, the Roman Empire became divided in two, the western half governed from Rome or Ravenna, the eastern half from Constantinople. The division of the Empire was a process rather than an event. The Emperor Gallienus (260–268) temporarily allowed the eastern and the western ends of the Empire to be independently defended, administered, and financed, while he himself retained control of the center. Shortly afterwards, Diocletian (284–305) institutionalized a separation between the two parts. In 285, he shared his power with Maximian voluntarily and equally, dividing the Empire and taking the eastern half for himself. Sometimes reunited, but often governed by separate rulers, from this point on the two halves of the Empire remained a reality. Then in 330, on the site of ancient Byzantium, Constantine inaugurated a new capital for the Eastern Empire, which he modestly called Constantinople (today it is Istanbul). This event helped sharpen the division, as did, upon the death of the Emperor Theodosius in 395, the assignment of each half to one of his sons. Whereas the Western Empire was dismembered in the fifth century and barbarian kingdoms put in its place, the Eastern Empire continued to maintain itself, not losing substantial territory until the Islamic onslaught in the early seventh century. Even so, the Eastern (or Byzantine) Empire struggled on, amazingly, until 1453, when its last stronghold, the city of Constantinople itself, fell to the Ottoman Turks.

The barbarians have now entered our story, in which they are going to play a prominent role. As their effect on Latin and Romance speech has been deep and lasting, so the word *barbarian* itself has had a long and branching history in the modern languages. In examining the meanings of the word and its derivatives, it is astonishing to see how a term that in origin referred to linguistic inability came to indicate very different, even opposing, characteristics. The tale includes transformations that would baffle an alchemist.

Ultimately, *barbarian* was onomatopoeic; that is, it imitated the sound made by what it denoted. Someone who said "bar bar" was a stutterer. In Sanskrit the adjective *barbarah* meant "stuttering," while in the plural ("the stutterers") it also designated foreign people. The connection was that those whose speech was unintelligible, for whatever reason, did not belong to one's own group. The word passed into the European lexicon through Greek, in which it first denoted those who did not speak Greek, foreigners. For several centuries it remained a neutral term, applicable even to those non-Greeks who were recognized as belonging to a more advanced civilization, such as the Egyptians. But after the Persians invaded Greece twice in the early years of the fifth century B.C.E., *barbaros* acquired the meanings we most often give it today, "uncivilized; brutal, violent." For the Romans, who got the term from the Greeks, it had the same range of meanings – except that they generously classed the Greeks along with themselves as the non-barbarians. Later, the Christians used *barbarus* for non-Christians; it thus became a synonym for *gentilis* "gentile" and *paganus* "pagan."

The extent to which the word came to designate simple otherness can be gauged from a pair of remarkable passages. In the apocrypha to the Hebrew Bible (*Second Book of Maccabees* 2.21), the Jewish author, writing in Greek, calls the oppressors of the Jews "barbarians." Who are the barbarians here? The Seleucid rulers of their country, successors to Alexander the Great – that is to say, Greeks! Then the Latin playwright Plautus, whose comedies unfold in a Greek setting, has one of his "Greek" characters piquantly refer to Plautus's fellow-author and fellow-Roman, Gnaeus Naevius, as *poeta barbarus* "barbarian poet" (*The Braggart Soldier* 211).

In Late Latin, *barbarus* became *brabu. The change probably happened by these stages: *bárbarus* > *barbru (the vowel following the accented syllable was lost, as often happens) > *babru (the first *r* was dropped – this is called "dissimilation") > *brabu (the *r* changed its position). The word has continued in the modern languages (Italian, Spanish *bravo*, French *brave*) and has prospered, with a variety of meanings. On the one hand, it retains the opprobrious meanings of *barbarus*: "uncivilized; violent, cruel; fierce, wild." In Spanish, a *río bravo* is a rugged, stony river (a John Wayne movie is entitled *Rio Bravo*). On the other hand, starting from the notion of "courageous" – the good face of "fierce" – it has acquired many favorable meanings: "brave; proud; splendid, noble; excellent, good," even "handsome." The range of meanings has changed over time and varies from one language to another. In English, which got the word from French, *brave* has only positive senses. Besides "courageous," it could mean in Shakespeare's day "splendid," as when in *The Tempest* Miranda exclaims "O brave new world / That has such people in 't!" And in all these modern languages, to shout "bravo!" after a performance is to express hearty approval.

(An alternative etymology for *bravus* derives it from *pravus*, which in Classical Latin meant "crooked, corrupt, faulty" (compare *depraved*), and then in Late Latin, when applied to lands or animals, "uncultivated, wild.")

Akin to *barbarus* is the Latin adjective *balbus* "stuttering, stammering." It too has lived on in the Romance languages. In Italian *balbo* is an obsolete, literary term for "stuttering," yet the verb *balbettare* means not only "to stutter" but also "to speak (a language) brokenly" – physical handicap is again associated with linguistic incompetence. Spanish has associated the word with intellectual incompetence: *bobo* means "foolish, stupid." And French has given it still another turn: *ébaubi* in addition to "tongue-tied" means "speechless, flabbergasted." English *babble*, finally, is also related.

Latin Versus the Empire's Other Languages

Whereas the linguistic consequences of the Germanic invasions were dramatic and enduring, lasting down to today, the consequences of the Empire's division into two were negligible, since that political boundary had previously existed for a long time as a linguistic boundary. The western half of the Empire had been dominated by Latin speech, the eastern half by Greek. When the Romans conquered Italy and then the remainder of western Europe, they succeeded in imposing their language upon their subjects. The other languages of Italy persisted, to be sure, for a couple of centuries after conquest, but eventually, soon after the start of the Common Era, they died out, except for Greek. Similarly, northern Italy, the Alpine regions, Gaul, the Low Countries, the Iberian peninsula, and Sicily and Sardinia gave up their own languages and began to speak Latin instead; so too did the inhabitants of central and western north Africa.

Latin's success in taking the place of other languages is a vital step in our story. It may seem natural that political domination brings in its train linguistic domination. Natural, perhaps, but not necessary. The Basques have been ruled by Spain for many centuries, yet their difficult language continues in vigorous use, nor have seven hundred years of English rule quite managed to exterminate Welsh. Examples like these urge us to consider why Latin was so successful in taking the place of the languages spoken by the people whom Rome conquered. It is nearly inevitable that people grow up speaking the language their parents speak. Why then did so many people give up their ancestral language?

The answer lies in the nature of Rome's empire and the way she controlled and maintained it. The Roman Empire, though surrounding the Mediterranean Sea – *mare nostrum,* as they called it, "our sea" – was very much a land empire. When the Greek cities sent out colonies, their commerce, culture, and language were limited to sea coasts and nearby river banks; the same was true for Carthage. Roman control, however, penetrated to the interior of the lands; they occupied entire regions, not just strips of land adjoining water.

Conquering soldiers came first, of course, and large standing armies thereafter assured that many military men were garrisoned in the provinces. The historian Tacitus describes a vivid scene during a military campaign. Two brothers belonging to a Germanic tribe stand on opposite banks of a river and spiritedly debate the proper stance to be taken towards the Romans: one urges alliance with them, while for the other this represents treachery and slavery (*Annals* 2.9–10). In narrating the episode, from the year 16 C.E., Tacitus manages to present within his history opposing views on collaboration with the Romans and, by extension, on the nature of Roman rule. And when he mentions that the debate was conducted mostly in Latin and explains that the brothers had learned the language through military service with the Roman army, he indicates one way by which familiarity with Latin spread among native people.

In the wake of the soldiers came a swarm of other Romans – governors and judges, customs officers and tax farmers, lawyers and bankers, merchants and other businessmen. Women too: in provincial households presided over by Roman women, the children would naturally be raised speaking Latin. The Romans tended to incorporate the conquered, to some extent, into their government and state as well as their army. They strove in particular to co-opt the local elites, a ready source of potential officers and administrators, and one of the best ways of doing this was to encourage education on the Roman plan. Several provincial cities were made seats of learning specifically for the sons of the nobility: already in the 70's B.C.E. Sertorius, rebelling against Rome, drew the Spaniards to his cause by establishing a school at Huesca and promising the young men positions of importance, and later, under the Emperor Tiberius (14–37 C.E.), the Gallic capital of Autun served the same purpose.

And the natives responded, not with resentment, but with alacrity. The same Tacitus recounts, in another work, how his father-in-law Agricola, in conquering and settling Britain, used education as a tool. "He had the sons of the leading men trained in the liberal arts, and regarded the British as more able than the Gauls. As a result, those who recently had rejected the Latin language now eagerly desired to become eloquent" (*Agricola* 21.2). And indeed they achieved their desire. Britain, Gaul, Spain, and north Africa were soon producing distinguished orators and writers, teachers and scholars. From Spain came the family of the Senecas, including the famous tragedian and Stoic philosopher Seneca and the epic poet Lucan. To such an extent did Latin penetrate at least the governing classes of the western provinces.

In these ways Latin, the language of the conquerors, the language of the army and the law court, of school and administration and business (and often of the nursery as well), became the road to preferment. Equipped with a literature, it was also a language of cultural prestige. The adoption of Latin, far from being a mere occurrence, represented a conscious decision taken by the Romans. A passage from Augustine (354–430 C.E.) reveals his view that the Roman government followed a policy of cementing its empire together with the Latin language. In speaking of how linguistic differences separate men from one another, he observes: "the imperial city, it might be argued, aimed to impose on the people it defeated not only its yoke but also its language, as a peaceful bond" (*On the City of God* 19.7). Yet he is far from endorsing such a policy, for he adds: "but at the expense of how many vast wars, how much human slaughter and bloodshed, was this achieved?"

Mention of Augustine touches on another force that added to the urgency of learning Latin. Christianity, which arose as an organized religion in the eastern half of the Empire and therefore in the Greek language, soon came to operate in Latin as well. Merely tolerated at first and occasionally persecuted, then encouraged and strengthened as a religion of the Empire by Constantine (who ruled until 337), it gave further impetus to learning the language.

By what stages did Latin, whether in Italy or abroad, come to replace the other languages? We do not know, to be sure, but, on the basis of what has occurred elsewhere, we can make an informed guess. After contact with the Romans a number of the conquered people must have become bilingual. In time the native language, which lacked a written form, came to seem inferior

37

and was relegated to domestic and local matters, the humble business of daily life. Bilingualism then became a burden, which was relieved by shedding the native language. Only Latin remained. Some such sequence of events must have occurred, first in the cities of the Empire. Later, and far more slowly, it got repeated in the countryside. Like the Latin language, the Christian religion too put down its roots in urban settings and only afterwards spread to rural areas.

Latin's victory was neither immediate nor complete, as is made plain by two Fathers of the Church. Jerome (*ca.* 347–420 C.E.) writes: "besides Greek, which the entire East speaks, the Galatians possess their own language, which is almost the same as that found in Trier" (*Commentaries on the Epistle to the Galatians* 2.3). Trier, located in eastern Gaul, was evidently a city in which Gaulish was still spoken, nearly five centuries after the territory had been conquered by Julius Caesar. Jerome's comment on the use of Greek also deserves notice: "the entire East speaks it." Latin's incomplete success is confirmed for another part of the Empire by Augustine. As the Bishop of Hippo, in north Africa, he says to his flock: "there is a familiar Punic saying, which I will tell you in Latin, since not all of you know Punic" (*Sermons on the Scriptures* 167.4). Punic, the Semitic language of the Carthaginians, who had colonized the region over a millennium earlier, evidently had not yet been wholly extirpated in favor of Latin, despite more than four and a half centuries of Roman rule, since Augustine implies that at least some part of his audience does know Punic. (It is possible that with "Punic" he refers to the current native language, which might have been Berber.) Clearly, Augustine himself, who was born in Africa, was familiar with Punic. It is ironic that not long after its triumph in north Africa Latin would be rapidly replaced in turn by another Semitic language, Arabic.

In the end, however, the Roman Empire wrought a vast linguistic transformation: by late antiquity it had induced the people of its western half to abandon their various languages and speak Latin instead. But here another question arises: having established itself as described, how did Latin maintain itself in the face of Roman military defeat and political decline at the hands of people who spoke Germanic languages? Why did the language of these conquerors not have the same success as that of those earlier conquerors, the Romans themselves? Some part of the answer lies in the nature of the barbarian invaders. To begin with, they were always small in numbers, amounting, it has been estimated, to somewhere between two and five percent of the population of the various provinces. Moreover, they were not so eager to replace the Romans as to win acceptance from them, they often showed eagerness to maintain Roman civilization rather than destroy it, and they recognized that the chief structures of civil society – law, commerce, administration – would better continue to operate in Latin.

Another factor was religion. Nearly all the barbarian people were adherents of Arianism, a form of Christianity opposed, and considered heretical, by the orthodox, and indeed the barbarians had come to regard Arianism as an essential element of their communal identity. When in the course of the fourth century Arianism was defeated, on the battlefield as well as in Church councils, the tribes' feelings of distinct identity were diminished, and they yielded the more readily to the Roman Church and to the language in which it conducted its rites.

The linguistic picture was very different in the eastern half of the Empire. Though Greece itself was only a small part of that territory, Greek had long been the dominant language of both public life and culture. Alexander the Great and his successors on the thrones of the several Hellenistic kingdoms that were carved out of his empire had brought the eastern side of the Mediterranean (and much territory farther east as well) within the Greek orbit. While the majority of inhabitants continued to speak their own language, whether Egyptian or Aramaic or Lydian, the official language was everywhere Greek. "Greek," it has been observed, "was used as a colonial language, more or less as English is in India and in various African states" (Tore Janson, *Speak: A Short History of Languages*, 2002, p. 82). The contrast is clear with the other half of the Roman Empire, in which over time the language of administration supplanted, and did not merely supplement, the native languages.

With the advent of the Romans, the situation in the East hardly changed. Latin, to be sure, was used in Roman colonies for official inscriptions, military orders, and public documents, and a school of Roman law at Beirut was conducted in Latin until the early fifth century, so the elite must often have learned it. But because Greek had long been in use, and because it was regarded as a fine and prestigious language, being the vehicle of a glorious literature, it was not replaced by Latin; this is attested in the quotation from Jerome. So the division of the Empire did not affect the career of Latin in the East, for there Latin had scarcely enjoyed a career.

Three Romance Regions

With the division of the Roman Empire in two and the barbarian invasions of it, especially its western half, political and linguistic history became fragmented too. In each of what would emerge as the three major areas of Romance speech, the forces shaping the changes to the Latin language were different.

The Iberian Peninsula

The Iberian peninsula, which had begun to come under Roman rule in the third century B.C.E., did not suffer serious barbarian invasion until the early fifth century C.E. In the year 409, two Germanic tribes, the Vandals and the Suebi, along with the Alans, who had crossed the Rhine in 406 and spent a couple of years ravaging Gaul, invaded Spain. Within two years, they controlled the peninsula and its Hispano-Roman population sufficiently to divide most of the territory among themselves. While the northeast remained in Roman hands, the south was occupied by one group of Vandals, the northwest by another group of Vandals, along with the Suebi, and the west by the Alans.

At this point, the Romans invited another Germanic tribe, the Visigoths, who earlier had been their attackers but at the moment were their allies, to settle in the still-Roman northeast and defend it. Soon, around 416, the Visigoths annihilated the Alans, in the west, and those Vandals who were in the south. When the Visigothic rescuers crossed back into Gaul in 418, they left the peninsula once again under Roman control except for the Suebi and Vandals in the northwest. By 429 the Vandals had departed, moving through southern Spain and then across the Strait of Gibraltar to north Africa, where they established a kingdom that would endure for about a century. Though the Vandals as a people have passed into history, the word *vandal* is still current, reminding us of their wanton destructiveness. Not all souvenirs of the Vandals are so grim, however: before exiting from Spain they left behind a name for its lovely southernmost region, *Andalusia* "land of the Vandals."

In the meantime, the Visigoths, still Rome's allies (or its mercenaries), had to be sent back from Gaul into Spain once more in order to check the predations of the sole remaining Germanic tribe, the Suebi (whose kingdom in the northwest they would not finally destroy until 584). But after the middle of the fifth century, as Roman authority became enfeebled, the Visigoths became more independent and established a kingdom of their own that straddled the Pyrenees, partly in southwestern Gaul, partly in Spain. Early in the sixth century, the Franks drove them out of Gaul, but their Iberian kingdom, now Christian and Romanized, endured for another two hundred years.

Though it was born of warfare and conquest and did not last long, the Visigothic kingdom of Spain was marked by assimilation and a certain amount of tolerance, a model that would be imitated occasionally in subsequent Spanish history. This was the setting for the remarkable career of Isidore, Bishop of Seville (600–636) and polymathic author, a figure as important to the political as to the cultural and spiritual life of his day. Isidore negotiated with the Visigothic kings, organized the Church in Spain, and wrote histories. He also has his part in our story.

Isidore composed several works about language, the most famous and influential of which is the *Etymologiae*, a kind of encyclopedia of the sciences organized by the terms that belong to them. Despite its limitations, this book was one of the great vehicles by which classical learning was transmitted to the Latin Middle Ages. As far as language goes, it contains both appallingly improbable etymologies and priceless evidence for the history of the Romance languages – sometimes the two together in the same entry. Thus, for the word *cattus* "cat" (the source of the names for "cat" in all the western European languages, a word possibly of African origin that replaced the Classical Latin *feles* – compare *feline*) Isidore suggests several possible etymologies: from *captura* "hunting," or perhaps, he says, from the verb *cattare* (earlier form *captare* "to try to capture, to hunt," < *capere* "to capture"), which he translates – surprisingly – as "to see." In the semantic shift from "hunt" to "see," the intermediate step, attested in late classical authors, was "try to perceive through the senses." The passage is interesting because it is the earliest mention of the verb with the meaning "to see," which in medieval Spanish would become common. *Catar* exists in Spanish today only with the specialized sense "to taste (wine)." Its earlier, more general sense of "to see" survives solely in a compound like *catalejo* "telescope" (literally, "sees from afar").

Some other Romance words recorded for the first time by Isidore are *cama* "bed" (of unknown origin), *colomellus* "little column" (a diminutive from Latin *columna* "column"), hence "fang," and *sarna* "mange" (native Iberian), all found exclusively on the Iberian peninsula. Two other such words with a link to English are *hosa* "hose" (Germanic, source of English *hose, hosiery*) and *capanna* "hut." The latter, of unknown origin, was the source of French *cabane* and also a later variant, *cabine*, which led in turn to Italian *cabina*, English *cabin*, and then to the diminutives, French and English *cabinet*; English *cabana* was taken directly from Spanish.

The kingdom of the Visigoths, under whom Isidore lived and wrote, was destroyed by the Arabs. ("Arabs" too is a shorthand term, traditional and convenient, but somewhat inaccurate: though all those invaders were Muslims, most were probably Berbers, from north Africa, joined with some warriors from Arabia.) The Arabs swept westward across north Africa, crossed into Spain, and defeated the Visigoths in a decisive battle at Jerez de la Frontera, in the year 711. From the name of this town, earlier pronounced /sher-es/ (slashes enclose representations of how a word was pronounced), came English *sherries*, designating the special type of wine produced there. Misunderstood as a plural, *sherries* gave birth to the presumed singular form *sherry*. Within a short time after that momentous battle the entire peninsula fell into the hands of the Arabs, with two small exceptions: a sliver of the northeast that was held by the Franks, their Spanish March, and the Kingdom of Asturias in the northwest, that mountainous region that always resisted ready conquest. From the latter the Reconquest would begin, which was to require nearly eight centuries to retake all lands from the Arabs.

France

Like the Iberian peninsula, Gaul had long been thoroughly Romanized when, early in the fifth century, the invaders arrived who would begin to disturb it. The Burgundians, a Germanic people who had resided around the middle of the Rhine, crossed the river into Roman territory in 406, establishing their capital at Worms. In 437, however, they suffered a devastating defeat at the hands of the Huns. The survivors settled in Savoy, near Lake Geneva. Here the Burgundians recovered sufficiently that they were soon expanding their territory towards the north, south, and west, eventually occupying what is now southeastern France and the adjoining region of Switzerland. Like the Visigoths in Spain, they assimilated to the Romanized population already there. Their kingdom lasted until 534, when they succumbed to the Franks.

The Burgundian kingdom, despite its brief existence, became the setting for a well-known heroic narrative. At the center of the *Nibelungenlied* ("Song of the Nibelungs"), an anonymous epic poem written around 1200 in Middle High German, stands the figure of Kriemhild. Sister to three Burgundian

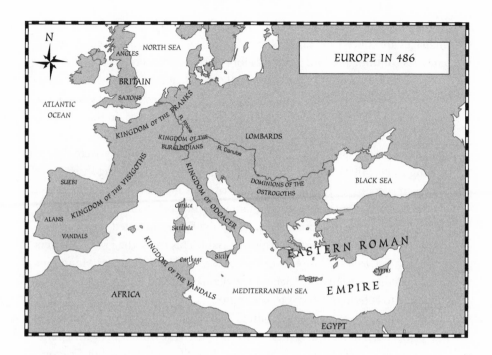

kings, she lives and is wooed at Worms. Kriemhild's second husband, called Etzel in the poem, is Attila, the leader of the Huns. (*Edsel* is a variant of *Etzel*.) Despite the links to actual times, places, and personages, the story is a historical impossibility. The plot revolves around Kriemhild's love for her first husband, Siegfried, and the long-delayed revenge she takes for his death.

Still another Germanic tribe, the Alamanni, took advantage of the Romans' abandonment of the Agri Decumates in the late third century and settled in that pocket between the Rhine and the Danube. Early in the fifth century they invaded the Empire by crossing the Rhine and moved southwards into what today is Alsace and northern Switzerland. Linguistically, however, they behaved differently from other people. Whereas the Burgundians and (later) the Franks adopted the Latin spoken by the Gallo-Roman population among whom they found themselves, the Alamanni continued with their native Germanic language. Thus they drove a Germanic-speaking wedge between two Latin-speaking people, the Burgundians to the west and the Romanized Alpine province to the south, which was called Rhaetia. In time, the Alamanni pushed

43

the Rhaetians further south into a few isolated valleys. The latter, whose various languages are collectively called Rheto-Romance, have during the subsequent centuries continued to lose ground before German speakers.

The Franks, another Germanic people, both caused the Romans much trouble over the years and provided them with loyal soldiers and generals. Some were settled on Roman lands in exchange for military service. In the mid-fifth century, the Franks moved from the lower Rhine into the Low Countries and northern France. Starting at the end of the century, when they were united by King Clovis, they came to control all of Gaul by overthrowing three other powers in succession. In 486 at the battle of Soissons they defeated the forces of a Roman kingdom that had maintained its independence after the rest of the Western Empire collapsed. Next, in 507 the Franks defeated the Visigoths, who occupied the southwestern region of Gaul. This made the Franks masters of the land between the Loire River and, to the south, the Pyrenees Mountains and the Mediterranean Sea. Then with a victory over the Burgundians, in 534, they came to rule all of what is today France.

The Franks, of course, would soon give their name to France, its language, and former currency. From earliest times, they used the word *frank* with a political meaning, "free," because in their kingdom they alone had full freedom. Hence in English the medieval word *franklin* (source of the familiar surname), a wealthy landowner who was free although not noble, like the epicurean pilgrim in Chaucer's *Canterbury Tales*. *Frank* in this sense, when applied to objects rather than people, came to mean "exempt from taxation, charge, or other condition," whence *to frank* "to indicate that one has the right of sending (a letter) without payment," as in "members of Congress must not abuse their franking privileges." The word *franchise* originally meant "freedom," then "right, privilege" (these two senses coalesce when the word, used with the definite article, means "the right to vote," as in "they only acquired the franchise in 1920"), from which it is but a small step to the commonest current meaning, as in "he owns the Burger King franchise."

The name of the people also came to be employed outside the sphere of public life. In Modern English, a person who speaks sincerely and without dissimulation is called *frank*. Such a meaning arose as freedom became associated with directness and lack of artifice, an appealing if unpersuasive identification. This is also the origin of *frankincense*, incense that is genuine, pure. At the root of this development lies the (self-)identification of a governing class with a particular virtue. Other English words with a similar history are *gentle*

(< Latin *gentilis* "of one's clan"), *generous* (< *generosus* "of noble birth"), and *noble* (< *nobilis* "of the nobility").

Although the Franks controlled all the land that is France, they did not spread themselves evenly throughout it. They tended to live in the northern parts of the country. South of the Loire they governed but rarely dwelled. The linguistic influence they exerted was thus more or less confined to the north. The language of northern France, much affected by contact with the Franks, in time became standard Modern French; with its home in the region known as the Ile-de-France and its center at Paris, it is also called "Francien." The language spoken in southern France also continued to develop out of Latin but had little contact with the Germanic language of the Franks. In time it became a distinct language, which is called "Provençal" (or "Occitan"). Nowadays Provençal is a second language for some people; almost everyone in the region can speak the northern variety, and many can speak only that. Another pair of terms for the two languages is derived from their differing words for "yes": "Langue d'Oïl" (northern, = French, Francien) and "Langue d'Oc" (southern, = Provençal, Occitan).

One small part of the Frankish territory replaced Latin speech with Celtic. When, in the wake of the Roman withdrawal, Angles and Saxons began to invade Britain in the fifth century, some of the Celtic inhabitants fled from the island, crossed the Channel, and took refuge on the nearby peninsula in northwestern Gaul, displacing the Latin-speaking Gallo-Roman population there. Because they came from Britain, the peninsula became known as *Brittany*, and its speech, called *Breton*, is still Celtic. The Celtic-speaking area has now shrunk to the western half of the peninsula, and virtually everyone there uses French as well.

In the ninth century, Normans, sailing from Denmark, began raiding the northern coast of France, as well as Germany, the Low Countries, Britain, and Spain. Also known as "Northmen," "Norsemen," and "Danes," they belonged to a larger group of Scandinavian Vikings, some of whom ravaged as far east as Russia. In the year 911 Norman pirates who had settled on the lower Seine were recognized as a duchy by the French king and became autonomous. The center of their power was Rouen, and the area they possessed became known as Normandy, more recently the site of another momentous invasion. In later centuries the Normans would again reshape the history of western Europe, principally by conquering Anglo-Saxon Britain in the eleventh century and by recapturing southern Italy and Sicily from the Arabs in the twelfth. For the moment, though, we may leave them settled in northwestern France.

Italy

The Western Empire, fittingly, lasted longest in its homeland. Italy was at least nominally ruled by a Roman emperor until 476, when the last of the line – a child, a usurper, a puppet, bearing the ironic name Romulus Augustulus, which recalled both the founder of Rome and its first emperor – was deposed by Odoacer. Odoacer, king of still another Germanic tribe, the Heruli, had served under Roman commanders before he overthrew the enfeebled Roman regime. He was soon overthrown in turn by a commander from the east, Theoderic. Theoderic had previously united several Gothic tribes, who then became known as Ostrogoths, and had been militarily active in the Balkans. An uncomfortable ally for the emperor of the Eastern Empire, he was dispatched by him to recover Italy, where he defeated Odoacer in 489. From then on, while acknowledging the sovereignty of the eastern emperor, Theoderic ruled Italy as an independent kingdom. He was nicknamed "the Great" because during his long reign (493–526) he continued Roman law and administration – and Roman administrators – and did much to improve the economic conditions of Italy, repairing roads and dredging harbors. His policy, involving parallel structures of administration, churches, and legal codes, contrasts with the assimilationist model of the Visigoths.

From history, Theoderic passed into the realm of legend. Under the name Dietrich of Bern (Bern here is Verona, site of the decisive victory over Odoacer), he appears as a secondary figure in the *Nibelungenlied*. In his own right too he became a hero of Germanic literature, the type of the courageous warrior and good king. About his legendary exploits, which are virtually unconnected to the historical figure of Theoderic, stories abound. Most have to do with warfare, recovering and defending his kingdom, fighting giants and dragons, and so forth; some are romantic. Dietrich of Bern represents among the German people the same type of quasi-historical, mostly legendary heroic figure as King Arthur does among the British.

Despite Theoderic's achievements and fame, the Ostrogothic kingdom did not long survive his death, in 526. From 535 to 552 several generals of the Eastern Empire waged a successful campaign to retake Italy from the Ostrogoths. Sardinia too was retaken, in 553, having been in the hands of the Vandals for less than a century.

Then in 568, not twenty years after the Eastern Empire had re-established its rule, Italy was invaded by one last Germanic tribe, the Lombards. The

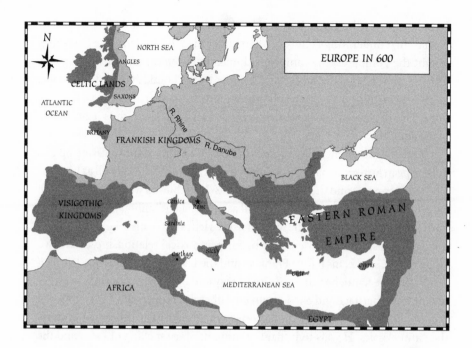

Lombards conquered a large part of Italy – the Po valley first, where they established their capital at Pavia, then Tuscany, Umbria, and much of the south. They did not conquer all of the peninsula, however. The Pope controlled certain lands, and the Eastern Empire held on to Liguria, Rome and Ravenna with their surrounding territories, and in the far south Apulia and Calabria. Not only was Italy now divided among several powers, but even the barbarians' lands were politically fragmented. The Lombards did not create a centralized kingdom, as had the Franks, but organized themselves loosely as a series of independent duchies. In this situation (not to mention the geography of the peninsula) lie the origins of that political disunity that Italy only succeeded in overcoming in the nineteenth century. The same circumstances conduced to the linguistic fragmentation of the peninsula, where even today, after a century and a half of statehood, and despite the mass media and a centralized educational system, one still hears a large variety of different dialects, and indeed a number of distinct languages.

Given the distance and weakness of the Eastern (or Byzantine) Empire and its increasingly divergent brand of Christianity, the Pope, as Bishop of Rome, perforce became the leader of Roman Italy. When the Lombards seized

Ravenna in 751, the Pope, Stephen II, appealed to the Franks for help. The Franks, first under King Pepin and then under his son Charlemagne (742–814), fought the Lombards, the campaign climaxing in the capture of Pavia in 774. The conquered Lombard lands were donated by the Frankish kings to the Pope, an enlargement of his temporal power. In return, on Christmas Day, 800, the Pope, Leo III, crowned Charlemagne Emperor of the West, thus legitimizing his conquests.

Charlemagne (French for "Charles the Great") is one of the towering figures in European history, a man who yoked together, in his person as well as his policies, the Germanic and the Roman traditions. He achieved what he did through cultural and linguistic programs as well as political and military moves, and in particular made mastery of the written word a leitmotif of his reign. An intriguing light is cast upon Charlemagne by his paradoxical relationship to the two languages he spoke, his native Frankish and the Latin he subsequently learned.

On the one hand, he put immense energy and other resources into preserving the Latin heritage and encouraging the liberal arts generally. He established schools, both at court and in monasteries, where clergy and others could study the Latin classics. He saw to it that the contemporary spelling of Latin and the penmanship of scribes were reformed. He had hundreds of ancient manuscripts collected from throughout his realm and copied; they have preserved the great bulk of the Latin literature that we possess. With these manuscripts in hand, he tried to re-establish classical standards for writing in Latin. Nor were personal efforts wanting: Charlemagne also learned Latin well enough to speak it no less fluently than Frankish. The literary and intellectual flowering he sponsored is aptly called the Carolingian Renaissance (literally "rebirth").

On the other hand, Charlemagne was eager for his subjects to use Frankish names instead of Latin for the months and the winds, and so he invented names for this purpose: instead of February he proposed *Hornung* ("the corner" or "turn" of the year, from *horn*); instead of July, *Heuuimanoth* ("the hay month"); instead of December, *Heilagmanoth* ("holy month").

Sad to say, this patron of literature and all learning was himself never able to learn to write: he started too late in life, explains his biographer. This information is reported by Einhard (*Life of Charlemagne* 25, 29), who himself illustrates some of the king's accomplishments. Einhard (*ca.* 770–840), educated at a monastic school, was a friend and adviser to Charlemagne. His biography of the king is written in correct Latin, according to the norms of the classical language, which had long been forgotten or neglected, and it imitates in its format the lives of the Roman emperors composed by the biographer Suetonius seven centuries earlier. His book is a testimonial to what Charlemagne had wrought in the world of letters and learning.

Epilogue: People and Names

The description of the dissolution of the Roman Empire, which has dwelt on the movements of the barbarians and teems with the names of their tribes, leads me to two concluding, contrasting observations, one about the abundance of names for a single barbarian people, and the other about the application of a single name to a host of peoples.

In English, we call the linguistic and ethnic group *Germans*, relying on the Latin term *Germani*, which Julius Caesar may have learned from the Gauls. The French today, applying the name of one tribe (the Alamanni) to the whole people, call them *allemands*; similarly, for the Spanish they are *alemanes*. (In the same way, we follow the Romans in calling *Greeks* the people who have always called themselves *Hellenes*: the *Graeci* were probably a Greek tribe who came early to the notice of the Romans and then disappeared, leaving only their name behind.)

The Italians use still another name. To them the Germans are *tedeschi*, which, despite appearances, is close to what the Germans call themselves. The Italian word goes back to Germanic *theudisk*. This in Old High German became *diutisc*, whence Modern German *deutsch*. (This is the source of English *Dutch*, which still means "German" in the phrase *Pennsylvania Dutch*, but otherwise refers to Holland or the Netherlands.) The first element of *theudisk* is cognate with Gaulish *teuta-*, the source of *Teutonic*. (The second element, *-isk*, is an adjective-forming suffix, seen also in *English* and *Gaulish*.) The same element, Germanic *theud-*, interestingly, has cognates in other western Indo-European language families, including Old Irish *tuath* (Celtic family), Oscan *touto* (Italic), and Old Lithuanian *tauta* (Baltic), all of which mean simply and plainly "the people." One could say that, in a sense, the polynomic Germans have no distinctive name for themselves.

No less intriguing than the abundance of different names for the Germans is the variety of applications of the single ethnic adjective that is the root of *Welsh*, *Walloon*, and other names. This story begins with the Germanic term *Walhos*, which referred to a particular neighboring Celtic tribe, called *Volcae* by the Romans. It was then generalized to refer to all Celts, not just those of the one tribe. The name *Gaul* (Latin *Gallia*) for the central territory inhabited by the Celtic people comes from the same source. The Germanic people who later invaded Britain carried the name with them, applying it to the Celtic people they found there. It thus meant "Briton" and by extension – such were relations between the two peoples – "foreigner; slave." By the twelfth century, it had narrowed its reference again, being restricted to the *Welsh*; hence also *Wales* and *Cornwall* (of which the first element may be Celtic *corn* "horn," with reference to the shape of the Cornish peninsula). It also survives in the surnames *Welsh*, *Walsh*, and (Scottish) *Wallace*. The Welsh, who do not find their own language foreign, call it *Cymric*, by the way, and call themselves *Cymry*.

Back on the continent, *Walhos* also became generalized, designating not the Celts alone, but non-Germans of any kind, strangers, foreigners. It thus – ironically – got applied to the Romans, that is to say, to the Latin- (or Romance-) speaking people with whom the Germans were in contact. This meaning has persisted down to the present. In German, *welsch* denotes "the foreigner," especially one who speaks a Romance language. It may be a neutral term, as in *die welsche Schweiz*, the French-speaking part of Switzerland, or derogatory, as in the phrase *welsche Treue*, referring to an unreliable loyalty. In Dutch, *Waalsch* designates the French-speaking people of Belgium, whom we call *Walloons*.

The same word also traveled eastwards, being taken over from the Germanic people by the Slavic. A historic name for southern Rumania is *Walachia*, for its people *Vlach* (in German, *Wallach*, also familiar as a surname). The Polish word for "Italian" is *Wloch*.

Returning to English, we can now see that *walnut* has the same origin. Introduced from Gaul and Italy and contrasted with the native hazel nut, the word originally meant "foreign nut." The verb *to welsh* (or *welch*) as in "welsh on a bet," first recorded in the nineteenth century, has sometimes been connected with the word under consideration, but there is no evidence for this, and the etymology remains unknown.

OTHER ROMANCE TONGUES, OTHER PLACES

Other Romance Languages in Europe

In the remainder of this book I trace out how the national languages of Spain, France, and Italy developed from Latin. These are by no means the only

Romance languages, merely those I have chosen. Many others exist. Because they do not figure in the remainder of these pages, I will deal with them now. I group these languages by geography and convenience rather than by science, and avoid getting involved with dialects.

A dialect is a version of a language perceived as different from a standard or other version. Drawing a clear distinction between a dialect and a language is an old, familiar, and formidable challenge. Here perhaps it can simply be accepted that "language" and "dialect" are two terms lying on a continuum of terms for speech differentiation. (Others would be "idiolect," the speech peculiar to a single person, which is the smallest group, and "language family," which describes a grouping larger than "language," such as the Indo-European family or the Germanic.) Although in many cases everybody would approve of one term or the other – that Rumanian is a separate language is as widely acknowledged as that Aragonese is a Spanish dialect – the distinction between language and dialect often remains a matter of interpretation and controversy. Because I'm not dealing with dialects here, the colorful, varied mosaic of speech found in Romance-speaking Europe is drastically reduced to the standard forms of the three languages; I'm sacrificing richness and completeness to simplicity and clarity. What follows is a modest attempt to restore a little fullness to the picture.

Our survey of the Latin-speaking lands of the Roman Empire begins in the south and moves clockwise. Most traces of the Latin language in central and western north Africa were wiped out by the Arab conquest in the seventh century. The native population, however, by then thoroughly Romanized and Christianized, especially in the cities, did retain a number of words they had adopted from Latin into their Berber language, where they live on today: *akartassu* "cork" (< Latin *corticea* "bark"), *akiker* "chickpea" (< *cicer*), *asentil* "rye" (< *centenum*), *grana* "frog" (< *rana*), *imik* "crumb" (< *mica*).

In the same way, Latin was all but eliminated from Britain in the fifth century, when the Angles and Saxons invaded the island, which had recently been abandoned by the Romans.

On the Iberian peninsula, the language most widely spoken is Spanish (also called "Castilian"). Yet it is not alone. The broad strip of land lying along the western (Atlantic) coast is, except in the far north, the country of Portugal, whose national language is Portuguese, another major Romance language, with a rich literature of its own. Because of their geographical position, maritime experience, and boldness, the Portuguese played a prominent role in exploring

51

the western and eastern coasts of Africa (and from there the Indian Ocean) as well as South America.

The northern piece of the western coast, called Galicia, belongs to Spain politically, yet its speech is closer to that of Portugal. In the Middle Ages, Galician was the medium of much refined lyric poetry, used even by those whose language was not Galician – for example, King Alfonso X of Castile (1221–1284, nicknamed "the Wise").

The broad northeastern strip of the Spanish coast, lying along the Mediterranean, is home to another language, Catalan. Catalonia, whose principal city is Barcelona, was a great commercial power in the western Mediterranean during late medieval times. It conquered the Balearic Islands in the early thirteenth century, and the language spoken there remains Catalan.

Within the borders of France we find, in addition to the national language, Provençal, which is of the south. Like Galician in Spain, Provençal was an important literary language in the Middle Ages, used especially for lyric poetry (the verse of the troubadours in particular) and sometimes by poets whose native language it was not. A roughly triangular region in the southeastern central part of the country is the home of Franco-Provençal, the name of which indicates its intermediate position between the two other speeches.

Several other areas lying just outside the borders of France are also French-speaking. Southern Belgium is home to the Walloons, who speak French (the northern part of the country speaks Flemish, a Germanic language akin to Dutch). In Luxembourg the language of administration and education is French. The native language of those living in western Switzerland, the Suisse Romande, is French as well. The same is true for Monaco, on the Mediterranean shore.

A remarkable diversity of dialects still flourishes in Italy. Italian is also spoken in Istria and Dalmatia, formerly parts of Yugoslavia, and in southern Switzerland.

Sardinian, however, is a separate language and the most conservative among all the Romance languages. It preserves a number of Latin features that other Romance languages do not, and it has not been affected by non-Romance languages, as the others all have.

Northeastern Italy and eastern Switzerland are home to a series of speeches that, though collectively called "Rhaeto-Romance" by convention, in fact do not have a common ancestry other than Latin: that is to say, after the collapse of Roman rule they were never again united politically, administratively, or

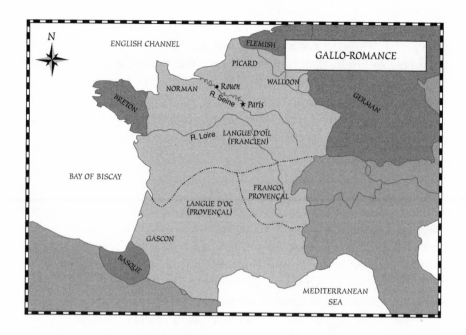

culturally. As a result, they do not share many characteristics. Of the three Rhaeto-Romance subgroups, the two smaller – Romantsch (in Switzerland) and Ladin (in Italy) – are both found in mountainous areas, and both proclaim their link with Rome and its language in the names they apply to themselves. The third, spoken by many more people, is Friulan (called by the people themselves "Furlano"), located in Italy to the northeast of Venice.

Further south along the eastern coast of the Adriatic, another Romance language was once spoken, Dalmatian. The last speaker of it died in 1898, though not without leaving some record of his speech: he had been interrogated by a linguist.

We come finally to Rumanian, which also through its name proclaims its membership in the Romance family. The language was not unequivocally recognized as Romance until the nineteenth century because it had changed so much from Latin, in particular incorporating many words of Slavic origin. But once linguists were certain of Rumanian's ancestry, they faced a puzzle that has not yet been solved. How did a Latin-based language come to be the speech of so large a population in that area? One theory is that Latin persisted north of the Danube, in the province called Dacia, just as it did in Spain and Gaul.

But the Romans occupied Dacia for only about 170 years before abandoning it, in 271 C.E. This does not look like a long enough period for Latin to have taken hold so firmly. Hence the rival theory, that the language disappeared but was brought back later by settlers from south of the Danube who were forced to emigrate by the arrival of Slavic tribes. Because we know so little about Rumanian's early history – the first preserved text dates only from the sixteenth century – we may never be in a position to decide the question.

Romance Languages beyond Europe

The course of history has carried several Romance languages beyond their European homeland to other parts of the world. Emigration, exile, and the desire for colonial expansion have introduced Portuguese, Spanish, French, and Italian to new lands on every continent.

As part of their exploration and exploitation of Africa and the East, the Portuguese established colonies in the Cape Verde islands (west of Senegal), in Guinea-Bissau, Angola, and Mozambique (all three along the western coast of Africa), and at various points on the coasts of India (Goa, for one), Ceylon, Timor, Java, Malaysia, and China (Macao). In all these places, now independent of the mother country, the mother tongue persists. Portugal also pushed westwards, into the New World. Portuguese is the language of two Atlantic archipelagos, Madeira and the Azores, and of Brazil, South America's largest and most populous country.

In one and the same year, 1492, two movements began that carried the Spanish language beyond its historical borders. Isabel and Ferdinand, *los Reyes Católicos* "the Catholic Monarchs," expelled the large population of Spanish Jews from the peninsula. The Jews took their language, nowadays most often called "Judeo-Spanish" (also "Ladino" and "Judezmo"), with them to the places of their exile, which included all parts of the Mediterranean basin, especially the Balkans: Thessalonica had a thriving Jewish community until the Second World War. And in the same year, Columbus, sailing under the flag of Spain, discovered America, where eventually all the lands between the Rio Grande and Tierra del Fuego, except Brazil and a couple of small adjoining states, would become Spanish-speaking. Much of the Caribbean also uses Spanish (Cuba and Puerto Rico), as does a considerable population in the United States. Some of the latter belong to families who have resided for centuries in the southwestern parts of the country, descendants of the original Spanish settlers;

many others are more recent immigrants from the Caribbean and Central and South America. Spanish is also spoken in the Canary Islands and Equatorial Guinea.

French has not had the same extraordinary expansion as its Iberian cousins, and yet it too is found on all continents. A sizeable French-speaking population lives in the Canadian province of Quebec. Earlier French colonists, known as Cajuns, left eastern Canada and settled in Louisiana, where they continue to speak a French-based language. French is the official language of Haiti and some smaller islands in the West Indies. Africa too was an object of French colonization, so the language still plays some role in Morocco, Algeria, and Tunisia, all bordering the Mediterranean, and also throughout the western and central regions of the continent, from Senegal to Zaire, in the Malagasy Republic, and in the Congo (a former Belgian colony). On the sea-lanes to Asia, the French established outposts in Mauritius, Seychelles, and Reunion, where their language is still spoken. From the countries of southeastern Asia, by contrast, Vietnam, Laos, and Cambodia, formerly French possessions, the French language has more or less disappeared.

Italian is much less diffused beyond its borders than French. A small pocket of Italian speakers is found in Italy's former African colony, Eritrea. And steady emigration has produced substantial Italian-speaking communities that have maintained themselves in Australia, Canada, the United States, Brazil, and Argentina.

All in all, Romance or Romance-based languages are used by well over half a billion people scattered across six continents and three oceans. Rome, the point of origin for all these languages, was the principal city of a plain no larger than the state of Delaware.

CHAPTER FOUR

LATIN AT WORK, I

Nature of the Language; Names and Qualities; Pronunciation

LATIN: AN INFLECTED LANGUAGE

We have observed the Indo-European ancestry of Latin and traced its recorded history from being the language of a city-state in central Italy to the language of a vastly larger territory, and then, as a result of the Empire's collapse and invasion, the language of a smaller but still significant part of Europe, which, in a later age of colonization, carried it to the Americas and other parts of the world – vast expansion, then shrinkage, followed long after by a second diffusion. But that is the external history of Latin, its career through time and space. What is the nature of this language that has lasted so long and traveled so far? In order to grasp the sometimes dramatic ways in which Latin changed, it is not necessary to study or learn it, but merely to understand how it worked, which is quite simple.

What makes the history of Latin becoming the Romance languages so fascinating is the combination of remarkable continuity with dramatic changes. The similarities between the mother and the daughters are close and palpable. And yet a great revolution has occurred in the course of the centuries, and the nature of the daughter languages is fundamentally different from that of the mother. Latin is an inflected language, whereas French, Spanish, and Italian – at least in regard to nouns and adjectives – are not. Rather, they are of a type called "isolating." Over time, that is to say, an inflected language (Latin) has evolved into isolating languages (the modern Romance languages) – a profound alteration in language type. Inflection, a fundamental trait that Latin and its kindred languages inherited from their Indo-European ancestor, was largely given up. We may understand inflection more fully by considering our own language, which is not inflected, or hardly so.

56

In English, a noun is always said and written in the same way. *Window, frustration,* and *child* are the words used to name certain things and people. To refer to more than one of them we say *windows, frustrations,* and *children.* No other forms exist in the modern language, except those with *-'s,* which indicate possession ("the window's dimensions," "the children's toys"). An English noun has one form for the singular and another for the plural, and that is all. It makes no difference whether the noun performs the action of the verb ("the window let light into the room"), or experiences it ("you broke the window"), or is used with a preposition ("a breeze entered through the window"). We never think of such distinctions in regard to English nouns, nor do we need to. The word is always *window* or *windows.*

In Latin, by contrast, the same word exists in a number of different forms: *fenestra, fenestrae, fenestram, fenestris* are a few of the forms of the word for "window." They are pronounced and written differently from one another. The difference is found at the end of the word. *Fenestr-,* which is the stem, remains the same, but the endings (or inflections) attached to it vary: *-a, -ae, -am, -is.* Which of the various forms is used depends on what job the word is doing in its sentence. Is it performing the action of the verb, as in "the window let light into the room"? Then we use one form (*fenestra*). Is it, rather, experiencing or suffering the action of the verb, as in "you broke the window"? In that case we use another form (*fenestram*). A language like Latin that relies very heavily on inflections is an inflected language.

Here is a simple example that brings out the inflected nature of Latin through contrast with English. Consider two English sentences: "Peter kills Paul" and "Paul kills Peter." Certainly there is a dramatic difference of meaning between the two, and each meaning is unmistakable. But what is it that produces the different meanings? It is not the words in themselves. Taken individually, the three words are identical in each sentence, said and written exactly alike. The different meanings are established exclusively by the *order* of the words: the noun before the verb performs the action (in grammar this is called the "subject" of the verb); the noun after it receives or suffers the action (the "object" of the verb).

If we translate "Peter kills Paul" into Latin now, it might come out like this: *Petrus Paulum interficit.* In this version, the word order runs: subject – object – verb. But what establishes *Petrus* as the subject is not its position at the head of the sentence or before the verb, but its form, which is determined by its ending, or inflection, *-us;* this ending tells us Peter performs the action of the verb.

Similarly, the inflection -*um* in *Paulum* tells us Paul experiences the action of the verb. The verb *interficit* means "(he) kills." Thus, "Peter kills Paul," and not the other way around.

The inflections, as we will see, are many. Yet in exchange, as it were, for its multiplicity of inflections, Latin possesses a kind of gift. Because inflections, not word order, determine the subject and the object, speakers are free to arrange the words in any order they would like: *Paulum Petrus interficit,* or *interficit Petrus Paulum,* or *Petrus interficit Paulum,* etc. The emphasis may shift from one version to another – in the first perhaps some emphasis falls on the victim of the crime, in the second on the action itself – but all six permutations of these three words have precisely the same meaning. The gift of a relatively free word order is a great one, much exploited by writers of both prose and verse.

The reverse situation, "Paul kills Peter," might be rendered *Paulus Petrum interficit,* where the inflection of *Paulus* indicates it is the subject of the verb and that of *Petrum* indicates it is the object. Change the inflections and you change the meaning of the sentence. Again, word order does not affect meaning; any arrangement is possible. We may formulate Latin's way of establishing meaning like this: FORMS > SYNTAX. ("Syntax" means a language's systems for defining the relationships among the various components of the sentence, and thus creating and conveying the intended meaning of the whole.) For English (and the modern Romance languages too) the corresponding formulation, with some simplification, would be: WORD ORDER > SYNTAX.

Now let us add a judgment and a weapon to the event in our original sentence: "wicked Peter kills Paul with a sword." We recognize that the adjective *wicked* applies to *Peter,* not to *Paul* or *sword,* solely because it is positioned next to *Peter* (contrast "Peter kills wicked Paul" or "with a wicked sword"). The prepositional phrase with *with* indicates by what means Peter does the dirty deed. In Latin this might be: *Petrus malus Paulum gladio interficit.* The adjective *malus* "wicked" does appear beside *Petrus,* to be sure, but, though common, this is neither necessary nor significant. The *form* of the adjective indicates unmistakably that Peter is identified as wicked: a grammatical rule of Latin is that an adjective has the same form as the noun it modifies. Here, accordingly, the adjective modifies *Petrus,* and it would modify *Petrus* even if it appeared at a different place in the sentence, as occurs often in poetry. The word *gladio* is a form of the noun *gladius* that indicates means or instrument, "with (by, by means of) a sword"; to express this relation in English we need to use a prepositional phrase.

In summary, English does have some inflections (singular and plural forms of the noun), but they make up so small a part of the grammar that we do not call it an inflected language. Instead, most of the meaning is created by word order and by prepositions. Latin, which, to be sure, does have prepositions, tends strongly to create meaning through the forms of the words – through inflections.

To illustrate the similarity between the Romance languages and English and the difference between all of them and Latin, we may translate the last sentence: French *Pierre le méchant tue Paul avec une épée,* Italian *il cattivo Pietro uccide Paolo con una spada,* Spanish *Pedro el malo mata a Pablo con una espada.* These languages have the same grammatical rule for adjectives as Latin, so the adjectives (*méchant, cattivo, malo* "wicked" – notice the variety, though all come from Latin!) are all in the masculine singular form, showing that they agree with *Peter* – they convey information about him. (Despite this rule, the adjectives must also appear next to the nouns they modify.) Yet for the rest, the Romance languages differ from Latin and resemble English: meaning is created very much by word order (notice the near identity thereof in the three sentences) and also by prepositions, only a little by inflected forms.

This illustrates Latin's evolution from an inflected language into one of a different kind. The evolution of English from its Germanic ancestor is parallel to that of the Romance languages from Latin; both Germanic and Latin were much more heavily inflected than their modern descendants. Indeed, the reducing of inflections is the single most prominent feature in the entire history of the Indo-European languages.

Forms of Nouns

Descriptors of Noun Forms

Latin nouns appear in a variety of forms, that is, with various endings, or inflections. To identify the different forms of the noun and to distinguish them from one another, three types of descriptors are employed: gender, number, and case. Every Latin noun met in speech or writing has a gender, a number, and a case. The modern languages have simplified this. English nouns have only number, and Romance nouns have both number and gender. Case has completely disappeared.

Like Ancient Greek and Modern German, Latin has three genders, masculine, feminine, and neuter. Gender is a grammatical term here, for the most part unconnected to sex. A noun's gender is a given in the language. It is not a matter of choice for the speaker, and it cannot be altered. A noun simply exists as either masculine or feminine or neuter. Sometimes the grammatical gender corresponds to natural gender: the word for "virgin" is feminine (*virgo*), for "king" masculine (*rex*), for "cow" feminine (*vacca*), for "bull" masculine (*taurus*). This seems straightforward, but the number of nouns possessing natural gender is tiny. For the vast majority, the gender appears arbitrary. Why is *lignum* ("wood") neuter yet *arbor* ("tree") feminine? How is it that the word for "window" (*fenestra*) is feminine, for "wall" (*paries*) masculine, for "floor" (*solum*) neuter? Why one noun is feminine, another masculine, and still another neuter remains a puzzle. In many nouns, it may have to do with the stem: usually stems in -*o* are masculine, those in -*a* feminine. (That in turn, if we wanted to pursue the matter, would lead to the question of why certain words have certain stems.)

Whereas Latin operates with three genders, its daughter languages have only two, masculine and feminine; we will deal later with the fate of the Latin neuter words. For English speakers learning Latin or a modern Romance language, having to memorize the gender of each noun is irksome and a regular source of trouble. By the same token, the fact that Modern English nouns have no gender is doubtless one of the features that makes the language easier for learners.

All these languages coincide, however, in having two numbers, singular and plural: Latin *amicus amici*, Italian *amico amici*, Spanish *amigo amigos*, French *ami amis*, English *friend friends*. If we know only those languages, we may suppose that no other number is conceivable, that singular and plural exhaust the possibilities. That is not so, in fact. Curiously, Indo-European also had a dual number, a special set of forms to refer to two. The dual survived for a while in Greek: in Classical Attic Greek (fifth and fourth centuries B.C.E.) it was already confined to words referring to natural pairs, like eyes and oxen, but it is completely unknown to the writers of the New Testament (first century C.E.). The dual has left a couple of traces in Latin: *duo* "two" and *ambo* "both" still show an old dual ending in -*o* (compare Greek *ophthalmo* "two eyes"). Today the dual still survives in Lithuanian and Icelandic, a truly ancient relic of Indo-European. Latin, however, operates with just singular and plural, as do its daughter languages.

The descendants of one of the duals that did manage to survive in Latin, *duo*, are easy to recognize: consider *dual, duo, duet, deuce*. The descendants of *ambo*, however, are more elusive and more intriguing. *Ambo*, in its combinative form *ambi-*, is found in *ambidextrous* (second element from Latin *dexter* "right") "having both right (hands), using the two hands equally well," *ambivalence* (< *valere* "to be strong") "strength in both (that is, two opposing) ways, contradictory attitude toward someone or something," and *ambiguous* (*-ig-* < *agere* "to act") "acting in two (opposing) ways, capable of being understood in two ways."

From its proper, local meaning, "on both sides," *ambi-* developed a looser one, "around, about," which is seen in *ambient* (*-i-* < *ire* "to go") "going around, surrounding on all sides," *ambition* (at first "going around" for the purpose of seeking votes in order to win elective office, then any similar eager striving for rank or power), and *ambulant* (second element not an independent word) "walking around." Related to *ambulant*, in turn, are *amble* and *ambulance*, the latter originally an adjective in the French phrase *hôpital ambulant* "a walking (that is, mobile) hospital." The Greek adverb/preposition cognate with *ambo* is *amphi*, still seen in *amphibious* "living in both ways (that is, on land and in the water)" and *amphitheater* "a place for looking (at something) from all around."

The word that has followed the most extraordinary, twisting path away from *ambo* is English *bust*: who would guess they were related? The Latin word *bustum* originally meant "funeral pyre" and was derived from *amb-ustum* "burnt all around," from *ambi-* and *ustum* "burnt." A false perception then altered the word. Misunderstood by the Romans (through what linguists call "misdivision") as *am-bustum*, it lost its presumed prefix and became shortened to *bustum*. *Bustum* soon developed, beside "funeral pyre," the more general sense of "burial place, tomb" without reference to cremation, and during the Classical Latin period those were the only meanings it had. When the word later reappeared in Italian, it no longer referred to a burial place, but rather to a type of statuary that represented the human figure from the chest upwards, and also to the trunk or torso. The presumed connection is that statues of this sort were associated with tombs. From the statuary type the word came to designate the female chest, the breasts. With these meanings, it soon passed from Italian into French (and thence English). The sound of *b* is all that remains from *ambi-*.

After gender and number, the third descriptor of a noun's form is case. Case is the feature that indicates the job the noun does in the sentence – whether the noun, for instance, performs the action of the verb or experiences it. The earlier description of *Petrus Paulum interficit* "Peter kills Paul" may now be rephrased in more precise grammatical terms: a Latin speaker identifies *Petrus* as the subject of the verb because it is in the nominative case, and *Paulum* as the object of the verb because it is in the accusative case. For all practical purposes, the language operates with five cases. In addition to the nominative and accusative, a Latin noun exists in the genitive, dative, and ablative cases. I will describe their use shortly.

Indo-European appears to have had three other cases besides: a vocative, a locative, and an instrumental, traces of the first two of which are still found in Latin. Just as in the passage from Indo-European to Latin the number of the noun's cases was reduced from eight to five, so in the passage from Latin to the modern Romance languages the number continued to be reduced, from five to two and then to one. Why and how French, Italian, and Spanish came eventually to lack cases altogether is an essential part of our story, and the clearest example of their conversion from inflected to isolating languages.

The Five Declensions

Every noun in Latin has a single, inalterable gender. The noun can be used in singular and plural, and in any one of five cases. Every noun, therefore, exists in a total of ten forms. The complete set of a noun's forms is called a "declension." (The word derives from *declinare* "to lean away from": the ancient grammarians pictured the other four cases as "leaning away from," that is, deviating from, the nominative.) Here is the declension of the noun *porta* "gate."

THE FIRST DECLENSION		
	Singular	**Plural**
Nominative	*port-ă*	*port-ae*
Genitive	*port-ae*	*port-arum*
Dative	*port-ae*	*port-is*
Accusative	*port-am*	*port-as*
Ablative	*port-ā*	*port-is*

We can see at once that the ten forms of *porta* do not consist of ten wholly different words, but rather of only seven. Within the declension there is some overlap of forms. *Portae* could be genitive or dative singular or nominative plural, *portis* either dative or ablative plural. Since each of the forms plays a different syntactical role, the overlap might seem worrisome. Nonetheless, the room for confusion is small – at least for Latin speakers. In context, in a given sentence or discourse, it was clear which of the possibilities was intended; if it weren't, the Latin speaker presumably would have expressed herself otherwise. It should be noted, however, that the nominative and the ablative singular are *not* identical. The ablative is distinguished by ending in a long *ā* (which we moderns mark with a macron) instead of a short. Though written the same by the Romans, the two vowels were pronounced with a clearly perceptible difference. To the Roman ear *portă* nominative could not be confused with *portā* ablative – no more than the verb in "I always used to read magazines" sounds like the verb in "yesterday I read a new magazine."

The forms of *porta* are written here with a hyphen to show clearly the two parts of the word: the stem *port-*, which does not change and which carries the meaning "gate," and the endings, which do change and show the job the word does in its sentence. The set of endings (*-a, -ae, -ae, -am*, etc.) is not unique to this word. On the contrary, the Latin language includes thousands of words with precisely the same endings. Here is the declension of *rota* "wheel": (singular) *rot-ă, rot-ae, rot-ae, rot-am, rot-ā*; (plural) *rot-ae, rot-arum, rot-is, rot-as, rot-is*. Once you learn the forms of *porta*, you also know the forms of *rota* and all other such words. This set of endings, this pattern of declension is called the first declension. (Thus, the term "declension" can refer either to the pattern of endings or to its application in a particular noun.) Practically all the nouns of the first declension, like *porta* and *rota*, are feminine in gender.

A number of phrases familiar in English still retain the endings of the Latin first declension nouns that are their origin. I'll reserve examples of nominative singulars and plurals for later, but here are phrases illustrating some of the other cases:

- Genitive singular (translated "of") in *-ae*: *lapsus linguae* "a slip of the tongue"; *aqua vitae* "the water of life," a strong alcoholic drink, the term probably derived from the use of brandy for medicine – or a kind of tippler's joke (the word *whiskey*, incidentally, originates in the Gaelic phrase *uisge beatha* "the water of life," itself likely to be a translation from Medieval Latin).

- Accusative singular (object of preposition) in *-am*: *ad nauseam* "to (the point of) nausea," as in "she talked ad nauseam about how wealthy her family used to be."
- Ablative singular (used with prepositions) in *-ā*: *subpoena*, from Latin *sub poena* "under penalty (of ...)," the threatening first words of the writ ordering someone to appear in court; *ex cathedra* "from the chair," made or done by virtue of one's office or authority, as in "his ex cathedra pronouncements on psychiatry," the chair being a symbol of office or authority (*cathedra* is a Greek word by origin, the source of *chair* and also of *cathedral*, the church where a bishop has his seat); *deux ex machina* "the god from the machine," that is, from the stage machinery (a crane or a revolving platform), which enabled a divinity to appear suddenly at the end of a play in order to resolve an irresoluble situation, Artemis, for example, in the *Hippolytus* by Euripides or Jupiter in Plautus's *Amphitruo*.
- Ablative plural (expressing cause) in *-is*: *gratis* < Classical Latin *gratiis* "because of kindnesses, (hence) without compensation."

See how much Latin you knew without realizing it?

Latin has four additional declensions, that is to say, four more groups of nouns, each group with its own set of distinctive endings. Here is a typical noun from the second declension, *amicus* "friend."

THE SECOND DECLENSION, MASCULINE		
	Singular	Plural
Nominative	*amic-us*	*amic-i*
Genitive	*amic-i*	*amic-orum*
Dative	*amic-o*	*amic-is*
Accusative	*amic-um*	*amic-os*
Ablative	*amic-o*	*amic-is*

Most second declension nouns end in *-us* and are masculine, like *amicus*. Two similarities to *porta* that you can spot here will play a very important part in the later history of Latin. A characteristic vowel is found in a number of the forms (here *o*, in the first declension *a*): in Spanish and Italian, many masculine nouns still end in *-o* and many feminine nouns in *-a*. Moreover, the accusatives singular and plural end in *-m* and *-s*, respectively (*-am* and *-as* in the first declension, *-um* and *-os* in the second): the *-m*, scarcely pronounced in Latin, will soon disappear, and Spanish and French (and therefore English) still make their plurals with *-s*.

As with *porta* and first declension nouns, the endings exemplified in *amicus* are the same for all second declension masculine nouns; if you can decline *amicus*, you can also decline *numerus* "number" and thousands of others. A number of endings of the second declension somewhat resemble those of the first: in addition to the accusatives, the ablative singulars -*ā* and -*ō*, genitive plurals -*arum* and -*orum*, dative and ablative plurals -*is*. The endings of the remaining three declensions will be seen to be quite different.

The second declension also includes a good number of neuter nouns, for instance, *spatium* "space."

THE SECOND DECLENSION, NEUTER		
	Singular	Plural
Nominative	*spati-um*	*spati-ă*
Genitive	*spati-i*	*spati-orum*
Dative	*spati-o*	*spati-is*
Accusative	*spati-um*	*spati-ă*
Ablative	*spati-o*	*spati-is*

Notice that the nominative and accusative plurals are identical and end in -*ă*. This is true for all neuter nouns in the language. It too will prove to be significant in the history of the Romance languages.

Quite a few English words and phrases still retain the endings of the Latin second declension:

- Genitive singular (translated "of") in -*i*: *anno Domini*, abbreviated A.D., "in the year of the Lord"; *lapsus calami* "a slip of the pen," the counterpart to *lapsus linguae*; *horror vacui* "dread of a vacuum," a term in art history for an artist's inability to leave empty space in her or his work; *exempli gratia*, abbreviated *e.g.*, "for the sake of example."
- Accusative singular (here used as object of preposition) in -*um*: *per annum* "per year," as in "her salary is $82,000 per annum."
- Ablative singular (with prepositions) in -*o*: *pro bono* "for the sake of good," work (usually legal) performed without a fee; *ex officio* "on the basis of one's office (or position)," as in "the chairman is a member ex officio of the executive committee"; *in vino veritas* "in wine (is) truth."
- Genitive plural (translated "of") in -*orum*: *variorum*, usually in the phrase "variorum edition," a text printed with the notes of several scholars, a shortening of the full phrase *editio cum notis variorum* "edition with the notes of various people"; *novus ordo seclorum* (a more classical spelling

would be *saeculorum*) "the new order of the ages," a motto from the Great
Seal of the United States, found on the back of a $1 bill.

- Dative plural (translated "to" or "for") in *-is*: *annuit coeptis* "he (that
  is, God) has given his approval to our undertakings," another motto of
  the same origin; *sic semper tyrannis* "thus always to tyrants," the words
  shouted by John Wilkes Booth after shooting Abraham Lincoln.

The third declension, well populated with nouns, is also important. Our
examples are *pes* "foot" and *corpus* "body."

THE THIRD DECLENSION				
	Pes, masculine		*Corpus*, neuter	
	Singular	Plural	Singular	Plural
Nominative	pes	ped-es	corpus	corpor-a
Genitive	ped-is	ped-um	corpor-is	corpor-um
Dative	ped-i	ped-ibus	corpor-i	corpor-ibus
Accusative	ped-em	ped-es	corpus	corpor-a
Ablative	ped-e	ped-ibus	corpor-e	corpor-ibus

(Feminine nouns of the third declension have endings identical to those of
pes.) Although the endings of *pes* are almost wholly different from those of
porta or *amicus*, we do notice again that the accusatives singular and plural
end in *-m* and *-s*. Third declension nouns do not incline toward one gender or
another.

Besides the different endings, something else sets this declension apart from
the others, and this too was to become important in post-classical times. The
relation between the nominative and the full stem (as shown by the genitive
singular) is unpredictable, unstable: *pes* nominative : *ped-is* genitive; *caput*
nominative : *capit-is* genitive (contrast the consistent stems *port-* and *amic-*).
The full stem is invariably reflected in English derivatives: compare *pedal* and
capital. The result is that the nominative sometimes looks isolated, not firmly
wedded to the rest of the declension. Further examples are: *tempus* : *tempor-
is* "time," *princeps* : *princip-is* "chief," and *homo* : *homin-is* "man" (compare
temporal, principal, hominid).

English words and phrases contain many examples of third declension
endings:

- Genitive singular (translated "of") in *-is*: *rigor mortis* "the stiffness of
  death"; *honoris causa* "for the sake of honor, honorary," as in "he was

awarded the degree Doctor of Humane Letters honoris causa"; *non compos mentis* "not in possession of one's mind."

- Accusative singular (object of some prepositions) in *-em*: *post mortem* "after death"; *infra dignitatem* "beneath one's dignity," often shortened to *infra dig*; *ad hominem* "at the person," used of arguments or attacks directed at one's opponent personally, not at the substance of the disagreement.
- Ablative singular (object of other prepostions) in *-e*: *pro tempore* "for the time being," as in "president pro tempore of the Senate," often shortened to *pro tem*; *sub judice*, literally "under a judge," with the meaning "under consideration by a court, not yet decided or resolved."
- Dative plural (translated "for") in *-ibus*: *omnibus* "(something) for all persons," most often (1) a mode of public transportation, nowadays shortened to *bus*, but sometimes (2) a book collecting various writings, intended for wide public diffusion, and also (3) used in the legislative phrase "omnibus bill," one that includes a miscellany of provisions, "something for everybody," as it were.
- Accusative plural (here used with a preposition) in *-es*: *primus inter pares* "first among equals," a familiar oxymoron.
- Ablative plural (with a preposition) in *-ibus*: *e pluribus unum* "out of many, one," the motto of the United States, referring to the creation of a central national government out of individual states.

The fourth and fifth declensions are not heavily populated. Of the fourth, our example is *fructus* "fruit."

THE FOURTH DECLENSION		
	Singular	Plural
Nominative	*fruct-ŭs*	*fruct-ūs*
Genitive	*fruct-ūs*	*fruct-uum*
Dative	*fruct-ui*	*fruct-ibus*
Accusative	*fruct-um*	*fruct-ūs*
Ablative	*fruct-u*	*fruct-ibus*

Though written alike, *fructŭs* nominative singular was pronounced differently from *fructūs* genitive singular or nominative or accusative plural. Again, accusative singular and plural end in *-m* and *-s*. Almost all fourth declension nouns are masculine.

A few fourth declension endings are preserved in English phrases:

- Accusative singular (object of preposition) in -*um*: *post partum* "after childbirth," as in "post partum depression."
- Ablative singular (object of preposition) in -*u*: *in situ* "in place, in the original position," as in "the grave goods were photographed in situ by the archaeologists"; *pari passu* "at the same pace," as in "his debility increased pari passu with the spread of the cancer."

Of the fifth declension, our example is *res* "thing":

THE FIFTH DECLENSION		
	Singular	Plural
Nominative	*r-es*	*r-es*
Genitive	*r-ei*	*r-erum*
Dative	*r-ei*	*r-ebus*
Accusative	*r-em*	*r-es*
Ablative	*r-e*	*r-ebus*

Once again the accusatives end in -*m* and -*s*. Virtually all fifth declension nouns are feminine. In the course of time the fourth and fifth declensions, underpopulated to begin with, disappeared.

The fifth declension too can show some survivals in English:

- Accusative singular (object of preposition or direct object of verb) in -*em*: *ante* (or *post*) *meridiem* "before (or after) mid-day," abbreviated to A.M. or P.M.; *requiem* "rest," a mass sung at funerals, the name derived from the service's opening words, *requiem aeternam dona eis, Domine* "grant them, Lord, eternal rest"; *carpe diem* "pluck the day," a phrase familiar from Horace (*Odes* 1.11.8, where the context suggests that the image of plucking ripe fruit is intended, rather than the violence implied in the usual translation, "seize the day," as in the title of a novel by Saul Bellow).
- Ablative singular (with prepositions or in adverbial phrases) in -*e*: *sine die* "without a day," parliamentary phrase used of adjournments made without a day being fixed for the next meeting; *prima facie* "on first appearance," meaning "on its face, self-evident," applied to evidence, arguments, cases.
- Accusative plural (object of preposition) in -*es*: *in medias res* "into the midst of things," another famous phrase from Horace (*Art of Poetry* 148),

endorsing the narrative skill of Homer, who in the *Iliad* plunges his reader into the thick of the Trojan War instead of starting at the beginning.

- Ablative plural (expressing means) in *-ebus*: *rebus* "by means of things," a form of puzzle message in which the meaning is created partly through letters, partly through drawings of things: the word *cub* could be represented by a picture of a cube followed by $-E$ (minus E).

The survey of the five declensions may be summarized as follows. Some regularities are found across the declensions, along with a certain amount of potential confusion. All accusative singulars and plurals end in *-m* and *-s*, at least for masculine and feminine nouns. Feminine singulars of the first declension and all neuter plurals end in *-ă*. Within each declension, several forms overlap with one another. Vowel length, realized in pronunciation, sometimes distinguishes identically written forms. Our overriding impression is of many declensions and cases, and consequently a large total number of forms that need to be mastered in order to speak the language.

Examining the manifold forms of Latin nouns may bring to mind some English words taken from Latin that are still regarded as being so close to Latin that they make their plural as Latin words do rather than with the familiar *-s* of English. It is invariably a question of the nominatives singular and plural.

- First declension (plural *-ae*): *alumna alumnae, alga algae*;
- Second declension masculine (*-i*): *alumnus alumni, nucleus nuclei, fungus fungi*;
- Second declension neuter (*-a*): *stratum strata, medium media*;
- Third declension masculine (*-es*): *index indices, vertex vertices*;
- Third declension feminine (*-es*): *thesis theses, matrix matrices*;
- Third declension neuter (*-a*): *genus genera, corpus corpora*.

Such words, few in number and somewhat specialized in use (academic life, biology, geology, mathematics), remind us of the forms of the nominatives – at least for the first three declensions. Several of the words are found with Latin plurals in scientific or technical writing, but with English *-(e)s* in general use: thus *indices* in economics but *indexes* otherwise, and *formulas* ordinarily but *formulae* in scientific prose.

English does have some words that are in origin Latin nouns of the fourth declension: *apparatus, hiatus, impetus, lapsus, status*. The Latin plurals ended in *-ūs*, but in English today these words, unlike those just cited, never have

Latin plurals. Most often they are simply avoided in the plural. It is not an accident that no examples of Latin plurals used in English can be produced for either the fourth or the fifth declension.

Syntax of Nouns

Much of what the Romance languages (and English) communicate through word order and prepositions, Latin communicates through the form of the noun, through the different cases. The *use* of the cases, in contrast to their forms, remains the same throughout the language. Whether the noun is neuter or feminine or masculine, singular or plural, and regardless of which declension it belongs to, the nominative case always performs a certain function; the same holds for the other cases.

The nominative case expresses the subject of the verb:

Milites   pugnant.
soldiers   fight

"The soldiers fight."

In this sentence, *milites* is in the nominative plural; it is the subject of the verb *pugnant.* The soldiers are doing the fighting.

The genitive case most often expresses possession, as with *Catulli* here:

Carmina   Catulli   laudamus.
poems   of Catullus   we praise

"We praise the poems of Catullus (or: Catullus's poems)."

English expresses possession with a preposition, *of* (or in some circumstances, -'s). The Romance languages also express possession with a preposition, *de* in French and Spanish, *di* in Italian.

The dative case most often expresses the indirect object of the verb, the person(s) to or for whom something is done:

Fructum   amico   das.
fruit   to friend you give

"You give the fruit to a (or: the) friend."

Id *nobis* *facite.*
it   for us   do

"Do it for us."

The words *amico* and *nobis*, both in the dative case, indicate the indirect object. Once again, the Romance languages and English express this relation by means of a preposition (Spanish, Italian *a*, French *à*, English *to* or *for*).

The accusative case most often expresses the direct object of the verb:

Petrus *Paulum* *interficit.*
Peter   Paul   kills

"Peter kills Paul."

Further examples are found in the three previous sentences (*carmina, fructum, id*). The accusative is often used also as the object of certain prepositions, *ad* "to, towards," for instance:

Feminae *ad*   *portas* *urbis*   *currunt.*
women   towards gates   of the city   they run

"The women are running towards the gates of the city."

We arrive finally at the ablative case, which is the most difficult to define. The ablative is used in dozens of ways; it is Latin's jack-of-all-trades case. To describe three of the most important uses will be enough here. The ablative case expresses the means or instrument by which something is done:

Stilo   *pugnabitis,*   *non* *gladio.*
by the pen   you will fight   not   by the sword

"You will fight with the pen, not with the sword."

In this use, the ablative is found without a preposition; the case all by itself conveys the notion of means. Several phrases familiar to us in English are originally Latin ablatives of means: *ipso facto*, for one, "by the fact itself." Another is *via* "by way (of)" (< Latin *viā* "road, street"), as in "we drove to Lucerne via Milan" or, in a transferred sense, "the word entered English via Old French."

The ablative can also express the manner in which something is done, sometimes with the preposition *cum* "with," sometimes without:

Patriam	*magno*	*gaudio*	*aspicit.*
homeland	great	with joy	she beholds

"She beholds her homeland with great joy."

Magno modifies *gaudio*, and the phrase describes in what manner she beholds her homeland, "with great joy, very joyfully." Again, we are familiar with several English phrases that are in origin Latin ablatives of manner. A *bona fide* offer of sale or employment is an offer made "in good faith," and if you did exceptionally well in college, perhaps you graduated *summa cum laude* "with highest praise, in a very praiseworthy manner."

The ablative also serves as the object of certain prepositions:

Ab	*Asia*	*sine*	*praemiis*	*veniunt.*
from	Asia	without	rewards	they come

"They come from Asia without rewards."

Ab and *sine* are two prepositions used with the ablative.

ADJECTIVES

An adjective is a word that supplies information about a noun; it indicates a quality or attribute: "the tall woman," "red shoes," "a frustrating experience." Adjectives are declined in Latin to correspond to the noun they modify. Depending on the noun, an adjective may need to be now in the genitive plural feminine, now in the accusative singular neuter, now in the nominative plural masculine. An adjective, therefore, must exist in all cases and genders and in both numbers – a large number of forms.

Latin has two types of adjectives, both of which have persisted into the Romance languages. Though differing from one another in their forms, the two types are used the same way. The first is an adjective like *latus lata latum* "broad" (in citing an adjective one traditionally gives the nominative singulars in the masculine, feminine, and neuter), which has endings identical to those of nouns of the first and second declensions – *amicus*, *porta*, and *spatium*. The second type is an adjective like *fortis forte* "brave," which has endings identical to those of nouns of the third declension – *pes* and *corpus*; the masculine and feminine forms are the same.

All adjectives in Latin exist as either the one type or the other; like the declension and the gender of nouns, this is simply a given in the language. Either type may modify nouns from any declension.

Ad	*villam*	*via*	<u>*lata*</u>	*perveniunt.*
to	country house	by a road	broad	they come through

"They reach the country house by a broad road."

In this sentence, *lata* is an adjective (ablative singular feminine) modifying the ablative of means *via*.

Sometimes we desire, not to register the presence of a quality or an attribute in someone or something, but rather to measure it against its presence in someone or something else. For this purpose we use the comparative (English examples: *braver, more suitable*) and superlative (*bravest, most suitable*) degrees of the adjective. In forming the comparative and superlative, both types of Latin adjective follow the same procedures. To make the comparative degree we add to the stem of the adjective *-ior*: hence, *latior* "broader," and *fortior* "braver."

Haec	*via*	<u>*latior*</u>	*est*	*quam*	*illa.*
this	road	broader	is	than	that

"This road is broader than that one."

The ending of the masculine/feminine form of the comparative adjective, *-ior*, is still preserved in some English words. Thus *junior* (< *juvenis* "young") means "younger," and *senior* (< *senex* "old") means "older." Two terms in logic, *a fortiori* "from the stronger" and *a priori* "from the earlier," also involve Latin comparatives. The ending *-ior* is in fact cognate with the English *-er*.

To make the superlative degree we add to the stem of the adjective the highly distinctive element *-issim-*: hence, *latissimus* "broadest" (or sometimes just "very broad") and *fortissimus* "bravest" (or "very brave").

Via	*Appia*	*omnium*	*est*	<u>*latissima.*</u>
road	Appian	of all	is	broadest

"The Appian Way is the broadest of all (roads)."

The superlative endings are perhaps most readily recognized today in some musical terms derived from Italian: *fortissimo* "very loud," *pianissimo* "very soft," *prestissimo* "very quick."

Not all the adjectives in Latin follow these procedures, though the vast majority do. For ease in pronunciation, some adjectives that have a stem ending in a vowel make their comparative by combining the positive degree with *magis* "more": thus, instead of *idonĕĭŏr* with its succession of three short vowels, considered harsh on the ear, the Romans said *magis idoneus* "more suitable." Such a procedure for forming the comparative, although applied to a very limited number of adjectives in Latin, was to find great fortune later in the Romance languages; adjectives like *idoneus* served as a wedge opening a door. English also has two ways of forming the comparative and superlative degrees: synthetically with -*er* and -*est* (*braver*, *bravest*) or analytically with *more* and *most* (*more suitable, most suitable*).

The term *synthetic*, by the way, is derived from Greek words that mean "putting (the information) together (in a single word)"; since different endings are one way of accomplishing this, *synthetic* may be regarded as nearly synonymous with *inflected*. Similarly, *analytic*, derived from Greek words that mean "breaking (the information) up (into separate words)," may be regarded as nearly synonymous with *isolating*.

A few adjectives – all very common – are simply irregular in the comparative and superlative degrees. The commonest consist of two pairs of opposites:

ADJECTIVES WITH IRREGULAR COMPARATIVES AND SUPERLATIVES		
Positive	Comparative	Superlative
bonus	*melior*	*optimus*
"good"	"better"	"best"
malus	*pejor*	*pessimus*
"bad"	"worse"	"worst"
magnus	*major*	*maximus*
"great"	"greater"	"greatest"
parvus	*minor*	*minimus*
"small"	"smaller"	"smallest"

Every one of these has English derivatives:

- *melior* "better": *ameliorate;*
- *optimus* "best": *optimum, optimism;*
- *pejor* "worse": *pejorative;*
- *pessimus* "worst": *pessimism;*

- *major* "greater": *majority, major, mayor;*
- *maximus* "greatest": *maximum, maxim;*
- *minor* "smaller": *minority, minor;*
- *minimus* "smallest": *minimum, minim.*

The irregular superlative *optimus* "best" deserves special attention because of the odd history of a word derived from it. Though nowadays *optimism* refers to a personal characteristic of temperament or outlook – it could be glossed as "hopefulness" – originally it identified an academic philosophy, that of the German thinker Gottfried Wilhelm Leibniz (1646–1716), to the effect that this is the "best" (in Latin, *optimus*) of all possible worlds. The doctrine, rendered material and misrepresented, was notably lampooned by Voltaire (1694–1778) in his novel *Candide* (published 1759), which is sub-titled *Or Optimism*. From French the word made its way into other European languages. Similarly, in the course of the twentieth century *pragmatic* was transformed from a precise philosophic doctrine into a term in general use as an equivalent of *practical.*

Thus, a curious shift has occurred between Latin and the Romance languages in regard to adjectives. The modern languages have preserved the *irregular* synthetic comparatives and superlatives of Latin, like *pessimus, optimus, pejor, melior,* and the others (French *meilleur,* Italian *migliore,* Spanish *mejor* "better"). Yet at the same time they have eliminated all the *regular* synthetic forms (*altior*) and replaced them with analytic (French *plus haut,* Italian *più alto,* Spanish *más alto* "higher"). The comparative and superlative degrees of the English adjectives *good* and *bad* are irregular in the same way as Latin *bonus* and *malus.*

PRONOUNS

A pronoun is a word that stands in the place of a noun (< *pro* "in place of" + *nomen* "noun"). Thus, *it* is a pronoun that can replace *the football,* as in "I fumbled and lost it," and *she* is a pronoun that can stand in place of *my mother,* as in "she encouraged me to study languages." In Latin, pronouns are declined also. Here I will say only a few words about the personal pronouns. Their forms are highly irregular, with the first person singular pronoun even drawing on two different stems (*ego* : *me*; compare English *I* : *me*, which are both cognate with the Latin), among other oddities. The nominative is used for emphasis only, never being needed to express the subject of the sentence, which is conveyed by the ending of the verb.

<u>*Ego*</u>	*altior*	*sum*	*quam*	<u>*tu*</u>.
I	taller	I am	than	you (singular)

"I am taller than you."

In this sentence, *ego* (nominative) could have been omitted. The verb *sum* would still mean "I am," but the contrast with *tu* would be less sharply marked.

The Latin personal pronouns have left their traces in a number of English words. The most direct borrowing is the word *ego* "I," which was used in various European philosophical systems as early as the seventeenth century, before its employment by psychoanalysis at the beginning of the twentieth. *Te deum* is a hymn of thanksgiving to God, written probably in the fifth century and often set to music: *te* is the second person pronoun "you," from the opening phrase of the hymn, *Te deum laudamus* "we praise you, God." (The phrase, by the way, is unrelated to *tedium*, which in Latin is *taedium*.) The genitive of the third person reflexive, *sui* "of oneself," is the first element in *suicide* "the killing of oneself," from Modern Latin *suicidium*, the second element deriving from the verb *caedere* "to kill." The accusative of the same pronoun is found in *per se* "by itself (herself, himself)."

To this small group we might add several English words derived, not from the personal pronouns themselves, but from the corresponding possessive adjectives. Thus *meus* "my" (from *me*) is the source of the first element in *madame* and *madonna* (originally French and Italian, respectively, for "my lady," with the second element coming from Latin *domina* "mistress") and also in *monsieur* (originally French for "my lord," the second element coming from Latin *senior* "older," which became a general term of respect). The English word *nostrum*, meaning a secret medical remedy recommended by its maker but really ineffective, is a shortening of the Latin phrase *nostrum* (< *nos* "we") *remedium* "our remedy," the "our" referring to the maker/recommender.

In personal pronouns, and in verbs as well, Latin makes a distinction between *you* singular (*tu*) and *you* plural (*vos*), and the modern Romance languages faithfully continue to make it. The history of that distinction in English, however, is not nearly so simple. Though nowadays nearly all of us say *you* in all situations, it was not always so, nor is it quite so today everywhere in the English-speaking world. Up until the period of Middle English, the language did distinguish a second person singular (*thou, thee*) from a second person plural (*you*). (I give the pronouns in a consistent, modern form.) In other words, English at that time was in the same position as Latin; indeed, *thou* is cognate with Latin *tu*. During the fourteenth century, however, under the influence of French, a new distinction emerged between the two forms: *you*, formerly plural, came to be considered a polite or formal *singular*, an appropriately deferential way of addressing one's superior, while *thou* was preferred for one's intimates, equals, or inferiors. Then, as time went on, *you*, the polite form now, became employed so much more widely, towards inferiors as well as superiors, that by the end of the eighteenth century it had driven *thou* out of general use. This remains the situation now (except for some speakers of English regional dialects, archaizing poets, and the Amish).

English today, therefore, can distinguish neither second person singular from plural, nor formal address from informal. About the loss of the latter distinction, opinion varies. "English is the only language that has got rid of this useless distinction" (Otto Jespersen, *Growth and Structure of the English Language*, 9th ed., 1938, p. 250), the "democratic" point of view. But "in losing this distinction English obviously has lost a useful device" (Thomas Pyles and John Algeo, *The Origins and Development of the English Language*, 4th ed., 1993, p. 188). The difference between formal and informal address did not exist in Latin at all, by the way, but is an innovation of the Romance languages.

The difference between singular and plural, however, has not altogether disappeared from English, but has held on tenaciously in some versions of the language. I grew up in Brooklyn, New York, hearing some people say *yous(e)*, as surely a plural as it was an object of censure for our teachers. In certain British dialects and, in particular, among speakers of Irish English, *yous(e)* is also heard. We sometimes use *you guys*, our southern cousins often say *you all* or *y'all*, folks in certain parts of Pennsylvania employ *you 'uns*, and some other varieties of British speech employ *you lot* to express a distinct plural.

Latin has no articles. The Romance languages developed both definite articles (in English *the*) and indefinite (*a, an*), and indeed developed them from Latin words, but Classical Latin itself had neither. The lack of these common little words contributes to the reader's feeling that a good Latin sentence resembles a wall constructed of solid blocks well fitted together, without mortar or small stones.

The Pronunciation of Latin

Pointers on Pronunciation

It is easy to learn to pronounce Latin correctly, since the written symbols of the language – the letters – correspond each to a single sound (more or less); exceptions are the vowels, which have two pronunciations apiece. The following recommendations are approximate and disregard certain niceties, but the approximations should serve our purposes well enough. The consonants *b, d, f, h, k, l, m, n, p, q* (always followed by *u*), *r, s, t, x,* and *z* are pronounced as they commonly would be in English. The letters *c* and *g* always have a "hard" pronunciation: *c* is always pronounced like *k*, as in *cat* (never as in *civil*), *g* always as in *gas* (never as in *giant*). The letter *i*, when a consonant, was pronounced like our *y* (*iacere* "to throw," three syllables, /ya-ke-re/). Consonantal *u* was pronounced like our *w* (*uallum* "rampart," /wal-lum/) until the first century c.e., when it came to be pronounced like *v*. (Thus, English *wine* and *-wick*, derived from Latin *vinum* and *vicus*, are revealed as early borrowings.) The Roman alphabet did not have distinct letters for consonantal *i* and *u*, with *j* and *v* taking on these functions only in early modern times; nonetheless, I use *j* and *v* here, unhistorically, for the sake of clarity and easy recognition. The Roman alphabet lacked the letter *w* as well, and *y* and *z* were found only in words of Greek origin.

The letters of the Roman alphabet corresponded closely to the sounds of the Latin language. For the most part, each letter had only one sound. The alphabet, in other words, was well fitted to the language – a claim that can hardly be made for English: compare the pronunciations of *though, through, thought, tough,* and in British English *plough*. But as the sounds of Latin changed, as the Romance languages began developing sounds that had not existed in Latin, the inherited alphabet became increasingly ill-suited to represent those languages. Even now, Italian, Spanish, and French represent their many different sounds by relying exclusively on letters they got from Latin; *w* appears to be an exception, but none of the languages uses it except in a few words of foreign, mostly English, origin. Indeed, one fascinating feature in early Romance texts is experimentation with the alphabet, attempts to fit the familiar letters to novel sounds.

Though the Roman alphabet did do, on the whole, a good job of representing the sounds of the Latin language, it was not always so, as a curious usage reminds us. The given names of Roman males were so few in number that they early acquired standard abbreviations: thus, *T.* = *Titus*, *M.* = *Marcus*, *P.* = *Publius*, and so on. For the names *Gaius* and *Gnaeus*, however, the abbreviations were *C.* and *Cn.*, not the *G.* and *Gn.* you would have expected. The explanation for this oddity takes us back to the Etruscans, who passed on to the Romans the alphabet they themselves had received from the Greeks. The third letter of the Greek alphabet, gamma, representing the sound of *g* (as in *gas*), was taken over by the Etruscans along with the others, but came to be used for a different sound. Because the Etruscans did not have the sound of *g* in their language, they used this letter, which they wrote *C*, to represent the sound of *k*. After a while they stopped using the now redundant Greek kappa to represent that sound, leaving only *C*. Thus, the alphabet the Romans received contained the letter *C*, pronounced like *k*.

But this created a certain difficulty for them. Unlike the Etruscans, the Romans *did* have in their language the sound of *g*, and, unable to represent it with the Etruscan alphabet, they were forced at first to use the same letter *C* for it. Later, they modified *C* for this purpose by adding a cross-bar, thus creating the letter *G*. So the Roman alphabet required a little tailoring before it became the close-fitting garment of classical times. But before that step was taken, the abbreviations of men's given names had already become standardized, and the use of *C.* and *Cn.* for *Gaius* and *Gnaeus* was frozen.

The very act of writing tends to enforce a certain conservatism, and names resist change more readily than other words. Most Latin nouns passed into the Romance languages in the accusative case, but the *-s* at the end of the following modern names shows that *they* passed into the Romance languages in the nominative, the form in which they were probably recorded in registries or other documents: French, English *Charles*, Spanish *Carlos* (< *Carolus*); French *Jacques*, English *James* (< *Jacobus*, of which there was a Late Latin variant, *Jacomus*). Abbreviations commonly used in legal or commercial settings can also be harbors for obsolete usages: consider *lbs.* for *pounds* (< Latin *libras*) and *no.* for *number* (< Italian *numero*).

Both the conservatism displayed in the abbreviations *C.* and *Cn.* and the early imperfection of the Latin alphabet that it illustrates throw into relief the generally excellent fit between symbol and sound. The later, more nearly perfect, alphabet developed two wrinkles, however. The pronunciation of *h* was weak and uncertain in the period of Classical Latin, with the result that it was often dropped altogether. And the letter *m*, when found at the end of words, was not pronounced as it was at the beginning or in the middle, but rather disappeared, nasalizing the vowel before it. The word written *amicum* "friend" was pronounced /amicu/, with the final vowel given a nasal pronunciation. These features were to have strong consequences in the Romance languages. The non-pronunciation of *h* is the single sound trait shared by all the Romance languages, and the non-pronunciation of final *m* wreaked havoc on the relics of Latin's declensional system: all masculine and feminine accusative singulars ended in *-m*, so the loss of that sound impaired the distinctiveness of those forms and thus challenged the declensional system, which depended on just such distinctions.

So much for the consonants. Classical Latin had a neat set of five pairs of vowels, each consisting of both a short and a long version: ă ā, ĕ ē, ĭ ī, ŏ ō, ŭ ū. The long vowels were longer than the short in the literal temporal sense: to pronounce long ā, one continued the sound of short ă for more time. Moreover, the difference between the long and the short versions was significant because it performed a function. Thus, *portă* with short *ă* is nominative and the subject of its sentence, whereas *portā* with long *ā* is ablative and performs some other function, such as indicating means. Similarly, the verb *vĕnit* (short *ĕ*) is present, "she comes"; *vēnit* (long *ē*) is past, "she came." With a long *ā*, *mālum* is the noun meaning "apple," with a short *ă* the unrelated adjective meaning "bad, wicked."

Latin also has three common diphthongs: *ae*, pronounced as in *aisle*; *oe*, pronounced as in *boil*; and *au*, pronounced as in *how*.

A last issue in pronunciation is the accenting of words. Latin accented words as English does, by stressing a syllable. Words of two syllables were always stressed on the first syllable: *hó-nor*, *Pét-rus*. With words of three or more syllables, the stress was determined by the next-to-last syllable. If that syllable was heavy, then it itself was accented: *ho-nó-rem*, *in-ter-fé-cit*, *re-púg-nat*, *fu-ís-sem*, *le-aé-na*. What makes a syllable heavy? A syllable was heavy if its vowel was long (*ho-nō-rem*, *in-ter-fē-cit*), or was followed by two consonants (*re-púg-nat*, *fu-ís-sem*), or was a diphthong (*le-aé-na*). If the penultimate syllable was light, the accent fell on the preceding syllable: *glá-dĭ-o*, *in-tér-fĭ-cit*, *cé-dĕ-rent*. The matter of which syllable was accented played a significant role in the development of Latin into the Romance languages.

How Do We Know How Latin Was Pronounced?

You may be wondering at this point by what means we can know how to pronounce a dead language like Latin. After all, we can't chat with a native speaker or listen to an old recording. Nonetheless, and perhaps surprisingly, we can determine quite closely what the pronunciation was, by relying on several sources.

Ancient writers sometimes make explicit statements about pronunciation. Quintilian, the late-first century C.E. teacher of oratory, tells us that *b* before *s* was pronounced like *p*, so the word for "city," though written *urbs*, was spoken /urps/ (*Education of an Orator* 1.7.7). The same author also tells us that final -*m* in a word was hardly perceptible before a following vowel (9.4.40). A poem of Catullus's (number 84) pokes fun at a man who, in his eagerness to speak correctly and not omit his aitches, overshoots the mark and adds aitches where they do not belong, pronouncing the word for "ambush" *hinsidias* instead of *insidias* (compare *insidious*). We learn from this that the pronunciation of *h* was already a source of trouble by the middle of the first century B.C.E.

Transcription into other languages can be helpful. The name of Cicero, when transcribed into Greek, is spelled with two kappas (the Greek letter *k*), and kappa, we know, always had the pronunciation of our *k*. Thus, we learn that *c* was pronounced hard.

Inscriptions are an especially valuable source of information about speech. An inscription is a text not transmitted by manuscript, which would have been subject to repeated copying and correction, but engraved on a durable material like stone and thereby preserved intact. Inscriptions may be tombstones, milestones, laws, decrees, legionary discharges, dedications, and many other things besides. What they have in common is that they have not been corrected or otherwise altered since they were written in antiquity. The number of preserved Roman inscriptions is vast, amounting to well over a hundred thousand, and most were carved by ordinary workmen. If certain spelling mistakes are encountered repeatedly, that suggests that the inscriptions represent current (if perhaps informal or uneducated) pronunciation. Thus, when on inscriptions we read *onorem* again and again (in place of *honorem*) and many another such misspelling, we safely conclude that the letter *h* was not pronounced; this confirms the evidence offered by Catullus's poem. Similarly, future scholars, if all records of contemporary pronunciation were lost, might realize that the *tonite* they often came across was a variant spelling of *tonight*, and they thus, ignoring the traditional spelling, might arrive at our current pronunciation.

Puns and other linguistic situations in which more than one meaning can be understood may serve to show that two sounds were close enough to be confused with each other, and thus provide further clues about pronunciation.

Here is an example from Roman history, recounted by Cicero (*On Divination* 2.84). The general Crassus, about to set forth on a military expedition to Parthia, happened to hear a figseller crying *Cauneas* ("Cauneans" were a type of fig). When the expedition had ended in utter disaster, it was recognized that Crassus should have heeded the omen, for *Cauneas* could have been understood as *cave ne eas* "take care not to go." This example teaches us several things: that consonantal *u* (written here with a *v*) could become a vowel (thus, /kau-e/ instead of /ka-we/); that *e* at the end of a word was sometimes not pronounced (/kau/ rather than /kau-e/); and that elision took place between the *e* at the end of *ne* and the one at the beginning of *eas*. ("Elision" means that the first of the two vowels in contact was not pronounced, thus *n' eas*, two syllables instead of three.) Were all three conclusions not valid, the story would be pointless; in fact, they are confirmed by other evidence.

Rhyme, you might expect, could similarly contribute to our knowledge of pronunciation. When we find *join* and *divine* rhyming in English poetry of the seventeenth century, we conclude that at that time they were pronounced alike, as in *sign*. A billboard near my house proclaims "No Heat? Pick up the Phone and Call Viglione." I reckon that a rhyme is intended, and deduce that the gentleman in question no longer pronounces his name as in Italian /vil-yo-ne/, but rather /vig-lee-ohn/. Unfortunately, rhyme was not a constitutive element in Latin poetry until the Christian centuries, so we get no help from that quarter.

What did provide the basis of Classical Latin verse was not rhyme, but meter, which consisted of strictly prescribed sequences of heavy and light syllables. A grotesque-sounding verse by Catullus (73.6) illustrates dramatically what may be learned about pronunciation from meter. The verse appears written thus: *quam modo qui me unum atque unicum amicum habuit*, " ... as he who recently had me as his one and only friend." The line seems to contain eighteen syllables, which is impossibly long for the meter. In fact, the number of syllables is thirteen – once account is taken of the five elisions, which are not prevented when the first word ends in *-m* or the second begins with *h-*: these sounds were weak, and the evidence of meter confirms it. Here is the verse rewritten so as to convey the way it was pronounced: *quam modo qui m' un' atqu' unic' amic' 'abuit.*

Using such resources as these, we arrive at a detailed and accurate notion of how ancient Latin was pronounced.

CHAPTER FIVE

LATIN AT WORK, II

Actions and States

FORM OF VERBS

The previous chapter described both the varying forms of Latin nouns, grouped in sets called declensions, and their uses. This chapter does the same for verbs. What Latin nouns and verbs have in common is that they are inflected: the form of the word, with the variable, distinguishing part usually found at the end, tells how it is used.

The complete set of forms for a verb is called a "conjugation" (< *con-* "together" + *jungere* "to join"). Latin has four conjugations, that is to say, four (slightly) differing sets of verbal forms. Every verb belongs to one of those four conjugations; which conjugation it belongs to is a given in the language, as the declension is for nouns. The number of irregular verbs (that is to say, those falling outside the four conjugations) is tiny, a mere half dozen. Among the conjugations, moreover, regularity is demonstrably greater than among the declensions: three of the six tenses (times) of the indicative, for instance, are formed exactly the same for all verbs in the language, including the irregulars; the same is true for three of the four tenses of the subjunctive. (I'll explain *indicative* and *subjunctive* shortly.) In the history of the Indo-European languages, Latin's dramatic regularization of the verb forms must be accounted one of its noteworthy achievements. The Romance languages in some ways regularized the verb even more, and in some ways made it more complicated too.

Descriptors of Verb Forms

The descriptors of verbs are person and number, tense, voice, and mood. All these bits of information are encoded in a single form. The one word *laudabitur*, from *laudare* "to praise," by its form declares that the subject is third person singular, the tense future, the voice passive, the mood indicative: "she (he, it) will be praised." English characteristically conveys this information by using separate words: the pronoun *she* announces the subject, the auxiliary verb *will* sets the action in the future, and *be* joined with the past participle indicates the passive. The Romance languages fall somewhere between Latin's synthetic way of working and English's characteristically analytic way.

Like nouns, verbs have two numbers, singular and plural. The first person refers to the speaker (*I*, in the plural *we*); the second, to the person or persons addressed (*you* both singular and plural); the third, to someone or something else (*he, she, it, they*). Latin does have personal pronouns: *ego* "I," for example, and *tu* "you (singular)." Yet because the inflection of the verb indicates the person and number of the subject, a subject pronoun is ordinarily superfluous. Although not required, it may be added for emphasis. Thus, *laudo* all by itself means "I praise" and is the usual form of expression. In *ego laudo*, which also means "I praise," the pronoun *ego* is inessential, but stresses the "I," perhaps implying a contrast with someone else who does not praise.

Unlike Latin, English verbs require an expressed subject, because the verb itself does not change: *I sing, you sing, we sing, they sing*. If it were not for the pronouns *I, you*, etc., the listener would not know who was performing the action. The only exception is the third person singular, which ends in -*s* (*he, she, it sings*), but even with the third person singular a subject needs to be stated. In the matter of needing expressed subjects, our three Romance languages differ from one another. Whereas Spanish and Italian still resemble Latin in preserving endings that are distinctive enough not to require an expressed subject (Latin *canto* : *cantat*, Spanish, Italian *canto* : *canta* "I sing : he sings"), French now is like English and does require one, because for the most part it no longer has distinctive endings (*je chante* : *il chante*).

The Latin verb has six tenses, which fall into two groups, or systems: the present tense (*she praises*), the imperfect (*she was praising*), and the future (*she will praise*), composing the present system; and the perfect tense (*she praised*), the pluperfect (*she had praised*), and the future perfect (*she will have praised*), composing the perfect system. A single stem serves to form the present, imperfect, and future, while another forms the remaining tenses. The Romance languages have added a few other tenses to these six. English has a still larger number of tenses: an example of one that cannot be readily expressed in Latin or her daughter languages is *she has been praising*.

The verb has two voices, active and passive. In the active voice (< *agere actus* "to do"), the grammatical subject performs the action of the verb: *I praise*, or *Peter will kill*. Who is doing the praising? I am. Who will be doing the killing? Peter. In the passive voice (< *pati passus* "to experience, suffer"), the grammatical subject undergoes or suffers the action of the verb: *I am praised*, or *Peter will be killed*. I am receiving the praise now, not dishing it out, and Peter will be the victim this time, not the perpetrator. Provided that the verb is transitive (that is, capable of taking a direct object: *to break* is a transitive verb, *to go* is not), a statement made in the active voice can be turned into an equivalent statement in the passive: "Caesar invaded Britain" (active), or "Britain was invaded by Caesar" (passive). The rhetoric of the two sentences differs somewhat – the former putting the agent Caesar in the foreground, the latter putting Britain there and possibly omitting all mention of the agent ("Britain was invaded") – but they both communicate the same information. English and the Romance languages also distinguish active voice from passive.

Finally, the verb has three moods: indicative, imperative, and subjunctive. The indicative is the usual, ordinary mood of the verb, making statements, relating facts or opinions: *laudabitur* "it will be praised," or *laudaverant* "they had praised." The imperative is the mood of command: "fetch the bone!," or "be quiet for a moment!" It has only a couple of forms. English and the Romance languages possess indicative and imperative moods of the verb too.

The Latin verb possesses another mood as well, the subjunctive, best described as an alternative to the indicative: *laudemus* "let us praise," which is an exhortation rather than a statement or a command. The subjunctive is also used in many kinds of subordinate clauses; hence its name, from *sub* "beneath" + *jungere junctus* "to join." No less for the subjunctive mood of the verb than for the ablative case of the noun, it is impossible to give a clear and helpful definition, because it is used in so many different ways. Since there is no global definition (except that it contrasts with the indicative), the simplest course is to identify a few of the various grammatical situations that require the subjunctive.

The positions of English and the Romance languages with regard to the subjunctive are very distant from one another. Like Latin, the Romance languages still tend to have distinctive subjunctive forms (French not so much as Spanish and Italian) and a large number of grammatical situations that call for them. In English, however, the subjunctive has become nearly invisible. We can catch sight of it by contrasting "she <u>plays</u> the piano" and "her parents insist that she play the piano." In the latter sentence, *play*, without the final *-s*, is a subjunctive. But in the pair "I play the clarinet" and "my parents insist that I play the clarinet" the difference is effaced. The subjunctive is indistinguishable from the indicative in English except in the third person singular (where the *-s* of the indicative is dropped for the subjunctive). In Indo-European, by contrast, it had a large number of distinct forms.

For a given Latin verb, then, the number of forms – indicative, imperative, subjunctive – is large, about 125 altogether (with the verbal adjectives included, double that). And yet this plethora is rather easily managed because the Latin verb is remarkably regular.

Readers more stirred by the plethora than by the regularity may be feeling tense or moody themselves at this point, as they encounter the terms used to describe the many forms of the Latin verb. To avoid misleading associations, they should keep in mind that the grammatical term *tense* has nothing whatever to do with *tense* in the meaning "stretched tight, under psychological strain." Both come into English via French, but the latter is from Latin *tendere tensus* "to stretch" (compare *tendon, tendency, tent*), whereas the former is from *tempus* "time" (compare *temporal*). Nor is the grammatical term *mood* related in any way to *mood* meaning "dominant feeling or temper." The latter is part of the ancestral vocabulary of English, cognate with German *Mut* "courage, spirit," whereas the former is derived through French from Latin *modus* "mode, manner." (English, notoriously, abounds in homonyms like these – *carrot, carat,* and *caret.*) Etymologically informed, we are unlikely to suppose that the study of grammar is tied to uncomfortable emotional states. Those still in need of encouragement may be cheered to learn that *glamour* comes from *grammar*. Among the unlettered, writing (grammar) was sometimes associated with occult learning, with magic and spells. In Scottish the word became *glamour*, which soon developed its current sense, "bewitching beauty or charm." Its passage into general use is owed to Sir Walter Scott (1771–1832), who introduced the word to readers in his popular novels.

System of Conjugations

All the many forms of the Latin verb can be unfolded from what are called its principal parts. These are four particular forms that give the bases for all the others. A verb in English has three principal parts: *sing sang sung,* or *play played played*, in which the first form is the present, the second the simple past, the third the past participle.

Very often, the relations among a Latin verb's four principal parts vary and are not wholly predictable. Here are the principal parts of three sample verbs: *laudo laudare laudavi laudatus* "to praise," *fallo fallere fefelli falsus* "to deceive," *dico dicere dixi dictus* "to say." You cannot start with *dico* and know for certain what the remaining principal parts are going to be. There is one class of exceptions, however. Verbs like *laudare*, whose second principal part (the infinitive, "to praise") ends in *-are*, nearly all follow the same pattern: compare *canto cantare cantavi cantatus* "to sing" and *dono donare donavi donatus* "to give." Verbs like these, belonging to the first conjugation, of which there are hundreds, have a perfectly predictable set of principal parts, ending in *-o -are -avi -atus*. Such great regularity makes verbs of the first conjugation exceptionally easy to handle. This fact had large consequences in the history of both Latin and her daughter languages, all of which have markedly favored first conjugation verbs.

The other principal part that demands attention is the fourth, which is the perfect passive participle (*laudatus* "having been praised"). The participle is both very common, being used even more extensively in the Romance languages than in Latin, and apparently subject to certain irregularities; many of the apparent irregularities can still be found reflected in English words.

The Latin perfect passive participle is formed by adding *-tus* to the present stem: *laudatus* "having been praised" from *laudare*, *dictus* "having been said" from *dicere*, and so on. Sometimes, however, the stem ends in *-sus* rather than *-tus*: *falsus* "having been deceived" from *fallere*, *missus* "having been sent" from *mittere*. And sometimes the stem appears in the participle in altered form. A consonant at the end of the stem may be affected by coming into contact with the *-t-* of the participle and accommodating itself thereto: from *scribere* "to write" the participle is *scriptus* (not *scribtus, which is awkward to pronounce); from *agere* "to do, drive" it is *actus* (not *agtus). An *-n-* of the present stem may be absent from the participle: from *vincere* "to conquer" the participle is *victus*; from *scindere* "to split" it is *scissus*. To speakers of the language, if they are aware of such things at all, these perfect passive participles seem like mild deviations or anomalies (although the philologist knows they obey certain rules).

Despite appearances, the participle *scissus* (from *scindere* "to split") is *not* the source of the English word *scissors*, which, via Old French *cisoires* and

Vulgar Latin *cisoria* (both plural in form, like *scissors*), goes back rather to the past participle *caesus* or *cisus (from *caedere* "to cut"). The modern spelling, however, was influenced by an imagined connection with *scissus* – an instance of folk etymology at work. *Scindo scissus* does have (distant) English relatives: it is cognate with Greek *schizein* "to split," the source of *schism* and of the first element in *schizophrenia*, literally "split-mindedness."

The discrepancies between the present stem and the fourth principal part, whatever their origin, have interesting consequences in the modern languages. Many of the discrepant perfect passive participles, especially from common verbs, are preserved in the Romance languages, where they are perceived as irregular. In Italian, verbs whose infinitive ends in *-ere* nowadays mostly make their past participle with *-uto*: *credere creduto* "to believe." Against this pattern, *rompere rotto* (not *romputo as one might have expected) "to break" appears irregular, yet in fact it closely reflects its Latin ancestor, *rumpere ruptus*. Spanish has eliminated – or, more precisely, regularized – many more such participles than Italian, with the result that the remaining "exceptions" or "irregularities" stand out more conspicuously. For Spanish verbs with the infinitive in either *-ir* or *-er*, the participle regularly ends in *-ido*: *vivir vivido* "to live," and *responder respondido* "to respond." Against this pattern, *escribir escrito* (not *escribido) "to write" and *poner puesto* (not *ponido) "to put, place" look irregular, although both are in fact faithful to their Latin ancestors, *scribere scriptus* and *ponere positus*. The French verb has changed so drastically from Latin that one cannot point to similarly clear examples in that language.

The discrepancies that crop up between the present stem and the perfect passive participle of Latin verbs are also reflected in English, which often possesses two sets of words derived from the same Latin verb, one from each of the stems. We can now see what the links are between words that we may have dimly felt to be related before. A few examples, from among hundreds:

- *agere actus* "to do, drive": *agent*, but *action, active*;
- *augere auctus* "to increase": *augment*, but *auction*, a form of sale with bids that increase;
- *legere lectus* "to read": *legible, legend*, but *lecture, lectern*;
- *pellere pulsus* "to drive": *repel, compel*, but *repulsive, compulsion*;
- *ponere positus* "to put, place": *opponent*, but *position, opposition*;
- *scribere scriptus* "to write": *scribe, describe*, but *script, description*;
- *videre visus* "to see": *video*, but *visual, visible*.

Conjugated Forms of the Verb

The present tense consists simply of the present stem plus the personal endings. Of the verb *laudare* the present is: *laud-o* "I praise," *lauda-s* "you (singular) praise," *lauda-t* "he, she, it praises," *lauda-mus* "we praise," *lauda-tis* "you (plural) praise," *lauda-nt* "they praise." The stem of this verb (and all the others like it) includes the characteristic vowel -a-, which appears in nearly every form; with verbs of other conjugations the characteristic vowel is -e- or -i-. The personal endings, which are the same for all verbs and here, for the sake of clarity, were separated from the stem by a hyphen, are: -o, sometimes -m (first person singular, "I"), -s (second person singular, "you"), -t (third person singular, "he, she, it"), -mus (first person plural, "we"), -tis (second person plural, "you"), -nt (third person plural, "they").

English, although it belongs to the Germanic family of languages, not the Latin, and even though over the centuries it has shed virtually all personal endings to the verb, nevertheless retains in its vocabulary a few traces of the personal endings used in Latin:

- First person singular -o (sometimes -m): The -o ending is familiar from *credo*, a statement of what "I believe" (thus, from an etymological point of view, "my own personal credo" is very redundant), and also from *veto*, which means "I forbid": *veto* was the term used by a tribune of the plebs, an elected Roman official, when exercising his characteristic power, that of halting proceedings of which he disapproved; his mere assertion "I forbid" was sufficient to prevent a law from being passed, an election from being held, and so on. Sometimes the ending -m marks the first person singular. A trace of this ancient inheritance from Indo-European remains as well: the -m in *am*.
- First person plural -mus: This ending can be recognized in *ignoramus*, literally "we do not know." Originally a legal term expressing a grand jury's opinion of a case in which the evidence was insufficient, it was later used for the name of the central character in a play well-known in its day, *Ignoramus*, by George Ruggles, performed in 1615; Ignoramus is a lawyer who is ridiculed. From here it was a small step to the word's being applied to any ignorant individual. The ending is also found in another word of legal origin, *mandamus* "we command," a writ in which a higher court orders a lower court to do something.

- Third person singular -*t* and third person plural -*nt*: Several words that were in origin third person singular Latin verbs are now English nouns. *Tenet* has gone from meaning "he, she holds (that something is true)" to "deeply held belief, principle." Something similar occurred with *habitat* "(the animal) inhabits" and *caret* "it is lacking" (a caret is an inverted v, the mark used in proofreading to indicate where something needs to be added to the text as set). The third person singular and plural endings are nicely exemplified in the old stage directions: *exit* "she, or he, (the actress or actor in question) leaves (the stage)," and *exeunt omnes* "they all leave."

The imperfect is one of the past tenses of the verb, also made from the present stem. Of the verb *laudare* two of the imperfect forms are *lauda-ba-m* "I was praising" and *lauda-ba-nt* "they were praising" (again, hyphens are added for clarity). The unvarying syllable -*ba*-, inserted between the present stem and the personal endings, marks this tense unmistakably.

The last tense built on the present stem, the future, is somewhat different from the first two, because, in place of uniformity among the conjugations, we find diversity. Some verbs make their future by inserting a syllable between the stem and the endings, *laudare* for instance: *lauda-bi-t* "he, she will praise." Others, however, mark their future with the vowel -*e*-, *ducere* for instance: *duc-e-t* "he, she will lead." Diversity creates difficulty. The speaker of Latin had to learn two different patterns of the future and know which to apply to a given verb. This duality was one strong reason why the Romance languages eventually rejected both and developed an altogether novel way of expressing futurity – one that was the same for all verbs.

The former of the two patterns for making the future tense is still present to us in a couple of words. With the phrase *lavabo inter innocentes manus meas* "I shall wash my hands among the innocents" (Psalm 25), the priest used to begin the part of the Mass following the offertory. By association, the first word, *lavabo* "I shall wash," came to designate the ritual washing of the hands and eventually the receptacle for the water. As a result *lavabo* became the name of a fixture intended for the washing of hands, at first those of the priest and then, as the word moved out of the sacristy and into the home, of anyone. It is now a general term in the Romance languages, and it exists, marginally, in English as well. Another reminder of one of Latin's ways of forming the future is *placebo*

"I shall be pleasing" (to the patient). It is possible that the word *gazebo*, coined in the eighteenth century, was a facetious formation of the verb *gaze*, modeled on the future of Latin verbs like *videbo* "I shall see," and meaning presumably "I shall gaze." A gazebo is a structure, such as a summerhouse, from which one enjoys a fine view.

Once we leave the present system behind, however, and pass on to the perfect system, complete uniformity among the conjugations becomes the inviolate rule. Of the verb *laudare* these are two forms of the perfect tense: *laudav-it* "he, she praised" and *laudav-erunt* "they praised." The perfect stem is employed (the third principal part of the verb), along with a somewhat different set of personal endings.

The ending of the third person singular, *-it*, can still be seen in a couple of English nouns. *Affidavit*, a written statement sworn to before witnesses, literally means "he has sworn under oath." It is from the Medieval Latin verb *affidare*, derived from the same root as *fides* "trust, promise." *Floruit*, the period during which someone or something flourished, as in "scholars put his floruit around the year 160," comes from the verb *florere* and means "he flourished."

The two remaining tenses can be illustrated with one example apiece: *laudav-era-nt* "they had praised" (pluperfect) and *laudav-eri-nt* "they will have praised" (future perfect).

The present passive system is formed by starting with the same stem and tense marker as for the active and simply adding a different set of personal endings, distinctively passive: *-r* ("I"), *-ris* ("you" singular), *-tur* ("he, she, it"), *-mur* ("we"), *-mini* ("you" plural), *-ntur* ("they"). Thus, beside *lauda-t* "he praises" (active) we have *lauda-tur* "he is praised" (passive); beside *lauda-ba-nt* "they were praising," *lauda-ba-ntur* "they were being praised." The ending alone signals the different voice.

The third person plural passive ending *-ntur* is preserved, curiously, in the English word *debenture*, meaning "a document that acknowledges a debt." *Debentur*, the original form of the noun, is Latin for "they (that is, sums of money) are owed." The current spelling is due to a false analogy with nouns that end in *-ure*, such as *stature* and *picture*.

In the perfect passive system, as in the perfect active, the forms are created in precisely the same way for every single verb in the language, including irregulars. For these three tenses the perfect passive participle is combined with a form of the verb *esse* "to be." Only here does the verb consist of two words.

The perfect passive tense combines the perfect passive participle with the present tense of the verb "to be": for example, *laudatus est* "he was praised" and *laudati sunt* "they were praised." (The participle has a different ending in the two examples because it agrees with the subject, which is now singular, now plural.)

In English, as we saw, the subjunctive has become all but invisible. In the grammars of Latin and the Romance languages, however, maintaining the difference between indicative and subjunctive is essential, so the forms of the subjunctive are distinctive. These we turn to now. Becuase the subjunctive in Latin is used in so many ways and almost never corresponds to a discernible subjunctive in English, translations are impractical, and so I make no attempt here.

The present subjunctive differs from the present indicative in the vowel that precedes the personal endings. If the characteristic vowel of the indicative is *-a-*, the subjunctive is marked by *-e-* (*laud-a-t* indicative : *laud-e-t* subjunctive); otherwise, the subjunctive is marked by *-a-* (*dic-i-t* indicative : *dic-a-t* subjunctive). The stem and the personal endings remain the same, but the vowel indicates which mood the verb is in.

The pluperfect subjunctive, formed the same for all verbs in the language, is highly distinctive and easily recognizable: *laudavisset, dixissent.* Two other tenses exist, and all the passive forms of the subjunctive are made in ways analogous to the indicative.

We can now appreciate the fact that the Latin verb is remarkably regular. The sets of personal endings vary little. The relation between active and passive in the present system is consistent. The markers of several sets of forms – for instance, the imperfect indicative (*-ba-*) – are uniform or nearly so. The perfect systems, both active and passive, for the indicative as well as the subjunctive, follow each a single plan. Moreover, they and most subjunctives are identical for all conjugations. The number of irregular verbs is very small.

Nonetheless, our overwhelming impression of the Latin verb is that it consists of a very large number of forms – just as with the nouns, only far more so. We also observe that a sharp distinction is drawn between indicative and subjunctive, and that the vast majority of the forms are synthetic – that is to say, all the information about the verb (person, number, tense, voice, mood) is encoded in a single word (recall the Latin *laudabitur* and the English *she will be praised*).

The fates of the inflections for nouns and verbs differ sharply. In the history of Latin as it becomes the Romance languages, the number of noun forms shrinks dramatically: the cases are reduced to one, genders to two, declensions to three or two – a more than twelvefold reduction! All change in the nouns moves in one direction; it is pure simplification. With the verbs the situation is more complicated. The forms of the verbs increase in number. With some variation from one language to another – French increases the least – Latin's tenses are all preserved, new ones are added to them, and the number of irregular verbs rises. At the same time, the ways the tenses are formed, which are sometimes novel, tend towards greater uniformity. As a result, it is hard to say whether the verb is easier to handle in Latin or in the languages derived from it. In any event, the changes in how the tenses are formed, which are often radical, and the introduction of tenses that did not exist in Latin will engage us later.

Verbal Nouns and Adjectives

Numerous as the conjugated forms are, they are not the entirety of the verb. Several of Latin's verbal nouns and adjectives also play a role in the daughter languages.

The form we call the infinitive (*to praise, to err, to disagree*) is a verbal noun, that is to say, a noun of the verb: it names the activity or state in question. Using English examples, we can readily recognize the noun quality of the infinitive when it is the subject or the object of a verb, as in "to err is human" (*to err* is the subject of *is*: compare "error is human") and "I hate to disagree" (*to disagree* is the object of *hate*: compare "I hate disagreement").

The infinitive, which is a Latin verb's second principal part, identifies to which conjugation the verb belongs. The four conjugations are thus represented by *laud-āre* "to praise," *mon-ēre* "to warn," *duc-ĕre* "to lead," and *aud-īre* "to hear." The term "infinitive" means "unbounded" (< *in-* "not" + *finitus* "bounded"), that is, unbounded in regard to its subject: unlike conjugated forms of the verb, the infinitive refers to the activity without referring to any particular person or thing performing it.

The gerund is another important Latin verbal noun. It corresponds to the English verbal noun that ends in *-ing*: *making* in the sentence "making mistakes is human." From *laudare* the gerund has these forms: *laudandi* "of praising" (genitive), *laudando* "for praising" (dative), *laudandum* "praising" (accusative), *laudando* "by praising" (ablative). The cases of the gerund, all with the distinctive element *-nd-*, perform the same role as those of other nouns. Here is an example of the gerund in the genitive case:

Milites	*cupidi*	*pugnandi*	*erant.*
soldiers	desirous	of fighting	were

"The soldiers were desirous of fighting."

The genitive is used here with the adjective *cupidus* "desirous"; the writer could have said *cupidi pugnae* "desirous of a fight," where *pugnae* is the genitive of an ordinary noun.

The genitive of a gerund appears in an English phrase familiar to all of us who watch police programs on television: don't we often hear about the perp's *modus operandi* "method of operating," customarily shortened to *M.O.*? The genitive of another gerund can be recognized in *modus vivendi* "a way of living (co-existing)." The motto of my university, founded in 1893 as a teacher's college, includes a gerund in the ablative case, where the ablative expresses the means employed: *docendo discimus* "by teaching we learn."

The infinitive and the gerund are both verbal nouns. Of verbal adjectives the commonest are the participles. Examples of participles in English are *praising* and *praised*, as in: "praising their ancestors, she drew attention to their steadfastness," and "praised (or, more fully: having been praised) by his parents excessively, he never lived up to people's expectations of him." The participle is an adjective because it modifies – supplies additional information about – someone or something mentioned in the sentence. Latin, like English, makes extensive use of its participles, which number three. Not only are Latin's participles, at least the first two, still in use in the Romance languages, but they can also serve as the key to recognizing thousands of words, both in those languages and in English.

The present active participle has a stem ending in *-nt-* : *laudant-em* "praising." The form is employed less often in the modern languages than in Latin and to a large extent has been replaced by another. Nowadays it is more prominent by virtue of the immense vocabulary it has contributed. The languages contain hundreds of words derived from a Latin present participle, invariably marked by the letters *-nt-* of its stem. Here is a small selection of English adjectives; cognates of most are found in the Romance languages (the participles are cited in the accusative singular):

- *adjacent* < *adjacentem* "lying near" (< *ad* "near" + *jacere* "to lie");
- *concurrent* < *concurrentem* "running together" (< *con* "together" + *currere* "to run");
- *potent* < *potentem* "being able, capable, powerful" (< *posse* "to be able," irregular verb);
- *Protestant* < *protestantem* "testifying, declaring publicly, protesting" (< *pro* "publicly" + *testari* "to testify");
- *recalcitrant* < *recalcitrantem* "kicking back (as a sign of resistance)" (< *recalcitrare* < *re-* "against" + *calcitrare* "to kick with the heels" < *calc-* "heel");
- *redundant* < *redundantem* "flowing back, overflowing, superfluous" (< *red-* "back" + *undare* "to surge" < *unda* "wave");
- *resilient* < *resilientem* "springing back" (< *re-* "back" + *salire* "to jump").

Like other adjectives, participles can serve as nouns. Latin present participles have accordingly furnished the modern languages with many nouns also:

- *agent* < *agentem* "one doing, one who does" (< *agere* "to do");
- *current* < *currentem* "something that runs" (< *currere* "to run");
- *detergent* < *detergentem* "something that cleans" (< *de* "away" + *tergere* "to wipe");
- *insurgent* < *insurgentem* "one who rises up against" (< *in* "against" + *surgere* "to rise");
- *president* < *praesidentem* "one who sits in front, one who presides (< *prae* "in front" + *sedere* "to sit").

From the same stem as that of the present active participles, Latin also derives a series of abstract nouns ending in *-ntia*. Of these also, both English and the Romance languages possess a huge number of examples. In English they end in *-nce* or *-ncy*:

- *stance* < *stantia* "quality or fact of standing" < *stant-* "standing" < *stare* "to stand";
- *constancy* < *constantia* < *constant-* < *constare* "to remain unchanged";
- *intelligence* < *intellegentia* < *intellegent-* < *intellegere* "to understand";
- *fluency* < *fluentia* < *fluent-* < *fluere* "to flow";
- *convenience* < *convenientia* < *convenient-* < *convenire* "to be suitable";
- *leniency* < *lenientia* < *lenient-* < *lenire* "to soften."

Classical Latin in fact created few such abstract nouns; most of the English and Romance words are derived from nouns that were formed in Medieval or Modern Latin.

The other participle used commonly in Latin and even more so in the Romance languages is the perfect passive participle, which is the fourth principal part of the verb: *laudatus* "having been praised."

The perfect passive participles of Latin have also supplied the modern languages with an immense number of adjectives and nouns. Some adjectives:

- *content* < *contentum* "contained, self-contained, satisfied" < *continere* "to hold together, contain" (< *con-* "together" + *tenere* "to hold");
- *obtuse* < *obtusum* "beaten against, pounded, dull" < *obtundere* (< *ob* "against" + *tundere* "to beat");
- *replete* < *repletum* "filled up" < *replere* (< *re-* "duly" + *plere* "to fill").

A few nouns derived from the participle:

- *fact* < *factum* "something done" < *facere* "to do";
- *prelate* < *praelatum* "one preferred" < *praeferre* "to prefer" (< *prae* "in front" + *ferre latus* "to carry" – the principal parts of this verb are irregular);
- *recluse* < *reclusum* "one shut up" < *recludere* (< *re-* + *claudere* "to close, shut");
- *subject* < *subjectum* "one placed below, inferior in status" < *subjicere* "to cast down" (< *sub* "below" + *jacere* "to throw").

In addition, Latin regularly adds to the stem of the perfect passive participle the suffix *-or* to produce an agent noun – the name of one who performs the action of the verb. Of this too the modern languages show innumerable examples:

- *monitor* < *monitorem* "one who warns" < *monitum* < *monere* "to warn, advise";
- *doctor* (originally meaning "teacher") < *doctorem* < *doctum* < *docere* "to teach" (so those who hold a Ph.D. have greater etymological right to be styled "doctor" than do physicians);
- *sculptor* < *sculptorem* < *sculptum* < *sculpere* "to carve."

Though originally denoting people, such agent nouns in time came to denote also devices that do something: *elevator, motor, radiator,* etc.

Even vaster is the number of abstract nouns derived from the stem of the perfect passive participle; these end in *-io* (stem *-ion-*). The corresponding English nouns end mostly in *-tion*, sometimes in *-sion*:

- *action* < *actionem* "a doing" < *actum* < *agere* "to do";
- *education* < *educationem* < *educatum* < *educare* "to educate";
- *emission* < *emissionem* < *emissum* < *emittere* (< *e-* "forth" + *mittere* "to send").

Classical Latin does not have nearly as many words so formed as do the modern languages. (In general, Latin, unlike Greek or German, is not fertile in forming abstract words; the language has a decided bent towards the concrete.)

Latin has one more participle, the future active, far less common and of much less consequence for its daughter languages. It is formed with the distinctive syllable *-ur-* before the endings: *laudat-ur-us* "going to praise." It is easy to recognize if we think of the word *future*, which itself comes from a future participle, *futurum*, of the verb "to be": *futurum* means literally "that which is going to be."

Another English souvenir of the future participle is *adventure*, which derives from *adventura*, the future participle of *advenire* "to happen." At first it meant "things about to happen" (neuter plural), then, when reinterpreted as an abstract noun (feminine singular, identical in appearance to the neuter plural), "chance, hazard," and finally "hazardous undertaking," a concrete meaning again. Apart from these words, the Romance languages have lost all trace of Latin's future participle – except for literary Italian, which retains a few isolated items: *perituro* "going to perish" (as in *l'uomo è perituro* "man is destined to perish") and *venturo* "going to come" (as in *sabato venturo* "next Saturday").

The Ablative Absolute

Closely linked to Latin's participles is a famous (or notorious) participial construction, the ablative absolute, remembered by every schoolboy who ever studied the language. The ablative absolute consists of a noun or pronoun in the ablative case and a participle modifying it, sometimes the perfect passive, sometimes the present active. Joined to each other, the two words float free in the sentence, modifying neither the subject nor the object of the verb nor anything else; the term "absolute" here has its etymolgical sense of "set free from (the rest of the sentence)" (< *ab* "from" + *solvere solutus* "to set free"). The ablative absolute indicates the circumstances under which the main action takes place. A simple example is:

Hostibus	*fugatis,*	*Romani*	*castra*	*expugnaverunt.*
enemy	having been routed	Romans	camp	attacked

"The enemy having been routed, the Romans attacked the camp."

Romani is the subject of the verb *expugnaverunt,* and *castra* is its object. By themselves the three words constitute a complete sentence: "the Romans attacked the camp." Yet the author also wants to mention an earlier action that has some bearing on the attack; he wants to include that in the sentence but assign it a secondary role, as preparing the way for the attack. He uses the ablative absolute *hostibus fugatis*: *hostibus* is a noun in the ablative, *fugatis* a perfect passive participle agreeing with it. The phrase is compact.

Although it may seem remote from our language, English actually contains quite a few phrases and words shaped by the Latin construction. *Vice versa* is in origin nothing other than an ablative absolute meaning "with the role (*vice*) having been reversed (*versa* < *vertere* "to turn, change, exchange")." And besides this set phrase of Latin, the absolute construction is still available in English also, as we may recognize from the familiar phrases in these sentences: "all things considered, I suppose you're right"; "I know no one, present company excepted, who is up to the task"; "there were, all told, six candidates for the position"; "absent malice, my client cannot be convicted"; "we will all meet again soon, God willing." The last would be expressed *deo volente* in Latin, where *deo* is a noun in the ablative and *volente* is the present participle, ablative singular, of the verb "to wish, will."

Ablative absolutes of this last type are still lurking in the modern languages, but they are invisible. The reason is that they go about disguised – as prepositions. The phrase *durante pestilentia* was such an ablative absolute, meaning "with the plague lasting" or "so long as the plague lasts," *durante* being the ablative singular of the present participle of *durare* "to last" and modifying *pestilentia.* As phrases like this got used more commonly, *durante* began to function as a temporal preposition meaning "in the course of" and thus came to be used even with plural nouns. It is still so used in the Romance languages: French *durant,* Spanish, Italian *durante.* English did not take over the new preposition; rather, it imitated the construction, employing its own equivalent present participle, *during*. Every time we say the word *during*, we are reiterating a Latin ablative absolute. In like manner, *absent* employed in phrases such as *absent malice* has recently been spreading from lawyers to the general population, and is on the way to becoming a preposition meaning "in the absence of, without." It is following the same path as *during*, in other words.

Very similar is the origin of two other (uncommon) prepositions. English *pending* imitates an ablative absolute like *pendente lite* "with the lawsuit hanging, in suspense, not decided" (*pendente* the ablative of the present participle of *pendere* "to hang" – compare *pendant*). In time, it too became a preposition, as in "pending the judge's decision, we simply must wait." Medieval legal procedure, regularly conducted in Latin, also gave rise to the ablative absolute *non obstante* "not being an obstacle," as in *non obstante priore sententia* "the earlier judgment not being an obstacle" (*obstante* the ablative of the present participle of *obstare* "to stand in the way, be an obstacle"). Hence the preposition/adverb in the Romance languages: Spanish *nono(b)stante*, French *nonobstant*, Italian *nonostante* "despite, in spite of, nonetheless." In the late fourteenth century, this was translated literally into English by Wyclif as *notwithstanding* (where *with* has its earlier meaning of "against," still seen in *withdraw* and *withhold*). Ablative absolutes all.

Excessive familiarity with the Latin ablative absolute likely led a great scholar astray. Richard Bentley (1662–1742), regarded as the most brilliant of English classicists, famous for his editions of Horace and Terence and for many textual and other philological accomplishments besides, notorious Master of Trinity College, Cambridge, satirized by his contemporaries – by Swift in *The Battle of the Books* (published 1704) and by Pope in *The Dunciad* (1728) – turned in his old age to editing an English classic, Milton's *Paradise Lost*. Among the hundreds of ill-advised emendations he made to that text are several curious instances of replacing Milton's nominative absolute, which is the historically correct construction in English, with something like a Latin ablative absolute. For "Thou looking on" (9.312) he substituted "Thee looking on," and for "I extinct" (9.829) "Me extinct."

The Gerundive

In addition to its three participles, Latin possesses another verbal adjective, the gerundive. Built on the present stem and with the distinctive formant

-nd- (laudandus), the gerundive has an unusual meaning. It is passive in sense and includes the notion of necessity or obligation; hence *laudandus* means "must (should, ought to) be praised."

English contains a number of words that in origin were Latin gerundives: *reverend* "one who ought to be revered," and *dividend* "that which needs to be divided (as among shareholders)." Other such living fossils are *memorandum* "that which ought to be remembered" and *addenda et corrigenda* "things that need to be added and corrected (in a book already printed)," also *propaganda* and *referendum*. *Agenda* was originally a neuter plural "things that need to be done" (< *agere* "to do"), but has now become singular and has developed its own plural, *agendas*.

The word *legend*, formed the same way, has an interesting history. The earliest meaning of *legenda* "things that ought to be read" (< *legere* "to read") is preserved when *legend* refers to the words accompanying an image, as on a coin or map. In medieval times a special meaning developed: a *legenda* (now singular) was a saint's life, read to monks in the refectory, or at matins, or on other occasions. Thus, the *Legenda Aurea* "Golden Legend," that popular classic compiled by Jacobus de Voragine around 1260 and extensively mined for centuries by visual artists, is a collection of saints' lives. Then, since saints' lives typically contained miraculous events, the word became applied to any marvelous, traditional account of past events that was regarded as less than fully authentic.

In the Romance languages too, we see former gerundives still at work. Italian *mutande* comes from Latin *mutandae* (< *mutare* "to change"). The unexpressed noun that it modified was *vestes* "articles of clothing," so *mutande* meant "(articles of clothing) that need to be changed," in a word "underwear." The Spanish word *hacienda*, not unfamiliar now in American English, has a twisting, curious history. Descended from the Latin gerundive *facienda* "things that need to be done" (< *facere* "to do" – the metamorphosis of initial Latin *f-* into Spanish *h-* is a notorious oddity of the Castilian dialect), *hacienda* soon came to mean "affairs," and then in a concrete sense "goods, possessions." At this point its path forked, as the word acquired both the abstract meaning "the administration of goods" (as still in *Hacienda* "the Treasury") and also the more specific, concrete meaning "cattle," which have usually been a particularly important form of possession. From the latter, or maybe from the general notion of "possessions," it was a short step to the commonest meaning of *hacienda* today, "ranch, estate."

A final example: from *lavanda* "things that need to be washed" (< *lavare* "to wash") derives French *lavandière* "a place for washing," from which in turn comes English *laundry*, still showing, after all its mutations, the distinctive -*nd*- of the Latin gerundive.

An appropriate way to round off the description of Latin's verbal adjectives is to explain the phrase *mutatis mutandis.* This is an ablative absolute with gerundive that means "with the things that need to be changed having been changed" (*mutatis* the perfect passive participle of *mutare* "to change," *mutandis* the gerundive), that is, "with the necessary changes having been made."

Despite the presence of a few such words in our vocabulary, the gerundive has not been a productive source for more than a thousand years. Speakers of the languages can no longer produce a gerundive for any verb in the language, as they once could; remnants do exist, but their number cannot be increased any more. A similar fate has befallen nearly all the non-conjugated forms of the verb. The present infinitive and the perfect passive participle are the only such forms still alive and relatively unchanged. The other four infinitives, the gerund, the other two participles, and the gerundive have all, as such, disappeared from the Romance languages.

Syntax of Verbs

Tenses of the Indicative

The Latin verb exists in six tenses of the indicative.

- Present: *carmina Horatii laudas* "you (singular) praise Horace's poems." As translated, this sentence looks like the statement of a general truth. But, since Latin has no progressive or emphatic verb forms, it might equally well, in context, be translated "you are praising" (happening right now) or "you do praise" (opposing a denial). Spanish and Italian do have progressive forms of the verb, but French does not; none of the three has emphatic forms like English's.
- Future: *carmina Horatii laudabis* "you will praise Horace's poems."
- Imperfect: *carmina Horatii laudabas.* As the name suggests (< *in-* "not" + *perfectum* "completed"), this tense of the verb communicates past actions that were in some sense incomplete: either in progress ("you were

praising") or habitual ("you used to praise") or perhaps persisted in ("you kept praising") or even conative – that is, describing attempts ("you tried to praise"). English handily distinguishes all these possibilities.

- Perfect: *carmina Horatii laudavisti*. Here too the Latin form corresponds to more than one English form of the verb. It might represent either the simple past ("you praised") or the past perfect ("you have praised"), which conveys more than the simple recording of a past event: it adds the notion that the activity extended into some time period that includes the present ("you have praised Horace's poems often in our conversations"). The distinction between the two, "you praised" and "you have praised," which we make in English and regard as useful, Latin has no way of making; French and Italian have no way of making it either, and the distinction is, in effect, unavailable to many speakers of Spanish as well.
- Pluperfect: *carmina Horatii laudaveras* "you had praised Horace's poems."
- Future perfect: *carmina Horatii laudaveris* "you will have praised Horace's poems."

Uses of the Subjunctive

The subjunctive – when does one use it?, in which form? – makes up a considerable part of Latin verbal syntax. The language has a large number of grammatical situations that require the verb to be in the subjunctive. Here we may limit ourselves to a representative handful that persisted in the Romance languages.

Sometimes the subjunctive is the main verb of a sentence. When it is, it can convey an indirect command; this is called the "hortatory" use of the subjunctive. In English it is translated with "let":

Illustres	*nunc*	*laudemus.*
famous men	now	let us praise

"Let us now praise famous men" – Ecclesiasticus 44.1, also the title of a book by James Agee. *Illustres* is an adjective used as a noun, the object of the verb. *Laudemus* is the present subjunctive, expressing an exhortation.

The hortatory subjunctive can still be seen embodied in several English nouns. An *imprimatur* (literally, "let it be printed") is a license to print something, or (more generally) permission, approval, as in "the treatise was published without the archbishop's imprimatur." A *caveat* ("let him beware") is a warning or caution, as in "I do endorse the suggestion, but with one caveat," as also in the legal doctrine *caveat emptor* "let the buyer beware." A *fiat* ("let it be done"), finally, is an authoritative decree, sometimes connoting arbitrariness, as in "the funds were impounded by royal fiat."

Fiat, the Italian car, is unconnected, by the way, to the word *fiat*: it is an acronym of Fabbrica Italiana Automobili Torino "Italian Automobile Factory – Turin." But there are two other European cars that really are Latin verbs: the Swedish Volvo ("I turn," appropriate for a wheeled vehicle) and the German Audi ("listen!"). The story of the latter is amusing. An early German car-maker, August Horch, was forced out of the company he had founded and named for himself. Forbidden from using his name, which in German means "listen," he created a rival car company and, translating his name into Latin, called it Audi.

Another hortatory subjunctive is found in the proofreader's term *stet* ("let it stand"), indicating that a change marked on the proof is cancelled and the text should remain as set.

Here is a quirky little tale. Our three Romance languages share a conjunction that in origin is a hortatory subjunctive. French *soit*, Spanish *sea*, and Italian *sia* are all subjunctives of the verb *to be* and, when used in this way, originally meant "let it be." They serve to mark alternatives, as in these sentences: French *je découvrirai le criminel, soit cette année, soit la prochaine*; Spanish *descubriré el criminal, sea este año, sea el próximo*; Italian *scoprirò il criminale, sia quest' anno, sia il prossimo*. Literally, these mean "I will discover the criminal, let it be this year, let it be the next." The words correspond to the English correlative pair *whether . . . or*, and from this disjunctive use they have developed others besides.

Besides indirect command, the subjunctive as main verb may also express a wish, and of this too our world possesses several traces – in the tombstone formula *Requiescat in pace* "may he, she rest in peace," or in the drinker's toast *prosit*, more often shortened to *prost*, "may it be beneficial."

More often the Latin subjunctive is found in subordinate clauses of one sort or another. In contrary-to-fact conditional sentences, for instance, the subjunctive appears in both the main clause, where it expresses potential, and the subordinate clause with *si* "if":

Si	*cantavissem,*	*laeta*	*fuissem.*
If	I had sung	happy	I would have been

"If I had sung [as in fact I did not], I would have been happy."

Cantavissem and *fuissem* are both in the pluperfect tense of the subjunctive. Together they indicate that the supposition (that I sang) is in fact false, and therefore the conclusion is also; the whole expression is avowedly and purely hypothetical. Notice that where English relies on auxiliary verbs (*would have*), Latin simply uses a particular tense of the subjunctive.

In clauses that express purpose the subjunctive is obligatory; the conjunction is *ut* (negative *ne*). In this sentence *celebreris* is passive subjunctive:

Carmina	*scribis*	*ut*	*celebreris.*
poems	you write	so that	you may be extolled

"You write poems so that you may be extolled."

In English, purpose may be expressed with the simple infinitive ("to be extolled") or in several other ways. In Latin, however, the verb of the purpose clause must be in the subjunctive: this is simply a rule of Latin grammar.

Most verbs that express requests, commands, exhortations, warnings, etc. – they are many and common – have for their object, not a noun or pronoun, but an entire clause. In Latin, such clauses, introduced by *ut* (or, if negative, *ne*) and called "noun clauses," must have their verb in the subjunctive. This is another grammatical situation in which the subjunctive form of the verb is required.

Rogamus	*ut*	*cantetis.*
we ask	that	you (plural) sing

"We ask that you sing (or: We ask you to sing)."

Here the entire clause *ut cantetis* is the object of *rogamus* (what do we ask? that you sing), and *cantetis* accordingly is the subjunctive. In English the object of such verbs is often an infinitive, as in "we ask you to sing" or "she orders him to leave." A familiar phrase that illustrates this use is the writ of *habeas corpus* (*habeas* is the subjunctive, dependent on an understood phrase like "the court commands"), an order "that you have the body," that is, that a detained person be brought before the court. The Romance languages still follow Latin and employ the subjunctive in such a situation. In fact, as we will see later when examining some of the earliest Romance texts, the modern languages still use the subjunctive very often and usually where Latin had used it.

Our final example of situations that require the subjunctive is clauses of fear. These have an additional and special interest because they shed light on the historical development of syntax. They demonstrate how the subjunctive came to be required in so many types of subordinate clauses. This can be shown with exceptional clarity in clauses of fear because of the decidedly peculiar way the conjunctions are used. The rule for clauses that depend on verbs of fearing is that the verb goes into the subjunctive; the conjunction is *ne* if the subject fears something will happen and *ut* if he fears something will not happen:

Timemus	*ne*	*Caesar*	*vincat.*
we are afraid	that	Caesar	be victorious

"We are afraid that Caesar will be victorious."

Timemus	*ut*	*Caesar*	*vincat.*
we are afraid	that (not)	Caesar	be victorious

"We are afraid that Caesar will not be victorious."

In both sentences, *timemus* is the main verb, expressing fear, and *vincat* is the subjunctive in the clause that is the object of *timemus*. The employment of the conjunctions is striking: in purpose and noun clauses (and others besides) *ut* introduces something positive, not negative. The reversal of the conjunctions' usual employment provides a clue to how the subjunctive came to be used in this situation to begin with. Originally, the two parts of such sentences were independent of one another. *Timemus* stood on its own and meant "we are afraid," and *Ne Caesar vincat!* also stood on its own, the subjunctive expressing a wish, "May Caesar not be victorious!" Of course, since that is what we *wish for*, we are *afraid* that the outcome will be otherwise. Similarly, *Ut Caesar vincat!* originally expressed the wish "May Caesar be victorious!" when we feared he would not. In time the second clause came to be understood as subordinate to the first:

Timemus. Ne Caesar vincat! > *Timemus ne Caesar vincat.*

Timemus. Ut Caesar vincat! > *Timemus ut Caesar vincat.*

What we witness here is the transition from co-ordination (the two clauses stand side by side as independent equals) to subordination (one clause is dependent upon the other). The transition has left its unmistakable trace in the apparently reversed roles of the conjunctions.

Other uses of the subjunctive in subordinate clauses presumably arose in a similar way, as evolutions from original independent uses. Just as the special nature of this piece of syntactic history allows us to glimpse backwards to the period when Classical Latin grammar was taking shape, so it projects itself deep into the future as well. The Romance languages, even after so many centuries, still show the effect of the odd Latin construction. Incredibly, in all three languages, clauses of fear still occasionally employ the anomalous, superfluous negative: French *nous avons peur que César ne vainque* "we are afraid that Caesar will be victorious." It needs to be added that this use, which, to be sure, is disappearing, has a discontinuous history. It is not a feature that was faithfully preserved in the natural spoken language, but rather a restoration brought about in the early modern period by grammarians who wanted to codify the grammar in a Latin mold. Such a move towards restoration, for which there are many parallels in the lexicon, is another reminder of Latin's unflagging influence, exercised in this case at a rather recent date.

CHAPTER SIX

VULGAR LATIN

CANONIZATION OF CLASSICAL LATIN

Up to this point, I have called the language simply "Latin," as if it were a single, unified entity. Now is the time to make an important distinction. The works of such writers as Cicero and Caesar were written in a specially refined, grammatically uniform Latin. This variety of the language, described in the preceding chapters, may be called "Classical Latin." It is still present in the modern world. The Latin that is taught in school, the Latin that has always been taught in the schools, is an "eternal" Classical Latin, with unchanging vocabulary, syntax, and forms.

But Classical Latin is not exactly the ancestor of the modern languages; the Latin written by Cicero and Caesar and taught at school was not the direct source of Spanish, Italian, and French. Instead, those languages derive from a different variety, which may be called "Vulgar Latin." "Vulgar" is not a judgmental term here, but has its etymological sense, "of the *vulgus*, the common people."

We stand at a fork in the road of our story, and from here on must abandon Classical Latin and follow the course of Vulgar. Nonetheless, Classical, though not the direct parent of the Romance languages, continued to affect them mightily at every stage. As we just saw, it shaped some syntactic norms in modern times, and it has always been available as a source when new terms were needed – *optimism* in the eighteenth century. The continuing role of Classical Latin makes it worthwhile to pause briefly and dwell on its formation and its future.

Classical Latin is a highly artificial language. It is artificial in that it has remained unaltered for two millennia, exempt from the changes that touch every natural language. Yet it is also artificial in that it was not a natural language to begin with, but was, to a considerable extent, consciously constructed by men. Though exemplified in Caesar's histories and Cicero's essays and speeches, it was a language spoken by virtually no one. It was, rather, a Latin that had been deliberately purified, proposed as an ideal, established by convention, and assiduously propagated. It was derived from and based on the natural language as it had been spoken during the earlier centuries of Latin's life, but it was different. And while the natural, spoken language continued to flourish and to change somewhat from generation to generation, as it always had, Classical Latin, once fixed, remained frozen in time, the same in 950 or 1950 C.E. as in 50 B.C.E. The stages by which Latin was classicized, and then canonized, make for a story that can, for intrinsic interest, almost be put beside the story of Rome's military and political conquests.

The Campaign

The earliest continuous Latin texts we have date from the late third and early second centuries B.C.E., beginning with the comedies of Plautus. The Latin in these and the other texts that follow them for the next century displays a certain amount of variety, as we might expect: a large and expressive vocabulary, some freedom with genders, declensions, and conjugations, a certain diversity in inflections and syntax. But in the first half of the first century B.C.E., this changed quickly and definitively. A group of men set about to find and fix a suitable form for the language. Their goal was to settle the language once and for all, and, in an important sense, they succeeded. These men, of whom the two most familiar are Caesar (100–44 B.C.E.) and Cicero (106–43 B.C.E.), did not constitute an academy of the Latin language, like those established in modern times for French and Spanish. Instead, by their own conscious practice they shaped the language into a form that seemed pure and worthy.

Their concerted effort to give the Latin language a fixed form was driven in part by the linguistic unsettledness and disorder they perceived around them. Language – actual spoken language – perhaps always appears messy to the ears and eyes of some, but at that time and place the messiness may have been very marked. Rome from its beginnings had been a city of immigrants, and the conquests abroad and other social upheavals of the preceding century had brought into the capital a swarm of people who did not speak Latin as their native language or were not familiar with the variety characteristic of the city. Some men consequently feared the disappearance of authentic, correct Latin. In his history of Roman oratory, Cicero links the deplorable linguistic situation of his day with social changes: "In those days [a century earlier] nearly everybody who had lived in this city and not been corrupted by home-bred provincialism spoke correctly. But the passage of time unquestionably changed the situation for the worse, no less at Rome than in Greece. Many people from different places who spoke a debased language poured into Athens and into this city. The language therefore needs to be purified" (*Brutus* 258).

Another impetus was the recognition that the linguistic situation, if grave, was not irremediable. Here the model of the Greek language played an important part. As Cicero draws a parallel between the problems at Rome and those at Athens, so he and his contemporaries looked to the latter for guidance in finding a solution. The dialect of Athens, known as Attic, which had established itself among the various Greek dialects as the one most prestigious and most suitable for refined speech and writing, had itself passed through a period of conscious purification; this purified Attic Greek served the Romans as an example. And at the same time that Attic offered a model to imitate, Greek rhetoricians were extolling the virtues of language that was logical, unambiguous, and otherwise clear.

Goaded by the current unhappy state of Latin and drawn by a vision of how it might be bettered, Caesar, Cicero, and others set about the task of purifying Latin. They shunned *rusticitas* "rusticity," anything that smacked of the countryside. They strove for *urbanitas* "urbanity, refinement," and in the sphere of language this was synonymous with *Latinitas* "(genuine) Latin-ness"; this equation is evident in the passage quoted from Cicero, who identifies as the genuine and desirable variety of Latin the one that had been spoken in the city of Rome by native Romans.

The Consequences

A certain variability or freedom found earlier in the different departments of the language was now suppressed, and it was replaced by consistency, uniformity, and a resolve to use one and only one form or construction for each grammatical situation. The word *clivus* "slope," for example – English *incline*, *recline*, and *decline* come from the same stem – had occasionally been neuter, but from now on was exclusively masculine. The genitive singular of words like *lingua* now always ended in *-ae* (*linguae* "of the tongue"), whereas in earlier days it could also end in *-ai* or *-as* (the Romans did preserve the latter obsolete ending in the word *paterfamilias* "head of the household," which we occasionally still use). The verb meaning "to smell," at first belonging to either one conjugation (infinitive *olēre*) or another (*olĕre*), with quite different forms, now came to belong invariably to the former. Some writers before Cicero's day had used *posivi* "I placed" as the perfect of the verb *ponere*, but thenceforth another form, *posui*, was the only one permitted.

Regularization extended to syntax as well. Now *si* was restricted to meaning "if" in formal prose, and could no longer be used for "whether." The infinitive could no longer be employed to express purpose. An indirect question is a question embedded in a sentence, as in "I asked how old he was," where the direct question was "how old are you?" Classical Latin made the subjunctive mood of the verb obligatory in indirect questions; in earlier days the indicative had also been permitted. (This use of the subjunctive is not continued in the Romance languages.)

Word choice was also restricted. The verb *fabulari* "to speak," common in early Latin, never appears in the works of Cicero, Caesar, or any other author of the day. And yet it must have continued in the spoken language because it is still alive in Spanish *hablar*. The classicizers banished it, as they did many another word. Earlier writers, Plautus in particular, had enjoyed great freedom in creating new words. They often resorted to expressive formations such as diminutives of nouns, for instance *morsiunculae* "little bites." There existed in Latin a type of verb called "frequentative," which indicated that the action in question was performed repeatedly. Since such verbs were more expressive, early writers liked using them: instead of the standard *ducere* "to lead," the frequentative *ductare*, which authors of the classical period later shunned.

The classicizers also set the pronunciation. They strove to maintain the sounding of the letter *h*, which was liable to be lost. Cicero himself, when he came to Rome – he was born in Arpinum, sixty miles away to the east-southeast – had to learn to mind his aitches, and he did.

To form a rough idea of how a certain variety of Latin got canonized, we might fancifully imagine that a group of contemporaries, centered perhaps in New York, by virtue of their knowledge, understanding, discrimination, prestige, and zeal, propose to establish a variety of the English language as the best. According to them, the plural of *roof* is *roofs*, and the past participle of *get* is *gotten* (as in "the money was gotten by fair means"); *rooves* and *got* are no longer accepted. *Center* is so spelled, not *centre*. One should say "a historical novel," pronouncing the *h*, not "an historical novel" with silent *h*. At the head of expressions of doubt, uncertainty, etc., *whether* is correct (and *if* incorrect), as in "I wonder whether it'll rain." *Aggravate* ought to be limited in meaning to "make worse," as in "the illness was aggravated by the damp climate"; it ought not to be used for "annoy." Likewise, *reference* should serve only as a noun, not a verb, so phrases like "that article you referenced" are banished. And so with many other features of contemporary English. All the rejected variants would still be available and be acceptable to many speakers, and some, to be sure, originate far back in the language's history, but the purifiers, in this imaginary scenario, choose to exclude them and narrow the possibilities to just one for each situation. If they were to succeed, somehow, in having schools adopt their norms as a standard and maintain them for two millennia, their achievement would resemble that of the Roman authors in question.

Academies and Schools

That achievement is considerable, as can be seen in a comparison with other attempts to purify and fix a language. In 1635 the Académie Française, or French Academy, was founded, sponsored by Cardinal Richelieu, and in 1713 the Real Academia Española de la Lengua, or Royal Spanish Academy of the Language. Both were charged with improving and settling the language of their country. The Spanish Academy's mission is summed up in its motto *limpia, fija y da esplendor* "purify, settle, and make splendid," and the dictionary it publishes, from the first edition (1726–39) onwards, has always been called the *Diccionario de autoridades* "Dictionary of Authorities," because it cites earlier, canonical authors for the meanings it endorses. Nonetheless, the Spanish has generally not been as conservative as the French Academy, whose members are styled "the Immortals." Reactionary in its earliest days – its goal was stated as *nettoyer des ordures qu'elle a contractées* "to cleanse [the French language] of the excrement it has gathered" – the French Academy has recently held to a hands-off policy, preferring to register rather than attempt to regulate the language in use.

Historically, the Spanish Academy has been chiefly responsible for establishing the sensible spelling of the language that is the norm today. The French Academy, facing a more intractable task, has also achieved much in this line, though both later and less than the Spanish. But in the other areas of linguistic performance – pronunciation, syntax, choice of vocabulary – the two academies, despite the prestige they enjoy, have had little influence over the vast majority of speakers. The handbooks of grammar they sponsored have been widely ignored. Both have tended to recognize and accept popular usage, when they do, only after much delay and hesitation. By contrast, the unchartered, unfunded, informal academy of Latin succeeded in perpetuating one form of it, at least for writing, without alteration.

The vehicle by which Classical Latin was faithfully transmitted has been, of course, the schools. Although (or perhaps, because) the natural, spoken language diverged from it more and more, Classical Latin was upheld by schoolmasters as the ideal form of the language, the model to be imitated by all learners. Towards the end of the first century C.E., Quintilian, the Spanish-born orator, teacher, and author of a marvelous book on the education of the orator, vigorously championed Classical Latin. He was a partisan of Cicero in particular, whose writings, he hoped, would spur a renewal that was no less moral than linguistic – a dream dreamt by many another after him. The writers who, chiefly in the fourth and fifth centuries, composed the many Latin grammatical treatises that have been preserved championed the same cause. So too did the Emperor Charlemagne.

Throughout the Middle Ages, the Renaissance, and more modern times, the learned men and women of Europe communicated with one another, either face to face or through writing, in Latin. Desiderius Erasmus (1466–1536), after whom my Brooklyn public high school used to be named, whether he was in Rotterdam, London, or Basel, conversed in Latin, smoothly, wittily, forcefully. In the public sphere, the Hungarian Diet conducted its sessions in Latin until 1868. As far as writing goes, Dante Alighieri (1265–1321) broke new ground in composing the *Divine Comedy* in Italian, a language thenceforth recognized as the peer of any for all forms of literary expression. But he also wrote in Latin, among other works, an essay *De Vulgari Eloquentia* "On the Expressiveness of the Common Language," which is the first book to deal with the Romance languages. In the seventeenth century René Descartes (1596–1650) wrote his *Meditations* in a pure and pellucid Latin, which was subsequently translated into French. His contemporary John Milton (1608–1674) in youth wrote elegies and other poems that are perhaps unsurpassed by any other works of post-Classical Latin, and later, as Latin secretary to Cromwell's government, fired volleys of pamphlets at its enemies, all composed in correct, Ciceronian Latin.

A reminder of Latin's persistence, especially in the academy, where its use has always been a badge of honor, is the large number of Latin abbreviations that still skulk about, even now, in scholarly writing, haunting footnotes especially:

op. cit. (*opere citato* "in the work cited"), ibid. (*ibidem* "in the same place"), passim "everywhere," q. v. (*quod vide* "which see"), cf. (*confer* "compare"), s. v. (*sub voce* "under the entry"), not to mention i. e. (*id est* "that is"), e.g. (*exempli gratia* "for the sake of example"), etc. (*et cetera* "and the rest"), and et al. (*et alii, aliae, alia* "and others"). That they are no longer invariably italicized suggests that they may have made themselves at home in English.

In the middle of the twentieth century, the Pope's Latin Secretary, Cardinal Angelo Bacci, faced a pretty problem: how to name modern institutions, ideas, and objects in appropriate language? Some of the solutions he hit upon were *promulsis* for "antipasto," *tabellarius* for "mailman," and *repraesentatio* for "cash" – and each of these choices he supports by reference to Ciceronian usage (*Lexicon Vocabulorum Quae Difficilius Latine Redduntur*, 4th ed., 1963). At all times and in every situation, the Latin on which these writers modeled their speech was Classical Latin.

CLASSICAL LATIN, VULGAR LATIN

The luxuriant abundance of earlier Latin was severely pruned in the first century B.C.E. by the classicizers, who artificially created Classical Latin and canonized it for all time. The unregulated, unreformed language used by nearly everyone – Vulgar Latin – continued to develop and change, however, and in time became French, Italian, and Spanish.

Vulgar Latin is a variety of the language that overlaps with Classical yet is distinct in many points. It belongs more to the masses, is less affected by schooling, and is rooted in speech rather than writing. Naturally, many features of Vulgar Latin are the same as in Classical Latin. The origin of the Romance words for "bull" (Italian, Spanish *toro*, French *taure*) is *taurus*, which is the same as Classical Latin. The Romance infinitives of verbs like *cantare* come from the Classical Latin: Latin *cantare* "to sing" > Italian *cantare*, Spanish *cantar*, French *chanter*. But many features do *not* originate with the correct, prescribed forms. Whereas the Classical Latin word for "milk" was *lac*, the Vulgar Latin *lactem* is the parent of Italian *latte*, Spanish *leche*, French *lait*. Vulgar Latin strongly preferred *plorare* as the word for "to weep" over Classical *flere*. In Classical Latin, the *c* in a word like *cera* "wax" was pronounced like a *k*, yet in Vulgar Latin it was pronounced differently, since it comes up in the modern languages sounding like *s* or like *ch* or like the *th* in *thin*.

One might think of Vulgar as popular Latin. The very term Vulgar Latin, which is traditional, conveys that it was the language of a particular social class, and the association is appropriate. The great mass of the Roman people – farmers, slaves, soldiers, artisans, traders – hardly exerted itself to speak in a special, somewhat complicated and unnatural way, no more than the masses of other peoples have done. The only persons striving to conform to Classical Latin must have been certain members of the educated class, and in the ancient world education was limited to the well-off, and the well-off were few.

One might also associate the practice of Classical Latin with writing, which for the same reason was limited to the few. Written language is always more careful, more formal than spoken, because, by virtue of the very act of writing, it is less spontaneous and more self-conscious. The person who picks up a pen or a stylus is likely to be not only more educated than someone else, but also more aware of his own use of language – even more than he himself would be when conversing. Written Latin, by its very nature, tends towards the Classical.

Vulgar Latin is that form of Latin that was the origin of the Romance languages. It comprises those features of vocabulary, pronunciation, forms, and syntax that have passed as a joint inheritance into the modern languages. Many of these features can be found in actual preserved texts (like *lactem* as the word for "milk"), but many are established only through reconstruction, that is, by working backwards from the evidence of the modern languages to the hypothetical form that was the original – the same procedure used for reconstructing Indo-European.

Vulgar Latin is not a language separate from Classical, but rather a set of individual features and tendencies that in time moved the spoken language so far from the Classical that the two became, at some point, mutually unintelligible. At that point the Romance languages may be said to have begun their existence.

THE *APPENDIX PROBI*

The merest accident has preserved a text that sheds invaluable light on Vulgar Latin. In the seventh or eighth century, a copyist working in the monastery of Bobbio, in northern Italy, rubbed out and effaced a Latin translation of the book of Kings, and wrote over it first a treatise on grammar and then several short works about language. (A manuscript so handled is called a "palimpsest," from Greek words meaning "scraped again," and such handling was more practicable when the manuscript was written on parchment rather than paper.) The name *Appendix Probi* "Appendix to Probus" is applied to one of those shorter works, a guide to correct Latin usage composed some time between 200 and 320 C.E. Had this one manuscript gone missing (it is now housed in a Naples library), or had the *Appendix* been removed from it, we would have no knowledge of this priceless work.

The *Appendix Probi* is a fascinating document, and, by virtue of its format, it allows immediate access to the revelations about Vulgar Latin that it contains. The *Appendix* consists of 227 entries, all of the type *X, not X'*, where *X* is the correct form of a word and *X'* a variant judged incorrect. In *numquam non numqua*, the anonymous author, a champion of Classical Latin, teaches the reader that the word for "never" is supposed to have an -*m* at the end (compare the incorrect form with the Spanish word for "never," *nunca*). The first, approved half of each entry is Classical Latin, the second, rejected half a deviation from it – the indications given by the format itself are unmistakable. Treating the individual word, the smallest readily intelligible unit of speech, the entries provide clear clues to Vulgar Latin. By the same token, they shed no light, unfortunately, on important questions like syntax or word order. The entries are mostly nouns, with some adjectives and a few verbs and adverbs.

No one would take the trouble to correct errors that were never committed, so one infers that the second part of the entry represents a genuine and common error. What is the nature of the error? A few entries like *crista non crysta* "crest," where the pronunciation would have been identical for the two forms, suggest that it was the spelling of the written word that came in for correction. The *Appendix* would thus appear directed to those who write. But in Classical Latin, where the letters still corresponded closely to the sounds, a spelling error was almost certain to reflect an error in pronunciation. This can be seen in modern languages. The commonest spelling error made by children learning Spanish is the omission of the letter *h*, spelling *hablar* "to speak" as *ablar*. Why? Because in Spanish *h* is silent. Most entries in the *Appendix* therefore are to be taken as revealing current mispronunciations of Latin.

The *Appendix* is like a transparent window that allows us to see through the façade of Classical Latin and get a glimpse of what the actual spoken language was like in the third century. What then does it reveal about those divergences from Classical Latin that were already appearing, many of them destined to continue into the Romance languages?

Changes in Pronunciation

Entries like *numquam non numqua* "never" and *idem non ide* "same" (compare *identical*) show that final *-m* was commonly not pronounced in Vulgar Latin, while *adhuc non aduc* "so far" and *hostiae non ostiae* "sacrificial animals" show that *h* was not pronounced either. (The last is the source of English *host* in the sense of "eucharistic wafer.") Both these developments had already begun in Classical Latin, so the *Appendix* here simply confirms other evidence.

The entry *cithara non citera* "lyre" shows that the sound of *th* was simplified in Vulgar Latin to *t*. Because the two letters were not pronounced as they are in either *thin* or *then*, but separately, like the *th* in *outhouse*, the loss of *h* here is comparable to that in *adhuc*. This change also continued in the Romance languages. Although French does faithfully write the combination *th*, it pronounces it /t/, just as Italian and Spanish do: Latin *theatrum* "theater" > French *théâtre*, Italian, Spanish *teatro*. This particular entry is no less interesting to the etymologist than to the phonologist. From Latin, *cithara* moved along two diverging paths, each of which led in time to an English word. *Cithara* was taken into Arabic as *kītâra*, then became Spanish *guitarra*, the source of *guitar*. The same word was taken into German as *Zither*, the source of English *zither*, another stringed instrument with fretted keyboard. The names for two other musical instruments, the *cittern* of the European Renaissance and the Indian *sitar*, are also cognate.

From the neatly paired items *baculus non vaclus* "rod" and *alveus non albeus* "trough," we learn that the sounds of *b* and *v* were liable to be confused with each other in Vulgar Latin. (Diminutives of both these words, it so happens, have provided modern medical terms: *bacillus* "small rod" is a rod-like bacterium, and *alveolus* "small hollow" is a cavity, such as an air sac in the lungs.) The confusion and interchange of the two sounds has played a continuing role in the Romance languages. The Latin word *mirabilia* "marvelous things" has come into the modern languages with a *v* sound in place of *b*: Italian *meraviglia*, Spanish *maravilla*, French *merveille* "marvel."

One entry in the *Appendix, sibilus non sifilus* "hissing, whistling," reminds us that dialectal differences between the Romans and their neighbors had not disappeared altogether; we recall other pairs, like *rubeus* and *rufus* "red." And another entry, *plebs non pleps* "common people" (compare *plebeian*), confirms Quintilian's statement that the combination *-bs*, though so written, was in fact pronounced /ps/, as also with *urbs* "city."

The *Appendix* reveals another alteration affecting consonants. When the same sound occurs twice in a word, and one of them is then changed to a differing sound, that change is called "dissimilation." In *flagellum non fragellum* "whip" (compare *flagellate*) the first *l* has been altered to *r* by some speakers, whereas in *terebra non telebra* "drill" the first *r* has been altered to *l*. It is not surprising that the *Appendix* includes this neatly contrasting pair of examples, because the sounds of *l* and *r* are especially prone to being interchanged. An example from English is *marble*, which comes from French *marbre*. Sometimes the reverse occurs, and one of two different sounds within a word comes to resemble the other; this is called "assimilation." An instance is seen in the *Appendix* entry *pancarpus non parcarpus* "composed of all kinds of fruits," where the *n* was assimilated to the *r* following.

An instance of dissimilation, from the prehistoric period of Latin, that is also of etymological interest is the word *meridies* "mid-day, noon," derived from *medidies*, in which the first element is easily recognized as *medi-* "middle," as in *medium*, and the second is the word for "day." The first *d* of *medidies* was dissimilated to *r*. From *meridies* Late Latin derived the adjectives *meridianus* and *meridionalis*, the modern descendants of which refer to the sun's behavior, as seen either globally or locally. A "meridian circle" of the earth's surface is one that passes through both north and south poles, and a "meridian line" (generally shortened to "meridian") is a segment of such a circle. They are so called because at the equator the sun crosses them at mid-day. The Romance languages also possess learned adjectives derived from *meridionalis* and meaning "southern." What is the connection between noon and the south? The entire Mediterranean basin, including Rome, lies in the northern hemisphere, so at mid-day the sun is to the south.

A striking and important change in pronunciation affecting the vowels is seen in the *Appendix* entries *viridis non virdis* "green" and *calida non calda* "hot." In each case some speakers evidently dropped the short, unstressed vowel that followed the stressed vowel. It looks as if the stress on one vowel weakened the next vowel to the point of disappearance. Linguists call this "syncope," a Greek term meaning "striking together." Examples of the same in English are *vegetable* pronounced (as is customary) with three syllables and *Wednesday*: the second *e* of both words, though written, is no longer spoken. Each of the shortened Vulgar Latin forms has Romance progeny, which is to say that the forms corrected by the *Appendix* prevailed nonetheless: Italian, Spanish *verde*, French *vert*; Italian *calda*, French *chaude* (and compare Spanish *caldo* "broth").

An anecdote told of the Emperor Augustus (reigned 27 B.C.E.–14 C.E.) shows that a pronunciation castigated by the *Appendix* could sometimes be heard in the highest circles of Roman society: Augustus reproached a grandson for *not* saying *caldus*, but rather *calidus*, which the emperor regarded as affected and offensive.

The *Appendix* contains, moreover, more than a dozen items like *vinea non vinia* "vineyard" and *lancea non lancia* "lance." The sheer number invites attention to this change in pronunciation also. Here the author is correcting the tendency to introduce the sound of *y* (as in *yes*) into certain words. *Vinea* was originally pronounced /veén-eh-ah/, with three syllables, which became /veén-ya/, with two syllables – the pronunciation here reproved. That the attempt to correct had no effect on the spoken language can be seen in the Romance results: Italian *vigna*, Spanish *viña*, French *vigne* – all still retaining the /ny/ sound.

Decline of the Declensions

Most of what the *Appendix Probi* teaches about Vulgar Latin has to do with pronunciation, but it also sometimes illuminates what was happening to the declensions of nouns and adjectives, and this is significant too. A pair of items, *nobiscum non noscum* "with us" and *vobiscum non voscum* "with you (plural)," point to the coming collapse of the declensional system. Some prepositions in Classical Latin were followed by the accusative case; others, including *cum*, by the ablative. Yet certain speakers, as one can see here, used *cum* with the accusative (*nos, vos*). This shows the tendency to eliminate the ablative in favor of the accusative with *all* prepositions. In time, as prepositions took over the functions of genitive, dative, and ablative, this would lead to the elimination of all cases except the nominative and accusative.

Unlike her daughter languages, Classical Latin had three genders of noun, with neuter in addition to masculine and feminine. During the passage from one stage of the language to the other, and beginning already in Vulgar Latin, the neuter vanished. One way by which Latin's neuter nouns survived even as the category of neuter was disappearing depended upon a coincidence. It so happened that all neuter plurals of the language ended in -*ă* (*spatia* "spaces"), and -*ă* was also the singular ending of thousands of feminine nouns (*porta* "gate"). That is the background to one of the most fascinating entries in the *Appendix*: *vico castrorum non vico castrae* "the street of the camp" (*vicus* could mean "street" as well as "village"). Both *castrorum* and *castrae* (genitives) come from a nominative *castra*, but the *castra* implied by *castrorum* is the correct neuter plural (like *spatia*), whereas the one implied by *castrae* is feminine singular (like *porta*). The neuter plural ending -*a* has been misunderstood as feminine singular. One fate of Latin's neuter nouns, then, was to be absorbed into the group that included *porta*.

The *Appendix* also demonstrates the tendency of speakers to absorb nouns and adjectives properly belonging to other declensions into the first (ending in -*a*) and the second (ending in -*us*). Speakers preferred these declensions because they were more common and more regular, hence more familiar and easier to use. With *palumbes non palumbus* "wood pigeon, dove" and *tristis non tristus* "sad," the author is correcting those who converted words of the third declension into the second (Vulgar Latin *palumbus* "dove," not Classical *palumbes*, is the ancestor of Italian *palombo* and Spanish *palomo* – from a diminutive of which *palomino* is derived, a horse with the creamy color of a dove). With *auris non oricla* "ear," the author is correcting those who converted a noun from the third declension to the first; here the conversion is done through a diminutive suffix.

In short, the *Appendix Probi* reveals the ways in which, already in the third century, the complex inflectional system of Classical Latin's declensions was in retreat: the number of cases was shrinking (from five towards two), the number of genders also (from three to two) and of declensions (from five towards two or three). Another language was emerging in its stead, simplified and differently structured.

When studying the *Appendix* with my classes, I have sometimes set them the exercise of creating a modern equivalent in English, and the examples they have come up with are instructive, illustrating not only the nature but also the limitations of the *Appendix*. Items like *receive, not recieve* or *tomatoes, not tomatos* that turned up in the exercises are spelling corrections, because both versions would be pronounced alike – compare the *Appendix* entry *crista non crysta*. When the two versions would not be said alike, however, something more is indicated. *Getting, not gettin* reveals a faulty, or at least an informal, pronunciation – compare *numquam non numqua*. To what extent the pronunciation of English can deviate from the spelling is illustrated in another student's entry, *Wednesday, not Wensday*, where one witnesses the preservation of a spelling eight centuries old, even though the sound of the word has changed. Foreign to the *Appendix*, however, are *socks, not sox* and *easy, not e-z*, where the intentionally "incorrect" spellings are influenced by advertising or other commercial consideration (*Boston Red Sox, E-Z Pass*). Finally, *alright, not alrite* shows that sometimes the would-be corrector needs correcting, and this too is found in the Latin text, whose author writes *calatus non galatus* "basket": the correct spelling was actually *calathus*.

The *Appendix Probi*, a work doubtless dull in its own day, compiled perhaps by a dozing schoolmaster disturbed by the sloppy language he heard all around him, is for us a priceless document. Its very format makes as clear and sharp as possible the split between Classical and Vulgar Latin. And when coming upon entries like *aqua non acqua* "water" (compare Italian *acqua*) and *auctor non autor* "author" (compare Spanish *autor*), it is easy to feel we are watching the Romance languages being born before our eyes.

OTHER EVIDENCE OF VULGAR LATIN

Though outstanding in the simplicity and clarity of its presentation, the *Appendix Probi* is hardly our only source of knowledge about Vulgar Latin. Many different texts shed light on how the natural language was developing. A brief sampling suggests the variety of materials at our disposal and introduces a few additional features of Vulgar Latin.

An excellent source of Vulgar Latin is Petronius's *Satyrica*, a rollicking, episodic novel written during the reign of the Emperor Nero (54–68 C.E.). Its longest and most famous scene finds the narrator and his companion, both educated rascals, dining at the home of a rich freedman; many of the other guests are also ex-slaves. The Latin of the narrator and his companion is correct, Classical. The language used by the freedmen, however, diverges at several points. Instead of *bubulus* "of a bull," a freedman uses the shortened form *bublus*. For the neuters *vinum* "wine," *fatum* "fate," and *lac* "milk," freedmen say *vinus, fatus,* and *lactem* (accusative), altering the gender of the nouns to masculine. Rather than the correct, third declension forms *palumbes* "wood pigeon, dove" and *strabo* "squinty-eyed," they employ the second declension forms *palumbus* and *strabonus*. With the verb *persuadere* "to persuade" the accusative case is found in place of the correct dative. Petronius characterizes the figures in his novel by such subtle linguistic means.

The myriads of Latin inscriptions found all over the Roman world naturally provide countless instances of Vulgar Latin forms. Unfortunately, it is difficult or impossible to date most of them. The commonest type of inscription is the funerary dedication. One stone registers the sad fact that a girl *vixit annis septe, mensibus dece, diebus XII* "lived seven years, ten months, twelve days": the numbers *septe* and *dece* are written without their final *-m*. (All the inscriptions are cited from Gerhard Rohlfs, *Sermo Vulgaris Latinus: Vulgärlateinisches Lesebuch*, 2nd ed., 1956, pp. 5–7; this is number 24, from Africa.) A certain Vibius Crescens erects a monument *coiugi incomparavili* "to his incomparable wife" (number 40, from Italy), which more correctly would have read *coniugi incomparabili*: *v* here was substituted for *b*, another indication of actual pronunciation. A Valerius Antoninus declares that he *ispose rarissime fecit* "made [this tombstone] for his very special wife" (number 28, from Africa), where a more careful author (or carver) would have written *sponsae rarissimae*. Several features deserve note here. The ending of the dative singular, the diphthong *-ae*, has been reduced to *-e*. Also, the *n* before the *s* of *sponsae* has been dropped, as must have been common. The husband of the earlier inscription actually spells his name *Cresces* rather than *Crescens*, and in another inscription (number 23, from Rome) the writers identify themselves as *de isula* "from the [Tiber] island," for which the correct form is *insula* (with *isula* compare Italian *isola*, Spanish *isla*, French *île*). This error, reducing the sound of *ns* to *s*, also is stigmatized by the *Appendix*: *mensa non mesa* "table" (compare Spanish *mesa*, familiar in English as the name of a topographical feature found in the western United States). The pronunciation must have been not only widespread but ancient, since *cos.* is the universal abbreviation for *consul* in Latin.

Most interesting is the *i-* here prefixed to the word (*ispose* instead of *sponsae*), which looks forward to a pronunciation prominent in a couple of the modern languages. Spanish and French (but not Italian) avoid beginning words with the combination of *s* plus another consonant (*sp-*, *sc-*, *st-*, etc.). To do this, they regularly prefix the vowel *e-*: Latin *sperare* "to hope" > Spanish *esperar*, French *espérer* (but Italian *sperare*). This change is already adumbrated in our inscription, as well as in another (number 49, from Italy), which is very touching: a father erects a memorial to his son, saying to him "I hoped you would do this for me," where "I hoped" is expressed *ego isperabi*, more correctly *speravi*.

Noteworthy too is a riddling inscription (number 4, from Hungary) that begins *hic quescunt duas matres, duas filias, numero tres facunt* "here rest two mothers, two daughters: in number they make three" (grandmother, mother, daughter). The arresting feature of the language is the use of the accusative case for the *subjects* of the verb, which should have been, in the nominative, *duae matres, duae filiae*. A similar example (number 11, from Rhaetia) is:

Bene	quiescant	reliquias	Maximini.
well	may they rest	the remains	of Maximinus

"May the remains of Maximinus rest well."

Reliquias, though in the accusative case, must be the subject of the sentence (the nominative would be *reliquiae*). These examples foreshadow the stage of the language at which, left with only two cases, the nominative and the accusative, it preferred the latter. Nearly all Latin nouns in the Romance vocabulary derive from the accusative case, not the nominative. (For that reason, from here on Latin nouns and adjectives are usually cited in the accusative.)

One of the richest mines of Vulgar Latin is a work entitled *Pilgrimage to the Holy Places*, an account of a trip to the Holy Land. The author, a nun perhaps from Spain, whose name was Egeria or Aetheria, probably wrote her detailed and fascinating description in the fourth century. She was wealthy, well connected, and, as is indicated by certain features of her style, also well educated. Her language is marked nonetheless by many deviations from Classical Latin, and, since it is continuous narrative, it illustrates changes in syntax and vocabulary as well as in sounds and forms.

For example, the author pens the phrase *toti illi montes* (2.6), which in context clearly means "all the mountains." In Classical Latin *toti* meant "entire" rather than "all," for which the proper word was *omnes* (though instances of *toti* so used are already found as early as Plautus). And *illi*, in Classical Latin a demonstrative ("those"), has grown weaker and here has merely the force of a definite article ("the"), which Classical Latin lacked altogether. Both these features were continued in the Romance languages: forms of *ille* supplied them with the definite articles (compare Latin *ille, illa* "that," masculine and feminine singular, respectively, with French *le, la*, Italian *il, la*, Spanish *el, la* "the"), and *omnes* was driven out by *toti* (compare French *touts*, Spanish *todos*, Italian *tutti* – the Italian word is familiar as a musical direction that all the players or singers should perform at the same time).

Elsewhere the nun writes:

Vallem	nos	traversare	habebamus.
valley	we	to cross	we had

"We had to cross the valley."

The fascinating feature of the sentence is the use of the infinitive joined with *habere* "to have" to express obligation: "we had to cross." Starting as the notion of what one was *obliged* to do, such a combination soon came to express, by a small shift, what one was *going* to do. These two elements, the verb *habere* and the infinitive, would eventually provide the Romance languages with their future tense, completely ousting the inherited Latin way of forming the future.

From these texts, and many others besides (veterinary handbooks, Frankish law codes, histories, translations of the Bible, etc.), we gather evidence about the paths that Vulgar Latin was following.

Let me conclude with an old philologists' joke:

Q: When does Latin stop and the Romance languages begin?
A: With Plautus.

PART TWO

THE ROMANCE
VOCABULARY

CHAPTER SEVEN

THE LEXICON IN GENERAL; SHIFTS IN THE MEANING OF WORDS

OVER-ALL SHAPE OF THE LEXICON

For the moment, the curtain is rung down on the developing grammar and sounds of Vulgar Latin; when it rises again, the spotlight will be on Proto-Romance. In the meantime, while the action takes place off stage – which is to say, the period when many changes go virtually undocumented – we have the opportunity to examine the vocabulary of the Romance languages, its sources and subsequent alterations.

The great bulk of the vocabulary in our three Romance languages is inherited from Latin or based on Latin. Many of the common, workaday words come from Latin: *et* "and" > French *et*, Italian *e*, Spanish *y*; *de* "of; from" > French, Spanish *de*, Italian *di*; *quando* "when" > Italian *quando*, Spanish *cuando*, French *quand*. Other languages also contributed words, to be sure. In the earlier centuries, they entered Latin first, which received and then passed them on: *carrum* "wagon" from Celtic, or *episcopum* "bishop" from Greek. Later they seem to have been taken into the Romance languages directly and independently: Germanic *werra* "war" > Italian, Spanish *guerra*, French *guerre*, and Arabic *súkkar* "sugar" > French *sucre*, Italian *zucchero*, Spanish *azucar*. Nonetheless, it remains true that Latin bequeathed the vast majority of the words to the Romance languages.

To dramatize this fact, when studying the Romance lexicon with my classes, I have sometimes assigned them a tricky exercise. They were first to choose a passage in one of the Romance languages, about forty words in length and taken from any sort of writing (poem, advertisement, magazine article, novel, etc.); then, with the aid of an etymological dictionary, for every word in the passage to indicate from which language family (Latin, Greek, Germanic, Celtic, Arabic, other) it entered the modern language; and finally, to tabulate the results. This seemed straightforward to the students. The abbreviated model of the exercise I gave them, a Spanish sentence I composed, was deliberately deceptive, however: *¡busquemos las tarifas en la guía!* "let's look up the rates in the guidebook!" Here is the analysis of the words' origins:

Latin	Germanic	Arabic	Other
las, en, la	*guía*	*tarifas*	*busquemos*
3/6 = 50%	1/6 = 17%	1/6 = 17%	1/6 = 17%

It invariably happened, in the days before the assignment was due, that a number of conscientious students, working from this model, came by my office, frantic, to confess that they must have made a serious error, because in their passage nearly all the words, not merely half, came from Latin! That was precisely the point, of course: *Quod Erat Demonstrandum*. Regardless of the passage chosen, the results varied little: the Latin portion never dropped below 90 percent, and usually reached 95, sometimes 100 percent. One student chose the two opening tercets of Dante's *Divine Comedy*:

Nel mezzo del cammin di nostra vita
mi ritrovai per una selva oscura,
che la diritta via era smarrita.

Ahi quanto a dir qual era è cosa dura
esta selva selvaggia e aspra e forte
che nel pensier rinova la paura!

"In the middle of the journey of our life I found myself in a dark forest, since the straight path was lost. Ah!, how hard it is to say what this forest was, wild, rugged, and harsh; the thought of it renews my fear."

Ignoring the exclamation *ahi* "ah!," the passage contains forty words, of which one is Celtic (*cammin* "journey, path"), one Germanic (*smarrita* "lost"), and the rest Latin, constituting 95 percent.

Perhaps it occurs to you that Dante is too literary, too steeped in Latin himself, to provide a fair gauge of the Latin element in the Romance languages. Then let us consider this Spanish sentence from a contemporary newspaper, chosen by another student: *Los precios del crudo volvieron a subir el martes a niveles históricos, mientras el suministro mundial se ve acechado por el fantasma de la escasez, lo que frena los esfuerzos para fortalecer los inventarios de petróleo de cara al invierno.* "The prices of crude oil rose to historic levels again on Thursday, at the same time as the world supply seems haunted by the specter of shortages; the situation is hindering efforts to beef up petroleum inventories in anticipation of winter." Four of the forty words are of Greek origin, one that has been present in Spanish all along (*cara* "face") and three coined from Greek in modern times (*históricos* "historic," *fantasma* "specter," *petróleo* "petroleum"). All the others are Latin, for a total of 90 percent.

Here is a final passage, from a delightful French comic-book series by Goscinny and Uderzo, set in the time of Julius Caesar and starring Astérix the Gaul. The exchange, the language of which is distinctly colloquial, takes place between Astérix and a fellow-Gaul as they are walloping the Romans: *Je les trouve un peu mous aujourd'hui, pas toi? – Oui, ils n'ont pas bonne mine... Ils devraient se soigner, manger une nourriture saine. – Il n'en reste plus. – Si on les ranimait, pour recommencer? – Non, viens, il se fait bien tard.* "I find them a little feeble today, don't you? – Yes, they don't look well.... They should take care of themselves, eat healthy food. – None of them are left. – What if we brought them back to life, to start all over? – No, come on, it's getting pretty late." Here *soigner* "take care" is of Germanic origin and *mine* "appearance" may be Celtic, while the remaining forty words are Latin: even in the language of this comic book, 95 percent of the vocabulary comes from Latin. The predominant source of the Romance vocabulary is unmistakable.

Nonetheless, there is Latin, and then there is Latin. The Latin language has actually bequeathed to its Romance offspring two separate word stocks, which might be termed "popular" and "learned." One consists of the words inherited directly from Latin, continuously present in the language, passed on without interruption from one generation of speakers to the next; the other, of words not native, not present all along, but introduced at some later time and adopted from written Latin (also from Greek). On the one hand, the words for "eye" are Italian *occhio*, Spanish *ojo*, and French *oeil* (familiar from the phrase *trompe l'oeil* "deceives the eye"), all derived from Latin *oculum*. (The French word, typically, is more remote from its origin than the Italian or Spanish.) On the other hand, adjectives meaning "having to do with the eye" were re-created in early modern times by learned men familiar with Latin: Italian *oculare*, Spanish *ocular*, French *oculaire*, all based on *ocularem*, which in turn is a derivative of *oculum*. The words in the first set, having undergone all the changes in sounds that took place over the centuries, are audibly, as well as visibly, altered from the Latin. Those in the second set, by contrast, are nearly full, faithful reproductions of Latin *ocularem*, with some adaptation of the endings to the patterns of the modern languages. The two sets, in fact, are different enough that most speakers of the languages are probably unaware they are related to one another.

Here now are several more samples of the Romance languages' two vocabulary stocks. It is not necessarily the case that the following pairs are the same part of speech or have precisely the same meanings. They present separate stems indicating more or less the same thing. In each instance, the second set consists of words introduced at a later date directly from Latin or Greek:

- Spanish *enemigo*, French *ennemi*, Italian *nemico* "enemy," from Latin *inimicum* "(personal or political) enemy" : Spanish *hostil*, Italian *ostile*, French *hostile* "hostile," all re-created in early modern times from Latin *hostilem*, from *hostem* "(foreign) enemy";
- Italian *gatto*, Spanish *gato*, French *chat* "cat," from Latin *cattum* "(wild) cat" : Italian, Spanish *felino*, French *félin* "feline," all borrowed in the nineteenth century from Latin *felinum*, from *felem* "(domestic) cat";
- Italian *amore*, Spanish *amor*, French *amour* "love," from Latin *amorem* : Italian *erotico*, Spanish *erótico*, French *érotique* "erotic," ultimately from Greek *eros* "love (usually sexual)."

The possession of two separate word stocks, far from being a redundancy, is a precious resource. The somewhat diverging denotations, connotations, or stylistic attributes that belong to the two stems, by creating the possibility of fine distinction and nuance, enrich the languages. Consider in English the subtle differences between *inimical* and *hostile*, *catty* and *feline*, *amorous* and *erotic*. English, indeed, has an advantage over the Romance languages in this regard, because it possesses, not two, but three separate word stocks: Anglo-Saxon words of Germanic origin found in Old English; words from Old French or Norman French (nearly all of Latin origin ultimately) that entered English within the first centuries after the Normans conquered England, in 1066; and learned words of Latin or Greek origin re-created or invented in more recent times. The second and third groups correspond to the two identified in the Romance languages; the first, the Germanic, is what distinguishes English. (English's three-fold word stock is the principal theme, engagingly developed, of Geoffrey Hughes, *A History of English Words*, 2000.)

A small selection of examples not found in Hughes illustrates this feature (each set is presented in the same, chronological order: Anglo-Saxon, popular Latin, learned Latin or Greek): *foe, enemy, opponent; love, amorous, erotic* (Greek); *begin* and *start, commence, initiate; snake, serpent, herpetology* (Greek); *deadly, mortal, lethal* (Greek); *witty, humorous, sarcastic* (Greek); *building, edifice, construction; answer, respond* and *reply, retort; wheel* (verb), *pivot, rotate; teaching, instruction, pedagogy* (Greek); *fiend* and *devil, diabolical, demon* (Greek). Our language's triple word stock is even reflected in suffixes: given certain adjectives, verbs indicating the creation of the quality denoted by the adjective can be formed with either the Anglo-Saxon *-en* (*soften, weaken*), or the Latin *-ify* (*purify, justify*), or the learned *-ize* (*publicize, realize*).

We should also note that a not inconsiderable number of Germanic words from the Scandinavian branch of the family entered English with the Danes (or Vikings), who began invading and settling northern England in the late eighth century. A few examples of common words so acquired are *die, egg, leg, low, steak, take,* and *window.*

A Pair of Polar Opposites . . . and the Ground Between

To survey the Romance vocabulary thoroughly would be a daunting task. The subject is as wide as the total vocabulary of all the languages involved, which is vast. Moreover, it is axiomatic in etymological studies that each word has its own, unique history, which requires careful investigation. Often several processes are at work in a word's history, and they cannot always be neatly disentangled from one another. Nevertheless, certain recurring patterns can be traced, as I propose to do in this chapter. Such patterns, however, are never predictions. It is true for etymology, and language generally, that the observer, when looking back on a given history, may be able to identify each separate element as familiar, as exampled elsewhere, but when looking forward, cannot predict what is going to happen.

On the path between Latin and the vocabularies of the present, many words have shifted their meaning. To begin surveying the relations between a later meaning of a word and an earlier one, it is helpful to consider the English words *father* and *groggy*, which define the extreme possibilities for semantic shift.

From Indo-European **pater-* was derived Germanic **fadar* (as well as Latin *pater*), from which came in turn both English *father* and German *Vater* (it is a convention of Modern German that common nouns are capitalized).

All denote the same thing, so here is an example of a word that, over the course of six millennia, has maintained its meaning – as extreme a case of semantic stability as can be found. And yet, we must admit, the words are not quite identical, not perfectly synonymous (words rarely are); each has slightly different connotations. The Indo-European term designated a man in his capacity less as the progenitor of children than as the head of a household. (Similarly, English *husband*, though it came to denote a male spouse, at first denoted the master of a house, a sense preserved in *husbandry* "management of a household.") Moreover, Modern German uses *Vater* in ways English does not use *father*. *Vaterstadt*, literally "father-city," is one's home town, and the colloquial *Doktorvater* "doctor-father" is a graduate student's dissertation supervisor: to neither one would English-speakers apply *father*. The edges of the words' territories do not match. Still, the central meaning is clear and unchanged.

Around 1740, Admiral Edward Vernon of the British Navy ordered water to be added to the ration of rum served to the sailors under his command. Because he usually wore a cloak made of a coarse fabric called *grogram* (< French *gros grain* "coarse grain"), the Admiral had been nicknamed "Old Grog." Thence the sailors began calling the unwelcome drink he had concocted *grog*. By 1770, *groggy* could describe anyone who was hazy and unsteady, whether from drink or otherwise. Unlike *father*, which represents virtually complete identity and continuity with its ancestor, *groggy* is the result of an utterly unpredictable circumstance, a sheer coincidence: nothing inherent in French *gros grain* even hints at the Modern English meaning.

Some of the possibilities for semantic shift that lie between these two poles can be illustrated from the various Romance words for *strike* (in the sense of "work stoppage"). Italian is straightforward. The verb for "to strike" is *scioperare*, from **ex-operare* "to cease working," from Latin *operare* "to work," from *opera* "work." Italian has had recourse to a compound formed with the prepositional prefix *ex-*.

In Spanish, the noun for "strike" is *huelga*, from the verb *holgar*, earlier *folgar*, meaning "to be at leisure, be idle," which is not quite the same as ceasing to work: it refers only to the state of rest, not what preceded it. *Folgar* itself came from Late Latin *follicare* "to pant." The semantic connection is evident: a person panting for breath is obliged to stand still and rest, be idle. *Follicare* in turn was derived from the noun *follem* "a leather sack filled with air; (specifically) a balloon, or (in the plural) bellows." The last gave *follicare* its

The Lexicon in General; Shifts in the Meaning of Words

meaning of "to pant": by an imaginative simile – both apt and vivid – panting lungs were likened to bellows at work. The story of *huelga* thus includes several turns. Each is modest and comprehensible, but taken together they travel from "leather sack" to "work stoppage," a considerable distance.

The history of the French word for "strike" resembles that of *groggy*. A Celtic word **grava*, at first meaning "pebble, sand" (a diminutive of which became *gravel*), developed the sense "pebbly or sandy stretch alongside a river." On the Right Bank of the Seine, in Paris, the spot where the Hôtel de Ville (or City Hall) now sits used to be called the *Place de Grève* "Pebbly Bank Plaza," and there, it so happened, workers without work used to congregate. From the phrases *faire grève* "to do a (*Place de*) *Grève*" and *en grève* "in the (*Place de*) *Grève*" the word *grève* eventually detached itself and came to stand on its own as the term for "strike."

All these patterns of shift in meaning, and others besides, will be seen in play in the following pages.

Some Patterns of Semantic Shift

General and Specific

A common shift in the meaning of a word as it passed from Latin into the modern languages was from general to specific, or the other way around. A clear English example of the former process is *deer*, the cognates of which (German *Tier*, for one) show that the original meaning was "wild animal." In its earliest uses in English the word had that general meaning still, but by the fifteenth century, perhaps because it designated *the* wild animal, the one most sought after by hunters, it had acquired the more precise meaning it has today. The deer, when served up at the dinner table, could be called *venison* or *meat*. The word *meat* is another example of the process of specialization. Its original meaning was "food," as in the old phrase "meat and drink," but it later developed the narrower sense of "animal flesh," which for many was (and for some still is) *the* food par excellence.

By the same process, Latin *potionem* "drink" became French *poison* "medicated or poisoned drink; poison." (Another common shift is seen in *potionem* itself, which in Classical Latin went from the abstract "act of drinking" to the concrete "drink, beverage.") In the same semantic field, the Vulgar Latin word

133

vivenda, altered to *vivanda*, originally a gerundive meaning "things necessary for living" (< *vivere* "to live"), gave rise to the nouns: Italian *vivanda*, Spanish *vianda*, French *viande* "food," which is certainly a necessity of life. (The French term meant "food" in the early days, to be sure, but it then underwent a second specialization, as a result of which it acquired the meaning it usually has today, "meat, animal flesh.") The same Vulgar Latin word was also specialized by Spanish in a different direction: *vivienda* means "housing," another of life's necessities.

The Latin *collocare* "to put in place" (< *locum* "place") produced Romance verbs that went in specific yet opposite directions. On the one hand, Italian *coricare* and French *coucher* (parent of English *couch*) mean "to lay down" (as a baby on a bed); this narrower sense already begins to appear in antiquity. On the other hand, Spanish *colgar* means "to hang up" (as curtains on a rod). With these verbs now possessing specialized meanings, the modern languages had to create learned words that recovered the original, general meaning: Italian *collocare*, Spanish *colocar*, French *colloquer* (the last now obsolete and literary) "to put in place" – a further instance of the languages' two sets of Latin-derived words.

Among the items in Latin's well-stocked arsenal of terms for "to kill" is *necare*. Used by classical writers for death brought about by any means (poison, sword, disease, etc.), the verb, for some reason, later was applied to killing without weapons, such as by suffocation. In Late Latin the verb acquired the still more specialized meaning "to drown": French *noyer*, Italian *annegare* (with prefix *ad-*), Spanish *anegar* (of which "to drown" was the earlier meaning, and the current one, reached by association, is "to flood"). Or consider *pacare*, originally "to reach an agreement," derived from *pax* (accusative *pacem*) "agreement; peace treaty; peace." In time the verb acquired the specific meaning "to satisfy a creditor (by paying him)," then simply "to pay (a person, a bill)." This is the origin of Italian *pagare*, Spanish *pagar*, French *payer* "to pay."

Spanish provides an example of an adjective undergoing this process, an example which is especially interesting because of its influence on United States toponymy. *Colorado* had always meant "colored" in Spanish, but in the fifteenth century it acquired the specific meaning "red." In the early seventeenth century, the Spaniards named a large, long river in their North American territories the Colorado because of the distinctive color created by the soil through which it flowed. The state later took its name from the river. What we call a "dirty joke" is called in Spanish *chiste colorado* "red joke." Whereas our term refers to the nature of the joke's content, the Spanish refers to the reception of the content by the hearers: it causes them to become red, to blush.

The reverse – a specific meaning supplanted by a general one – also happens, although perhaps less often. Think of the English word *place*, which indicates geographical location in the most general terms. Yet in origin it had a precise reference. Derived from a Greek word meaning "broad, flat" (a *platypus* is literally "flat foot," and English *flat* is cognate), in Latin a *plateam* was a "street," that is, an open space wide and level enough to allow passage. The Romance terms, derived from Vulgar Latin *platteam*, all developed a somewhat different, though equally precise sense: Spanish *plaza*, Italian *piazza*, French *place* "open square in a city." World capitals provide familiar examples: the Place de la Concorde in Paris, the Piazza Navona in Rome, the Plaza San Martín in Córdoba, Argentina, and Grand Army Plaza in Brooklyn, New York. Even in the earliest French examples, however, and in English as well, the word *place* possesses a very general meaning.

Generalization can be seen at work elsewhere in the Romance vocabulary. In Classical Latin a *passerem* was a "sparrow" (compare *passerine*). Yet its derivative in Spanish, *pájaro*, is the general term for "bird." (*Passar*, a stage intermediate between *passer* and *pájaro*, is attested in the *Appendix Probi*.) The story of the Latin verb *afflare* is a twisting, fascinating drama in several acts, between the first or second of which and the final its meaning has shifted from specific to general. Composed of *ad* and *flare*, it originally meant "to blow toward." The subsequent changes took place in the context of hunting and hunting dogs. From "to blow toward" the word developed the meaning "to graze with one's breath," next "to smell the trail of (a deer or some other prey)," and then "to meet up with, find" – no longer the process, but the result. In Modern Spanish, *hallar* (< *afflare*) has lost all connection to trailing or tracking and means simply "to find."

As final examples of generalization, let me mention the all-purpose terms for "to clean" in the modern languages. Each has followed its own course and generalized a different Latin word: Italian *pulire* < Latin *polire* "to polish," Spanish *limpiar* < *limpidare* "to make clear" (< *limpidum* "clear, transparent"), and French *nettoyer* < *nitidiare* "to make bright, shining" (< *nitidum* "bright" – the French adjective *net* "clean" has entered English with the meaning "free from charges or other subtractions").

Abstract and Concrete

Another shift we often come across is between abstract and concrete. Whereas Latin *civitatem* meant "state," in the sense of "polity, political entity," its Romance progeny have become the words for "city": Italian *città*, Spanish *ciudad*, French *cité*. (Nowadays, to be sure, the French word for "city" is *ville*, while *cité* has a more restricted use, such as "citadel.") They are linked by the fact that in the Greco-Roman world the customary unit of political organization was the city-state, comprising a city together with the adjoining territory. Before it was an empire, Rome too was a city-state. The original meaning of *civitatem* is still preserved in the derived nouns, Italian *cittadino*, French *citoyen*, Spanish *ciudadano*, all meaning *inter alia* "citizen." Another fine example is Latin *potestatem* "power," which has yielded Italian *podestà* "mayor."

Sationem, formed like *potionem*, had at first a similarly abstract sense, "a sowing." In time, however, it came to designate "the season for sowing" and then, more generally, "season," as seen in French *saison* (> *season*). *Mansionem* too had an abstract sense in the beginning, "an awaiting, an abiding." Within the period of Classical Latin it developed the senses "stopping point on a journey" and, more concretely, "place to stay, inn," and then later, in French *maison*, it became "house." Because the *n* dropped out before the *s* of *mansionem*, we may be confident that *maison* was a popular word, one that existed continuously in the language. But from *mansionem* too a learned form was later created, which became English *mansion* "the house of the lord of a manor," then simply "a large house." Both *manor* and *manse* come from the same Latin word as well.

While *maison* is the French word for "house," in Spanish and Italian it is *casa*, which in Classical Latin meant "cottage, hut," even "hovel." What happened to *domum*, the standard and common Latin word? For some reason it got dropped from the lexicon. It continued its life, nevertheless, in the phrase *domum episcopi* "the house of the bishop," which, abridged to *domum*, became Italian *duomo* "cathedral."

An engaging story of the opposite move, a word beginning with a concrete and changing to an abstract meaning, is that of Latin *stilum* "pointed metal rod; (specifically) stylus." For composing and casual writing, the ancients most often used wax tablets into which they incised the letters with a stylus, a thin metal rod sharpened at one end for writing and flattened at the other for smoothing the wax again or "erasing" – hence Horace's advice to writers who wish to be read more than once: *saepe stilum vertas* "invert the stylus often" (*Satires* 1.10.72). *Stilum* quickly came to mean "the practice of writing" and then "manner of writing, literary style." All this took place within the classical period. Only in much later times was *style* applied outside the sphere of writing, to other arts or to characteristic forms of behavior, dress, management, etc. – far from a pointy piece of metal. The French (and English) spelling *style* is due to a false association with Greek *stylos* "pillar, column."

Technical and Popular

If not by car, train, or airplane, the ancients could still travel by a variety of means: by foot, in a litter, astride a mule or horse, in a cart, by boat or ship. It is curious therefore that the general Romance terms for reaching a destination are all drawn from only one mode of transport. The several words meaning "to arrive" also illustrate how a word employed in a fairly precise, technical way by a few can become the property of all – and therewith shift its meaning. The Latin word for the "bank" of a river, sometimes also the "shore" of a lake or sea, is *ripam*, from which, combined with the prefix *ad-* "to," was derived the compound verb **arripare* "to come to the bank, the shore," applied to travelers by water putting in at their destination. Because the sound of *p* between vowels has become *v* in French (regularly) and in Italian (occasionally), the results are French *arriver* and Italian *arrivare*. No longer a term of sailing, the verb means simply "to arrive," regardless of mode of transport.

Ripam itself has not been lost from the Romance and English lexicons. It is preserved in various guises: with *p* intact, in English *riparian* (as in "riparian flora"); with *p* altered to *v*, in Italian *Riviera*, in French *rive* (the Hôtel de Ville sits on the *Rive Droite* "Right Bank" of the Seine), and, via French, in English *river*; and, with *p* altered to *b*, in Old Spanish *riba*, the origin of the adverb *arriba*, at first perhaps "upstream" but now more generally "up."

In Spanish, the verb for "to arrive" is *llegar*. The latest stages of its development are clear and beyond dispute, but for its ultimate origin two rival accounts have been proposed. (*Rival*, by the way, is derived from Latin *rivum* "stream": rivals were originally men who drew water from the same stream, with contentious consequences that can readily be imagined. *Rivum*, unrelated to *ripam*, is the source of English *rivulet*, which leads to the surprising recognition that *river* and *rivulet* are not related!) Spanish *llegar* comes from *plecare*, and *plecare* in turn comes from *plicare* "to fold." But how did *plicare* acquire the meaning "to arrive"? According to some, *plicare* was used with the word "sails" understood: you folded your sails when you had arrived at your destination. But *plicare*, according to the rival theory, is a shortening of the compound verb *applicare*, which in Classical Latin was said of ships and meant "to put in" and in Late Latin signified more generally "to approach." *Aplekare* in a tenth-century Spanish glossary and similar forms found in other languages and dialects, all meaning "approach" or "arrive," make the latter view more plausible. In any event, a term once employed in sailing has given Spanish too its term for "arrive." So various words connected with voyaging illustrate the journey from a narrower, technical meaning to a broader one.

Part and Whole, Other Natural Associations

It seems a natural feature of speech to mention a part as a way of representing the whole. No one would misunderstand "a hundred head of cattle" as one hundred bovine heads separated from the bodies, or "a fleet of twenty sail" as so many pieces of canvas without hulls, masts, or rigging. With the passage of time some words identifying a part have shifted their reference and are now established as denoting the whole. The Latin word *testam* at first meant "shell; ceramic pot," and then, by virtue of a perceived resemblance, "cranium," the rounded, thin, pot-like casing of the brain. Soon it designated the whole of which the cranium is a part, the head. It already has this meaning in a fourth-century poem by the Latin author Ausonius, who speaks of a *glabra testa* "hairless head" (*Epigrams* 76). As a result, Italian *testa* and French *tête* are the words for "head," having ousted Classical Latin *caput.* (The circumflex mark in French, as over the first *e* of *tête*, is almost always a souvenir of an *s* that has been lost: compare *île* "island" < *insula.*) A similar resemblance must have been noted in the history of German, one of whose words for "head," *Kopf,* cognate with English *cup,* originally meant "bowl, drinking vessel."

Another etymological narrative that touches upon body parts amply illustrates the workings of association in altering the meaning of a word. From Greek, Latin took over the word *spatham* "broad blade," which in Vulgar Latin became *spatam.* A *spatam* might be made of wood and perhaps serve as a batten in weaving, or be of metal and form the business end of a sword. With some specialization of meaning, and with the part used for the whole, in the Romance languages (as occasionally in Classical Latin already) *spatam* became the word for "sword": Italian *spada,* Spanish *espada,* French *épée.* So firmly did the new reference cleave to it that the modern languages had to develop alternative words for "blade."

Spatulam, in form a diminutive of *spatam*, underwent more remarkable and instructive changes. Similarity of shape led the word to be applied to the "shoulder *blade*," as we also call it in English. From that it came to designate the shoulder itself, of which it was but a part: a fourth-century Roman cookbook refers to *spatula porcina* "pork shoulder" (Apicius, *On Cooking* 4.174). All three Romance languages show this shift from part to whole: Spanish *espalda*, Italian *spalla*, French *épaule* (source of *epaulets*, the ornamental fringed pads worn on the shoulders of a uniform). Once *spatulam* moved on to indicating the shoulder, another term was needed to take its place for referring to the shoulder blade. Spanish *espalda* did not stop there, however. From "shoulder" it shifted its meaning once again, and by association became the word for the "back" (and *hombro* is now the Spanish word for "shoulder"). Similarly, Italian *spalle* "shoulders" can equally well mean "back" today. Unlike Indo-European **pater-*, most words do not stand still, and one change often entails another.

Latin *spatulam* was later re-introduced into the Romance languages as the name for various implements used by masons, cooks, etc.: Italian *spatola*, French *spatule*, Spanish *espátula*. This set of learned words reflects only minimal adjustments of the Latin, whereas the other, popular set was subject to all the phonological changes that occurred during their history.

In Latin, *tabulam* was originally "board, plank of wood." But it soon came to designate a board used for a particular purpose, most often writing, but also painting and playing games. Not until the Middle Ages did it refer to a piece of furniture with a flat top and legs: Italian *tavola*, French *table* "table." A handy tool for making a table is the saw, the Latin word for which was *serra* (compare *serrated*). The resemblance between the teeth of a saw and the jagged edges of a mountaintop produced Spanish *sierra* "chain of mountains," which is familiar from topographic names in the United States, such as *Sierra Nevada* ("Snowy Sawtooth") and *Sierra Madre* ("Mother Mountain"). Like *mesa* – and for the same reasons – *sierra* is never found east of the Mississippi.

The meanings of words are altered by a wide variety of associations, not merely those of physical resemblance and of part with whole, and these too feel natural. The Latin verb *navigare* "to sail" has become French *nager* "to swim." The verb *mollire* "to soften" has become Spanish *mojar* "to make wet." The Latin word for "fire," *ignem*, has disappeared completely from popular speech (though revived in words like *ignition*). Its place has been taken by *focum*, originally "hearth": Italian *fuoco*, Spanish *fuego*, French *feu* "fire." From a derived noun *focarium* French developed *foyer* "hearth," which got passed along to English, where, to be sure, it now denotes something different.

Yet the Latin word *focus* itself took on new life in modern times. It was re-introduced by Johannes Kepler, who gave it the meaning "burning point, point at which the rays of a lens or mirror converge" – a brilliant adaptation. From his treatise, written in Latin, naturally, the word passed into the modern languages, where within a couple of centuries it developed the more general sense "center of activity or interest."

A different type of association was at work in the history of the Latin word *follem*, "a leather sack filled with air; (specifically) a balloon" (*follem* is cognate with English *ball*). Through a kind of simile, an imaginative perception of likeness, it is already found in fifth-century writers such as Augustine and Jerome with the meaning "a person full of air, an 'air head,' a fool." A modern derivative with the same sense is French *fou* (feminine *folle*), the source of English *fool, foolish, folly*.

SITUATION AND SPEAKER: TWO OBSERVATIONS ON SHIFTS IN MEANING

From this assortment of material, I should like to draw a complementary pair of general observations and amplify the particular points with a few further examples.

A shift in meaning often occurs because of a particular situation, setting, or context – historical or linguistic – in which a word is used and from which it takes on a new meaning; the particular situation may be called a "matrix." *Groggy* is a transparent instance, because the name for a type of cloth came to be applied to a state of stupor only because of a precise historical circumstance. Similarly, *ignoramus* passed into the general lexicon because of a seventeenth-century play. The matrix in which *arripare* acquired a general meaning was travel by boat. Once a word goes off in a new direction, the matrix that gave birth to it is usually forgotten, left behind like the booster stage of a rocket. When we hear that someone "awoke groggy," we probably do not think of rum and certainly do not think of grogram, and so far are we from limiting the use of *arrive* to travel by water that we readily apply it not only to other means of transport but even to abstract destinations, as in "arrive at a conclusion."

The story of some Romance words for "cheese" follows a common pattern. The Latin term, *caseum*, straightforwardly led to Spanish *queso* and Italian *cacio*; entering Old English directly at an early date, it also became the parent of English *cheese* (*casein*, a milk protein, is a learned term, created in the nineteenth century). But in France and in some parts of Italy, the north particularly, the word for "cheese" is different: French *fromage*, Italian *formaggio*. Where did it come from? In this case, the matrix is a phrase, *caseum formaticum* "cheese made in a mold" (< *forma* "mold"), which, through regular employment, got shortened to the adjective alone, *formaticum*, and then was applied to cheese made by any means, in a sieve or basket, for instance.

The matrix – or perhaps it could be called the "mold" – of the Romance and English words for "date" was the activity of letter writing. Latin letters regularly ended or began with an indication like *data ante diem quartum Nonas Iunias* "given on June 2nd" (literally "given on the fourth day before the Nones of June" – the Roman system for reckoning the days of the month was complicated and cumbersome). The "giving" referred to handing over the letter to the messenger who would deliver it, and *data* "given" (< *dare* "to give") is feminine because it agrees with the unexpressed feminine noun *epistula* "letter," or perhaps *carta* "document." From its employment in letters, the word spread to other situations in which temporal specification was needed. In Italian the word is *data*, in French *date*. In Spanish, however, it is *fecha*, originally "done," from Latin *facta* (< *facere* "to do"), referring to the completion of the letter rather than its dispatch. Thus Cervantes has Don Quixote end a letter to his beloved Dulcinea: *fecha... a veinte y dos de agosto deste presente año* "done... on August the 22nd of the present year" (*Don Quixote* 1.25).

From the verb *cadere* "to fall," Vulgar Latin created the noun *cadentia "a fall." On the one hand, *cadentia led to the creation of two learned musical terms in early modern times: Italian *cadenza* "conclusion of a piece of music; (later) bravura passage, often improvised by the performer, usually near the end of a movement"; and, from the Italian word, French *cadence*, meaning "rhythm" (English uses both these terms). On the other hand – and this is the more interesting piece of the story – in the spoken language *cadentia became specialized in the sense "the fall of the dice," and then in the Middle Ages, dicing being what it is (think of English *dicey*), "unknown outcome, random event, luck." These are the senses found in French (and English) *chance*. In the matrix of gambling, then, "fall" became "chance, luck." Related is the French adjective *méchant*, of which the first element is *mé-*, elsewhere *mes-*, a negative prefix derived from Germanic and corresponding to English *mis-* (as in *mistake, misunderstand*). *Méchant* originally described one who has back luck, to whom bad things happen ("unfortunate"), but later it developed the active sense it has today, one who does bad things ("wicked").

Another French word for "wicked" is *chétif* (brother to Italian *cattivo* and parent of obsolete English *caitiff*), which has an even stranger history, in that the matrix is a group of different phrases. Latin *captivum* "captive, prisoner" was used by Stoic philosophers (Seneca the Younger, for one) in a moral rather than physical sense; it is found combined with words like *irae* "prisoner of anger," one so subject to anger that he is not in control of himself. Christian writers continued the usage with similar phrases, such as *captivum libidinis* "prisoner of lust." Augustine and the translators of the Vulgate often spoke of a *captivum diaboli* "prisoner of the devil." From phrases like these, and especially the last, the word *captivum* emerged so firmly associated with evil-doing that it came to stand on its own as signifying "wicked."

One of the clearest and most dramatic examples of the effects of a matrix, an etymology so renowned in Romance linguistics as to be considered a classic, is the word for "liver." The Latin name for the organ is *iecur*, which has survived nowhere. Now the Romans, like the Greeks, highly esteemed a certain culinary specialty, the liver of a goose that had been fed on figs, for which their term was *iecur ficatum*. *Ficatum*, literally "figged" (< *ficum* "fig"), modeled on a Greek word, is shorthand for "belonging to a fig-fed goose." Like *captivum* and *formaticum*, the adjective *ficatum*, through regular use (it is already found alone in Apicius's cookbook) came to represent the entire phrase. It then passed through two successive stages of generalization. From a goose liver specially prepared, it came to denote a goose liver, and soon the liver of any animal or person. It thus became the parent of the Romance words for "liver": Italian *fegato*, Spanish *hígado*, French *foie* (the last again unrecognizably remote from its origin). Out of the matrix, therefore, emerged a word for "liver" that had once referred to figs. Nothing intrinsic connects the two, and, for reasons of sound as well as semantics, few speakers perceive a relation between the word for "liver" and that for "fig" (Italian *fico*, Spanish *higo*, French *figue*).

A change in a word's meaning often corresponds to a change in the population that uses it: this is the second general observation. *Arripare* at some point ceased to belong to sailors and travelers by boat and became, with an enlarged sense, an item in everybody's vocabulary. Similarly, *testam* in the sense of "cranium" may at the start have been medical slang, which then spread to society at large. The history of the name for another body part involves a similar shift in those employing it, and is arresting too for the variety of words it has spawned. The Greek noun *kampē* meant "bending, flexure of a member" and was applied especially to the legs of quadrupeds, horses above all. Adopted in the fourth century c.e. by the authors of Latin treatises on veterinary medicine as *gambam*, the word passed from the restricted circle of veterinarians and those who raised and trained horses out to the general populace and acquired the meaning "leg." Its quality of being slang – in this case occupational slang – may well have added to its appeal; the same is true of *testam*. In this story not only does a part represent the whole, but a shift in sense corresponds to a shift in users.

Gambam survives in Italian *gamba* (compare the *viola da gamba*, "viol for the legs," an early bowed stringed instrument that was held between the legs, like a cello) and French *jambe* "leg," the latter of which has sired in turn a number of English words. In both *gambol* "to run and jump about in a frisky, playful way, like a colt" and *gambrel* "type of roof with two slopes on each side," so called from its resemblance to the hind leg of a horse, the connection with horses is still felt. Association with equines is absent, however, from *gam* "a person's leg" (slang) and *jamb* "the vertical side piece of a doorway." The same word again was specialized by French in the sense "leg of a pig," which became *jambon* "ham," whence Spanish acquired its current word for "ham," *jamón*. (English *ham*, of Germanic origin, is unrelated.) On the long road between "flexure" and "ham," one of the turnings is due to the change in the people employing the word.

These are several of the patterns and principles involved in a word's changing its meaning over time. But sometimes instead of its reference a word changes its form.

CHAPTER EIGHT

CHANGES IN THE FORM OF WORDS

Words, then, certainly do shift their meanings. Words often also change their form, their outward appearance, in one way or another, and in that new form sometimes they retain their earlier meanings, sometimes they acquire new ones. In surveying now the changes of this sort that took place, it makes sense to continue limiting the examples to words that entered the Romance languages from Latin, because the latter already possessed a considerable variety of means for creating fresh word forms. With vocabulary, as with other features, Latin provided not only the model of a language that could change and grow, but also the blueprints and the tools for the process.

NOUNS

Nouns from Adjectives

Sometimes an adjective is so regularly attached to a noun by speakers that it begins to represent the entire phrase, eventually becoming a noun in its own right; this might be more exactly described as a change in part of speech than a change in form. We have already seen that in certain regions, after Latin *caseum* "cheese" gave way to the phrase *caseum formaticum* "cheese made in a mold," the adjective *formaticum* alone came to represent the phrase, in the end turning into the noun that named the food. Similarly, and with a startling shift of reference, the Latin phrase *iecur ficatum* got reduced to *ficatum*, now meaning "liver."

Examples of such natural changes abound in English too. If you sat down in a diner and asked for "a side of French" rather than "a side of French fries," would you not be confident of getting just what you wanted? A few other examples, among hundreds: *finals* (with *examinations* understood), *capital* (in one sense *city* is understood, in another *letter*), *fundamental* (as in "the fundamentals of baseball," with no particular noun understood), *cereal* (originally "belonging to Ceres," the Roman goddess of grain), *adhesive, vegetable, emetic, uniform.* Nor are examples lacking within the history of Classical Latin. *Merum* in Latin was an adjective meaning "unmixed, pure"; often used in the phrase *merum vinum* "unmixed wine," it became a noun with that meaning. The adjective is familiar as English *mere*, in which the sense has shifted from "with nothing added" to "no more than," as in "mere saber-rattling." A similar story with consequences for English is that of the adjective *persicum* "Persian": understood either in the feminine (*persicam*) with *arborem* "tree" or in the neuter (*persicum*) with *malum* "fruit, apple," after passing through the form *pessi-* (the *Appendix Probi* cites *persica non pessica*), it produced Romance words for "peach," Italian *pesca* and French *pêche*, the latter of which became English *peach*. *Impeach*, incidentally, is not related: it comes through French from Late Latin *impedicare* "to fetter" (< *pedicam* "fetter, shackle" < *pedem* "foot").

This process was repeated often in the history of the Romance languages. A good example involves another fruit. For the Romans, the *malum cotoneum* was a kind of fruit, related to the apple, that we call *quince*. The name in Italian is usually *mela cotogna*, which reproduces the Latin phrase in full, but sometimes it is just *cotogna* alone, with the adjective taking the place of the phrase. Similarly, in French it is *coing*, the origin of English *quince* (the *s* sound at the end reflects an earlier plural form). Latin *fontem* meant "spring, source of water; source" (> *fount*, as in "baptismal fount" or "fount of knowledge"). An adjective derived from *fontem* was so often combined by the Romans with the word for "water," in *aquam fontanam* "water from a source," that *fontanam* eventually turned into a noun: Italian *fontana*, French *fontaine* "fountain." *Singularem*, abbreviated from *porcum singularem* "single pig," originally designating a male pig who lived alone, produced a couple of Romance words for "boar": French *sanglier*, Italian *cinghiale*.

Several expressions dealing with time underwent a similar change. *Festam diem* "festive day" got shortened to mere *festam* "festival, party": Italian *festa*, Spanish *fiesta*, French *fête*. *Dominicam diem* "the Lord's day" (< *dominum* "master, lord") led to Italian *domenica* "Sunday," while *dominicum diem* (the adjective masculine here, because *diem*, though usually feminine in Latin, was sometimes masculine) led to Spanish *domingo* "Sunday." In both cases *diem* "day" dropped out, leaving the adjective to do its job. *Diem* itself lives on in Spanish *día*, but from the other two languages it has disappeared, and its place has been taken by words derived from the corresponding adjective. *Diurnum*, originally "daily, of the day," is the parent of Italian *giorno* and French *jour* "day" (compare *soup du jour* "soup of the day"); the latter in turn is the parent of English *journal, adjourn, journey* (at first "a day's travel"), and *journeyman* (originally "a man qualified for a day's wages," in contrast to an apprentice, whose compensation was merely the skill gained). The story of the words for "winter" is similar. Latin *hiemem* "winter" got replaced by *tempus hibernum* "wintry time," from which the adjective produced the Romance terms: Italian *inverno*, Spanish *invierno*, French *hiver*.

The adjective *crescentem* "growing" – it is the present participle of the verb *crescere* "to grow" – was often applied to *lunam* "moon" to describe the young moon. As a result *crescent* has come to designate that particular shape. The French equivalent, *croissant*, is familiar as the curved, flaky, buttery roll. In this case the noun understood with *crescentem* was a precise one. Not so, however, with Latin *mobilia* "movables" (< *movere* "to move"), which stands on its own, and which, through the legal sense "movable goods," has produced the modern words for "furniture": Italian *mobili*, French *meubles*, Spanish *muebles*. Similarly, English *regalia, insignia*, and *memorabilia* are nothing but Latin (neuter) adjectives now serving as nouns; originally, they meant "royal things," "distinguishing things," and "memorable things."

Diminutives and Other Words with Suffixes

All these are instances of nouns made from adjectives. Nouns also often change their form by adding some suffix, and of the various suffixes, none play a more varied, important, or interesting role than the diminutives. We have come across several already: from *columnam* "column," *colomellum* "little column," which became Spanish *colmillo* "fang"; from **morsionem* "bite," *morsiunculas* "little bites, nips," used by Plautus; from *spatam* "blade," *spatulam*, with its many offspring. Observe that Latin diminutives usually include the sound of *l*. We see reminders of that fact in modern scientific terms, such as *bacillus* "small rod," *alveolus* "small hollow," *particle* "small part" (< *particella* – from the same origin, via French, comes *parcel*, the etymology of which is inscribed in the phrase "part and parcel"). Latin *calcem* "limestone" (compare *calcium*) gave birth to the diminutive *calculum* "pebble," the origin of our *calculus* and *calculate*. The connection? Pebbles were often used for calculating. Similarly, *muscle* comes from Latin *musculum*, at first "small mouse" (< *mus* "mouse"), later "muscle," on account of the resemblance between the little rodent and a rippling biceps.

An interesting series of English etymologies climaxes in a double diminutive. In Latin *penem* meant "penis; tail." A diminutive, *peniculum*, meant "little tail" and so "brush, broom, sponge"; in his play *The Menaechmus Brothers*, which is the basis for Shakespeare's *Comedy of Errors*, Plautus bestows the apt name of Peniculus on a parasite who sponges off the other characters. From *peniculum* in turn was derived a further diminutive, *penicillum*, which has produced a pair of English words that one would never suspect of being cousins: *penicillin*, the antibiotic made from a mold that under the microscope resembles paint brushes, and *pencil*, which through the nineteenth century was still sometimes used with its original meaning of "paintbrush" (the current meaning of *pencil* arose in the sixteenth century).

Diminutives do sometimes express physical smallness, as with *spatulam* and *penicillum*. Yet a word like *morsiunculam* may not only denote smallness ("nips, nibblings"), but also convey a certain emotional coloring, such as the affection or ardor of a lover. In other instances, a diminutive appears not to carry any special weight or expressiveness, but to be merely an alternative available in the language. An example is **lusciniolum*, parent of the Romance words for "nightingale," a replacement for *luscinium*. It also happens sometimes that a diminutive is, in one way or another, a more useful or convenient form of a word. The Latin adjective *vetus* "old," despite ending in -*us*, was a somewhat anomalous adjective of the third declension (accusative *veterem*). The diminutive form *vetulum*, which became the parent of the Romance words for "old" (Italian *vecchio*, Spanish *viejo*, French *vieux*), may have been more expressive than *vetus* (Plautus preferred it), but certainly also recommended itself to speakers by being a completely regular adjective of the first and second declensions, like *latus lata latum* "broad."

The Latin term for "ear," *aurem*, presented a different sort of problem: at a time when *au* and *o* were coming to be pronounced alike, it could be confused with another body part, *os* (genitive *oris* – compare *oral*) "mouth." The diminutive *auriculam* evaded the difficulty, and also shifted the word from the third to the handier first declension. Thus *auriculam* – found in the earliest Latin texts, recorded in the *Appendix Probi* as *oricla* (with the sound change indicated and also with syncope), the source of the Romance words for "ear"

(French *oreille*, Spanish *oreja*, Italian *orecchio*), and recognizable in English *auricular* – survived and succeeded as a diminutive for reasons of ease, not because it referred to a little version of the organ of hearing.

Certainly the diminutive of Latin *solem* "sun," *soliculum*, did not indicate a heavenly body smaller than the one that rises each morning; probably because of its more substantial form, it has become the parent of French *soleil*, as in the designation of King Louis XIV as *le Roi Soleil* "the Sun King." The French word for "basket," *corbeille*, derives, not directly from Latin *corbem*, but from a diminutive *corbiculam*. Not *cultrum* "knife," but *cultellum* is the ancestor of Italian *coltello*, French *couteau*, and Spanish *cuchillo*. Not *genu* "knee" (of the fourth declension), but *genuculum* (of the handier second) is the ancestor of Italian *ginocchio*, French *genou*, and Spanish *hinojo* (nowadays found only in the phrase *de hinojos* "kneeling"). Not *avem* "bird," but *avicellum* is the ancestor of French *oiseau* and Italian *ucccello*. (The latter is recognizable to us as a proper noun: the Florentine painter Paolo di Dono (1386–1466) received the nickname "Uccello" because of his fondness for painting birds.) None of these diminutive forms necessarily referred to smaller sizes of the original item.

Productive though the diminutives were within Classical Latin and in the passage to the Romance languages, they became much more so in later times. This resource, however, is by no means uniformly available to speakers of the several languages. Our three languages agree in designating an unmarried woman through a diminutive: Italian *signorina* (< *signora*), Spanish *señorita* (< *señora*), French *mademoiselle* (< *madame*) "miss." But whereas Italian and Spanish make abundant and expressive use of diminutive endings (and of other suffixes as well), French hardly uses them at all. In this regard English resembles French.

Italian provides a fine illustration of the potential variety and utility of suffixes – not only diminutives, but also augmentatives (larger versions of the basic item, such as *cartone*), pejoratives (disparaged versions, such as *cartaccia*), and combinations (like the double diminutive *cartellino*). Here are some suffixed forms of the single word *carta* "paper," each identifying a distinctly different object: *cartina* "(cigarette) paper," *cartella* "briefcase," *cartellina* "folder," *cartaccia* "waste paper," *cartoccio* "wrapping paper," *cartone* "cardboard," *cartoncino* "card," *cartuccia* "cartridge," *cartello* "poster," *cartellino* "tag," *cartellone* "wall poster," *cartolina* "postcard." (These are taken from Anna Laura Lepschy and Giulio Lepschy, *The Italian Language Today*, 2nd ed., 1988, p. 182.)

The augmentative suffix *-on(e)*, as in *cartone* "thick paper, cardboard," turns up in the name of another Italian painter, Giorgio Barbarelli (*ca.* 1478–1510), called "Giorgione," something like "Big George." From Italian *viola* "viol" was formed the augmentative *violone* "bass viol," a diminutive of which is *violoncello*, more familiar in the clipped form *cello*. The name of Grand Teton National Park, in Wyoming, is a kind of redundancy: *Grand* does the same work as the suffix in *Teton*, literally "Big Teat," from Spanish *teta* "teat."

A few sets of Spanish examples of a different sort reveal the economy and the expressive range possible within a language that is rich in suffixes. The suffix *-ado* or *-ada* can indicate the fullness or the measure of something: thus, from *boca* "mouth," comes *bocado* "snack" (originally "mouthful"); from *pulgar* "thumb," *pulgada* "inch"; from *carretilla* "wheelbarrow" (a word with two suffixes already), *carretillada* "wheelbarrowful." The suffix *-azo* denotes a blow delivered by something: from *puño* "fist," *puñetazo* "punch"; from *dedo* "finger," *dedazo* "poke with a finger"; from *bala* "bullet," *balazo* "gun shot." The suffix *-al* indicates the place where a plant is grown: from *manzana* "apple" comes *manzanal* "apple orchard"; from *arroz* "rice," *arrozal* "rice paddy"; from *trigo* "wheat," *trigal* "wheat field"; from *naranja* "orange," *naranjal* "orange grove"; from *caña (de azucar)* "(sugar) cane," *cañaveral* "sugar cane plantation," as in Cape Canaveral, Florida, where the Kennedy Space Center is located. One notes the variety of English words required to translate each suffix, as the noun to which it is attached changes. This is only a small selection from the suffixes available in Italian and Spanish, but sufficient perhaps to suggest the place they occupy in those languages.

In French, by contrast, the number of suffixes is far smaller, and the freedom to employ them is much more restricted. (The sixteenth century did witness a fashion for imitating Italian in the ready formation and frequent use of diminutives, but it was short-lived.) On the basis of *maison* "house" we may speak of a *maisonnette* "small house"; on the basis of *chêne* "oak," of a *chênaie* "oak grove." From the adjective *pauvre* "poor" the expressive diminutive *pauvret* may be formed; the Italian and Spanish equivalents of the last would be *poverino* and *pobrecito*. But whereas Italian *-ino* and Spanish *-ito* are extremely common and applied to vast numbers of nouns and adjectives, French *-et* can be added to relatively few. Thus French lags far behind the other two languages in this particular resource. It prefers using analytic means to convey smallness: *petite soeur* "little sister" rather than *soeurette*.

English is in the same position as French. It does contain diminutives that are perceived as such: a *booklet* is a small book, a *cigarette* a little version of a cigar, *panties* a small pair of pants, *darling* an affectionate form of *dear*. A few words, like *hillock* and *bullock*, rely on an Old English diminutive suffix. Nonetheless, these suffixes are hardly productive nowadays; the number of words that contain them can scarcely be enlarged. So if one wants to refer to a sister who is petite or younger or an object of affection, one can only say *little sister*, not *sisterlet or *sisterette or *sisterling, all "impossible" words. Moreover, some words that in origin were diminutives are probably no longer perceived as such: *circle, gravel, idyll, luncheonette, napkin, toilet,* and *yearling*. So our language too, in contrast to Latin, Italian, and Spanish, more or less lacks this valuable linguistic asset.

English nonetheless has directly adopted from Romance languages a good number of words that were diminutives: *casino* (< Italian *casa* "house"), *stiletto* (< Italian *stilo* "dagger" < Latin *stilum* "pointed metal rod"), *libretto* (< Italian *libro* "book"), *umbrella* (< Italian *ombra* "shade"), *camisole* (< French < Provençal < Celtic *camisia* "shirt"), *roulette* (< French *roue* "wheel"), *peccadillo* (< Spanish *pecado* "sin"), *armadillo* (< Spanish *armado* "an armed man"), *guerrilla* (< Spanish *guerra* "war" – at first a small war, one of skirmishes, later the fighter waging it), not to mention a handful of pasta shapes, such as *spaghetti* (< Italian *spaghi* "strings") and *linguine* (< Italian *lingue* "tongues"). Though limited in its ability to imitate them, our language has enhanced its word stock through such imported formations.

English therefore – to give a chronological summary – possesses some diminutives inherited from Germanic (*duckling,* for instance, and *hillock*), some inherited from or based on French (*roulette, luncheonette*), some adopted directly from other Romance languages (*guerrilla*), and many coined on the basis of Latin (*bacillus*). A final pair of double diminutives may illustrate, again, our language's varied word stock. From Frankish *haim "home," which is cognate with English *home*, was derived the Old French diminutive *hamel* "village," and from that in turn, with a second diminutive suffix, came *hamlet* "small village." The other, more twisting story begins with Latin *bullam*, originally meaning "bubble" and then, because of the similarity of shape, "amulet; seal." In Late Latin the word came to designate that to which a seal was applied, "document; (especially) papal decree, bull." From this, Italian created the diminutives *bolletta* and then *bollettino*. The English word *bulletin* was taken from French, which imitated Italian.

Verbs

Frequentatives

In Classical Latin, adjectives could be altered at either end. In addition to the diminutives, which were formed through suffixes, like *vetulum* "old," the language contained adjectives the meanings of which were affected by prefixes: from *bonum* "good," Latin created *perbonum* "very good," and from *rusticum* "rustic," *subrusticum* "rather rustic." Adjectives of this type are rare in the modern languages, however. In Classical Latin, verbs too could be altered at either end, and changes at both sites influenced the forms of many verbs in the Romance languages.

Latin had a regular procedure for making from one verb another that included the notion of performing the action in question repeatedly; the result is called a "frequentative" verb. From *canere* "to sing" (perfect passive participle *cantus*) Latin created the frequentative *cantare*, basically of the same meaning as *canere* but often with the connotation of repetition: the *Oxford Latin Dictionary* gives definitions such as "to repeat; to speak constantly of; to speak in a sing-song tone." The procedure for forming a frequentative was to take the stem of the perfect passive participle, which usually ended in -*t*-, and make it the basis of a new first conjugation verb. In this way, Latin created a good number of frequentatives, some with distinctly different meanings: *habere habitus* "to have" > *habitare* "to inhabit"; *cedere cessus* "to yield, withdraw" > *cessare* "to desist"; *haerere haesus* "to cling" > *haesitare* "to hesitate" (with other changes too). All these pairs we recognize from English (*habeas* (*corpus*), *inhabit; cede, cease; adhere, hesitate*), doubtless without realizing that the second in each pair was once a Latin frequentative verb.

The pair *salire saltus* and *saltare*, related in the same way, are the start of an engaging etymological story. In Latin, *salire* meant "to jump, leap." The Romance derivatives of the simple verb have mostly lost the idea of jumping and taken on different, associated meanings. French *saillir*, to be sure, when used of a male animal, now means "to cover, mount (the female)," in which the sense of jumping may still be felt, yet it also means "to gush out; to stick out, project" (the latter sense reflected in English *salient*). Dropping the idea of jumping while preserving that of upward motion, Italian *salire* came to mean "to go up, climb, mount." The verb took still a different direction in Spanish: from "to jump" it acquired the sense "to jump outward, away" and then simply "to go out, leave," which is what *salir* means today. The verb *salire* seems to have leapt about, unpredictably, in various directions.

Its frequentative *saltare*, which in Classical Latin meant only "to dance," later recovered the original meaning of *salire* and became the source of Italian *saltare*, Spanish *saltar*, and French *sauter* "to jump." From foot and leg activity a couple of these verbs have come in turn to refer to hand and mouth activity – to cooking and eating. The Italian veal dish *saltimbocca* is so tasty it "jumps into your mouth" (*bocca* is Italian for "mouth" < Latin *bucca* "jaw, chaps"). And the French term *sauter* is familiar in English as well. When we fry something quickly in a small amount of fat and, by constant stirring, make the ingredients "jump" so they do not stick to the pan, we are *sautéing* them.

Apart from the special nuance or sheer colorfulness, frequentative verbs offered the speaker of Latin another important advantage: belonging now to the first conjugation, they were, with their completely uniform and predictable four principal parts, the most regular verbs possible. Instead of *cano canere cecini cantus*, there was now *canto cantare cantavi cantatus*; instead of *salio salire salui* (or *salii*) *saltus*, there was *salto saltare saltavi saltatus*. Frequentative verbs, invariably belonging to the first conjugation, could thus perform for speakers the same job as diminutive nouns, which invariably belonged to the first or second declension: by transferring the word in question to a more familiar and more regular class, they made it much easier to handle in speech.

It is this, and probably not the original frequentative nuance, that led *cantare* to win out as the Romance word for "to sing": Italian *cantare*, Spanish *cantar*, French *chanter*. The same story was repeated with many another verb. From *adiuvare adiutus* "to help, assist," the Romans had formed *adiutare* and were already using it as a synonym in the earliest texts; not the former, but the latter became the parent of Italian *aiutare*, Spanish *ayudar*, French *aider* (English derivatives are, from the Latin, *adjutant* and, from the French, *aid, aide*). Similarly, in post-classical times, from *radere rasus* "to scrape, scratch" the frequentative **rasare* was created, the origin of Italian *rasare* and French *raser* "to shave" (Latin *rasorium* "implement for scraping" became French *rasoir* and then English *razor*).

The common Latin verb *capere captus* "to take, capture," gave rise, within classical times, to *captare*, meaning not so much "to take repeatedly" as "to try to take, try to capture." Further lengthened to **captiare* by the addition of *-i-*, the verb has continued in the Romance languages down to today:

Italian *cacciare*, Spanish *cazar*, French *chasser* (> English *chase*), all having the more specialized sense "to hunt." With or without the original frequentative connotation, and often for reasons of convenience, such verbs have prospered in post-classical times. English too can be said to have frequentative verbs: *sparkle, suckle, gabble, wrestle, huddle* (< *hide*), *putter* (< *put*), *flutter* (< *float*).

In the modern languages, Italian in particular, verbs can still be modified by suffixes. Thus, from Italian *girare* "to go around" is created *girellare* "to stroll," and from *dormire* "to sleep" is created *dormicchiare* "to snooze." Like the latter is Spanish *dormitar* "to snooze." These almost seem to be "diminutive" verbs.

Compounds

It was always possible to add something to the front end of a Latin verb as well, in order to alter the meaning. The classical language used prefixes freely and productively. Out of *gradi gressus* "to pace, step, go" (< *gradus* "pace, step") it built a series of compound verbs: *egredi* "to go forth," *ingredi* "to go in," *progredi* "to go forward," *regredi* "to go back," *congredi* "to come together," et al., all recognizable in English from their past participles: *egress, ingress, progress, regress, congress*. Many such compound verbs persisted in the Romance languages, and some new ones were created.

What is of interest here is the use of prefixes to create compound verbs that had the same meaning but were felt, at least at first, to be intensive: popular speech often strives for forcefulness or colorfulness. The Classical Latin compound *comedere*, with the intensive prefix *com-*, was stronger than the simple verb and meant "to eat up, consume." From this comes Spanish *comer* "to eat," no longer forceful or colorful, just the ordinary term. A remarkable saga of compounding illustrates, in its second half, the same process. From *ire itus* "to go," Latin formed the compound *inire* "to go in, enter upon, begin," and from that in turn the noun *initium* "beginning" (compare *initial*) and the frequentative verb *initiare* "to initiate, introduce." The latter was then reinforced by *com-* to produce **cominitiare*, which is the parent of the Romance words: Italian *cominciare*, Spanish *comenzar*, French *commencer* "to begin." But the story does not quite end there. Italian, perhaps feeling this was not as forceful as it could be, tacked on still another prefix and created the synonym *incominciare*, a kind of double intensive compound verb.

All these new types of words are said to be formed by derivation – a noun deriving from an adjective, a diminutive from a base noun, etc. The other principal process is composition – the joining together of existing words to form a new one. English examples of composition would be *skyscraper, blackbird*, and *wallpaper*. Composition is found in Latin and the Romance languages – Latin *agricultura* (< *agri-* "field" + *cultura* "cultivation") or Italian *grattacielo*, Spanish *rascacielo*, French *gratte-ciel* "skyscraper," all made from the words for "scrape" and "sky" – but it occupies nowhere so large a place as it does in English and the other Germanic languages, one of whose marked characteristics is precisely this facility. The more usual pattern is contrast between an English compound word and a phrase in the Romance languages: between *wallpaper* and Italian *carta da parati*, French *papier peint*, Spanish *papel de empapelar*.

OTHER PARTS OF SPEECH

Not only did nouns, adjectives, and verbs often change their forms between Latin and the Romance languages, but so too did invariable parts of speech like prepositions, adverbs, and conjunctions. The story of these is, in outline, the same as of the diminutive nouns and compound verbs. The lengthened forms, because they were more substantial, vigorous, or colorful, were at first preferred by speakers. Then they replaced the shorter original forms. Now, when they no longer contrast with others, the longer words or phrases are not special, but standard; they are the only ones available to do the job. Something similar can be observed in English. The Germanic preposition *before* used in a spatial sense, as in *Two Years Before the Mast* (the memoir by Richard Henry Dana), though acceptable, is obsolete nowadays, its place taken by a phrase: one is far more likely to say "the altar in front of the temple" than "the altar before the temple."

A few examples from the Romance languages should suffice. In Latin, the preposition *ante* meant "before" in both spatial and temporal senses. Its place came to be taken by *de in ante* in Vulgar Latin, longer and more emphatic but signifying the same. This yielded Italian *dinanzi* and Old Spanish *denante* "in front of"; the latter, through dissimilation, became Modern Spanish *delante*. Both are now regularly followed by a fourth preposition: "in front of the temple" would be *dinanzi del tempio* in Italian and *delante del templo* in Spanish, considerably longer than Latin *ante templum*. French *jusque* "up to, as far as" was compounded of Latin *usque*, meaning the same, plus *de*; it too is regularly followed by an additional preposition, as in *jusqu' à nos jours* "up to our days." The Italian adverb and conjunction *dove* "where" is derived from *de* plus *ubi* "where"; the Spanish equivalent, *donde*, is derived from *de* plus *unde* "from where." You can see that *de*, in Latin a preposition indicating "down, from," became an all-purpose particle of place. An especially extended instance is the French *au-devant de* "in front of," < *ad* + *de* + *ab* + *ante* + *de*. Two of those elements, *ab* "from" and *ante* "in front," were also combined into a verb, **abantear*, the source of *advance* (and *advantage*), in which the *d* arose through misunderstanding the first element as *ad* "toward."

Another pair of such adverb/prepositions are the start of some interesting etymologies. From the stem of the noun *forem* "door" (the English is actually cognate) Latin derived two adverbs, *foris* and *foras*, both meaning originally "at the door" and then "outside." (The semantic connection appears tighter if we keep in mind that *forem* referred particularly to a door that opened outwards; the Indo-European term indicated egress from an enclosure rather than a house.) Already in the earliest Latin texts these adverbs were often preceded by *de* or *ab* "away." All the more predictably, then, do we find the Latin words replaced by prepositional phrases in the modern languages: Italian *fuori di* and Spanish *afuera de* "outside of." The French equivalent is longer still, *au dehors de* (from *ad* + *de* + *foris* + *de*). The Latin adverbs begat the Late Latin adjectives *foranum* and *forestem* "outside," from the former of which came *foreign*, while the latter, through the phrase *forestam silvam* "outside woods," produced *forest*, another former adjective we now use as a noun.

A few words that are prepositions in the modern languages, in English no less than the others, did not begin their lives as prepositions or conglomerations thereof, but had a completely different start. They originally were used, like *during* and *pending*, in ablative absolutes. Latin *excepto* was a perfect passive participle, "(having been) excepted, excluded." Employed in sentences like *omnes redierunt, excepto Marco* "all returned, Marcus excluded," *excepto* came to be understood as a preposition meaning "except," with its form now fixed and unvarying. This is the origin of English *except* and its Romance cognates. Nearly identical is the story of the obsolete English preposition *save*, which goes back to Latin sentences like *omnes perierunt, salvo Marco* "all perished, Marcus (being) safe," where the last phrase is again an ablative absolute. Later this would be rendered "all perished save Marcus." In this way a participle and an adjective turned into prepositions.

155

Size and Substance

Because size and substance have featured in a number of word histories, I may fitly conclude this chapter with a pair of contrasting observations thereon.

It happens occasionally that speakers lose sight of a particular element in a word and so, sensing the lack, restore that element. From a historical point of view, this results in redundancy. Examples of redundancy in English phrases that we sometimes hear are "PIN number" (where PIN = "personal identity number") and "please RSVP" (where SVP = *si vous plait*, French for "please"). The Latin expression for "with me" was *mecum*, which in Spanish became *migo*. But once the word reached that form, the element *cum* "with" was no longer recognized by speakers (and this preposition being attached at the end, which is idiomatic with personal pronouns in Latin, added to the confusion). As an independent preposition, *cum* had become *con*, to which *go* did not sound at all similar. Consequently, the preposition *con* was added at the beginning, to form *conmigo*, which is thus the result of a historical redundancy: *cum* + *me* + *cum* "with me with."

French *aujourd'hui* "today" has a similar story. Formed by compounding from *ad* + *diurnum* + *de* + *hodie*, in which both *diurnum* "day" and *hodie* "today" (< *hoc die* "on this day") go back to *diem* "day," the adverb, historically analyzed, means "upon the day today." Of course, speakers of Spanish and French do not sense any redundancy in these words – no more than do speakers of English who use the word *saltcellar*. The first element here is obvious. The second, unconnected to *cellar* "store room," comes instead from French *salière* "saltcellar," < Latin *sal* "salt." The first element of the word therefore, from a historical point of view, is unnecessary and redundant.

The history of the Romance languages also includes what might be considered the opposite phenomenon – remarkable shortenings of words. Shortening, sometimes called "clipping," is familiar from English, which sometimes clips the front of a word, as with (*omni*)*bus* and (*we*)*blog*, sometimes the back, as with *auto*(*mobile*) and *fan*(*atic*), and occasionally both, as with (*in*)*flu*(*enza*) and (*de*)*tec*(*tive*). The Romance languages include some exceptionally dramatic examples, a few of which have passed into Germanic languages. From Latin *jejunum* "fasting" (compare English *jejune* "undernourished, immature") was derived the verb **disjejunare* "to cease fasting," the source of Spanish *desayunar* "to breakfast" (notice the exact equivalence of the English term) and also of French *déjeuner*, which originally referred to the first meal of the day but during the nineteenth century came to designate the mid-day meal. (In Manet's painting, *Déjeuner sur l'herbe* "Luncheon upon the grass," from 1863, the light makes it evident that the time is not morning.) In medieval France, however, alongside the other a shortened form of the verb had arisen, *disjunare*, which became *disner* in Old French, Modern French *dîner* (and English *dine*, four syllables shorter than the original Latin verb!). This term indicated at first the mid-day meal but then, in consequence of the shift in *déjeuner*, the evening meal. From an etymological point of view, therefore, all three of a French speaker's daily meals (*petit déjeuner* "breakfast," *déjeuner*, *dîner*) are the same. And, since they all represent breaking a fast, why shouldn't they be?

The six-syllable Greek word *eleëmosyne* "pity, mercy; charity" became in Vulgar Latin *alemosina*, the source of Italian *limosina* (four syllables), Spanish *limosna* (three), French *aumône* (two), and English *alms* (one!). The word actually entered English, not through the French, but through the Germanic, which is prone to drastic reductions, as may be seen from a final example. The Late Latin *paraveredum* "extra horse" was a strange hybrid at its birth, combining Greek genetic material (*para* "beside; secondary") with Celtic (*veredum* "light horse"). It produced in turn Medieval Latin *palaveredum* (with dissimilation of *r – r* into *l – r*), the parent of both Old French *palefrei* (> English *palfrey*) and German *Pferd* "horse," which has just one-fifth the number of syllables of the original term.

CHAPTER NINE

WHEN WORDS COLLIDE

Conflict and Resolution in the Lexicon

Though much of Latin's vocabulary has continued into the Romance languages, many common Latin words have disappeared, as we saw, and their places have sometimes been taken by other words, sometimes by different forms of the same one. In the modern languages, *ignem*, for instance, has been replaced by *focum* as the term for "fire," *iecur* by *ficatum* for "liver," *domum* by *casam* or *mansionem* for "house." *Hibernum* has come to be used for "winter" instead of *hiemem*, *cantare* for "to sing" instead of *canere*, *auriculam* for "ear" instead of *aurem*. Some reasons have already been suggested for these preferences. Yet the question deserves further and more systematic consideration if we want, not merely to accept that vocabulary is always in flux, even more than other features of language are, but to understand how and why this is so.

VICTORIOUS CAUSES

In outline, every story of words in conflict is the same. At a given time in the history of the language it happens that more than one word is available to express a certain notion – both *ignem* and *focum*, for instance, or both *aurem* and *auriculam*. It does not matter whether the two terms are exact synonyms (they never really are) or just loosely associated with each other, nor whether one or the other is well established in the language or but newly coined. Regardless of history or semantics, the two words have at a certain point come to be regarded as equivalent. The decisive moment in the story of words in conflict is the elimination of one in favor of the other. One word is victorious and continues in the language, while the other drops out of use. Or sometimes they continue to co-exist, although usually with different meanings. Having observed earlier several of the processes by which two terms arrived at being considered equivalent, we may now look more closely into the reasons why one eventually ousted the other – reasons which are varied, being sometimes straightforward, sometimes multiple, sometimes obscure.

Convenience

Vulgar Latin came to prefer the diminutives *genuculum* "knee," *soliculum* "sun," and *vetulum* "old," to the simple forms, *genu, solem,* and *veterem.* There can be no question of these diminutives being preferred because of the added notion of littleness, which does not apply to any of them. In each case, rather, the new form belonged to the first or second declension, whereas the older one belonged to the third (*solem, veterem*) or the fourth (*genu*). Now, the first two declensions were both more similar to one another than to the other declensions (the accusative plurals ended in *-as* and *-os*, for instance, the genitive plurals in *-arum* and *-orum*) and more familiar because they contained larger numbers of nouns. As a result, nouns of the first two declensions were more convenient to handle. In shifting nouns and adjectives in this direction, therefore, speakers sought regularity, which brought ease of use. The *Appendix Probi* already showed signs of this shift: *palumbes non palumbus* "pigeon" and *tristis non tristus* "sad," in each case a third declension form replaced by an "incorrect" second declension form. The latter alteration may also have been influenced by the fact that a synonym (*maestus* "sad") and an antonym (*laetus* "happy") belonged to the first and second declensions.

Even when it was a question of different words for the same notion, and not just differing forms, the same inclination toward convenience played a role. Thus *gambam* "leg," *focum* "fire," and *ficatum* "liver" have in common the fact that they all belonged to the first two declensions, whereas the words they drove out belonged to the third: *crus, ignem, iecur.* And the adjectives *hibernum* and *diurnum* more easily supplanted *hiemem* "winter" (third declension) and *diem* "day" (fifth) for the same reason.

Convenience also explains the popularity of frequentative verbs, all of which belonged to the first conjugation. We already saw that *cantare*, no longer meaning "to sing repeatedly," was favored over *canere* because the principal parts of a first conjugation verb were much more predictable than those of other verbs, and other features of the conjugation were more regular as well. Here too, regularity made for ease of handling. A similar process can be seen in English.

Our language possesses verbs with complicated patterns of principal parts (*sing sang sung* or *speak spoke spoken*), called "strong verbs." It also possesses verbs that follow a single, much simpler pattern (*play played played* and *help helped helped*), called "weak verbs." Throughout history English speakers, in pursuit of regularity, have been adapting strong verbs to the pattern of the weak. Thus, the past participle of *help* was *holpen* at first, only later *helped*, and before it became *stepped* the past tense of *step* was *stope*. English verbs have trended towards this pattern as Latin verbs did towards the first conjugation, and for the same reason.

The simple verb *canere* was not irregular in Latin, merely less easily predictable in its forms than *cantare*. The verbs that the Romans themselves perceived as irregular – few in number, but all in common use – were subject to special pressure to conform to the more familiar, easier patterns. The irregular *posse* "to be able" was remodeled as a regular second conjugation verb, *potere* (like *monere*). Derived from *potere* are Italian *potere*, Spanish *poder*, French *pouvoir*. (*Posse* is still alive in English, nonetheless. British Medieval Latin used the infinitive as a noun meaning "power, force," and out of the phrase *posse comitatus* "the force of the county" arose our present use of *posse* for a group of men whom the sheriff calls upon in a crisis. Thus, a term we might associate with the Sheriff of Dodge City originated, so to speak, with the Sheriff of Nottingham.) Similarly, the irregular *velle* "to wish, want" got converted to the second conjugation verb *volere* (> Italian *volere*, French *vouloir*). *Ferre* "to carry," also an irregular verb (and familiar from a host of English compounds, such as *coniferous* "cone-carrying"), was not remodeled, but rather replaced with a verb that was regular: either *portare* (> Italian *portare*, French *porter*) or *levare*, at first "to lighten" (as a burden – *levare* comes from *levem* "light": compare *levity*, *levitate*), then "to lift up, carry" (> Spanish *llevar*).

Convenience of a different sort played a role in the stories of the Italian and Spanish words for "sister" and "brother." The Latin terms were *sororem* and *fratrem*, both third declension nouns, which passed smoothly into French as *soeur* and *frère*. Now, both Italian and Spanish tended to preserve a pattern from Latin whereby nouns ending in *-a* were feminine and those in *-o* were masculine. (The weakening and dropping of final vowels in French erased this handy pattern of gender distinctiveness.) Examples are Italian *zia*, *zio*, Spanish *tía*, *tío* "aunt" and "uncle," and Italian *nonna*, *nonno*, Spanish *abuela*, *abuelo* "grandmother" and "grandfather." Conformity to the pattern was desirable with another clearly gendered pair, "sister" and "brother," and the two languages did achieve this, although by different means. Italian resorted to diminutives, not of the same word, but clearly marked for gender nonetheless: *sorella* "sister" and *fratello* "brother." Italian was urged along this path by the fact that *frate* had early come to be used for "brother" in the religious sense: thus, *fratello* not only ended in *-o*, but also maintained a useful distinction. The Spanish words for "sister" and "brother" originated in phrases – *sororem germanam, fratrem germanum* – in which the adjective *germanum* "genuine" indicated sharing the same mother and father: "full sister, full brother." The phrases got shortened to just the adjectives, with the result that the Modern Spanish words are *hermana* and *hermano*, a contrasting pair of terms neatly marked for gender.

Distinctiveness

In some cases, we can discern more than one reason for the preference given to a word. One drawback to *aurem* "ear" was its membership in the third declension. A second drawback was its sound: as *au* became identical with *o* in Vulgar Latin pronunciation, *aurem* ran the risk of being confused with *os* (stem *or-*) "mouth." From this point of view *auriculam* was therapeutic: remedying the problems in *aurem*, it restored the word to health.

The imagery of illness and rehabilitation is not mine. Rather, it is prominent in the writings of a renowned Romance philologist, Jules Gilliéron (1854–1926), who in 1918 published a ground-breaking study, *Genealogy of the Words for "Bee."* This could be realized only because of an earlier project Gilliéron had designed, *The Linguistic Atlas of France*. In that work, carried out in collaboration and published between 1902 and 1912, the words for nearly two thousand items were recorded in more than six hundred localities of French speech. The painstaking and revolutionary compilation, which long served as a model of linguistic geography, revealed unmistakably the remarkable variety in vocabulary across the territory of what was traditionally regarded as a single language. (Despite its title, the *Atlas* included material from French-speaking parts of Belgium, Switzerland, and Italy as well.)

Pondering that variety and seeking its historical sources (the "genealogy" of the title), Gilliéron perceived that the cause for much innovation in the lexicon was homophonic clash, that is, two different words pronounced alike. This could lead to confusion, and speakers, he presumed, aim at being clear. The inherited Latin word for "bee," *apem*, was easily liable to confusion, since *p* between vowels often got altered. In Italy it was preserved: the Modern Italian word for "bee" is *ape*. But in several French dialects *apem* got reduced to *ep, ef,* and even *e*, forms so insubstantial as nearly to evanesce. In standard French, intervocalic *p* regularly changed to a *v* (Latin *ripa* > French *rive*, for instance). *Apem* thus ran the risk of being mistaken for *avem* "bird" and perhaps also *avum* "grandfather." Gilliéron identified two types of solutions to the difficulty. Some speeches abandoned the word altogether and substituted another, *mouche-à-miel*, for instance, "honey-fly," while others resorted to lengthened forms, such as the diminutives *avette* and *abeille*. The last, from Latin *apiculam*, is the standard term in Modern French.

Gilliéron and those who came after him discovered many other similar cases of homophonic clash followed by therapeutic action. It may not be a coincidence that the scholar who drew attention to this process so forcefully was a native speaker of French (he was born in Switzerland), for of our three Romance languages, French is the one that, having undergone the most dramatic abridgments and alterations, presents the largest number of homophonic clashes. Drawing upon the discoveries he had made about the words for "bee," Gilliéron went on to write a general treatment of the theme, *Pathology and Therapy of Words* (1915, 1921).

Like *abeille*, the French word for "sun" originated as a therapeutic diminutive, *soleil*, < Latin *soliculum*. And here too homophonic clash played a role, because the simple *solem* could be confused with *solum* "soil" and *solum* "alone," as well as with *soldum* "a sou (small coin)." The last word, quite apart from its potential conflict with *solem*, has an interesting history. It originated as the Latin adjective *solidum* "solid." In the fourth century c.e., *solidos nummos* "solid coins" began to be minted, of unalloyed gold. The phrase became regular enough that soon the coins were called simply *sólidos* or, with syncope of the post-tonic vowel (that is, the vowel following the accented one), *soldos*. Over the centuries the value of the coins so denominated diminished greatly, with the result that today French *sous* and Italian *soldi*, formerly small coins but now no longer even in circulation, both signify sums of little worth. The corresponding Spanish word, *sueldo*, means "salary." From *soldos* was derived the Medieval Latin term *soldarium*, "one who worked for pay; a soldier."

Sometimes homophonic conflict had already arisen in Classical Latin. Such was the case with the noun *bellum* "war" and the adjective *bellum* "pretty, beautiful." Brought into clever conjunction in the saying *bellum haud bellum* "war (is) hardly pretty," the two words had distinct origins. The term for "war," it was known, had earlier been *duellum*, which Roman folk etymology connected with *duo* "two": "war," accordingly, referred to the two opposing sides (and English *duel* derives from this folk etymology). The adjective, an affective word already popular in Classical Latin, eventually drove out its rival, *pulchrum* "handsome, beautiful." *Bellum* survives in French *beau* (feminine *belle*) and Italian *bello*. In Spanish, *bello* is rather literary and found in fixed phrases like *bellas artes* "fine arts"; the usual word for "beautiful" is *hermoso* (< Latin *formosum* "beautiful" – the island of Taiwan was named *Formosa* by the Portuguese).

The homophonic conflict between *bellum* and *bellum* was resolved by replacing the Latin word for "war" with a Germanic one, *werra (> Italian, Spanish *guerra*, French *guerre*), the earliest meaning of which was "confusion, disorder" (compare German *Wirren* "disturbance") – a natural enough association. Word histories are affected by historical events as well as by purely linguistic developments. Here, the solution to the conflict was favored by the historical circumstance that the Germanic peoples excelled at war and conquered large parts of the former Roman Empire. Similarly, the distinction maintained in Italian between *frate* and *fratello* presupposes Christian monasticism.

Avoidance of Monosyllables

One of the grave problems with the forms of *apem* that developed in certain French dialects (*ep, ef, e*) was their near insubstantiality. They were so small as to seem indistinct, insignificant, barely existing. Many Latin words were afflicted in this way. The term for "spring," *ver* (compare *vernal*), went out of circulation, replaced by polysyllables: in French, by *printemps* (< *primum tempus* "first time, first season"); in Spanish and Italian, by *primavera* (one thinks of Botticelli's painting of that name), derived from the phrase *primo vere* "at the beginning of spring."

The Classical Latin word *aes* (genitive *aeris*) referred to either copper or bronze. It was not strange that the Romans used the same word for the two metals, because bronze is an alloy of copper plus tin. (When they did need to make the distinction, the Romans called copper *aes Cyprium*, "Cyprian *aes*," the island of Cyprus being a rich source of copper ore from prehistoric times. The adjective is the source of English *copper*.) Already in Late Latin the monosyllable *aes* began to be replaced by the more substantial *aeramen*, which passed into the Romance languages with varying meanings: Italian *rame* "copper," French *airain* "bronze," Spanish *alambre* "wire." In the case of the Spanish word, the sequence of senses was "bronze, copper; object made of bronze or copper; copper wire; wire (made of any metal)." Again, speakers eschewed a monosyllable.

The very common (and irregular) Latin verb for "to go" was *ire*, many of the forms of which were monosyllables and hence vulnerable. That it was precisely monosyllabism, and nothing else, which speakers and writers found objectionable emerges unmistakably from a set of observations made and reported by Einar Löfstedt, the great Swedish scholar of Late and Vulgar Latin (1880–1955). He contrasts the use of *ire* with that of the verb *vadere*, also meaning "to go," all of whose forms are at least two syllables long. *Vadere*, though found widely, was not nearly so often used by writers of Classical Latin. In regard to the Vulgate (the Latin translation of the Bible made by Jerome in the late fourth century and expressed in every-day language), Löfstedt points out that the text never once has *it* "he, she goes," or *is* "you (singular) go," or *i* "go! (imperative singular)," but instead has *vadit* (21 times), *vadis* (10), and *vade* (181). In contrast, it has *ite* "go! (imperative plural)" 68 times and the corresponding *vadite* not once. The conclusion is inescapable: Jerome never used the verb *ire* in his translation when it would have been a one-syllable form, putting *vadere* always in its place, but he did use *ire* otherwise. (*Vadere* is the source of *invade*, literally "to go into, against.")

Similar data gathered by Löfstedt from other Vulgar Latin texts confirm these observations. Not a single one-syllable form of *ire* is found either in the prose of Petronius's *Satyrica* or in the so-called *Mulomedicina Chironis* "Chiron's Equine Medicine," a veterinary compilation made in the fourth or fifth century. The same holds for the *Pilgrimage to the Holy Places*, where some of the "objectionable" forms are replaced by *vadere*, others by *ambulare* "to walk." During the centuries since then, *ire* has nearly disappeared from the Romance languages (but it does still serve to form some future tenses: French *j'irai*, Spanish *iré* "I will go"). Its place has been taken variously by *vadere* (Italian *vado*, French *je vais*, Spanish *voy* "I go"), by the somewhat mysterious *andare (Italian *andiamo* "let us go"), and by the puzzling *alare* (French *allons* "let us go"; English *alley* comes from French *allée* "path," originally "a going"). Löfstedt makes the astonishing observation that the author of the *Pilgrimage*, writing in the fourth century, was already using exclusively those forms of *vadere* still alive in Modern French and Italian today! *Ire*, to the extent it was monosyllabic, obviously had to go.

Two other Latin verbs with many single-syllable forms were *flere* and *nare*, and, predictably, they too disappeared. *Flere* "to weep, wail" was replaced here by *plorare* (> French *pleurer*, Spanish *llorar*, compare English *implore*, originally "invoke by weeping"), there by *plangere*, earlier "to beat the breast as a sign of mourning," then "to mourn, bewail" (> Italian *piangere*; compare English *plangent, plaintive, complain, plaintiff*). Instead of *nare natus* "to swim," its frequentative *natare* was employed (> Spanish *nadar*, Italian *nuotare*), also *navigare*, originally "to sail" (> French *nager*), the association evidently being movement through water.

The prepositions, finally, many of them monosyllables, were often replaced by longer versions. To the earlier examples given, I may add another pair here. Classical Latin *sub* "under" lost out to *subtus*: Italian *sotto* (as in the phrase *sotto voce* "in an undertone," literally "under the voice"), French *sous* (as in *sous-chef* "under-, assistant-chef"), Old Spanish *soto* (the modern equivalent is the still lengthier *debajo de*). Similarly, *trans* "across" was replaced by the compound *ad transversum* (*de*), literally "towards crosswise (from)": Italian *attraverso*, French *au travers de*, Spanish *a través de*.

In the matter of monosyllables, a sharp contrast exists between English, on the one hand, and, on the other, the Romance languages and many others besides: English is the only European language that is hospitable to words of one syllable. It has been calculated that of the five hundred words most often used in English, four hundred are monosyllables. Many monosyllables, to be sure, are part of the language's Germanic inheritance: *fire, house, sing, ear, sun, knee, old, can, want, gold, bee, bank, shore, war*. Yet quite a few come from elsewhere: *curve* from Latin, *save* from French, *glen* from Gaelic, *gene* from Greek. And English has added to its stores of monosyllables by clipping words: *cab(riolet)*, *mob(ile vulgus)*, *(tele)phone*. It is therefore possible in English to write children's books using monosyllables alone and to compose, as the scholar-poet A. E. Housman sometimes did, whole stanzas of sophisticated verse with no more than one polysyllable or two.

Intensity, Color

The preferring of one word over another is not always settled solely on the basis of form – a word's convenience, distinctiveness, or substance. Often it has to do with content, with the reference or coloring or forcefulness or stylistic level of a word. Some diminutives, for instance, in addition to morphological convenience, were probably preferred because of their meaning: the notion of smallness lent the words an attractive emotional feeling. So *avicellum* "bird" and *auriculam* "ear" not only rescued the words from potential confusion and led to forms more easily handled, but also, at least in the beginning, may have conveyed a greater intensity of feeling – "cute little bird" or something such. Similarly, the frequentative verbs may have appeared to intensify the action in question: *cantare* "to sing repeatedly" perhaps later approached in sense "to really sing," only to lose its force eventually and mean merely "to sing," like the *canere* it had replaced. And *ad transversum de* probably seemed a more forceful way to express "across" than plain old *trans*.

The standard Classical Latin verb for "to eat" was *edo* (compare English *edible*; Germanic *eat* is cognate), which was irregular and liable to be confused with the verb "to be" (the infinitives were *ēsse* "to eat" and *ĕsse* "to be"), and which also included several monosyllabic forms. In addition to these other drawbacks, the verb may have appeared weak in content, without force or flavor. Already in Classical Latin the compound *comesse* (or, in regularized form, *comedere*) was often employed, meaning "to eat up, consume." This intensive form is the parent of Spanish *comer* "to eat." The intensive prefix *com-* also marked other compound verbs that outlived the simple forms: *cominitiare "to begin," for example, or *comparare* "to buy" (> Spanish *comprar*).

Many preferred words were more colorful than those they drove out; they presented to speakers a vivid image in place of a neutral term, until they themselves, from steady use, became ordinary too. The verbs *arripare and *plecare both summoned up a picture of a boat putting in at the shore, and so were more appealing means of expressing "to arrive" than Classical Latin *pervenire*, literally "to come through."

The common Latin verb for "to speak" was *loqui locutus* (compare *loquacious, eloquent, colloquium, interlocutor, circumlocution*), the forms of which were somewhat unusual. It disappeared from the Romance languages, and its place has been taken by a pair of verbs not only more regular but also more colorful. Spanish *hablar* "to speak" came from Latin *fabulare* "to converse, chat," which evoked a distinct social situation, an informal exchange of speech among acquaintances. The origin of the Italian and French words for "to speak" is more remote and complex. It started from the Greek noun *parabole* "comparison," and resulted from two converging lines of development. First, the Jewish authors of the Septuagint (the Greek translation of the Hebrew Bible, made in the third century B.C.E.), faithfully imitating the semantic range of a Hebrew term that meant "comparison," added to this meaning of *parabole* other meanings that the Hebrew term possessed, including "proverb" and "speech." That in turn prompted the translators of the Vulgate, working more than half a millennium later, to use *parabolam*, the Latin form, with the same expanded set of meanings. The word then became part of the Christian vocabulary, of common folk no less than Church fathers. Second, Christians applied *parabolam* to teachings of Jesus, because they often are in the form of comparisons (hence *parable*), and the speech of Jesus was regarded as the Word par excellence. By these routes, *parabolam*, ousting Classical *verbum*, became the general word for "word": Italian *parola*, Spanish *palabra* (the *l* and the *r* having exchanged places), French *parole*. (English *parole* was at first the word of honor of a prisoner who promised not to escape, later of a criminal who accepted release from prison on condition of obeying certain rules.) The derived verb *parabolare*, accordingly, meant "to speak": Italian *parlare*, French *parler* (compare *parlor* and *parliament*, both places for speaking). This story, obviously, could have unfolded only in the context of Christianity.

Another verb nicely illustrates again the success of the colorful. *Fervere* "to be hot" was also Latin's usual word for "to boil" (for the former sense, compare *fervent*, *fervid*; for the latter, *ferment*, *effervescent* – *fervere* is cognate with English *brew*). But *fervere* survived only in Spanish *hervir*. What did the other languages do? They replaced it with *bullire*, originally meaning "to bubble" (compare *ebullient*): bubbles rising through a liquid and bursting at the surface form a livelier picture of boiling than does heat. The result is Italian *bollire*, French *bouillir* (> *boil*, *bouillion*), and also Spanish *bullir*, which, however, is limited to figurative senses. (In this, *bullir* resembles English *seethe*, which originally meant "boil" but nowadays is used only in phrases like "seething with anger" or "seething mass of bodies on the dance floor.")

Commonness

Sometimes one Latin word was preferred over another for reasons of level or register: a common thing was aptly named with a word that was common – depreciative, familiar, rustic, coarse, low, or vulgar. The word was preferred because it had a certain punch to it, and the punch was given by its "social" status, its place within the language's various levels of usage. We may contrast, in contemporary English, *short-order cook* and *hash-slinger*. The latter is not the least bit formal, it might even be regarded as insulting, but it is a lot more vivid than the former. An example in the Romance languages is the Italian and Spanish word for "house," *casam*, originally "hut, cottage, hovel (in the country)," which supplanted the standard and dignified *domum*. The great majority of people in the Roman Empire, it must be remembered, lived in the country.

Spanish replaced Classical Latin's awkward *edere* "to eat" with *comer*. French *manger* and Italian *mangiare* "to eat" come instead from the colorful verb *manducare*, originally "to chew" (*mandible* is derived from the same stem), which because of its connotation of chomping or champing was likely considered somewhat gross. Accordingly, it is found chiefly in Latin comic and satiric authors. The word was used, however – and in the sense of "to eat" – by the Emperor Augustus himself, who wrote in a letter to his stepson Tiberius: *duas buccas manducavi* "I ate two mouthfuls" (Suetonius, *Life of Augustus* 76). Despite the emperor's authority, the sentence, far from refuting, tends to confirm the low status of *manducare*, since it is in collocation here with *bucca*, which is also a rather coarse word. (Augustus liked colloquial speech.) *Buccam*, originally indicating the chaps, the jaw, soon came through association to mean "mouth," eventually replacing the classical but compromised noun *os* (stem *or-*). The results in the modern languages are Italian *bocca*, Spanish *boca*, French *bouche*. (In the same chapter, Suetonius quotes Augustus as using *comedere* also.)

A pair of adjectives provides an interesting further example. *Magnum* "great" was very common in Latin (and is familiar to us from a host of learned words, such as *magnitude* and *magnificent*). It was declined in the convenient first two declensions, and there was nothing irregular about the word itself. Its comparative and superlative degrees, however, *maiorem* "greater" and *maximum* "greatest," are irregular in relation to it. The curious thing is that they have survived, while *magnum* itself has been lost from the Romance languages. A further surprise is that it was replaced by a third declension adjective, *grandem* (> Italian, Spanish *grande*, French *grand*). Moreover, *magnum* began giving way to *grandem* in spoken Latin fairly early, and by the fourth century the author of the *Pilgrimage to Holy Places* was using *grandem* almost to the exclusion of *magnum*.

What led *grandem* to be preferred to *magnum*, despite the latter's several advantages? Like *bullire* in relation to *fervere*, *grandem* was more concrete. It conveyed the picture of someone or something that had reached its full size. Though it could be used for anything large, *grandem* was most often applied to people who were grown up or plants that were mature, and was frequently used among farmers.

A notorious example of a depreciative word winning out is *caballum* "nag," which took the place of *equum* "horse" in the Romance languages: Spanish *caballo*, Italian *cavallo*, French *cheval*. About the level of *caballum* there can be no doubt, since, for a change, we have explicit ancient testimony. A poet from the time of Nero (reigned 54–68 C.E.), Persius, prefaces his satires with a sneering rejection of the traditional sources of poetic inspiration: "I didn't swill my lips in the Fountain of the Nag" (*fonte caballino*), he says, a reference to the famous Hippocrene spring, created, according to legend, by the winged horse Pegasus. About this verse an ancient commentator remarks: "he says 'of the Nag' (*caballino*) rather than 'of the Horse' (*equino*) because lowly things befit satire." The employment of the lowly *caballum* was to be ampler than the commentator could have known, and its victory over *equum* was not long in coming.

An inscription of the second century C.E. found in Portugal and concerning the leasing of state-owned mines contains the clause: *qui mulos mulas asinos asinas caballos equas sub praecone vendiderit* "he who shall have sold at auction mules (*mulos*) and she-mules (*mulas*), asses (*asinos*) and she-asses (*asinas*), horses (*caballos*) and mares (*equas*)." The first two pairs are alike in that the same stem is used for naming the animals, with different gender inflections for male (*-os*) and female (*-as*). But with the third pair the symmetry disappears: female horses are called *equas*, whereas the males are called, not *equos*, as we might have expected, but *caballos*. The Romance preference is already expressed here.

A certain depreciativeness, then, made *caballum* a colorful, appealing word. But why did a common word like *equum* give way to it? Perhaps because its distinctiveness was threatened, through three changes in pronunciation. As the diphthong *ae* converged in Vulgar Latin with *ĕ*, the adjective *aequum* "level, fair, just" (compare *equal*) began to sound like *equum*. Another phonological change affected *equum*. The /kw/ pronunciation of *qu* was tending to be reduced to /k/, as the *Appendix Probi* testifies: *equs non ecus*, also *coqus non cocus* "cook." And then, with the shift of intervocalic *c* to *g*, another regular sound change, *ecum* would have become a homonym of *ego* "I." Clearly, Classical Latin *equum* became a compromised word, and therefore was vulnerable. An interesting twist was given to the story by a certain phonological condition that came into play. The second of the changes, from *equum* to *ecum*, took place only before the sounds of *o* and *u*. As a consequence, the name of the male horse alone changed; *equam* was unaffected, and, unlike *equum*, it has continued in some Romance languages: Spanish *yegua*, Portuguese *egoa* "mare."

The horse, by whichever name called, was an important animal in the ancient world and, even more, in the medieval, chiefly because of its centrality in warfare. A whole series of terms attests to the special status of those who rode horses – or simply looked after them. Starting in the Middle Ages, many desirable moral and social qualities became associated with the notion of the horseman, who was called *caballero* in Spanish, *cavaliere* in Italian, *chevalier* in French. Some current English words derived from these encapsulate what the man on horseback, the knight, represented to earlier ages. *Chivalrous*, for instance, according to the full and fine definition in *Webster's Third New International Dictionary*, means "characteristic of or relating to the ideal knight of the feudal and Renaissance times according to modern romantic tradition," which is glossed as "marked by honor, fairness, generosity, and kindliness especially to foes, the weak and the lowly, and the vanquished." The adjective *cavalier*, however, shows the other side of the coin, the disagreeable qualities that such a man might develop: superciliousness, arrogance, highhandedness.

Today, a *constable* is a policeman, but his position in earlier times was considerably loftier. The term at first identified the chief official of a royal or noble household, then later a high officer with military, administrative, or judicial responsibilities. It comes from Late Latin *comitem stabuli* "the count (officer) of the stable," which serves as a reminder of how important that wing of the palace was. The term *marshal* now usually identifies a police or judicial officer in the United States. Though derived from Germanic, it has a history parallel to that of *constable*. Old French *mareschal*, a compound meaning "horse servant" (the first element is the same as *mare*), at the start designated a groom, and only later did it become the title of various high officers, as in the military "field marshal."

At lower levels of medieval society as well, the importance of horses and their care is reflected in language. Today a *henchman* is a trusted follower, often of a gangster or someone else sinister. The present meaning comes from generalizing the meaning of the Old English word, a compound of *hengist* "horse, stallion" plus *man*, so a henchman too, like a marshal, was a groom once upon a time. (Those two legendary Saxon brothers of early English history, Hengest and Horsa, may both have been named for the same animal.)

An *equerry*, who now is a personal attendant on royalty, used to be a man in charge of horses, a position that his title appears to reflect. The actual etymology, however, involves Late Latin *scutarium* "shield-carrier, guardsman" (< *scutum* "shield"), out of which arose both *squire* and *esquire* also. The modern spelling of *equerry*, which in Middle French had been *escuerie*, was influenced by *equum*, though that was not the actual source. Taken together, all these words constitute a monument to the horse's place in western history.

The preference shown for rustic or low words, like *casa* and *caballum*, has an obvious corollary. Literary words of Latin did not continue into the Romance languages; by definition, they had not formed part of the vocabulary of most speakers. Three terms for natural elements may serve as examples: although known to every Roman schoolboy (and to every modern schoolchild who has read the first hundred verses of the *Aeneid*), *tellus* "earth," *aequor* "sea," and *sidus* "star" vanished from the lexicon. The every-day words remained: *terra*, *mare*, *stella*.

Not all conflicts among words involve two parties. Several words are sometimes in competition, as with the set of *domum*, *casam*, and *mansionem*, from which different languages made different selections. Nor does the resolution of one conflict forestall further changes. As *espalda* in Spanish moved from meaning "shoulder blade" to "shoulder" to "back," other terms had to be brought in to fill the gaps left – *omóplato* for "shoulder blade" and *hombro* (< Latin *umerum*) for "shoulder." Then in the nineteenth century, to designate "bone of the upper arm," which in Latin had been designated by *umerum*, Spanish began to use the learned re-creation, *húmero*, a doublet of *hombro*. Often individual words are in motion, and a movement here dislocates something there, and entrains perhaps another movement, another dislocation.

Yet even knowledge of the various reasons why one word wins out over another and awareness of the need to consider lexical items within their wider semantic field are not always sufficient to explain the results. Often we just do not know why this term was chosen at the expense of that one. We may hope that further research will answer the question. And we may, at the same time, accept the notion that the random, the accidental, and the capricious play a role in the history of languages no less than of other human affairs.

Obscurity envelops the common Romance words for "small," all of which, it so happens, are easily recognizable to us from English. The Latin word, *parvum*, disappeared, and its place was taken by three other adjectives beginning with *p*, which may be related to one another and which seem to be onomatopoeic – they are expressive in the same way as children's talk often is. The French word for "small" is *petit*, which has given us *petite* and *petty*. It is related to Vulgar Latin *pitinnum*, as may also be Spanish *pequeño*, the source of *pickaninny*. And similar to the Spanish in turn is Italian *piccolo*. A shortening of the phrase *flauto piccolo* "small flute," this name of a musical instrument is another adjective that has become a noun.

There are other questions we can ask about the Romance vocabulary. Much study has been devoted to drawing distinctions within the Romance family, to differentiating eastern languages from western in lexical choices made, or central languages from peripheral. Some evidence suggests that the peripheral areas are often more conservative: consider the contrast in the terms for "beautiful" between classical *formosum* (maintained in Portuguese *formoso*, Spanish *hermoso*, Rumanian *frumos*) and popular *bellum* (French *beau*, Italian *bello*). Here, however, I have focused on the general grounds for one word's victory over another.

THE *REICHENAU GLOSSARY*, AND OTHERS

Just as the *Appendix Probi* presented in transparent format the changes in sounds and word forms as Vulgar Latin was moving away from the norms of Classical, so the wars between words are revealed transparently in a type of document called a "glossary." A glossary is a series of notes, added in the margins or between the lines of a text, explaining one word by means of another. It may also be a collection of such notes no longer attached to the original texts, but gathered together separately and reorganized, often alphabetically; in this case, a glossary resembles a primitive dictionary. A typical gloss is *pulcra : bella*. This demonstrates that the glossator believed *pulcra* would not be understood by a reader, and he therefore explained it, defining it with the more familiar term *bella* "beautiful." This gloss confirms what the history of the several languages shows, that *pulcra* "handsome, beautiful" was supplanted by the popular *bella*. Glossaries are often our earliest evidence for changes that were taking place in the lexicon. They indicate, for the time and place they were created, which words were in use in popular speech and which were not.

The example cited comes from a glossary that is fascinating for the story of the Romance languages, the *Reichenau Glossary*. It is so called because the unique manuscript of it once belonged to the Benedictine monastery at Reichenau, located on an island in Lake Constance, in southwestern Germany. It was composed, in the eighth century, chiefly to help readers of the Vulgate. In each entry, the first word is the fairly classical Latin of the original text, while the second, the gloss proper, is also Latin, but a Latin that reflects contemporary usage. The form of the words cited is set by the way they are employed in the glossed text.

The combination of several entries points unmistakably to France as the place where the glossary was composed. Among verbs we read *transgredere : ultra alare* "to go beyond" and *da : dona* "give!" Only in France were *alare* and *donare* used: compare French *aller* "to go" and *donner* "to give." The entry *vespertiliones : calvas sorices* "bats" (literally "bald mice") leads inescapably to the same conclusion: compare French *chauve-souris*.

In the *Reichenau Glossary* we come across many words we have met before:

- nouns: *plaustra : carra* "wagons," *hiems : ibernus* "winter," *passer : omnis minuta avis* "any small bird," *caseum : formaticum* "cheese," *iecore : ficato* "liver," *in ore : in bucca* "in the mouth";
- adjectives: *vorax : manducans* "greedily eating," *optimum : valde bonum* "very good";
- verbs: *cecinit : cantavit* "he, she sang," *emit : comparavit* "he, she bought," *fervet : bullit* "it boils," *comesta : manducata* "eaten," *submersi : necati* "drowned," *isset : ambulasset* "he, she had gone," *abio : vado* "I go," *si vis : si voles* "if you want";
- preposition: *preter : excepto* "except."

But the *Glossary* also brings us a number of novelties. The entry *rerum : causarum* "of things" illustrates that the common but colorless *rem*, of the fifth declension, has been replaced by the first declension noun *causam*, originally "cause, case (often with judicial reference)," but latterly "thing" (> Italian, Spanish *cosa*, French *chose*). The intermediate stage between the two meanings was "affair." Similarly with *ictus : colpus* "blow" (noun), where *colpus*, ultimately of Greek origin, has become the parent of the Romance words: Italian *colpo*, Spanish *golpe*, French *coup* (familiar to us in the phrase *coup d'état*). The dropping of *hic* "this" as a demonstrative adjective/pronoun in favor of *iste* (> Spanish *este*, Italian *questo*, French *cet*, the latter two with a prefix) is evident in *ab his : ab istis* "from these."

One entry in the *Glossary, iacere : iactare* "to throw," introduces the ancestor of a large number of familiar terms. We notice here the familiar replacement of the simple verb (*jacere jactus*) by its more convenient frequentative. A related form of the verb, **jectare*, yielded Italian *gettare*, Spanish *echar*, French *jeter* "to throw." The French in turn is the source of English *jet*, at first "spurt, stream of water," also of *jettison* (to throw overboard), *jetty* (something thrown up as a breakwater), and *jeté* (a certain leap in ballet). So a document from the eighth century reveals the birth of a word that would in time come to be used, for instance, in the phrase "jet propulsion." And the stem is recognizable in such words at *project, reject, interject, dejected* "thrown down," etc.

But the *Reichenau Glossary* reveals to us more than the directions the Romance vocabulary was taking. It occasionally supplies early evidence for morphological changes too. Thus, in *saniore : plus sano* "healthier" one observes the analytic form of the comparative superseding Latin's synthetic form. And *singulariter : solamente* "solely" looks ahead to what was becoming the standard procedure for forming adverbs in the Romance languages.

Furthermore, the *Glossary* contains indications of the vast historical events that had been taking place in western Europe. Entries such as *Gallia : Frantia* and *Italia : Longobardia* point to the replacement of Roman political authority by that of the several barbarian peoples who had overthrown and occupied the Empire. And that in turn is reflected here in the Frankish (Germanic) words that have already begun to enter the Gallo-Roman vocabulary, a number of them eventually making their way into English:

- *galea : helmus* "helmet": the Frankish word is the source of the English;
- *pignus : wadius* "pledge": in *wadius* lies the origin of English *gage* and *engage* as well as *wage, wager,* and *wed*;
- *respectant : rewardant* "they watch over": the meaning "compensate," as in English *reward*, would develop later – notice the adaptation of the Germanic verb to Latin's first conjugation (like *laudare*);
- *ocreas : husas* "greaves": because these were a type of armor unfamiliar to the Germanic tribes, they referred to them with a native word that meant "leg coverings" – *husas* is the parent of *hosiery* and *hose* "stocking," later "flexible rubber tube";
- *castro : heribergo* "military camp": *heribergo* went on to develop the sense "lodging" and became French *auberge* "inn," Italian *albergo* "hotel," Spanish *albergue* "shelter, hostel" – all familiar to travelers – and also,

via Old English, *harbor*, the original meaning of which was "refuge, place of safety," without reference to ships; in *heribergo* the first element is Germanic for "army" – both the verb *to harry* and the names *Herbert* and *Herman* derive from it also.

The *Reichenau Glossary* grants us glimpses into the making of European political history and of linguistic history, including our own, and this glossary is not unique. On the contrary, many others are preserved, some in different formats. In them we read *urbs : civitas* "city," and *genu : geniculum* "knee," and *testa : caput vel vas fictile* "head or ceramic pot," which shows that the earlier meaning of *testa* had not yet been lost sight of. And in a Greco-Latin glossary, *megaleura* "big" is defined with *grandia*, not *magna*.

After the *Reichenau Glossary*, the *Kassel Glossary* is of greatest interest for the story of the Romance languages. Named for the city to whose public library the manuscript belongs, it was found in another Benedictine monastery, Fulda, in central Germany, and was composed around 800. The *Kassel Glossary*, created for a different purpose than the *Reichenau*, differs accordingly in its format. Arranged for the most part systematically under various headings (people, farm animals, houses, etc.), it glosses Latin words – at this point we should rather consider them Romance – with German; it resembles a bilingual phrase-book such as a traveler might carry. For us the interest here is not the glosses themselves, which are German, but the words glossed: these were obviously the current Romance terms for the items in question. In this glossary too, therefore, we witness the outcomes of the wars between words. Both the Romance forms and the German are phonetically somewhat peculiar, because they are filtered through the Bavarian dialect of the compiler. To aid in identification, I give some of the Vulgar Latin forms between square brackets. The German glosses are cited only when recognizable by English speakers.

Here again we meet familiar Romance forms:

- *figido* [*ficatum*] *: lepara* "liver": compare German *Leber*, English *liver*;
- *casu : hus* "house": compare German *Haus*, English *house*;
- *cauallus : hros* "horse": compare German *Ross*, English *horse* – but that the earlier standard term had not yet disappeared and was still available is proved by the immediately following gloss, *equum : hengist* "horse."

So we conclude that *ficatum*, *casam*, and (to some extent) *caballum* were the current words of that place and time.

The glossary identifies several domestic animals with terms that were orig-. inally diminutives in Latin, and these are the parents of modern Romance vocabulary:

- *fidelli* [*vitelli*] "calves": the diminutive of *vitulum* is the source of Italian *vitello*, French *veau* (> *veal*);
- *agnelli* "lambs": the diminutive of *agnum* is the source of Italian *agnello*, French *agneau*;
- *ouiclas* [*oviculas*] : *auui* "sheep" (compare *ewe*): the diminutive of *ovem* is the source of Spanish *oveja*.

Two other diminutives attested in the *Kassel Glossary* have interesting off-spring in the modern languages. Late Latin *buttem* (or *buttiam*) referred to a small container; from it, through French, was derived English *butt* in the sense of "barrel for wine or beer." The diminutive appears in the glossary: *puti-cla* [*butticula*] : *flasca* "bottle" (compare *flask*), which yielded Italian *bottiglia*, Spanish *botella*, French *bouteille* (> *bottle*). The other word derives from Classi-cal Latin *botulum* "sausage" (*botulism* was so named in the nineteenth century because the illness was associated with eating tainted sausage). The diminutive *botellum* is recorded in the glossary as *putel*. From this came Italian *budello*, French *boyau* "gut, intestine," and from an Old French form *böel* came English *bowel*. Here, virtually at the dawn of the Romance languages, we find many novel items belonging to our own vocabulary.

In the realm of morphology, the glossary confirms a process observed ear-lier: what had been neuter plurals ending with -*a* in Classical Latin have become construed as feminine singulars, the plurals of which now end with -*as*: *mem-bras* "members" and *armentas* "herds" (contrast Classical *membrum membra* and *armentum armenta*). It is not possible to take leave of the *Kassel Glossary* without noticing two entries that carry us back to that extraordinarily produc-tive and far-reaching Germanic term *Walhos*, which at that time and place identified the Roman, that is to say, the Romance-speaking, foreigner: *romani : uualha* and *in romana : uualhum*.

NATIVES AND PARVENUS: DOUBLETS IN ROMANCE AND ENGLISH

Up to this point the material examined has been pairs of words one of which drove out the other. It is intriguing, in concluding, to consider a common phenomenon that is, in a way, the reverse – not "from two words, one," but rather "from one, two." It often happened that a single Latin word became part of a language twice, at two distinct times. First, it was continuously present in the spoken language and underwent the usual sound changes: this I call the "native." Later, it was also introduced in a form close to the Latin, as a learned borrowing: the "parvenu." The two versions of the same word, different in appearance (sometimes to the point that their kinship is unrecognizable) and usually with different meanings, exist together in the language today, side by side. Each half of such a pair is called a "doublet." An example repeated in all three languages is Latin *causam*, which continued in speech as the word meaning "thing" (Italian, Spanish *cosa*, French *chose*) and then was later re-introduced with the earlier meaning "cause" (Italian, Spanish *causa*, French *cause*). Other pairs of doublets already encountered are French *coucher* "to lay down" and *colloquer* "to set in place" (< *collocare* "to set in place"), and Spanish *espalda* "back" and *espátula* "spatula" (< *spatulam* "spatula").

Doublets are fascinating because they exemplify the two-fold word stock of the Romance languages. Often they are also surprising, for even native speakers are usually unaware that *cosa* and *causa* derive from the same word, not to mention *coucher* and *colloquer*. Similarly, which English speaker suspects that *forge* and *fabric* share the same origin, or *coy* and *quiet*? Moreover, the details of the stories – the shifts in form and meaning, the date and circumstances of the re-introduction – can be noteworthy. And in general, the existence of the doublets reminds us of the immense resource, eternally available, that Latin has been at every stage in the growth of the Romance languages.

A number of words we have already encountered turn out to have a doublet. Latin *plateam* "street" evolved into Italian *piazza*. Then, in the seventeenth century, as the modern enclosed theater building was beginning to take shape, Italian summoned *platea* back to active duty; it now designates the first floor of theater seating, in particular the area directly in front of the stage. Now *piazza* and *platea* co-exist in Italian – fraternal twins, as it were, even if unrecognized. Though they do not much resemble one another and their meanings differ, they are one in their birth.

Latin *parabolam* "comparison" developed into Spanish *palabra*, Italian *parola*, French *parole* "word." But it was also re-introduced in the late Middle Ages as a learned word meaning "parable": Spanish, Italian *parabola*, French *parabole*. (The term of geometry, *parabola*, was also re-created, in early modern times.) Similarly, Latin *navigare* "to sail" remained in spoken French and through association became the verb for "to swim," *nager*. In the late fifteenth century, *navigare* was taken up again as *naviguer* with the original meaning. Latin *papyrum* designated both the papyrus plant, native to Egypt, and the material made from it, which was the commonest writing material in antiquity. When rag paper, a Chinese invention, was introduced to Europe by the Arabs in the high Middle Ages, the word got applied to that: French *papier*, Spanish *papel* "paper." (The Italian word is *carta*.) Later still, in the sixteenth century, *papyrus* was brought back into use for the plant: French *papyrus*, Spanish *papiro*. In every case, necessarily, the newer form more nearly resembles the Latin.

The learned form of the word doesn't always recapture the sense of the original. Spanish continued Latin *rationem* "reason" as *razón* with the same meanings, but then re-created *ración* in the sense "portion, helping" (compare English *ration*). This is exceptional, however. Most often, along with the form the meaning of the original was reproduced. Thus, the Latin ordinal *sextam* "sixth" (feminine) was restored in Spanish as *sexta*. What happened to the form that had been in the language all along? That was *siesta*, which had acquired its own, very distinct meaning. To understand this story, we need to keep in mind how the ancient Romans told time: they divided the daylight into twelve equal parts and called each one an "hour," so an hour, although varying in length with the seasons of the year, was on any given day as long as every one of the others. The sixth hour – more precisely, the end of it – was therefore always the mid-point of the day. So *siesta*, feminine because it agrees with the implied noun *horam* "hour," went from marking a point in time to an activity appropriate to that time – a post-prandial mid-day nap. Once this had happened, Latinate *sexta* was required for the meaning "sixth."

Sometimes neither of the Romance doublets quite matches the meaning of the Latin original; the three words may be recognizably related in sense, yet overlap only a little. From the adjective *hospitalem* "hospitable," with perhaps *domum* "house" understood, French possesses *hôtel* "hotel; mansion" (the native) and also *hôpital* "hospital" (the parvenu). In Latin, *cameram* was "vaulted roof, vault." This turns up in French not only as *chambre* "room, chamber," without reference to how roofed, but also, because of its box-like appearance, as *caméra* "(motion picture or television) camera." "Purchase" was the meaning of Latin *redemptionem*, which, remaining in the spoken language, became French *rançon* "ransom," referring both to persons recovered from pirates or kidnappers and to souls recovered from sin; then in the thirteenth century the Latin word was brought back as *rédemption* "redemption" specifically for the religious sense.

It is not accidental that most of the examples of doublets have been French. The dramatic changes in sound experienced by French words have led, on the one hand, to many opportunities for the re-introduction of Latin terms as if novel and, on the other, to startling surprises occasioned by the great differences in sound and appearance between the native and the parvenu, which obscure their kinship. Often, moreover, the doublets have persisted into English. Latin *fabricam* "workshop" evolved into French *forge* with the specialized meaning "forge, smithy." But it was also re-created as *fabrique* "factory." (The common meaning of *fabric*, "cloth," represents a different application of the learned term.) Who by sense or sound would be led to believe that *forge* and *fabric* started as the same word? *Coy* entered English from Old French *coi*, earlier *quei*, derived in turn from Vulgar Latin **quetum*, from Classical *quietum* "at rest, calm"; the sequence of senses was "calm; reserved, bashful; affecting shyness, coquettish." But, through French again, English also adopted *quiet*, giving it the additional sense "silent."

French *grotte* and *crypte* are doublets of a different sort, since neither is a native. The latter was made directly from Latin *cryptam* "crypt," which had come from the Greek adjective meaning "hidden" (compare *cryptic, cryptography*, and in all likelihood *kryptonite*); the noun understood with it is probably *cameram* "chamber." *Grotte* came from the same source, although by a roundabout route. First *cryptam* became *grotta* in Italian. Then from Italian the word entered French. Both were later taken over into English (*grotto, crypt*). *Grotesque* originally referred to odd, unnatural representations of living beings such as had been found occasionally in Roman grottoes.

Here now is a small collection of additional English doublets presented without detail or comment. In each case the first derivative entered English through French (the native), whereas the second was created directly on the basis of Latin (the parvenu): Latin *abbreviare* "to make brief" > *abridge* and *abbreviate*; *antiquum* "ancient" > *antic* and *antique*; *capitalem* "having to do with the head" > *cattle, chattel* and *capital*; *crucem* "cross" > *cruise* and *cross*; *dignitatem* "dignity" > *dainty* and *dignity*; *factum* "deed" > *feat* and *fact*; *legalem* "legal" > *loyal* and *legal*. As an almost grotesque final instance of the phenomenon in question, and also as a symbol of how hospitable English has been to words from a variety of other languages, we may consider this set, all of which derive, by one path or another, from Latin *discum* "disk," which itself derives from Greek: *discus* and *disk/disc* (both directly from Latin), *dish* (from Old English), *dais* (from French), *desk* (from Italian). "Doublet" hardly seems an adequate term for this plethora.

CHAPTER TEN

IMMIGRANTS

Non-Latin Words in the Romance Languages

Although Latin is by far the leading source of words for the Romance languages, throughout their history both Latin herself and her offspring have adopted words from other languages. Similarly, English has been hospitable – exceptionally so – to words that arrived from elsewhere. The immigrant word typically gets adapted to the grammatical forms of its new setting (if a verb, for instance, it joins one of the conjugations, as we saw with *rewardant* in the *Reichenau Glossary*). Sometimes it meets with resistance, yet within a short period it may succeed in making itself at home, and then it is indistinguishable from the native-born. Just as speakers of the languages do not perceive a connection between *espalda* and *espátula* or *coy* and *quiet*, so they do not recognize *angel* as Greek, *shirt* as Scandinavian, or *sugar* as Arabic. The history of the language is hardly present to their minds. The words simply exist in the language and are available for use.

Why are words welcomed from other languages? Sometimes for reasons reviewed in the previous chapter: convenience of form, distinctiveness, or vividness, examples of which would be Germanic **werra* "war" and Greek *parabolam* "word." Sometimes, however, because the thing denoted by the word is imported from a foreign culture or associated with it: Etruscan *histrionem* "actor" or Celtic *carpentum* "wagon." Words of the latter type are especially interesting, since they chart the historical and cultural interactions of a people with others.

Immigrant words began arriving early in Latin. Even before the Romans conquered Latium and the rest of the Italian peninsula, words from other peoples had become part of the Latin language. We noted examples, recognizable in English, of lexical items coming from the other Italic dialects (*odorem* "smell," *lupum* "wolf") and from Etruscan (*satellitem* "bodyguard," *atrium* "reception hall"). The Celtic language also contributed words to Latin in the early centuries (*carrum* "wagon"), but, unlike those others, continued to do so long after. And, in much greater numbers than any other language, Greek contributed items to the vocabulary. These two languages require separate treatment.

GREEK

The Romans have always lived in the shadow of the Greeks. They themselves, or at least the culturally advanced among them, regularly regarded themselves as backwards and inferior. And in modern times, it has been customary, indeed, to grant the Romans distinction in several areas, such as political organization, administration, law, engineering, and technology, but to assert the general intellectual and creative superiority of the Greeks. That is unfair to the Romans, who for the past two centuries have been the victims of prejudice and bad press. However that may be, it is certainly true that many aspects of their life were deeply influenced by the Greeks, including their language.

At every stage of its history, even the earliest, Latin welcomed Greek words. *Poena* "penalty," for instance, which is found in the Laws of the Twelve Tables, a Roman legal code from the archaic period, was borrowed from the Greek. In time it developed an additional sense, "pain," and both these senses are preserved in the Romance languages as well as English (Spanish, Italian *pena*, French *peine*, English *penalty* and *pain*); the related verb *punire* "to punish" has also survived. So this term, which entered Latin from Greek two and a half millennia ago, is still with us, no longer an immigrant, now a well-established citizen indistinguishable from the others.

No period of Roman history, no arena of activity failed to adopt Greek words. In early writings we already meet *plateam* "street" and *scaenam* "stage building, stage." Colloquial in character are *colaphum* "clout on the head" (later to become *colpum* "blow"), *massam* "mass," and many words found in Cicero's letters to his intimates. In the realm of education and culture, the Romans adopted *poetam* "poet," *philosophum* "philosopher," and *rhetorem* "rhetorician." From the Greeks again the poets took over *aër* "air." Other words of the same origin that have already been met are: *theatrum* "theater," *citharam* "cithara," *spatam* "blade," *kampe* "flexure," *eleëmosyne* "pity," *cameram* "vaulted room," *cryptam* "crypt," *discum* "disk." Taken together, these items just scratch the surface, for the Greek contribution to the Latin vocabulary is substantial.

One Greek-derived word that met with great success was *scolam* "school," for which the genuine Latin word was *ludum*. (Originally, *schole* in Greek meant "leisure" and *ludum* meant "play, game," notions that at the moment seem remote from schools.) Returning to the *Kassel Glossary*, we encounter the entry *keminada* (*caminata*), derived from Greek *caminus* "oven, furnace, fireplace." At first *caminata* was an adjective meaning "provided with an oven, etc.," next a noun referring to a room so provided, then a name for the fire apparatus itself or the structure that vented it – the *chimney*. From Late Greek *thios* derive Spanish *tío*, Italian *zio* "uncle."

Yet of all the impulses towards introducing Greek words into Latin none was mightier than the Christian religion. Christianity originated in the eastern half of the Roman Empire and therefore took shape in the Greek language. Its earliest texts, including the New Testament itself, its doctrines, beliefs, and dogmas, its rituals and practices, were all written in Greek. It was only natural, then, that, as the new religion spread westwards, the terms already in use got transferred to Latin. The large numbers of religious words that entered Latin in this way are a monument to the influence of Christianity.

Often, the evolution of a word's meaning within Greek, from its traditional sense to its novel application by Christians, is striking. *Ecclesiam* meant "assembly" in Classical Greek, and then for the Christians, more specifically, "place of assembly of the faithful"; it is the parent of the Romance words for "church": Spanish *iglesia*, French *église*, Italian *chiesa*. (English *church*, Scottish *kirk*, and German *Kirche* also come from Greek, but derive from the adjective *kyriakon* "belonging to the Lord," with *doma* "house" understood.) The words for "priest," including the English, come from *presbyter*, literally "elder"; the term translates a Hebrew word used often in the Bible (compare *Presbyterian*, a sect governed by elders, and *presbyopia* "farsightedness," the typical vision problem of the elderly). Set over the priest was the bishop, Latin *episcopum*, from a Greek word meaning "overseer" (the root *scop-* "see" recurs in *scope*, *telescope, periscope, scopophilia*).

In Greek, a *propheta* is "one who speaks ahead of time," while a *martyr* is "a witness," in a Christian context, one of those who bore witness to their faith by the manner of their death. *Angelus* in Classical Greek is simply "messenger," specialized then by Christians into "messenger of God." The "good message" that Matthew, Mark, Luke, and John (and others) brought is the *evangelium*, in which the first element comes from Greek *eu-* "well, good," as in *eugenics* and *euphemism*. The word for "devil," *diabolus*, in Greek meant "slanderer, accuser"; its application to the Evil One imitates Hebrew usage. Greek *petra* "stone" drove out Latin *lapidem*, not only because it belonged to the first declension rather than the third, but also because it was associated with Peter, the first bishop of Rome, given that name in place of Simon because he was the rock on whom Jesus founded his church.

Our three Romance languages show interesting, parallel treatments of a verb taken over from Greek. *Blasphemare* meant "to blaspheme." In Vulgar Latin, it became *blastemare*, which everywhere acquired a more general meaning: Italian *biasimare*, French *blâmer* (> *blame*) "to blame," Spanish *lastimar* "to injure." Learned forms, closer to the original, were then used to recover the original sense: French *blasphémer*, Italian *bestemmiare*, Spanish *blasfemar* "to blaspheme."

Starting a millennium later, in the early modern period, many Greek words were re-created, or coined, as we saw, helping to enlarge the learned stock of the vocabulary: *petroleum, phantom, historic, erotic, herpetology, lethal, sarcastic, pedagogy, demon*. Greek too are *metaphor* (and virtually all other terms of rhetoric), *melancholy, metal, mechanic,* and *monochrome*. And the advancing complexity of western civilization has required thousands of new terms, many of them based on Greek (these examples, like the preceding ones, are cited in English alone since they are virtually identical in the Romance languages): *thermometer, telegraph, gastric, cybernetics,* and others. Over the years a number of hybrids have been born as well, half-Greek, half-Latin, such as *hypertension* (< Greek *hyper* "above, elevated" + Latin *tensionem* "pressure") and *television* (< Greek *tele-* "at a distance" + Latin *visionem* "seeing"). The Greek suffix *-ist,* denoting a person, is as productive as ever: witness *scientist, specialist, tourist, Marxist, classicist.*

PRE-LATIN WORDS

Greek has been present, then, throughout the history of Latin and the Romance languages. It began exerting its influence upon Latin before the Romans conquered the Greek-speaking lands (and before those lands "conquered" Rome culturally), and it continued to serve long after the Romans had relinquished political control. One traditional way of describing relations between languages is to identify some as "substrates" (Latin for "lying underneath"): these are languages that belong to a people dominated by another through political, military, economic, or cultural might. The language of the conquering or dominant people is a "superstrate" ("lying on top"). Neither of these terms fits well the complex relations between Latin and Greek. They are suitable, however, for Latin's relations with other languages.

Iberian

In the course of the more than two centuries that the Romans spent subduing the Iberian peninsula, they encountered mostly Celtic peoples there. But the Celts themselves, upon their arrival in the peninsula, not later than the fifth century B.C.E., had found others already inhabiting the land, who remained distinct for a while and have left linguistic traces of their existence. These few Iberian words represent the oldest substrate in the Latin-speaking west. Unlike the Celts, the earlier inhabitants did not speak Indo-European languages.

Words limited to the peninsula for which no other plausible source can be identified are usually judged to belong to the Iberian substrate. Such are Spanish *cama* "bed" and *sarna* "mange," first cited by Isidore of Seville, possibly also *capanna* "hut." The commonest such word is Spanish *izquierdo* "left," which took the place of Latin *sinister*, no doubt because of the latter's associations; as proof of how widespread it is, we may compare Portuguese *esquerdo*, Catalan *esquerre*, Basque *ezker*, and, on the French side of the Pyrenees, Gascon *esquerr* and Languedoc *esquer*. Some familiar animals are still called by Iberian names in Spanish – *zorro* "fox," *perro* "dog," *cachorro* "puppy" – and also a certain topographical feature, "land beside a river," which is *vega*. To Americans, *Zorro* is familiar as the legendary figure from Spanish California, and *Las Vegas* as the national capital of gambling. It is not coincidental that these Iberian words that survived into Spanish are associated with the western part of the country.

Celtic

The case is quite different with Celtic, a family of languages that was spread more broadly and contributed many more items to the Romance lexicon. If we keep in mind that virtually all Europe north and west of the river Po, including the British Isles, was populated by Celtic peoples during the centuries of the Roman Republic, this is hardly surprising. Gaul was, so to speak, the Celtic homeland, the central area, not completely conquered by the Romans until the time of Caesar, with the result that more Celtic words are found in French than the other languages.

Carrum and *carpentum*, two words for "wagon," and *veredum* "light horse" we have already met. (Celtic words are cited in Latinized form.) For the road along which the horse-drawn wagon traveled, the Romance languages still employ a term of Celtic origin, **camminum* "path, road," which led to Italian *cammino,* French *chemin,* Spanish *camino* (which makes us think of the *Camino Real* or "King's Highway," snaking its way through California). The horse might pick up a **grava* "stone," discussed before, or have to cross a *cumbam* "valley," recognizable still because of its appearance in English place names, such as Ilfracombe and High Wycombe.

The *Kassel Glossary* includes *camisam* (elsewhere written *camisiam*), Celtic for "shirt." This is continued in Spanish *camisa,* Italian *camicia,* French *chemise,* from the last of which came, with somewhat different meanings, English *chemise* and *camisole.* Originally the *camisiam* was a garment for a man, as were *bracas* "trousers," another Celtic word, with which English *breeches* is cognate. Beer, whether predominantly for men or not, is associated with several Celtic words that are still alive. Malt, the principal ingredient, was called *bracem* in Celtic (the word is identified as Gaulish by Pliny the Elder), and the verb meaning "to brew" was **braciare,* Modern French *brasser,* whence comes *brasserie,* originally "beer saloon" and now applicable to any informal eatery. Another glossary explains: *braces sunt unde fit cervisia* "malts are what beer is made from." *Cervisia* (elsewhere *cervesia*) "beer" turns out to be a Celtic word too, the source of Spanish *cerveza.*

We may fittingly conclude with one of the most successful of all Celtic survivals – an emblem of this book's theme – the common verb *cambiare* "to change." It is the source of Italian *cambiare,* Spanish *cambiar,* French *changer.* The word may be cognate with Greek *kampe* "bending, flexure," the ancestor of Latin *gambam* "leg." If so, the semantic link between the meanings would have a parallel in Latin *flectere,* at first "to bend," as in *flexible,* then "to change," as in *inflection.*

POST-LATIN WORDS

Latin overwhelmed, replaced, and, to a modest extent, absorbed the languages of the peoples who were conquered in western Europe and western Africa. The Roman Empire, however, which was its vehicle, although it lasted remarkably long, did not last forever. The tables were turned, and the Empire itself was now invaded, divided, and conquered. The linguistic consequences were surprising. Latin proved to be more successful at holding out against the languages of the invading peoples than, say, Celtic had been against Latin. It faced two great waves of assault, of which the first, breaking over it in the fourth and fifth centuries, was Germanic. To be sure, a number of the lands along Rome's northern frontier, the regions that are now western Germany, the Netherlands, northern Belgium, Britain, and German-speaking Switzerland, succumbed to Germanic arms and speech. But in the remainder of western Europe, Latin, though affected variously by the language of its conquerors, continued to predominate nonetheless, with the result that the entire Iberian and Italian peninsulas, the islands of the western Mediterranean, France, and southern Belgium, speak Romance languages lightly touched by German, and not a German touched by Latin. The western part of the African coast also continued to speak Latin for a while. The second wave of assault was that of the Arabs, in the eighth century, who did virtually wipe out Romance speech in north Africa, but, like the Germanic tribes, had only a modest effect on Iberia. Nevertheless, these two superstrates have played noteworthy roles in shaping the Romance lexicon.

Germanic

It is only to be expected that the Germans added to the Romance languages many words connected with warfare: *werra "war" itself we have already met, along with *heriberga* "camp" and *helm* "helmet." War included plunder: Germanic *raubon* produced Italian *rubare*, Spanish *robar*, Old French *rober* "to rob, steal." A war might be ended by a *triuwa* "truce" (> French *trève*, Spanish, Italian *tregua*).

Two Germanic verbs originally associated with war in its defensive aspect have been adopted as well, but with distinct shifts in their meanings. From *warjan* "to protect" are derived Italian *guarire*, French *guérir* "to cure, heal." (The original sense of protection is still to be caught in *garrison*, a stronghold or those manning it, and *garret*, now an attic, but at first a watchtower, place of refuge.) Related to *warjan* is the verb *wardōn* "to guard, defend," which has become Spanish *guardar*, French *garder* "to keep, preserve" (> *guard*). The corresponding Italian verb, *guardare*, developed in a different direction: the sequence of its senses was "to watch over, look after; look at"; the French compound *regarder* followed the same path, also ending up as "to look at."

Yet the Germanic languages, as reflected in Romance and English, are familiar with much besides war. Domestic life too plays a part, and we recall that *home* and *hamlet* originated in Germanic *haim* "village." It may be surprising, but it is true that the Romans, a people devoted to bathing, borrowed their term for "soap" from the Germans. In the first century C.E., Pliny the Elder recorded *saponem*, a substance for cleaning and dyeing the hair, which is the parent of Italian *sapone*, French *savon*, Spanish *jabón* "soap." Our *soup* and *supper* come from Germanic *suppa* "soup," as do Spanish *sopa*, French *soupe*, and Italian *zuppa*. One might eat supper while seated on a *banka*, a Germanic term that gave the Romance languages their words for both "bench" and "bank" (in the sense "place for keeping money"), the connection being the use of a bench-like counter for money transactions. (Similarly, in antiquity the Greek for "bank" was, as it still is today, *trapeza*, originally "table" – *trapeze* and *trapezoid* are related.) Germanic *want* "glove" produced French *gant* (> English *gauntlet*), Italian *guanto*, Spanish *guante*. The Romance words for "harp" all derive from Germanic *harpa*. Here we are far indeed from the battlefield.

A few other items of interest deserve mention. It is striking how many color terms Germanic has supplied: *blank* "white" (> French *blanc*, Spanish *blanco*, Italian *bianco*), replacing Latin *album*; *brūn* "brown" (> French *brun*, Italian, Spanish *bruno*); *grīsi* "gray" (> French, Spanish *gris*, Italian *grigio*). The colorless, general Germanic *wīsa* "manner, way" has given rise to Romance words with specific meanings. Italian, Spanish *guisa*, French *guise*, to be sure, can all still mean "manner, way." But at the same time Spanish specialized the word, first to "manner of preparing," and then even more to "manner of preparing food"; today *guiso* or *guisado* is more concrete and still more specific, "stew." And French derived from *guise* a verb *déguiser* "to change one's way of being, to render different"; used particularly for difference created by means of clothing, it acquired its present sense, "to disguise." *Guise* and *disguise* obviously came into English through French, whereas Germanic *wīsa* is the direct source of the *-wise* in *otherwise*, *clockwise*, *likewise*, literally "in like manner."

The words so far mentioned survive in all, or nearly all, our Romance languages. Some, like *saponem* "soap," were taken into Latin early enough to become diffused everywhere, whereas others may have been adopted separately in each language. It is possible to attempt to trace the precise path followed by individual words, to determine whether they entered a language through Latin or directly, from which of the various Germanic languages or dialects they may have entered, and when. For our purposes, it is sufficient to identify them as

Germanic. Still, it is worthwhile to point out a few words that directly entered only one language.

The presence of the Visigoths in the Iberian peninsula is responsible for some items in the Spanish vocabulary, *gana* "desire," for instance, derived from Gothic **ganō* "desire, eagerness." More complex is the story of *casta* "caste." Originating in Gothic **kasts* "group of animals," the word entered the languages of the Iberian peninsula with the sense "type of animal," and soon developed into "race of men" and later "class, condition of men." Then the Portuguese, the first Europeans to reach India by sea, applied the term to the castes they encountered there, a highly distinctive feature of Indian society, and from Portuguese it spread to the other modern languages.

The Lombards left some linguistic impress on Italian, naturally. From the Germanic verb *borōn* "to bore" was derived the name of the tool used in engraving, *burino*, which passed through French to become English *burin*. Germanic *balko* "scaffold, hayloft" yielded Italian *balcone* "balcony," which traveled thence into the other modern languages. And *skerzōn* "to jest" led to Italian *scherzare*, from which *scherzo* "jest, joke" became a term in music, indicating a movement that is quick and lively. Such examples remind us not only of the Germanic contribution to Italian, but also of the Italian contributions to music, architecture, the visual arts, and others.

Since the Franks dominated the lands they had conquered far more thoroughly than either the Visigoths or the Lombards – one could say that their domination never ended – the number of Germanic words in French is much higher. Several such words entered along with the Franks, and then moved from French into the other languages. In the realm of nature, the Franks contributed *busk* "woods," which became French *bois* (an earlier form with a more transparent etymology is the Old French diminutive *boschel*), and spread from there into Spanish (*bosque*) and Italian (*bosco*). English *ambush* also came from French, the original sense being "to lie in wait in the woods," and *bush* derives from the same stem. Another souvenir of this Germanic word is the name of the Flemish painter, Hieronymus Bosch (*ca.* 1450–1516): Bosch is not his real surname, rather a nickname given him for the town where he was born and he painted, s'Hertogenbosch "Duke's Wood."

A garden is an enclosed piece of nature, and for this too Frankish supplied the term: **gardō* "enclosure" became French *jardin* "garden," which also passed from French into Spanish (*jardín*) and Italian (*giardino*). From Germanic *troppum* "herd" derive both French *troupe* "troop; troupe" and *troupeau* "herd." The notion of "multitude" that was naturally associated with "herd" led to French *trop*, earlier "much," then "too much." In several Romance languages the word for "towel," like the one for "soap," is of Germanic origin: Frankish *thwahlja* > Old French *touaille* > English *towel*, Spanish *toalla* "towel," Italian *tovaglia* "tablecloth."

An extraordinarily diverse set of familiar words was produced from Frankish *bann*, which meant "proclamation." In feudal times it designated proclamations of many sorts, interdictions as well as injunctions, touching law, land, marriage, military service, and more. Accordingly, the results in English have been very varied. The basic notion of a proclamation is transparent in *banns*, the public notice of a proposed marriage. *Ban* and *banish* derive from proclamations that forbid a person to remain within a community, and a *bandit* (this from Italian, not Frankish directly) is someone so forbidden, that is to say, an outlaw (the specialization of meaning to "robber" is recent). From a lord's use of proclamation for summoning his vassals to military service, the word came to refer to a feudal levy, and *banner* designated the flag marking out a particular group. In another direction, *ban* referred to the area subject to the authority of a proclamation, specifically the public, or common, land. Something available for use by the whole community was therefore *banal*, which has developed pejorative senses. And Old French *bandon*, meaning "authority, power," is the origin of *abandon*, literally "to give oneself to the power (of another)," that is, "to surrender." All these words are owed to the same Frankish monosyllable.

Several adjectives describing characteristics of persons have also been contributed by Germanic. English *gay* and Italian *gaio* derive from French *gai*, itself stemming from Provençal *gai*, from Germanic *gahi* "quick, impetuous." Specifically Frankish was *hardjan* "to harden," which yielded French *hardi* "hardened, hardy," adopted in turn by Spanish (*ardido*) and Italian (*ardito*). What may be the most beloved adjective of all descends from Frankish *rīki*, which at first meant "powerful" (cognate with German *Reich* "empire, kingdom"), but in French soon acquired the specific sense "powerful by virtue of money": *riche* "rich."

Arabic

During the nearly eight centuries that went by between the battle of Jerez, in 711, and the overthrow of the last Moorish kingdom, in 1492, the Arabs were a prominent presence on the Iberian peninsula. Their rapid conquest was followed by much intermarriage, because the invading warriors, who had come without women, were obliged to take wives from the Christian, Hispano-Roman population. The result was extensive bilingualism, even within households, and in such a setting lies the chief explanation for the many Arabic words that have entered Spanish. Moreover, an Arabic word not rarely accompanied a novel import of the Arabs, who were responsible for introducing a number of new crops and crafts, along with much science and technology.

Spain was not the sole conduit of Arabic terms into the Romance languages. Trade, warfare, and occasional occupation brought other parts of the Romance world, Italy in particular, into contact with the Arabs, again with linguistic consequences. Spanish can usually be distinguished as the source of Arabic words by a certain historical oddity. Many Arabic terms were adopted into Spanish along with the definite article *al-*: thus, the word for "cotton," which was brought into European cultivation by the Arabs, is *cotone* in Italian, *coton* in French (> *cotton*), but *algodón* in Spanish. So in this case, it is clearly not the Spanish form which has been propagated throughout Europe.

Other plants and foodstuffs introduced to Europe by the Arabs and familiar under their Arabic names as first spoken in French or Italian are: *lemon* (< French *limon*), *sugar* (< French *sucre*), and – medicinal, if not refreshing – *syrup* (< French *sirop* or Italian *sciroppo*; *sherbet* is related). Italian was the specific locus of diffusion, however, for *arsenal* (< Italian *arsenale*, the name of Venice's vast complex of shipyards and arms factories). The same is true for *magazine*, which, via French, in which *magasin* now means "store," came from Italian *magazzino*; the original meaning in Arabic, "storehouse," is still evident in English, whether *magazine* refers to a chamber for ammunition or a publication containing a number of articles. The history of Arabic *zecca* "mint" (in the sense "place where money is coined") includes an interesting sartorial twist: a term of administration taken into Italian with the same meaning, it produced a diminutive, *zecchino* "gold coin," which passed into French as *sequin* "spangle, sequin."

To illustrate the remarkable diffusion of an Arabic term, here are the words for "sugar" in all the major modern European languages: Basque *azukreztu*, Breton *sukr*, Catalan *sucre*, Czech *cukr*, Danish *sukker*, Dutch *zucker*, English *sugar*, Estonian *suhkur*, Finnish *sokeri*, French *sucre*, German *Zucker*, Greek *sáchari*, Hungarian *cukor*, Irish *siúicre*, Italian *zucchero*, Latvian *cukura*, Lithuanian *cukrus*, Norwegian *sukker*, Polish *cukier*, Portuguese *açúcar*, Rumanian *zahar*, Russian *sachar*, Serbo-Croatian *secer*, Spanish *azucar*, Swedish *soker*,

Turkish *seker*, and Welsh *siwgr*. It is easy to see that, regardless of language family – Indo-European, Ural-Altaic, or other – and of proximity to the Mediterranean, all these go back to the same Arabic word.

Like Germanic in French, Arabic is more significant in Spanish, obviously, than in any other Romance language. Arabic contrasts sharply with Germanic in the spheres within which it contributed to the vocabulary. The Arabs, successful warriors too, did pass on to Spanish some words connected with warfare – one is *almirante* "admiral" – but a great many more having to do with agriculture, commerce, administration, science, and luxury – all activities that were foreign to the Germanic tribes. The Arabs were responsible for bringing features of a more refined civilization to Europe.

Arabic words have entered Spanish designating items of comfort, pleasure, and recreation: in the living room and elsewhere, *alfombra* "rug"; in the dining room, *taza* "cup"; in the bedroom, *almohada* "pillow." The bedroom or alcove in which one slept was an *alcoba*, where the walls might have been made of *adobe* and the floor covered with *azulejos* "enameled tiles" (< *azul* "blue," a favored color of enamel among the Arabs – compare Italian *azzurro*, French *azur*, English *azure*). Within Arabic, *zahr*, originally "flower," came to indicate "die" (singular of *dice*) because of the flower painted on one side of it. In the form *azzahr*, where *az-* is the definite article *al-* assimilated to the sound following, or simply *azar*, it entered Spanish, at first meaning "unfavorable face of the die," next "bad luck," and then "chance." The French word derived from it, *hasard*, with similar senses, led to English *hazard*.

Reminders of the advanced state of Arab knowledge during the early Middle Ages, many terms of science and technology passed from Arabic through Spanish into the mainstream of European vocabulary. In chemistry, *alcohol*, *elixir*, and *alchemy* are familiar all across the continent; in astronomy, *zenith* and *nadir*; in mathematics, *algebra*, *cipher*, and *zero*. The last two, astonishingly, come by different paths from the same Arabic word, meaning "empty; nought," and point to one of the most precious gifts received, the system of Arabic numerals, with its brilliant reliance on place-value and zero. In this, as in other matters, the Arabs themselves were intermediaries rather than originators, for what we call "Arabic numerals" had actually been invented by Indian mathematicians.

Then as now, the leisure and learning of some were made possible by the workaday occupations of the mass of the people, mostly agriculture but commerce as well, and this also is reflected in Arabic items in the vocabulary. In addition to *cotton* and *lemon*, the Arabs provided the names by which we know the *artichoke, rice* (ultimately a Greek word, *oryza*), and *apricot* (ultimately a Latin word, *praecoquum*), and the more exotic *jasmine* and *saffron*. A staple of the American breakfast table is orange juice. Though the tree is native to more easterly climes, the name comes from Arabic *naranj*. In Spanish, this was taken over straightforwardly as *naranja*. The Italian and French, as a result of misdivision, differ more from the original. In Italian "an orange tree" was *un narancio*, of which the second *n*, confused in sound with the *n* of the indefinite article, got lost, resulting in today's (*un*) *arancio*. Similarly, the initial *n-* has been lost in French *orange*. In the realm of commerce, the Arabs contributed to the European lexicon *tariff* and the words for "customs" (> Spanish *aduana*, Italian *dogana*, French *douane*, all familiar to travelers).

Algebra and *alcohol*, twin curses of high school, are further examples of the phenomenon noted earlier, that Spanish adopted many Arabic words along with the definite article. This is piquantly illustrated in the name of a California restaurant, The El Almadén, in which we have the definite article of three languages (English, Spanish, Arabic) set out in a row (*almadén* is an obsolete word for "mine"). In a curious re-enactment of the phenomenon many centuries later, several *Spanish* words were taken into American English along with their definite article. *Lariat* comes from Spanish *la reata* "the rope (especially as used for tying horses)," and *alligator* from *el lagarto* "the lizard."

But not every *al-* at the beginning of an English word signals an origin in Arabic. The *al-* in two common terms is not the Arabic definite article, nor part of the actual stem, but rather the preposition *a* combined with the Romance definite article. Both entered English from Old French, which had adopted them from Italian: *alert* < Italian *all'erta* "on the watch," and *alarm* < Italian *all'arme* "to arms!"

BORROWINGS WITHIN THE FAMILY

Sometimes a Romance language acquired a word neither by direct inheritance, whether from Latin or a non-Latin language, nor through learned re-creation, but rather from another Romance language – a sideways movement, as it were. This stands to reason. Even under the difficult circumstances of the Middle

Ages, when land travel remained cumbersome and extremely slow, all the more so without a strong central government to maintain the roads and the peace, and when sea travel was threatened by Arab control of much of the Mediterranean, the various language groups were nonetheless still in contact with one another. Then, in the early modern period interchange became much readier. I illustrate the sisterly sharing of words within the Romance family with a few examples, the first couple of which also illustrate on what basis we know this to have happened.

Words beginning with *ga-* retained that sound in Italian and Spanish: thus, Latin *gallum* "rooster" > Italian and Spanish *gallo*, and Latin *gambam* "leg" > Italian and (obsolete) Spanish *gamba*. The Italian derivative of Latin *galbinum* "yellow," however, is the unexpected *giallo* /dja-/ (*dj* represents the sounds in *judge*). What happened to explain this anomaly? The word did not enter Italian directly from Latin, but passed through French, in which /ga-/ had altered its pronunciation. By the fourteenth century, this had come to be pronounced /dja-/. Italian adopted the word in that period and has kept that sound. (Notice also how the pronunciation of *jaundice* reveals that that word entered English at about the same time.) The same happened with Frankish *gardo* "enclosure," which has resulted in Italian *giardino* /dj-/ and Spanish *jardín* /x-/ "garden" (/x/ represents the sound of *ch* in Scottish *loch* or in German *ach!*). Again, the Italian pronunciation represents that of Middle French. The French sound, however, continued to evolve, soon becoming /zh/, as it remains today (/zh/ represents the sound of *s* in *measure*). Spanish, when adopting the word in the late fifteenth century, gave it a pronunciation as close to that as it could manage, /x/. So the paths of both these words can be securely traced through French. Another example: from Vulgar Latin *cameratam* "roommate" (< *cameram* "vaulted roof; room") the regular result in French would have been *chambré*. The several divergences between that and the actual result, *camarade* "comrade," point to Spanish *camarada* as the immediate source.

By such phonological tests and other signs – such as the external history of a word, when and where it was first used and for what – it is usually possible to identify a term in one Romance language as deriving directly from another. Without any attempts to date, group, or characterize the various borrowings (such as were made in several fascinating studies of historical and cultural relations among the three languages), here are a few more examples, most of which we have already come across. French *garage* "garage" (from Frankish *warjan* "to protect, shelter") led to Italian *garage*, Spanish *garaje*.

Italian *cartuccia* "cartridge" (an augmentative form of *carta* "paper") produced Spanish *cartucho*, French *cartouche*. Spanish *chocolate* (from Nahuatl, the language of the Aztecs) gave rise to French *chocolat*, Italian *cioccolato*. To Spanish, French contributed *jamón* "ham" (< *jambon*) and *chimenea* "chimney" (< *cheminée*); to Italian, it contributed *grograna* "grogram" (< *gros grain*) and *gabinetto* "cabinet" (< *cabinet*). Italian gave French *brave* "brave" (< *bravo*) and *fiasco* "fiasco" (< *fiasco*); it gave Spanish *busto* "bust" (< *busto*) and *emboscar* "to ambush" (< *imboscare* "to hide in a wood"). To French, Spanish passed on *abricot* "apricot" (< *albaricoque*) and *tomate* "tomato" (< *tomate*, from Nahuatl); to Italian, it passed on *azienda* (< *hacienda*).

COLONIAL WORDS

Latin, Greek, substrates, superstrates, sisters – these do not exhaust the sources of the Romance vocabulary. At a much later date, when the European powers began seeking overseas empires, most strenuously in the Americas, they encountered plants, animals, and artifacts that were unfamiliar to them. They could deal with these in several ways. One was to adapt words from their own languages for the novelty. Thus, the Spaniards dubbed the sloth *el perezoso* "the lazy one" – and English *sloth* is just the abstract noun to *slow*, given then a concrete meaning. Commoner was the practice of adopting the words that the natives used. Here is a tiny list of English words acquired from colonial sources in the Americas, all with instantly recognizable cognates in our three Romance languages: from Algonquian, spoken broadly across northern North America, *moccasin*; from Arawakian, used in Haiti, Puerto Rico, and other Caribbean islands, *maize*; from Carib, *canoe*; from Nahuatl, *cacao*; from Quechua, the language of the Incas (Peru), *llama*; from Guarani, spoken in Paraguay, *petunia*. No less familiar colonial words originating outside the Americas are: *banana*, from west Africa; *chess*, from Persia; *pajamas*, from India; and *tea*, from China.

IMMIGRANTS IN ENGLISH

Many words that migrated into Romance from languages other than Latin have migrated into English as well. And yet, in respect to immigrant words, English is in a very different position from the other languages. For the Romance languages, Latin remains by far the most important lexical source, regularly constituting 90 percent of the words in a given passage, often more. Neither the Arabic element in Spanish nor the Frankish element in French alters this fact, not to mention the lesser contributions from elsewhere. English, by contrast, though a Germanic language, received such a vast number of Latin-derived words, mostly through French, that nowadays the vocabulary used by speakers is about half Latinate. Such an alteration of the basic lexicon, such an extensive mixing-in of a foreign element, is extraordinary and without near parallel in the Romance languages; Rumanian, containing many Slavic words, is the closest instance. The unusual historical position of English's vocabulary has deeply marked the language and given it some of the distinctive qualities it possesses, such as a special stylistic flexibility.

The following passage, a tour de force, is the penultimate paragraph of an outstandingly readable history of English (Thomas Pyles and John Algeo, *The Origin and Development of the English Language*, 4th ed., 1993, p. 311). I wonder how quickly the reader will grasp what is distinctive about it.

> But with all its manifold new words from other tongues, English could never have become anything but English. And as such it has sent out to the world, among many other things, some of the best books the world has ever known. It is not unlikely, in the light of writings by English speakers in earlier times, that this would have been so even if we had never taken any words from outside the word hoard that has come down to us from those times. It is true that what we have borrowed has brought greater wealth to our word stock, but the true Englishness of our mother tongue has in no way been lessened by such loans, as those who speak and write it lovingly will always keep in mind.

This is a marvelously self-exemplifying statement. These sentences about the Englishness of English, which is said to have no need for immigrant words, are in fact composed entirely of words from the native stock. Not a single item in the paragraph derives from Latin, French, Scandinavian, or any other language. The reverse, however, is impossible: no one could write an English paragraph without Germanic words, for that would involve dispensing with the articles, prepositions, nearly all pronouns, and most of the core vocabulary. To compose their paragraph, the authors say, required a "slight effort," which experiment suggests is a modest understatement. Yet, however that may be, it is obvious that to compose a paragraph in French, Spanish, or Italian with none but Latin words would be hardly any effort at all; indeed, many such paragraphs are written unintentionally or spoken spontaneously. Despite the immigrants present in their midst, the Romance languages remain thoroughly Latinate.

~

PART THREE

Proto-Romance, or What the Languages Share

CHAPTER ELEVEN

THE SOUND OF PROTO-ROMANCE

CHANGE IN LANGUAGE

Vulgar Latin, as we've seen, is that form of Latin from which the Romance languages originated. "Proto-Romance" is an equivalent name for it, an appropriate term to introduce at this point. Although identical in reference, "Vulgar Latin" and "Proto-Romance" are not interchangeable terms. They both indicate the same variety of the language, but they view it from different angles. Whereas "Vulgar Latin" emphasizes the difference from Classical Latin, the deviations from the variety that was the standard, "Proto-Romance" sees the same matter from the vantage point of the future, what Vulgar Latin ultimately developed into. Our subject now is Proto-Romance.

Up to this point, we have encountered illustrations of Vulgar Latin for the most part casually, as chance offered them in particular texts, and they represented sound changes more than anything else. But if we are to continue and track Vulgar Latin along its path to becoming French, Spanish, and Italian, then we need a more systematic and fuller treatment, in order to do justice to the scope of the changes that took place in sounds, forms, and syntax. Interesting themes that emerge from such a treatment are the inter-relatedness of these different aspects, and the remarkable combination of inheritance and innovation that distinguishes the story. In this part of the book, I sketch those significant changes to Classical Latin that are shared by our three Romance languages. In the next part, in contrast, I draw attention to their divergences from one another.

Sounds change more readily than other aspects of language, such as forms or syntax. Though often in motion, sounds do not move so rapidly as to lead quickly to incomprehension between speakers. Moreover, as they change, they

201

can affect other features. In the case of the Romance languages, sounds changed most rapidly and dramatically at the start, during late antiquity and the Middle Ages, before the standardizations that were attempted in early modern times. The forms of the Romance languages, by contrast, have changed the least over time; they, more than anything else, mark the current speeches as akin to one another.

Though my presentation here turns more systematic, I have been talking about language change all along. Now, the great fact about language change is the inexorability of it: languages never stand still, but are always changing, at whatever speed, in some way or other. The pace of change may sometimes be slow, as often happens in isolated communities, such as islands. Of the Romance languages, the most conservative in several points is Sardinian, which continues the five distinct vowels of Latin and persists in pronouncing *c* as /k/ before *e* and *i*. Within the Germanic family, Icelandic is so close to Old Norse (the language of the Vikings who settled the island in the ninth century) that, despite the passage of time, modern Icelanders can read their ancient sagas more easily, it is said, than contemporary English speakers can read Shakespeare. Sometimes change comes quite rapidly, as it did during the period of Middle English, when the language lost all its inherited gender distinctions and most of its inflections as well: -*s*, for instance, now served to mark all possessives (*Bob's*) and nearly all plurals (*books*), replacing a multitude of earlier endings. Yet, whatever the pace, languages are constantly in motion.

It is possible to describe, at least in a general way, why and how languages change. The crucial events in any change are two: a person avails herself or himself of a different possibility of expression – a word, pronunciation, form, or construction other than the one used before – and then this choice gets propagated throughout the community of speakers. The alternative may already exist in the language, be created by analogy, or arrive through contact with another language. It may arise through imperfect mastery of the language, error, or random variation. Speakers are always experimenting, trying new things. The alternative may be preferred because it is easier or stronger, more vivid or more forceful, or it may be imposed. The speaker may adopt the alternative consciously or otherwise. Then, the alternative becomes widespread – or it does not. As with genetic variations, many alternatives come into existence without succeeding in propagating themselves. Still, an alternative may be adopted by large numbers of people independently for the same reasons or because it comes to be seen as prestigious on account of its use by others. Like a wave, it spreads through a language community until it becomes dominant. Even then, some speakers may stick with the old way, so the alternative may enjoy only a partial victory: speech rarely remains unvarying across a population.

Since the term "Proto-Romance" has just been introduced, this is a convenient place to pause and explore the history of that remarkably enduring yet slippery term, *romance*, each stage of which has left traces in our current usage. In late ancient times, *romanice* designated a language derived from Latin, the speech of the Romans, as opposed to one derived from a Germanic language. Hence "Romance languages." Next, in Old French the word shifted to indicate a composition in such a language. Many of those early (and popular) compositions involved chivalrous knights, heroic adventures, and lovely damsels, all narrated with an air of imaginative unworldliness. Hence *romance*, a literary genre, as written by Chrétien de Troyes or Barbara Cartland. Hence too *romance* meaning something wild, extravagant, exciting. Finally – and this happened only about a century ago – the word got attached to another prominent feature of romances. Hence *romance* signifying "love, love affair."

CHANGES IN SOUND

Changes in sound tend to be regular, that is to say, uniform, even if unpredictable. One might claim that all the instances of a particular sound in a given language undergo the same change, but this would be putting the matter too baldly, since some qualification is frequently called for. Typically, the student of language notices a certain historical change in sound and formulates it – "*this* sound turned into *that* sound" – in what is usually termed a "rule," or even a "law." Next, the student often recognizes that it does not take place globally, but only in certain circumstances, in a particular part of the word, for instance, or in the vicinity of certain sounds. The rule then is reformulated, to take account of that. If further exceptions are noted, this might be repeated. The final result may be, not a single simple rule, but a complex set of rules describing how a particular sound changes – plus, perhaps, a few stubborn exceptions.

Sounds, though the very stuff of language, lie below the level of meaning, and sound changes may seem like the dreariest, most unpromising aspect of language history, the one most difficult to relate to intelligible utterances, to human life and human interest. But several considerations render it both accessible and fascinating. It is easy to make the sounds for yourself and re-enact the changes in your own person. It is exciting to discover with what remarkable uniformity a vast, ungoverned, supra-personal enterprise like language alters over time. It is intriguing to see unmistakable patterns emerge out of (apparent) chaos, out of the welter of different sounds that exist within a language or a language family, and then to find patterns inside those patterns: it is like gazing with increasing appreciation at an intricate textile design.

The observer can enjoy watching not only the individual languages as they change, but also the partialities and preferences that bring together now these languages, now those, in shifting patterns of likeness and difference. The evidence for changes in sound is a further source of interest. Because no recordings of earlier speech exist and explicit statements by writers are rare, how, we may wonder, can we know that *this* sound became *that*? Many of the changes described here are adumbrated already in the *Appendix Probi* and confirmed by inscriptions. Finally, understanding even a few of the principal changes in sound – the goal of this chapter – leads us to recognize the origin or kinship of many words that otherwise would remain obscure.

Because of the conjunction of two historical facts, this is especially true for us English speakers. A very large number of Latin words entered English through French, and French had altered the Latin sounds it inherited far more drastically than did Italian or Spanish. The result is that many English words are nearly impossible for the uninstructed eye or ear to recognize as the descendants of their Latin ancestors. We will come to understand how *friction* and *fray* are the same word in origin, as are *ligature* and *liaison*, and why the *-ti-* of *nation*, despite the spelling, is pronounced /sh/.

We may begin with two contrasting examples of rules for phonological change, which illustrate the extremes of simplicity and complexity, not to say obscurity. A straightforward example of marked regularity is the change undergone by Latin words beginning with *fl-*, *cl-*, and *pl-*. In Italian, in each case the *l* became written as *i* and pronounced /y/ as in *yes* (the sound is called "yod"): Latin *flammam* "flame" > Italian *fiamma*; Latin *florem* "flower" > Italian *fiore*; Latin **clesiam* (shortened from *ecclesiam*) "church" > Italian *chiesa* (the letter *h*, not pronounced itself, is added in Italian as a graphic signal that the preceding *c* is to be pronounced /k/); Latin *clarum* "clear" > Italian *chiaro* (as in the term from art history, *chiaroscuro* "bright-dark," applied to the sorts of dramatic lighting effects obtained in their paintings by Rembrandt and Caravaggio); Latin *planum* "level, smooth" > Italian *piano* "soft, gentle" (the original name of the musical instrument was *pianoforte* "soft-loud" – it is noteworthy that *pianoforte* and *chiaroscuro* are formed alike, each a pair of opposite adjectives yoked together); Latin *plateam* "street" > Italian *piazza* "open square in a city." This change affects a multitude of Italian words. Exceptions, in which the sound has not changed, such as *platea* "orchestra (seating area of a theater)," are learned re-creations, in this case from the seventeenth century.

The same Latin sounds move with equal regularity into French and Spanish. In French *pl-*, *cl-*, and *fl-* are uniformly retained, whereas in Spanish all three get changed to *ll-* (pronounced approximately /ly/, where *y* is as in *yes*, or in some dialects /zh/), at least in certain common words: Latin *pluviam* "rain" > French *pluie*, Spanish *lluvia*; Latin *clamare* "to shout" (compare *clamor*) > French *clamer*, Spanish *llamar* "to call"; Latin *flammam* "flame" > French *flamme*, Spanish *llama*. One might illustrate the convergence of *fl-* and *cl-* that has taken place in Spanish with a sentence like this, said perhaps of the moth: (Latin *illa flamma illam clamat* >) *la llama la llama* "the flame calls her" (*llama*, the name of the Andean mammal, is still another word, derived from Quechua).

A more complex example illustrates the difficulty of formulating rules for sound changes. Perhaps the most notorious change that took place between Latin and her daughter languages is in the sound of initial *f-*, which has become a silent (but written) *h* in Spanish: Latin *fabulare* "to converse, speak" > Spanish *hablar*; *ficatum* "figged" > *hígado* "liver"; *formosum* "beautiful" > *hermoso*; and dozens more words. The origin of this change is one of the knottiest puzzles in Romance philology.

Whatever the solution may be, exceptions to the observation begin to present themselves at once. In Late Latin, *defensam* meant "defense, prohibition," as reflected still in the sign familiar to travelers in France: *Défense de Fumer* "Prohibition of Smoking" (not "Defense of Smoking," which would indicate nearly the opposite of what is intended!). From the abstract "prohibition," *defensa* developed a concrete sense "fence," that which prohibited or kept out (English *fence* is a shortening of *defense*). Then, by association, in Spanish it came to indicate that which a fence enclosed: *dehesa* today means "pasture" (in the Middle Ages pastures were usually fenced in). In Spanish *dehesa*, then, the *h* results from an *f* that is in the middle of the word, not the beginning. How did that happen? The noun in this case was recognized as deriving from a compound, *de* + **fendere*, and the simple verb's initial *f-* was treated in the usual way. So *dehesa*, despite one's initial impression, can be brought under the rule already formulated.

Many other exceptions, however, still need to be faced. Some scholars, observing Latin *fortem* "strong, brave" > Spanish *fuerte, focum* "hearth" > *fuego* "fire," *fontem* "spring; source" > *fuente, foras* "outside" > *fuera,* and other such exceptions, proposed a modification of the rule, to the effect that initial *f-* appearing before *o* resisted the change to *h*. The proposal looks promising, but it itself runs into counter-examples: Latin *formam* "shape, form; beauty" > Spanish *horma* "shoemaker's last," *formicam* "ant" > *hormiga,* etc. So that appears to be a blind alley. And we would be justified, furthermore, in wondering whether such common, unchanged terms as *fiesta* "party" (< Latin *festam*), *fin* "end" (< *finem*), *frente* "front; forehead" (< Latin *frontem*), and others are all to be accounted for as learned or even semi-learned creations, as has been proposed. The rule now looks fuzzy. This sound change then, in contrast to the previous one, seems impossible to capture in a rule. Happily, most sound changes are more uniform than this.

I've illustrated the regularity of sound changes both just now, from the history of the Romance languages, and earlier, from the history of the Indo-European language families: Greek *h-* corresponding to Latin *s-* as with *hals* : *sal* "salt." The principle of regularity being established, it is time to examine several more instances of changes between Latin and her daughter languages. I have selected the few examples that follow, some of them touched upon earlier, for their variety and (relative) lack of complexity, their intrinsic interest (several astonish by the extent of alteration produced), and their explanatory power – that is, the numbers of words in the languages, including English, that they affect. They are, of course, only a selection, and should be understood as representing the whole, much larger, more complex set of sound changes that have been discovered and charted in the Romance languages.

One of my colleagues, while studying in Mexico, took a course on the history of the Romance languages that turned out to consist entirely of memorizing the changes in sound between Latin and Spanish; nothing was said about morphology, syntax, or vocabulary, not to mention the historical setting of the whole process. And a respected American textbook, *An Introduction to Romance Linguistics,* 1975, by D. Lincoln Canfield and J. Cary Davis, devotes two-thirds of its pages to phonology, and in that section, moreover, among the scores of words it cites as examples, it informs the reader of the meaning of not more than a half dozen: the rest remain meaningless ciphers illustrating phonological rules. Although not wanting to go to such extremes, we may readily agree that changes in sound must be an essential part of language history.

Quality and Number of Vowels

As Classical Latin turned into Vulgar, the altered pronunciation of the vowels, involving both simplification and complication, was fundamental. It explains, among other things, a basic gender pattern that emerged.

Two important changes were successively wrought in the vowels. First, instead of by length, the vowels within a pair became distinguished from one another by the quality of the sound; the sounds themselves were now different. Short ă came to be pronounced like the first *a* in *aha!*, long *ā* as in *father*; short *ĕ* as in *bet*, long *ē* as in *bay*; short *ĭ* as in *bit*, long *ī* as in *machine*; short *ŏ* as in *pot*, long *ō* as in *pole*; short *ŭ* as in *putt*, long *ū* as in *pool*. Vowel quality had replaced vowel quantity.

In physical terms, the difference within each pair now lay in where the tongue was positioned in relation to the roof of the mouth. The short vowels came to be pronounced in an open way, that is, with a greater opening between tongue and roof; the long vowels in a close way, with the tongue closer to the roof. It is therefore appropriate to change terminology and refer to the vowels, no longer as "long" and "short," but rather as "close" and "open." The change in pronunciation, though affecting all the vowels, was most consequential for *e* and *o*, and so we may use them to illustrate the aptness of the new terms. When you say *bet*, then *bay*, or *pot*, then *pole*, you can feel your tongue rising towards the roof.

The next change was a reduction in the total number of vowel sounds. Close *a* and open *a* collapsed into a single sound. And, more striking, in our three languages open *i* merged with close *e*, and open *u* merged with close *o*. The result was that Classical Latin *mālum* "apple" and *mălum* "evil," once distinct, were now pronounced identically, as were *vērum* "true" and *vĭrum* "man" (both with close *e*), and similarly *rōdens* "gnawing" and *rŭdens* "rope" (both with close *o*).

How do we know about the latter changes? Some early inscriptions show a revealing confusion on the part of the writers or the carvers. The tendency

of close *e* and open *i* to coincide is seen in the occasional use of the letter *e* to represent open *i* (*menus* for *minus* "less," *veces* for *vices* "turns" – the latter is the noun in the ablative absolute *vice versa* and is the source of *vicissitude*) and, conversely, in the use of the letter *i* to represent close *e* (*minsis* for *mensis* "month," *tris* for *tres* "three"). Obviously, the writers were trying to represent the sound as they heard it, but, because the same sound could be represented with either of two spellings, they sometimes got confused and chose the wrong one: their misspellings point to the converging pronunciations. Similarly, the tendency of close *o* and open *u* to coincide is seen in the occasional use of the letter *o* to represent open *u* (*corret* for *curret* "he, she will run," *colomna* for *columna* "column" – this from the *Appendix Probi*) and in the use of the letter *u* to represent close *o* (*octubris* for *octobris* "October," *punere* for *ponere* "to put, place").

The changes of vowel sound implicit in these deviations from Classical spelling are confirmed by the later history of our languages. The leveling of the difference between the close *a* and the open *a* of Classical Latin is evidenced by the Romance reflexes of *cārum* "dear" and *măre* "sea": Italian *caro, mare*; Spanish *caro, mar*; French *cher, mer*. We see that Italian and Spanish inherited the leveled *a* sound and did not change it. French did change the sound, but what is important to notice is that both versions of Latin *a* turned out the same there too.

The merging of close *e* and open *i* is seen in the identical Romance reflexes of *vērum* "true" and *crēdit* "he, she believes," on the one hand, and of *pĭrum* "pear" and *vĭdet* "he, she sees," on the other: Italian *vero, crede, pera, vede*; Spanish *vero, cree, pera, ve*; French *voir* (as in *voir dire*, literally "to speak true," a stage in jury selection), *croit, poire, voit*. French again has carried the inherited sound several stages beyond the other languages (the former close *e* of Vulgar Latin is now spelled *oi* and pronounced /wa/), but illustrates the convergence nonetheless. It is an arresting curiosity that the elements of the phrase *voir dire* (*verum* "truth" and *dicere dictus* "to say") recur in *verdict* – the very different activities at the opposite ends of the trial process are etymologically the same (like *engagement* and *wedding*, as we shall see)!

Similarly, the convergence of close *o* and open *u* is seen in the identical Romance reflexes of *flōrem* "flower" and *cōpulam* "band," on the one hand, and of *gŭlam* "gullet" and *cŭrtum* "short," on the other: Italian *fiore, coppia* "pair," *gola, corto*; Spanish *flor, copla* "stanza," *gola, corto*; Old French *flour*, French *couple* "pair," Old French *goule*, French *court* (> English *curt*), where *ou* is pronounced /oo/. These two convergences, like the loss of final -*m*, would soon have repercussions in Latin's declensional system.

Curt, by the way, has nothing whatever to do with English *court*, which derives, also through French, ultimately from Latin *cohortem*. That term has an exceptionally interesting history. It designated at first a rural enclosure, for animals or equipment or plants – it's cognate with Latin *hortum* "garden" (compare *horticulture*) – and then, in military language, a division of an army camp, hence the part of a legion quartered there (a Roman legion consisted of ten cohorts). The meaning shifted further when *cohortem* came to denote a body of troops detailed for a particular purpose (such as guarding a general), then the staff or entourage of a military or political official. From there it was a short couple of further steps, taken during the Middle Ages, to "royal household" and also, because the king and other important personages often constituted a tribunal, "court of justice." The word has traveled very far indeed, for who would associate the Supreme Court or the Court of St. James with a garden plot? The adjective *courteous* originally meant "befitting a court." Because the words are unconnected, it is not surprising that someone who is courteous is unlikely to be curt.

Now we are in a position to understand how one of the patterns most obvious, most helpful, and indeed fundamental to Italian and Spanish emerged, whereby virtually all nouns and adjectives ending in -*a* are feminine and virtually all ending in -*o* are masculine. First declension nouns, regularly feminine, ended in -*am* in the accusative singular (the accusative case is nearly always the source of the Romance words), and the *a* was retained in both languages (and final -*m* lost): Latin *portam* "gate" > Italian *porta*, Spanish *puerta* "door," all unmistakably feminine. Second declension nouns, regularly masculine, ended in –*u(m)* in the accusative singular, but the open *u* became *o*, as we observed: a fine double example is Latin *cŭrtŭm* "short," which led to Italian and Spanish *corto* – now the second *o* is the object of our interest, marking the adjective as unmistakably masculine. This created neatly paired terms like Italian *amica/amico*, Spanish *amiga/amigo* "female/male friend," and Italian *zia/zio*, Spanish *tía/tío* "aunt/uncle," and thousands of words in each language where the gender is instantly recognizable by this same principle. The following examples are spelled the same in both languages: *lana* "wool," *arena* "sand," *cera* "wax," *pagina* "page" – all feminine – and *arco* "bow," *grano* "grain," *maestro* "teacher," *libro* "book" – all masculine. In French, by contrast, where almost all final vowels were lost, no such clear-cut pattern exists: the feminines generally end in -*e* (*laine, cire, page*), whereas the masculines sometimes end in a consonant (*arc, grain*) but sometimes in -*e* also (*maître, livre*).

Diphthongs Subtracted and Added

The few, common diphthongs of Classical Latin also changed, becoming simple vowels. The diphthong *ae* became an open *e*: Latin *praestare* "to supply, furnish" > Italian *prestare*, Spanish *prestar*, French *prêter* "to lend." The diphthong *oe* became a close *e*: Latin *poenam* "punishment" > Italian, Spanish *pena*, French *peine*. And eventually the diphthong *au* became a close *o*: Latin *aurum* "gold" > Italian, Spanish *oro*, French *or*. These developments were under way in classical times. Thus, on inscriptions we read instructive misspellings, such as *questus* for *quaestus* "having been sought" and *ceperint* for *coeperint* "they began." As for the diphthong *au*, even literary texts written in Classical Latin use both *plaustrum* and *plostrum* "wagon," for instance, and both *caudam* and *codam* "tail" (the latter > Italian *coda*, familiar in English as a term for the concluding section of a piece of music). The *au* pronunciation was considered the more refined, as we learn from two anecdotes. In Cicero's day, a man named Publius Claudius Pulcher, born into one of Rome's most ancient families, the Claudii, deserted the aristocratic cause and joined the plebeians. To mark his new allegiance, he had himself adopted into one of the plebeian tribes – and also changed his name from Claudius to the more plebeian Clodius. In the next century, the Emperor Vespasian (who ruled from 69 to 79 c.e.), reproached by a certain Mestrius Florus for saying *plostra* rather than *plaustra*, retaliated upon his corrector the next day by addressing him as "Flaurus."

Although Proto-Romance lost the diphthongs of Classical Latin, it created many of its own. The open vowels *e* and *o*, when the accent fell on them, turned into diphthongs, with *e* becoming *ie* and *o* becoming *uo*. This is one of the most far-reaching sound changes of Proto-Romance. A few examples: Latin *pédem* "foot" > Italian *piede*, Spanish *pie*, French *pied* (as in *pied-à-terre*, literally "foot to the ground"); Latin *pétram* "rock" > Italian *pietra*, Spanish *piedra*, French *pierre* (the same as the proper name *Pierre* "Peter"); Latin *mél* "honey" > Italian *miele*, Spanish, French *miel*; Latin *nóvum* "new" > Italian *nuovo*, Spanish *nuevo*, Old French *nuef* (Modern *neuf*); Vulgar Latin *mórit* "he, she dies" > Italian *muore*, Spanish *muere*, French *meurt*.

For the vowels to become diphthongs, it was an essential condition that they be accented; unaccented vowels did not change. This can be demonstrated with clear contrasting examples such as are most easily supplied by Spanish. Whereas Vulgar Latin *pótet* "he, she can" became Spanish *puede*, which shows the change, *potémos* "we can" became Spanish *podemos*, which lacks it. Why so? In the latter the accent no longer fell on the *o*, which therefore did not become a diphthong. Similarly, Latin *fríco* "I rub" (compare *friction*) > Spanish *friego*, but *fricátis* "you (plural) rub" > *fregáis*.

How did this curious change, called "spontaneous diphthongization," come about? The accented vowel, because it was accented, was lengthened first: *pédem* "foot" /pe-de/ came to be pronounced /pe-e-de/. Then, by dissimilation, the first of the two sounds changed, resulting in /piede/. By a parallel process, accented *o* /o/ came to be pronounced /o-o/ and then /uo/. Thus, Vulgar Latin *morit* "he, she dies" > Italian *muore*; both Spanish and French once had the same diphthong as Italian, but then altered it further, resulting in *muere* and *meurt*.

A few additional examples of diphthongization: Latin *ténet* "he, she holds" (compare *tenet, tenacious*) > Italian, Spanish *tiene*, French *tient*; Latin *décem* "ten" (compare *decimal, dime*) > Italian *dieci*, Spanish *diez*, Old French *dieis* (Modern *dix* /dis/); Vulgar Latin *célum* "sky" (compare *celestial*) > Italian, Spanish *cielo*, French *ciel*; Latin *bóvem* "ox" (compare *bovine*) > Italian *bue*, Spanish *buey*, French *boeuf*; Latin *óvum* "egg" (compare *ovary, oval*) > Italian *uovo*, Spanish *huevo*, French *oeuf*.

Upon still closer study, a further refinement appears, a distinction between Spanish, on the one hand, and both French and Italian, on the other. The latter languages do not diphthongize accented *e* or *o* if the vowel is followed by a consonant within the same syllable (such a vowel is called "checked"; the opposite is a "free" vowel). Latin *tér-ram* "earth" (compare *terrestrial, terrain*), where the vowel is checked, leads to diphthongized *tierra* in Spanish but remains *terra* in Italian, *terre* in French. Similarly, Latin *pór-tum* "harbor" produces Spanish *puerto*, but Italian *porto*, French *port*.

Additional instances: Latin *mér-dam* "shit" > Spanish *mierda*, but Italian *merda*, French *merde*; Latin *cén-tum* "hundred" (compare *century, centennial, centurion*, a legionary officer in command of a hundred soldiers) > Spanish *ciento*, but Italian *cento*, French *cent*; Latin *cór-pus* "body" > Spanish *cuerpo*, but Italian *corpo*, French *corps*; Latin *mór-dit* "he, she bites" (compare *mordant*, adjective and noun) > Spanish *muerde*, but Italian *morde*, French *mord*. In all these cases, and many others besides, we can see that Italian and French do not turn checked vowels into diphthongs, whereas Spanish does.

Syncope

Accent played an important role in such diphthongization; indeed, it was indispensable. Accent was also central in another important change having to do with vowels, syncope, in which a vowel is lost from a word. The vowel lost is most often the one following the accented syllable. We encountered this in the *Appendix Probi: báculus non vaclus* "rod." The stress on the one vowel (here the *a*) detracted from the force given to the vowel following (the first *u*) to such an extent that the latter ceased to be pronounced. An example of syncope in English is the oft-heard British pronunciation of *medicine* with two syllables /med-sin/.

Syncope indeed had occurred often in the earlier history of Latin, as with *valde* "strongly" from *válide*, and *aetas* "age" from *aévitas*: both syncopated forms were regarded as correct. The *Appendix Probi*, through its repeated attempts to halt the phenomenon, reveals that syncope continued to be a prominent feature of spoken Latin: *angulus non anglus* "angle, corner" and *stabulum non stablum* "stable, shed, pen." The phenomenon was widespread in the history of the Romance languages, as can be seen from French derivatives of the syncopated forms, *angle* and *étable* (> English *angle* and *stable*). Here are some further instances, not recorded in the *Appendix* (the syncopated vowel is set between parentheses): Latin *pós(i)tam* "a putting, placing" (in various senses) > Spanish *puesta*, Italian *posta*, French *poste* (in the latter two languages one of the meanings is "mail," and from French *poste* are derived English *post*, *postal*); Latin *púl(i)cem* "flea" > Italian *pulce*, Spanish *pulga*, French *puce* (the source of the color *puce*); Latin *cóm(i)tem* "companion (of the emperor)" > Italian *conte*, Spanish *conde*, French *comte* "count"; Latin *íns(u)lam* "island" > Spanish *isla*, French *île* (but Italian *isola*).

Here again one has the pleasure of discovering, within the general phenomenon, various sub-rules that distinguish the languages. Syncope was most likely to take place in all three languages when the vowel following the accent (called the "post-tonic vowel") stood between certain combinations of sounds: a consonant and *l*, *l* and a consonant, and *r* and a consonant. Because *l* and *r* easily join with other consonants, the sounds that resulted from the vowel's being dropped and the consonants' thus coming to stand side by side were easy to pronounce, which favored the change. The *Appendix Probi* corrects a number of syncopes that were, despite its efforts, perpetuated in the Romance languages: *speculum non speclum* "mirror" (not the correct former, but the latter > Italian *specchio*, Spanish *espejo*), *viridis non virdis* "green" (the latter > Italian, Spanish *verde*, French *vert*).

When the post-tonic vowel was found between other combinations of consonants, however, Italian often differed from the other two languages in not allowing syncope to take place: Latin *duódecim* "twelve" (compare *duodenum*, the first segment of the small intestine, so called because twelve fingers' breadth long) > Spanish *doce*, French *douze*, but Italian *dodici*; Latin *fráxinum* "ash tree" > Spanish *fresno* (as in the name of the California city), French *frêne*, but Italian *frassino*; Latin *péctinem* "comb" > Spanish *peine*, French *peigne* (compare *peignoir*, originally a garment worn by a woman while combing her hair), but Italian *pettine*; Latin *lítteram* "letter" > Spanish *letra*, French *lettre*, but Italian *lettera*.

Occasionally syncope affected, not the vowel following, but the vowel preceding the accented syllable. Some examples: Latin *bon(i)tátem* "goodness" > Italian *bontà*, Spanish *bondad*, French *bonté*, in which the *i* before the tonic *a* has been lost; Latin *ver(e)cúndiam* "modesty, shame" > Italian *vergogna*, French *vergogne*, Spanish *vergüenza*; Latin *coll(o)cáre* "to put in place" > Spanish *colgar* "to hang," French *coucher* "to lay down, put to bed"; Latin *fab(u)láre* "to speak" > Spanish *hablar*.

SOME CHANGES IN CONSONANTS

Loss of h *and Final* m

Many of the changes in consonants that characterize Proto-Romance have also been observed already in the *Appendix Probi*. One trait that all the Romance languages share, and not just our three, is that they have lost the sound of *h*; indeed, it is the single phonological trait they all share. By the time it was castigated in the *Appendix* (*hostiae non ostiae* "sacrificial animals"), the dropping of aitches was already a lost cause. However wittily mocked by Catullus centuries earlier, it remained a problem in Latin, because *h* was always weakly pronounced – an aspiration, a puff of air practically. Grammarians again and again took up the cudgels in defense of sounding the *h*, but to no avail: hundreds of inscriptions, through spellings such as *omo* for *homo* "man" and *ora* for *hora* "hour," reveal the unaspirated pronunciation in actual use. This has persisted to today. The initial aitch in Latin *honorem* "honor," whether written in the derived languages (Spanish *honor*, French *honneur*) or not (Italian *onore*), is no longer sounded at all. (The contemporary Spanish and French spellings generally represent restoration rather than faithful preservation.) The same holds for Latin *humilem* "humble," which gave Spanish *humilde*, French *humble*, Italian *umile*, and for scores of other words. The *h* that once appeared in the middle of some Latin words is not written by any Romance language as a souvenir of the past: Latin *cohortem* > Italian, Spanish *corte*, French *court* "court"; Latin *prehendere* "to grasp, take" > Italian *prendere*, Spanish *prender*, French *prendre* (already in the late first century c.e. the grammarian Quintilian was recommending the spelling *prendere*). The Germanic languages, by contrast, have no problem with sounding the *h*. We recognize that English pronounces the *h* in *humble* and retains and pronounces the *h* in *apprehend*, not to mention Germanic words like *hose* and *hamlet*.

The feeble pronunciation of final -*m* in Latin words is also attested by the *Appendix*: *olim non oli* "formerly," and *passim non passi* "throughout." Rooted in Classical Latin, this sound change also, far from being begun in Proto-Romance, was merely continued in it. Nonetheless, unlike the loss of *h*, it had extremely far-reaching effects on the language, extending beyond the realm of sounds and affecting morphology and, in turn, syntax. For it so happens that the accusative singular of all Classical Latin nouns (and adjectives too), except for some neuters, ended in -*m*: *portam* "gate," *amicum* "friend," *donum* "gift," *pedem* "foot," *fructum* "fruit," *rem* "thing." At the moment it is enough to observe that, with the loss of final -*m*, many of those forms lost their distinctiveness, became liable to confusion with other forms, and so were seriously hampered in their functioning, because in an inflected language like Latin the form of the word declares its function. Take *portam* as an example: with loss of final *m* (and obliteration of the distinction between open and close *a*), all difference was effaced between Classical *portă* (nominative singular), *portam* (accusative), and *portā* (ablative). The loss of final -*m* thus threatened to make the direct objects of verbs unrecognizable as such, and this in turn would mean that some other system needed to be employed to mark them.

Virtually every Romance noun or adjective derived from Latin illustrates the loss of final -*m*, because virtually every one derives from the Latin accusative case singular. Some examples referring to the family: Latin *patre(m) bonu(m)* "good father" > Italian *padre buono*, Spanish *padre bueno*, French *père bon*; Latin *filia(m) juvene(m)* "young daughter" > Italian *figlia giovane*, Spanish *hija joven*, French *fille jeune*. The natural world: Latin *nocte(m) clara(m)* "clear night" > Italian *notte chiara*, Spanish *noche clara*, French *nuit claire*; Latin *caballu(m) feroce(m)* "fierce horse" > Italian *cavallo feroce*, Spanish *caballo feroz*, French *cheval féroce*. And so on, all the way through the dictionary: no trace of the final *-m* so common in Latin is to be found.

Confusion Between b and v

The *Appendix Probi* also revealed a persistent confusion between the sounds of *b* and *v: tolerabilis non toleravilis* "tolerable," to cite one instance in addition to the others noticed earlier. This error too is often found in inscriptions: *bivus* instead of *vivus* "alive," or *valneas* instead of *balneas* "baths." And here too such evidence testifies to an altered pronunciation. In Classical Latin, the letters *b* and *v* represented different sounds, as they do in English today. In Vulgar Latin, however, they merged into a single sound which was intermediate between the two (and which is foreign to English). That sound is made by positioning the tongue and lips as for *b*, but then vibrating the lips together as for *v* (such a sound is called a "fricative") and bringing the voicebox into play. The result is a sound distinct from both *b* and *v* yet similar to each, and therein lies the origin of the confusion.

The Vulgar Latin sound was preserved in Spanish, which nonetheless in writing is careful to discriminate *b* from *v*, as Classical Latin did. This reflects not so much a difference in pronunciation as, again, the success of the Royal Spanish Academy of the Language in imposing historically faithful spellings. The two sounds are pronounced so nearly alike, in fact, especially at the beginning of words, that the substitution of one for the other is the second most common spelling error among children learning the language, who, for instance, often write *baca* for *vaca* "cow." In both Italian and French, however, the same Vulgar Latin sound, when it occurred between vowels, changed consistently to *v*. Thus, from Latin *habere* "to have," which was soon to become an indispensable auxiliary verb, were derived Spanish *haber* (with the fricative pronunciation), but Italian *avere*, French *avoir* (pronounced /v/); from Latin *debere* "to owe," Spanish *deber*, but Italian *dovere*, French *devoir*; from Latin *caballum* "horse," Spanish *caballo*, but Italian *cavallo*, French *cheval*.

Yet *b* and *v* are so prone to be confused with one another that many instances appear to follow no pattern: Latin *tolerabilem* "tolerable" > French, Spanish *tolerable*, Italian *tollerabile*; yet Latin *honorabilem* "honorable" > French, Spanish *honorable*, but Italian *onorevole*; Late Latin *hibernum* "winter" > Italian *inverno*, Spanish *invierno*, French *hiver*.

The Classical Latin pronunciation of *v* as in English began in the first century C.E. Previously, the letter *v* had represented the sound of /w/, which in certain combinations tended to disappear. From the verb *movere* "to move" was created the noun **movimentum* "movement," which is only found as *momentum*, the syllable -*vi*- having been lost. The same happened with many verb forms: instead of *cantavisset* "that he sing," we read *cantasset*, even in literary texts.

Mutability of l and r

Still another case of consonantal interchange very influential upon the modern languages was heralded in the *Appendix Probi*, the mutability of *l* and *r*: *flagellum non fragellum* "whip," and *terebra non telebra* "drill." Both these liquid consonants combine with other consonants to form easily pronounced clusters. Yet they also often get exchanged with each other. This affects so many words in the Romance vocabulary that some further examples may usefully be gathered and grouped here. You will see that the phenomenon is by no means uniform within a language or between languages, but occurs erratically; Spanish seems especially prone to changing these sounds.

When two *rs* or two *ls* occur in a word, one of them sometimes gets altered to the other sound by dissimilation: Latin *arborem* "tree" > Italian *albero*, with dissimilation of the first *r*, and Spanish *árbol*, with dissimilation of the second (but French *arbre*, retaining the two *rs*); Latin *peregrinum* "foreigner" (compare *peregrine*, as in "peregrine falcon") > Vulgar Latin *pelegrinum* > Italian *pellegrino*, Old French *peligrin* (> *pilgrim*) "pilgrim" (but Spanish *peregrino*); Latin *Mercuri (diem)* "(day) of Mercury" > Italian *mercoledì*, Spanish *miércoles* "Wednesday" (but French *mercredi*); Latin *paraveredum* "extra horse" > French *palefroi* "a riding horse, of a sort suitable for a lady" (> *palfrey*); Latin **lusciniolum* "nightingale" > Vulgar Latin **rusciniolum* > Italian *rosignolo*, French *rossignol*, Spanish *ruiseñor* (the second *r* of this word was altered by folk etymology: the word was taken to be *Ruy señor* "Sir Roderick").

Occasionally *l* and *r* exchange places within a word: Latin *miraculum* "miracle" > Spanish *milagro* (but Italian *miracolo*, French *miracle*); Latin *periculum* "danger" > Spanish *peligro* (but Italian *pericolo*, French *péril*: compare *peril*).

The *l* or the *r* often mutates into the other: Latin *ancoram* "anchor" > Spanish *ancla*, with syncope (but Italian *ancora*, French *ancre*); Latin *papyrum* "papyrus" > Spanish *papel* "paper" (but French *papier*); Latin *bursam* "bag (especially for holding money)" (compare *bursitis*, inflammation of sacs in the body) > Spanish *bolsa* "bag; stock exchange" (but Italian *borsa*, French *bourse* – English *bursar* is derived from the last, whereas *purse*, of the same ultimate origin, entered the language earlier, adopted directly from Latin into Old English).

The closeness of *l* and *r* is reflected in a curiosity of English given names. A number of them change *r* to *l* in their pet forms: *Harry* > *Hal*, *Derek* > *Del*, *Sarah* > *Sally*, *Mary* > *Molly*.

Addition of Initial e

An inscription that we met before included the word *ispose* for *sponsae* "wife," in which the combination of *s* plus another consonant at the start of the word must have sounded intolerable and was therefore eased by the addition of a vowel in front of the *s*. That inscription was a harbinger of what was going to happen in Spanish and French. Those languages, but not Italian, regularly prefixed *e-* to such words: Latin *spiritum* "spirit" > Spanish *espíritu*, French *esprit* (compare *esprit de corps*), but Italian *spirito*; Latin *stipare* "to pack tight" (compare *constipation*) > Spanish *estivar* (source of *stevedore*, one who packs a ship), French *estiver*, but Italian *stivare*.

It often happened in French that the *s* itself eventually disappeared, leaving the *e* marked with an acute accent, which indicates a close *e* sound: Latin *scribere* "to write" > Spanish *escribir*, Old French *escrivre* > Modern French *écrire*; Latin *scolam* "school" > Spanish *escuela*, French *école*; Latin *spatam* "sword" > Spanish *espada*, French *épée*; Latin *scalam* "ladder" > Spanish *escala*, French *échelle*.

By contrast with Spanish and French, English contains hosts of words beginning with *s* + consonant, most of Germanic origin: *scratch, slack, snow, speed, squirt, strew, swerve*, and so on.

Voiceless Plosives

A set of consonant sounds underwent parallel changes between Latin and the Romance languages, and the changes are widespread, sometimes dramatic, and always interesting, not least because many of them are reflected in

English words. Moreover, in the patterns discovered here, we will find a couple of special features, that a number of different sounds get treated alike and that each language clearly represents a distinct stage of the evolution. The consonants in question are *p*, *t*, and *c*, which may appear to have nothing in common, but which are all voiceless plosives – "voiceless" because they are produced without use of the voicebox (see following discussion for the contrast between voiceless and voiced) and "plosives" because they are produced by a single slight explosion of breath (contrast sounds that can be continued, such as those of *v* or *l* or *s*). The developments in question took place where the consonant occurred between vowels. Each language dealt with that set of three consonants in a uniform manner, and we can discern a neat progression from one language to another. Italian retained the sounds as they were in Latin; Spanish changed them to their voiced equivalent; French also changed them to their voiced equivalent, but then changed them again, often in a way that obscured the earlier change.

The change in sound that took place in Spanish and French is not arbitrary. If a sound changes, it changes to another sound that is not very different from it. It would be extraordinary, for instance, to assert that in one step a *t* turned into an *r*. Here, however, the relation between the series *p t c* (voiceless) and the series *b d g* (voiced) is simple, and you can easily demonstrate it to yourself. If, holding a hand against your voicebox, you say *pet* and then *bet*, you'll recognize that for both consonants your lips and tongue are in the same position and the only difference is that for *bet* your voicebox is brought into action. You will discover the same difference between *t* and *d* and between *c* and *g*. A sound may change again, but each change is as modest as this one.

Of the voiceless plosives, then, intervocalic -*p*- of Latin remained -*p*- in Italian, changed to -*b*- in Spanish (with the fricative sound described), and in French ended up as -*v*-: Latin *leporem* "hare" > Italian *lepre*, Spanish *liebre*, French *lièvre* (compare *leveret*, a hare less than a year old); Latin *ripam* "bank, shore" > Italian *ripa*, Spanish *riba*, French *rive*; Latin *sapere* "to have a (certain) taste; to be intelligent" (compare *insipid* "without taste" and *homo sapiens* "man the intelligent") > Italian *sapere*, Spanish *saber*, French *savoir* (compare *savant*, "a knowing, learned person"). The initial change, from -*p*- to -*b*-, is also attested in inscriptions, where we read *labidem* for *lapidem* "stone." The fricative sound of Vulgar Latin *b*, intermediate between *b* and *v*, which was retained by Spanish, easily passed into a distinct *v* in French.

In parallel fashion, intervocalic -*t*- of Latin remained -*t*- in Italian, changed to -*d*-, its voiced equivalent, in Spanish and French, and in French then changed again to the point of disappearance: Latin *mutare* "to change" (compare *mutable*) > Italian *mutare*, Spanish *mudar*, French *muer*; Latin *vitam* "life" (compare *vital*) > Italian *vita*, Spanish *vida*, French *vie*; Latin *pratum* "meadow" > Italian *prato*, Spanish *prado* (as in Madrid's peerless art museum, called El Prado because of its location), French *pré*. What happened with French was this: it changed the -*t*- into -*d*- along with Spanish, but then continued onward, first turning that sound into the sound of *th* in English *then*, and later losing it altogether. Inscriptions provide instances of the voicing of -*t*- to -*d*- as well: *immudavit* is found for *immutavit* "he, she altered" and *amadus* for *amatus* "beloved."

The letter *c*, always pronounced /k/ in Classical Latin, presents a more complicated picture for when it appeared between vowels. What happened to the sound when it occurred before *e* or *i* – a dramatic tale – we will take up shortly. Before *a*, *o*, or *u*, however, the changes were parallel to those with the other voiceless plosives. Latin -*c*- remained in Italian, changed to -*g*- in Spanish, and changed still further in French (which we may leave aside for a moment): Latin *amicam* "female friend" > Italian *amica*, Spanish *amiga*; Latin *focum* "hearth" > Italian *fuoco*, Spanish *fuego* "fire"; Latin *securum* "secure, certain" > Italian *sicuro*, Spanish *seguro*. This change of pronunciation too is revealed in the misspellings of inscriptions, such as *negat* for *necat* "he, she slays" and *pagatus* for *pacatus* "settled, paid." The voicing of all three plosives is neatly illustrated in a single Spanish word: Latin *apotecam* "store-room" > Spanish *bodega* "cellar (especially for wines); grocery store." (From *apotecam* are also derived both *apothecary*, originally "shopkeeper," later "pharmacist," and, via French, *boutique*.)

French, after undergoing the same change with -*c*- as Spanish, treated the resulting -*g*- in two different ways, depending on the vowel that *preceded*. After *i*, *o*, or *u*, the -*g*- simply disappeared: Latin *amicam* "female friend" > French *amie*; Latin *advocatum* "advocate, lawyer" > French *avoué* (the learned term *avocat* is also in use – *avocado*, however, is unrelated, the word, like the fruit itself, coming from Mexico, from Nahuatl *ahuacatl* "testicle"); Latin *lactucam* "lettuce" > French *laitue*. After *a* or *e*, however, the -*g*- became -*ij*- /-iy-/: Latin *pacare* "to settle" > Old French *paiiyer*, Modern French *payer* "to pay" (> *pay*); Latin *decem* "ten" > Late Latin *decanum* "leader of ten" > Old French *deien* (> *dean*) > Modern French *doyen* "dean."

The etymology of the last item is engaging, since it reminds us of the origin of our colleges. In Late Latin a *decanum* was the leader of a group of ten – ten soldiers, ten monks, and so forth. In the Middle Ages, it came to designate the head of a chapter of priests attached to a cathedral, regardless of their number. And because European institutions of higher learning emerged out of ecclesiastical organizations, it was natural to call the head of a school or college *decanum* too. Hence our word *dean*. English has adopted the Modern French form of the word as well, but always uses it in a transferred sense: "Jean is the doyen (or: Jeanne is the doyenne) of contemporary literary critics."

The disappearance of intervocalic -*t*- and -*c*-, as in *vitam* > *vie* and *decanum* > *doyen*, opened up a gulf that separates many Latin words from their French offspring – a gulf often so wide that it prevents the kinship from being recognized. A few further examples: Latin *adjutare* "to help" (compare *adjutant*) > French *aider* (> *aid*); Latin *catenam* "chain" (compare *concatenation*) > French *chaîne* (> *chain*); Latin *nativum* "natural" > French *naïf* "ingenuous, artless" (> *naïve*); Latin *imperator* "general" > French *empéreur* "emperor"; Latin *traditionem* "handing over; surrender" (compare *tradition*) > Old French *traïson* "treason"; Latin *fricare* "to rub" (compare *friction*) > French *frayer* (> *fray*); Latin *locum* "place" (compare *local, locate*) > French *lieu* (> *lieu* in the phrase "in lieu of," also *lieutenant*, literally "place-holder"); Latin *securum* "secure, certain" > French *sûr* "sure" (> *sure*), which reveals that, from an etymological standpoint, a store's prosaic security is no different from France's famous *Sûreté*, inhabited by the shades of Inspectors Maigret and Clouseau.

A couple of other intervocalic consonants, -*d*- and -*g*-, also disappeared during the centuries that separated Latin and French, with the same result – transformation to the point of unrecognizability. Here, without explanation of the phonological changes, are a few instances: Latin *mercedem* "wage, payment, reward" (compare *mercenary*) > French *merci* "favor, thanks" (> *mercy*); Latin *gaudia* "pleasures" (neuter plural) > French *joie* "joy" (feminine singular, > *joy*); Latin *redemptionem* "purchase" > French *rançon* "ransom" (> *ransom*); Latin *praedam* "prey" (compare *predator*) > Old French *preie* (> *prey*); Latin *sedem* "seat" (compare *sedentary*) > Old French *sié* > (> *see*, as in "Holy See"); Latin *desiderare* "to desire" > French *désirer* (> *desire*); Latin *rugam* "crease, wrinkle, rut" (compare *corrugated*) > French *rue* "street"; Latin *regula* "ruler, pattern" > Old French *reule* (> *rule*); Latin *ligationem* "binding" (compare *ligature, league*) > French *liaison* "bond, connection" (> *liaison* – the original Latin *g* is also missing from the cognates *lien, ally, alloy*); Late Latin *exagium* "weighing, balance" > French *essai* "trial; essay" (> *essay – assay* is cognate).

Italian stands at the opposite end of the mutability scale from French: it tended to retain the Latin consonants faithfully. Nonetheless, more than the other two languages, Italian contains quite a few exceptions – that is to say, words in which the voiceless plosives were not retained, but did become voiced: *strada* "street" < Latin *stratam*; *scudo* "shield" < Latin *scutum*; *lago* "lake" < Latin *lacum*; *pagare* "to pay" < Latin *pacare*; *bottega* "shop" < Latin *apotecam* "store-room" – a double example. The explanation for the "exceptions" is this: standard Modern Italian, to a greater extent than the other standard languages of today, has been formed out of distinctly different varieties of speech, out of both the southern varieties, which usually preserve the consonants in question, and the northern, which are inclined to voice them. The latter therefore are the source of the apparently anomalous words.

Palatalization

The sound of *c* before the vowels *e* or *i* underwent astonishing transformations between Latin and the modern languages. Here too special interest lies in the remarkable nature of the changes, the large number of words affected (including many English words), and the fact that the modern languages stand at different points along the path of development, each one exemplifying a distinct stage. We will also see that Italian, though altered, remains closest to Latin, and that in this matter American Spanish aligns itself with French and differs from European Spanish.

Pronounced /k/ everywhere in Classical Latin, *c* before *e* or *i* turned into a variety of sounds all remote from their origin – ultimately into /tsh/ in Italian, /s/ in French and in American Spanish, and /th/, as in *thin*, in European Spanish. Each change along the way, each individual step, was small, and only the long series of steps taken together carried the sounds such a distance. This is the most complex of the sound changes I describe, yet it should be easy to follow. By making the sounds for yourself, you can readily observe the closeness of each to the one out of which it developed, and thus sense the ease, the naturalness, of every step. For illustration I use /ke/, but the same changes took place with /ki/.

The first change was that /ke/ developed a yod sound between consonant and vowel, /kye/, which is more relaxed. (/Kye/ does not rhyme with *rye*, but the *y* is as in *yes* and the *e* is pronounced.) The yod is called a "palatal" sound because it's made by pressing the front of the tongue against the hard palate. Say /ke/, then /kye/ and you'll feel this. Because it set off a kind of chain reaction, the whole process it began is often called, somewhat loosely, "palatalization": strictly speaking, the term applies only to this first step. The next change, produced by moving the tip of the tongue forward a little, so it touched the back of the teeth, was from /kye/ to /tye/. This sound in turn was then slightly relaxed by becoming /tshe/. Things had reached this stage in Proto-Romance before the languages separated from one another. In Italian the sound ceased to change at this point, whereas in the others it continued to develop. Next, /tshe/ was simplified to /tse/, whence two paths opened up, which led to the other current pronunciations. In both French and the Spanish of America, the dental element (/t/) from /tse/ was lost, and the sound became simplified to /se/. In European Spanish, however, the dental at first remained, assimilating the following consonant to itself, so /tse/ became /tthe/, and then that got simplified to /the/, pronounced as in *thin*. This sound, unknown in American Spanish, creates the "lisping" impression characteristic of European Spanish.

Here is a concrete example of how the sound changed. Latin *cervum* "stag" developed as follows: /kervu/ > /kyervo/ > /tyervo/ > /tshervo/ (the Italian pronunciation) > /tservo/, at which point the path forks; /tservo/ > /servo/ > French *cerf* /serf/ and, with diphthongization, American Spanish *ciervo* /syervo/, but /tservo/ also > /tthervo/ > /thervo/ > European Spanish *ciervo* /thyervo/. By the same series of steps, Latin *civitatem* "state, city" ended up as Italian *città* /tshita/, French *cité* /see-tay/, and Spanish *ciudad*, pronounced /syudad/ in Córdoba, Argentina, but /thyudad/ in Córdoba, Spain. Scores of other words changed in just this way.

Palatalization worked upon many other sounds in the Romance languages, altering, for instance, Latin *planum* "level, smooth" to Italian *piano* "soft." Indeed, perhaps no other kind of sound change affected so many words, and so deeply. Since our plan is to sample rather than survey, we may limit ourselves to just one other type of palatalization, which is similar to the first type and involves an even larger number of words. The *Appendix Probi* includes no fewer than fourteen examples of a single mistaken pronunciation (*vinea non vinia* "vineyard," for instance, and *lancea non lancia* "lance"): no other error is so often reproved. (*Vinea* in the sense of "vine" is, by the way, the unexpected

222

parent of *vignette*, which indicated at first a decorative design on a page, often in the form of vine tendrils, and then a little scene.)

The corrections attempted by the author of the *Appendix* attest to a change in pronunciation that was taking place. In these words, observe that the consonant was followed by two vowels (not one, as in *cervus*). The *e* in *lancea* and *vinea* (and similarly the *i* in others), when sounded before another vowel, tended to cease being a vowel and to develop into a consonant instead, the yod. Thus *lancea* /lan-ke-a/ was coming to be pronounced /lan-kya/, with two syllables instead of three. And here once again palatalization set off a chain reaction. The sound of /k/ before *e* or *i* developed like this: /k/ > /ky/ > /ty/ > /tsh/ (Italian) > /ts/ > both /s/ (French, American Spanish) and > /tth/ > /th/ (European Spanish). Thus, Latin *lancea* "lance" and *minacia* "threat" have resulted in the following: Italian *lancia* /lantsha/ and *minaccia* /minatsha/, French *lans* /lans/ and *menace* /menas/, and Spanish *lanza* and *menaza*, pronounced either /lansa/ and /menasa/, in America, or /lantha/ and /menatha/, in Europe. The corresponding English words, *lance* and *menace*, deriving of course from French, also give an /s/ sound to what once upon a time was /k/. Very different, indeed.

Before *e* or *i* and a second vowel, the sound of /t/ developed very much along the same line: /t/ > /ty/ > /tsh/ > /ts/ (Italian) > both /s/ (French, American Spanish) and /tth/ > /th/ (European Spanish). So Latin *plateam* "street" and *fortiam* "force," both trisyllables originally, have turned out as follows: Italian *piazza* /pyatsa/ and *forza* /fortsa/, French *place* /plas/ and *force* /fors/, and in Spanish *plaza* and *fuerza*, pronounced /plasa/ and /fwersa/ or /platha/ and /fwertha/. The words so affected in each of the languages easily number in the hundreds, and palatalization was again the first step in a process that gave the modern languages some of their most characteristic sounds.

The same process also provides nearly the whole of the explanation for why English words spelled -*tion* are nonetheless pronounced /-shun/. Such words, of which there are hundreds, began to enter the language during the Middle English period from French, and naturally they were pronounced as in the French of that day, with an /s/ sound, for instance, *nation* /nasyon/: all the changes detailed previously had already taken place. But in England, from /s/ the sound shifted during the next centuries to /sh/, the present pronunciation. Curiously, the shift from /s/ to /sh/ is also an instance of palatalization – to say /sh/ the tongue is pressed against the hard palate – so the long history that brought Latin *nationem* to be pronounced as it is in Modern English both begins and ends with the same phonological phenomenon.

These two sets of sound changes, provoked by palatalization and largely coinciding with one another, both involve many steps. How reliable is that lengthy sequence I described? What evidence, in addition to the *Appendix Probi* and the present-day outcomes, supports it? The evidence is abundant and pleasingly varied, with a prominent part again played by inscriptions. We saw that /k/ before *e* or *i* became /ky/, then /ty/, then /tsh/. That this stage was reached is inferred from inscriptions with such spellings as *Bintcente* for *Vincente* "Vincent" or *intcitamento* for *incitamento* "incentive": the *tc* combination looks like an attempt to represent the /tsh/ sound.

The /ty/ sound as heard in *nationem* evolved beyond /tsh/ to /ts/, as we also saw. This stage of the sequence is amply confirmed too. For a welcome change, a grammarian, a certain Papirius who lived not later than the early sixth century, states it directly: "in the word written *iustitia*, the third syllable is pronounced as if it consisted of the three letters *t*, *z*, and *i*" (fragment in Keil's edition of the grammarians, 7.216). The changed pronunciation is unmistakable too in an inscriptional spelling like *Crescentsianus* for *Crescentianus*, a man's name.

Finally, the evolution of the pronunciation of /ke/ to /tse/ is evidenced in what may seem an unlikely quarter, the Modern German language, where it is made crystal clear through contrast. Words spelled with *ce* or *ci* were adopted from Latin into Germanic in two distinct periods. In words borrowed during the time of the Roman Empire, the contemporary pronunciation was /k/, which has persisted in German to the present: Latin *Caesar* (the family name of Julius, later a title) > German *Kaiser*; Latin *cellarium* "store-room" > German *Keller* (*cellar* thus, our ears tell us, entered English through French, not German). But by the seventh century, at the latest, the sound of *c* in that position had changed to /ts/, so the words thenceforth adopted by the Germans were pronounced with that sound, represented today by the letter *z*: Latin *censum* "assessment, tax" > German *Zins* /tsins/ "interest"; Latin *crucem* "cross" > German *Kreuz*; Latin *citharam* "lyre" > German *Zither*.

Palatalization, of which only a pair of types have been cited, and the other sound changes mentioned before by no means constitute a full description of Proto-Romance phonology; on the contrary, they paint but a small piece of the picture of sound changes between Latin and Romance. They should be taken as merely representing the gamut of such changes.

Voltaire (1694–1778) is reported to have declared that etymology is a science in which the consonants count for little and the vowels for nothing at all. The witticism was at home in the eighteenth century, but is hardly so in the twenty-first, when we can reliably trace out and explain those changes, however extended or improbable, which have so conspicuously altered the sound and the look of the languages, and indeed have had an impact not on phonology alone but on morphology and syntax as well.

CHAPTER TWELVE

THE NOUN IN PROTO-ROMANCE

Nouns

The distinguishing quality of Latin, received as its principal legacy from Indo-European, was that it was a highly inflected, synthetic language. Through their form, Latin words declared what role they were playing in a sentence, and the number of forms for any given word was large. The revolution in the history of Latin as it became the Romance languages was precisely the loss of inflections, and a concomitant re-orientation in the nature of the language, from synthetic towards analytic. This segment of our story therefore has two parts: the number of forms that needed to be mastered and deployed was drastically reduced, and, accordingly, the tasks those forms had previously executed needed to be carried out by other means. Those are the themes of this chapter and the next. Of the noun, which is taken up first, the revolution abolished all forms but two. The verb managed to hold on to more of its inflected forms.

Wherever we look among the features of nouns, we find simplification. The number of noun classes was reduced, in the end, from five to three (or fewer), the number of genders from three to two, the number of cases from five to one. Whereas an ancient Roman needed to command about eighty noun forms altogether, the speaker of any of the modern languages makes do with no more than six. This part of our story can be set forth in almost full detail, and yet it is easy to follow.

Two sets of forces were at work in altering the noun, one based in the mind, so to speak, the other in the tongue and the ear. On the one hand, the moves to reduce the number of forms (and also to regularize them) were driven by a desire for greater simplicity and economy in speech. The language would be that much easier to learn and to use if the forms were fewer and more predictable. On the other hand, several of the sound changes described earlier were undermining from within Latin's system of noun declensions. Loss of final -*m*, for instance, rendered the accusative singular *portam* "gate" indistinguishable from the nominative singular *porta*, or the accusative singular *pedem* "foot" indistinguishable from the ablative singular *pede*. Similarly, the convergence of open *i* with close *e* made *pedis* (genitive singular) identical in sound to *pedes* (nominative/accusative plural). This would not have created problems, had Classical Latin not been a language that depended on just such distinctions. These two sets of forces, the interplay of which must have been complex but which operated in the same direction, profoundly altered the nature of the language. They wrecked the former system and replaced it with a new and different one.

Noun Classes

Latin possessed five noun classes – five different sets of noun forms, or declensions. The fourth and fifth declensions, which contained many fewer nouns than the first three, eventually disappeared; the *Appendix Probi* already gave indications of their approaching demise. What happened, then, to the nouns belonging to those declensions? They did not simply disappear from the language; rather, they were absorbed into other declensions, nouns of the fourth declension into the second declension, and those of the fifth into the first. The mechanisms of the absorption, however, were different.

The fourth declension consisted mostly of masculine nouns, with a few feminines and neuters. Exactly the same was true of the second declension, so the fit in terms of gender was good: a noun could readily retain its gender in moving from one declension to another. What motivated the absorption, however, was the similarity of endings. When the genitive, dative, and ablative cases fell into desuetude, only the nominative and accusative remained in common use. And it so happened that the endings of those two cases in the fourth declension singular (*fruct-us fruct-um*) were precisely the same as those for the second (*amic-us amic-um*). This was true for none of the remaining endings of the singular nor any of the plural, but it was for those two, and that was enough. The result was that in practice the two types became identical: *fructus* was handled exactly like *amicus*. In this process we observe that the singular was determinative rather than the plural, the forms of which differed conspicuously in nominative and accusative (contrast *amic-i amic-os* with *fruct-us fruct-us*). The simplified singular led the fourth declension noun into the camp of the second declension and caused a corresponding new plural to be created (*fructos, like *amicos*: compare Spanish *frutos*, French *fruits*). In this way Latin nouns of the fourth declension became indistinguishable from those of the second: Latin *fructum* "fruit" > Italian *frutto*, Spanish *fruto*, French *fruit*; Latin *mercatum* "market" > Italian *mercato*, Spanish *mercado*, French *marché*; Latin *exercitum* "army" > Italian *essercito*, Spanish *ejército* – all now belonging to the second class of nouns.

The fifth declension also disappeared, but its nouns got absorbed in a different way. The fifth declension resembled the first in that it consisted almost exclusively of feminine nouns. Classical Latin happened to possess a number of declensional doublets or alternatives, nouns formed from the same stem and with the same meaning that were found in both the first and the fifth declensions: *materiam/materiem* "material," for instance, and *luxuriam/luxuriem* "luxury." When such a pair existed, the outcome was that the first declension member of the pair prevailed over the fifth declension member, which disappeared. The first declension prevailed because its population was much bigger and so its forms were more familiar, and also because its forms were more similar to those of the second declension.

Then, in a second stage, the other nouns of the fifth declension, which did not have such a partner, joined the first anyway. From the Latin pair *materiam/materiem*, for instance, *materiam* had won out, which led to Italian, Spanish *materia*, French *matière* "material," as well as Spanish *madera* "wood," all indistinguishable from nouns of the first declension, like *portam*. Then, by analogy with such words, Classical Latin *rabiem* "frenzy" (fifth declension – compare *rabid*) changed to Vulgar Latin *rabiam (first declension), which became the parent of the Romance forms: Italian *rabbia*, Spanish *rabia*, French *rage* (> *rage*). Similarly, *diem* "day" became Spanish *día*.

Those are the separate but similar paths that nouns of the fourth and fifth declensions followed, and they look smooth and easily traveled. But what impelled the nouns to move along those paths? Given the two possibilities, why did they not remain as they were? Simplicity and ease were the chief impetus. The speaker needed to master and remember three patterns of nouns now, not five. Words that had appeared anomalous, because few in number, were eliminated. The clear, handy, appealing pattern by which nouns ending in *-a* were feminine and those ending in *-o* were masculine was reinforced. The result was that Proto-Romance came to possess nouns of only three types – the two just mentioned, representing descendants of Latin's first and second declensions, plus descendants of the third declension. The last proved more troublesome because they had a variety of endings and their gender was indeterminate: *colorem* "color" (masculine), *vallem* "valley" (feminine), *corpus* "body" (neuter), *mare* "sea" (neuter), *animal* "animal" (neuter). What pattern could be perceived in these?

Gender

Classical Latin possessed three genders – masculine, feminine, and neuter. In the Romance languages nearly all masculine and feminine nouns retained the gender they had had in Latin – a reminder of how rootedly features of Latin have persisted. A few nouns, however, did switch gender. Nearly all of these came from Latin's third declension, which, having no clear gender identification, was more prone to confusion: Latin *colorem* "color" (masculine) > Italian *colore* and Spanish *color* (masculine), but French *couleur* (feminine); Latin *vallem* "valley" (feminine) > Italian *valle* (feminine), but Spanish *valle* and French *val* (masculine). I can report that when I make mistakes of gender in Spanish, they are with nouns of this type.

In regard to gender, the dramatic change was the elimination of the neuters. Neuter words were not dropped from the vocabulary; instead, they were absorbed by the other genders, in one of two ways. The majority of neuter words became masculine. Those from the second declension already resembled the masculines of the same declension in most forms, including the accusative singular: compare *amicum* "friend" (masculine) and *spatium* "space" (neuter). Thus they easily passed over to the masculine gender: Latin *spatium* "space" (neuter) > Italian *spazio*, Spanish *espacio*, French *espace* (masculine); Latin *granum* "grain" (neuter) > Italian, Spanish *grano*, French *grain* (masculine). Neuters of the third declension experienced the same change: Latin *corpus* "body" (neuter) > Italian *corpo*, Spanish *cuerpo*, French *corps* (masculine); Latin *animal* "animal" (neuter) > Spanish, French *animal*, Italian *animale* (masculine).

Now, the nominative and accusative plurals of all Latin neuter nouns ended in -*ă*. This circumstance led to a number of neuters being absorbed by the feminines, which came about like this. Their plural forms ending in -*ă* got re-interpreted as feminine singulars, which also ended in -*ă*. The move from plural to singular was probably made first by such nouns as could easily take on a collective meaning, for instance, Latin *ligna* "pieces of firewood" (neuter plural) > Italian *legna*, Spanish *leña*, Old French *legne* "firewood" (feminine singulars). Then others followed: Latin *folia* "leaves" (neuter plural) > Italian *foglia*, French *feuille*, Spanish *hoja* "leaf" (feminine singulars, all with new plurals); Latin *gaudia* "joys" (neuter plural) > French *joie* "joy" (feminine singular); Latin *vota* "vows" (neuter plural) > Spanish *boda* "marriage vow, marriage" (feminine singular), now ordinarily used in the new plural, *bodas*. This change, already glimpsed in the *Appendix Probi*, we saw exampled in the *Kassel Glossary*: *membras* "members" instead of classical *membra*.

A couple of oddities deserve to be mentioned, as illustrating both the tenacity and the occasional laxity of Latin's influence. Striving to remain somewhat faithful to Latin, Italian possesses a number of words derived from Latin neuters which in the singular end in *-o* and are masculine, but which in the plural end in *-a* and are feminine (the strong association of *-a* with feminine singular is probably responsible): Latin *genuculum genucula* "knee knees" (neuter) > Italian *ginocchio* (singular, masculine) and *ginocchia* (plural, feminine); Latin *ovum ova* "egg eggs" (neuter) > Italian *uovo* (singular, masculine) and *uova* (plural, feminine). The *-a* ending in the plural is a striking anomaly within Italian, but by the same token a mark of Latin's persistence. Occasionally, the languages diverge in the gender they assign to what was formerly neuter: Latin *mare* "sea" (neuter) > Italian *mare*, Spanish *mar* (masculine), but French *mer* (feminine, as in the title of Debussy's tone poem, *La Mer*); in a few set phrases, such as *alta mar* "high sea," the word is feminine in Spanish as well.

The Cases in Vulgar Latin

The reductions in declensions and genders, however striking, seem almost trivial in their effects upon the language when compared with the reduction in cases, which, besides shrinking the number of forms that needed to be used, overthrew altogether the syntax of nouns. Classical Latin's five cases tended in Vulgar Latin towards two, nominative and accusative, and ended up eventually as one, which was the descendant of the accusative. In French documents written up to the thirteenth century, we still encounter distinct nominative and accusative forms, as we shall see. The same is not true for Italian and Spanish, from which the cases were eliminated so thoroughly that even the earliest texts show only the single form. In tracking the changes step by step from Classical through Vulgar Latin and then onwards, changes that are easy to grasp, we are witnessing the new languages unfold before our eyes.

How do we know that the accusative was the source of the Romance words, not the nominative, as might have been expected? Occasionally, we saw, an inscription employs the accusative in place of the nominative as the subject of a sentence: *hic quescunt duas matres, duas filias* "here rest two mothers, two daughters," where *duas* and *filias* are unmistakable accusatives. The reverse, nominative for accusative, is never found. Then too, both Spanish and French make their plurals with -*s*, which can only derive from the accusative plurals of Latin: Latin *portas* "gates" (contrast nominative plural *portae*) > Spanish *puertas*, French *portes*; Latin *amicos* "friends" (nominative plural *amici*) > Spanish *amigos*, French *amis*. (In the third declension, nominative and accusative plural both have the same ending, so no conclusion can be drawn from that.) Furthermore, with many nouns of the third declension the form of the nominative singular was somewhat different from that of the accusative, and the Romance words show unmistakably that their origin lies in the latter: Latin *partem* "part" (nominative *pars*) > Italian, Spanish *parte*, French *part*; Latin *leonem* "lion" (nominative *leo*) > Italian *leone*, Spanish *león*, French *lion*.

Romance nouns derive from the accusative, therefore – but not quite all of them. Some interesting exceptions are found. Whereas Latin *hominem* "man" (accusative) is the parent of French *homme*, Latin *homo* (nominative) led to French *on* "one," used in impersonal expressions, such as the proverb *quand on veut, on peut* "when one wants to, one can." (English *one*, the numeral, is therefore unconnected to French *on*.) It seems a shame that English lacks so handy a word, for our *one* sounds awkward in comparison. The French word for "son," *fils*, obviously comes from the Latin nominative *filius* (not the accusative *filium*). The nominative may have persisted here, exceptionally, because it was used in registries of birth and other records, which were ordinarily kept in Latin: *Josephus filius Philipi* "Joseph son of Philip." The French term is familiar (though perhaps unrecognized) in the English-speaking world as an element in certain surnames: *fils* (or rather, its earlier form *filz*) is the origin of *Fitz-* in names such as *Fitzgerald* and *Fitzwilliam*. From Norman times onwards, *Fitz-* was employed to create surnames for the illegitimate children of royalty, so "son" there carried a certain connotation: *Fitzgerald* in effect meant "bastard son of Gerald."

The reduced forms of the three declensions remaining in Vulgar Latin may be represented in a chart (the paradigms are *capra* "goat," *murus* "wall," *mons* "mountain").

		Classical Latin		Vulgar Latin	
		Singular	Plural	Singular	Plural
First Declension	Nominative	*capra*	*caprae*	*capra*	*capre*
	Accusative	*capram*	*capras*	*capra*	*capras*
Second Declension	Nominative	*murus*	*muri*	*murus*	*muri*
	Accusative	*murum*	*muros*	*muru*	*muros*
Third Declension	Nominative	*mons*	*montes*	*montis*	*montes*
	Accusative	*montem*	*montes*	*monte*	*montes*

Most of the changes in sound between the Classical and the Vulgar Latin forms have already been described: reduction of the diphthong *ae* to *e* (*caprae* > *capre*), and loss of final *-m* (*capram* > *capra, murum* > *muru, montem* > *monte*). How *mons* became *montis* (nominative singular) does need a word of explanation. A number of third declension nouns showed a kind of double irregularity, a discrepancy in stem and in length between the nominative singular, on the one hand, and, on the other, the genitive together with the other cases: *pars partis*, for instance. Vulgar Latin regularized these by remodeling them on the basis of other nouns, like *canis canis* "dog," and producing thereby new nominatives like **partis* and **montis*. In other words, by analogy with *canis canis, mons montis* became **montis montis*. Moreover, because open *u* had converged with close *o, murus* and *muros*, even though so written, had come to be pronounced alike. So too had *montis* and *montes*, on account of the convergence of open *i* with close *e*. Even when so reduced, the system of noun declensions presented problems: no set of forms was free from potential confusion.

The Cases in French

The confusions became especially acute in Early French. The two-case system that French did manage to maintain for several centuries was unstable, always threatened by its own inconsistency and uncertainty, and that situation in turn had been produced by two changes in pronunciation peculiar to the language.

		Vulgar Latin		Early French	
		Singular	Plural	Singular	Plural
First Noun Class	Nominative	*capra*	*capre*	*chevre*	*chevres*
	Accusative	*capra*	*capras*		
Second Noun Class	Nominative	*murus*	*muri*	*murs*	*mur*
	Accusative	*muru*	*muros*	*mur*	*murs*
Third Noun Class	Nominative	*montis*	*montes*	*monz*	*mont*
	Accusative	*monte*	*montes*	*mont*	*monz*

One change affecting the first noun class was that *a* became *e* in an open syllable, that is, a syllable that did not end with a consonant. The change affected both *a* sounds of *ca-pra*, which thus became *chevre* (consonant combinations like *pr* are not split, but go with the vowel following). For the singular, where no distinction existed even in Vulgar Latin between nominative and accusative, there could only be one form. The expected nominative plural (*chevre*) would have been identical with the singular, so it was dropped and the distinctive accusative plural was used. Now both singular and plural consisted of one form apiece.

The remaining noun classes, which did maintain two cases, were affected by a far more drastic change in pronunciation that took place. In French, all unaccented final vowels except *a* were lost: for instance, Latin *cantare* "to sing" > French *chanter*, in which the final -*e* was lost. This was to have extremely far-reaching consequences, and not only for nouns but for verbs as well, and indeed the whole verbal system. As a result, the forms match up in a confusing criss-cross way. The nominative singulars and accusative plurals became identical: both *murus* and *muros* > *murs*, and both *montis* and *montes* > *monz* (*z* representing the sound of /ts/). The accusative singulars and nominative plurals also became identical: both *muru* and *muri* > *mur*, and the nominative plural *montes*, which changed first into *monti and then into *mont*, became indistinguishable from the accusative singular. A speaker might not have been able to tell readily whether *murs* meant "wall" and was the subject of the verb or meant "walls" and was the object.

The instability of such a confusing two-case system led to its collapse. By the thirteenth century, the second and third noun classes followed the example of the first, and operated with just one form for the singular and another for the plural – the situation still obtaining in Modern French.

		Early French		Modern French	
		Singular	Plural	Singular	Plural
First Noun Class	Nominative	*chevre*	*chevres*	*chevre*	*chevres*
	Accusative				
Second Noun Class	Nominative	*murs*	*mur*	*mur*	*murs*
	Accusative	*mur*	*murs*		
Third Noun Class	Nominative	*monz*	*mont*	*mont*	*monts*
	Accusative	*mont*	*monz*		

The two-case system, a long-lasting relic of Latin's declensions, is gone. Only singular and plural remain, and all plurals are uniformly marked by -*s*.

This has important consequences for English as well. In Old English, the language as it was before the influence of French began to be felt (*ca.* 1100), many plurals were formed with -*s*, as they had been in Germanic: *engel* (singular) *englas* (plural) "angel." Yet many Old English plurals were formed in other ways also, with *u, a, e,* or *n*: *lim limu* "limb," *giefu giefa* "gift," *cwen cwene* "queen," *eage eagan* "eye." In time – partly by analogy with nouns like *engel*, and partly under the influence of French (which is to say, ultimately, the influence of Latin) – these native words also came to make their plurals in -*s*: *limbs, gifts, queens, eyes.* Moreover, all new words that have entered the language since then make their plurals the same way. Only a few of the old *s*-less plurals still remain in use, such as *oxen, teeth, mice.* But the handful of exceptions point up the vast success French had in imposing -*s* as a marker of the plural.

The Cases in Spanish and Italian

With Spanish the story is much simpler. No trace of two cases is found. The Latin accusatives, singular and plural, have led directly to the forms of the modern language. Again the plurals are marked by -*s*. This state of affairs is found in the earliest texts and continues today without alteration.

		Vulgar Latin		Spanish	
		Singular	Plural	Singular	Plural
First Noun Class	Nominative	*capra*	*capre*	*cabra*	*cabras*
	Accusative	*capra*	*capras*		
Second Noun Class	Nominative	*murus*	*muri*	*muro*	*muros*
	Accusative	*muru*	*muros*		
Third Noun Class	Nominative	*montis*	*montes*	*monte*	*montes*
	Accusative	*monte*	*montes*		

The Italian forms of nouns, however, present a somewhat differing pattern.

		Vulgar Latin		Italian	
		Singular	Plural	Singular	Plural
First Noun Class	Nominative	*capra*	*capre*	*capra*	*capre*
	Accusative	*capra*	*capras*		
Second Noun Class	Nominative	*murus*	*muri*	*muro*	*muri*
	Accusative	*muru*	*muros*		
Third Noun Class	Nominative	*montis*	*montes*	*monte*	*monti*
	Accusative	*monte*	*montes*		

The singulars derive straightforwardly from the Latin accusatives. The plurals, however, do not end in -*s*. Why is Italian different in this point from the other languages? Whereas the others used the accusative forms for the plurals too, Italian used the nominatives – except for nouns of the third class, which imitated those of the second in their ending, -*i*. The cause of both these divergences from the ruling pattern is the same: the loss of final -*s* in Italian, which occurred in other eastern Romance languages as well. Because of that loss, the Latin accusative plurals were not available to serve as forms distinct from the singulars: *capra* and *capra(s)* would have been the indistinguishable results in the first class, for instance, *muro* and *muro(s)* in the second, *monte* and *monte(s)* in the third. Resort was had, therefore, to the nominatives: *capre*, *muri*. Even so, with nouns of the third class this move would have been of no avail, since both the nominative and accusative plurals ended in -*s*, so the language employed the plural ending of the second noun class: *monti*.

Thus, whereas the Romance languages dropped all of Latin's distinctions between the cases, regarding them as no longer essential, they have retained its distinction between singular and plural. They also continue to make gender distinctions inherited from Latin. Speakers of the languages know whether each noun is masculine or feminine, and they make adjectives agree with them. For those learning the languages, however, this can be an arduous and annoying task – perhaps more annoying because, to English speakers, it seems unnecessary. English, which formerly made distinctions between masculine, feminine, and neuter nouns (as German still does), has shed them in the course of the centuries and gets by nicely without them. Still, the grip of Latin upon the Romance languages remains so strong that this feature has been retained.

Syntax of Nouns

In these ways, the multitudinous forms of Classical Latin's nouns got whittled down to a mere six: singular and plural for each of three noun classes. The most dramatic and most influential change was the eventual loss of all case distinctions. Whereas the loss of two noun classes and one gender required no repair, no compensatory response, because the words affected were simply absorbed into other existing groups, the loss of the cases could not possibly take place without some further alteration in the language. Their function, identifying the grammatical role played by the noun within the sentence, was indispensable to communication. What happened then? The jobs that had been performed by the cases in Classical Latin came to be performed in the Romance languages partly by prepositions and partly by word order. The tasks of the genitive, dative, and ablative cases were taken over by prepositions, and the distinction between the subject and the object of the verb, which had been indicated by the nominative and accusative, was now indicated by word order.

Latin had always had prepositions, but now their role was much expanded. The economy they introduced was this: instead of needing to use a certain specific case whose form differed from one declension to another and from singular to plural as well, the speaker could always use the same preposition along with the sole form of the noun that now remained. How particular prepositions got detailed to replace a particular case makes for an interesting story.

The genitive case, which can almost always be translated in English with "of," expressed several relations in Latin, two of the commonest being possession (*libri Ciceronis* "the books of Cicero, Cicero's books," where *Ciceronis* is genitive) and object of a noun that has some verbal idea (*direptio urbis* "the sack of the city," *urbis* genitive). Although not especially common, another use was to express the whole of which a part was mentioned: *unus amicorum* "one of the friends" (*amicorum* genitive). In Classical Latin, the last could equally well be expressed *unus de amicis*, literally "one from the friends." In one particular situation, then, *unus de amicis* was equivalent to *unus amicorum*, and therein lies the origin of the Romance development.

The restricted equivalence became generalized, so that *de* + noun in time came to be regarded as equivalent to the genitive case in *all* situations – and then speakers had no further use for the genitive, which shriveled up and disappeared. In other words, once a preposition was used, the case endings could fade away. The Romance languages now all use the same preposition for expressing the relationships that the genitive case had formerly expressed in Latin: Spanish *uno de los amigos,* Italian *uno degli amici* (*degli = de +* the definite article *gli*), French *un des amis* (*des = de +* the definite article *les*) "one of the friends"; Spanish *los libros de Cicerón,* Italian *i libri di Cicerone,* French *les livres de Cicéron* "the books of Cicero"; Spanish *el saqueo de la ciudad,* Italian *il saccheggio della città* (*della = de +* the definite article *la*), French *le sac de la ville* "the sack of the city."

The story of how the dative case got replaced is similar. In Latin the dative case most often designated the indirect object of the verb, the person to or for whom something was done ("to" and "for" are the usual English translations): *pecuniam viduae dedit* "she gave money to the widow" (*viduae* dative). In a certain very particular situation, the dative came close in meaning to the preposition *ad* "to, towards" + noun. Consider these two sentences: *litteras Caesari mittit* "he sends a letter for Caesar" (*Caesari* dative), and *litteras ad Caesarem mittit* "he sends a letter to(wards) Caesar" (*ad + Caesarem* accusative). Classical Latin perceives a subtle difference between the two: the former, more abstract, indicates the person for whose benefit the letter was intended (but perhaps it was sent to somebody else, to be handed over to Caesar and read by him), whereas the latter, more concrete, indicates in which direction the letter was sent (but perhaps Caesar was to turn it over to someone else for that person to read).

The difference was evanescent, however, and in time the two sentences were taken to be equivalent, and from this particular situation *ad* + noun was generalized to be the equivalent of the dative case. Today the Romance languages all use *a,* descendant of *ad,* to express the same relationship that had been expressed with Latin's dative case: Spanish *dio dinero a la viuda,* Italian *ha dato danaro alla vedova* (*alla = a +* the definitve article *la*), French *elle a donné d'argent a la veuve* "she gave money to the widow." The dative case too has disappeared.

The ablative case, which expressed a large variety of relations and was already often used with prepositions in Latin, disappeared in the same way. Its place was taken, not by any single preposition, but by a number. To give just one instance, Latin relied on the ablative case alone, without a preposition, to express the means or instrument by which something was done: *gladio interfecti sunt* "they were killed by a sword" (*gladio* ablative). In this situation the modern languages use one or another preposition: Italian *sono stati ammazzati per* (or *con*) *una spada*, Spanish *fueron matados por* (or *con*) *una espada*, French *ils ont été tués par* (or *avec*) *une épée*.

The prepositions that had been used with the ablative began, in Vulgar Latin, to be used with the accusative. In the *Appendix Probi* we already read *vobiscum non voscum* "with you (plural)," in which *cum* is incorrectly joined with the accusative. The same error recurs on an inscription from Pompeii, which therefore was written no later than 79 C.E.: *magister cum suos discentes* "the teacher with his pupils" (more correctly, *cum suis discentibus*).

The accusative thus became the form used for the object of all prepositions as well as for the object of the verb, while the nominative continued to serve as the subject of the verb. French, we saw, maintained a difference between the two cases for a while, but then, like its sister languages, it resorted to a single form, the descendant of the accusative case, for all grammatical functions. When that stage was reached in each language, how could speakers distinguish the subject of the verb from its object? Often, to be sure, the context and common sense made it clear: "the dog bit the man" is a more likely meaning than "the man bit the dog." Soon, however, word order came to be used to clarify matters: the subject could be identified because it preceded the verb, the object because it followed. The marvelous freedom of Latin word order was given up, and instead word order became relatively fixed, as it still is in the Romance languages (and English as well): subject, verb, object. Nowadays, with no cases available, the only thing that distinguishes "Peter killed Paul" from "Paul killed Peter" is the placement of the words. Instead of Latin's numerous forms and flexible word order, the modern languages operate with just two forms of each noun – singular and plural – a larger number of prepositional phrases, and a restricted word order. As far as the nouns are concerned, the Romance languages have become completely analytic: the tasks once performed by the inflections have been taken away from the word itself and assigned to either prepositions or word order.

The story of English is, in this regard, closely parallel. Like every Indo-European language, Germanic was highly inflected, and nearly all its descendants today remain inflected languages. For instance, Modern German still operates with three genders and four cases (although the system is weakening a bit). The great exception is English, which in the course of the centuries, chiefly during the Middle English period, has shed virtually all inflections. And what has taken their place? Prepositions and word order.

ARTICLES AND DEMONSTRATIVES

Latin had no articles, definite or indefinite. *Amicus* could be "friend," "a friend," or "the friend," and the distinctions among the three, which seem no less clear than dear to speakers of modern languages, could not have been drawn by an ancient Roman. But already in the fourth century, the author of the *Pilgrimage to Holy Places* had begun to employ *ille* as a definite article: *toti illi montes,* she wrote, meaning "all the mountains," not, as would have been the case with a writer of Classical Latin, "all those mountains." The usage grew over time, and *ille* "that," one of Latin's demonstratives, ended up supplying our three Romance languages with their definite articles. Depending on which was accented, sometimes the first syllable of the demonstrative provided the article, sometimes the second. The masculine *ille* is the source of the masculine singular articles (as in Italian *il libro*, Spanish *el libro*, but French *le livre* "the book"), as the feminine *illa* is of the feminine singulars (as in Italian *la vacca*, Spanish *la vaca*, French *la vache* "the cow").

The Latin numeral *unus* "one" has given the modern languages their indefinite articles, as in Italian, Spanish *un libro*, French *un livre* "a book," and Italian *una vacca*, Spanish *una vaca*, French *une vache* "a cow." Latin *vacca* "cow," by the way, is the source of *vaccine*, originally a cowpox serum used against smallpox, then a serum injected to fight any disease.

The stories of both the definite and the indefinite articles are the same in English as in the Romance languages. The word *the* originated in Old English as a demonstrative. A trace of this can still be glimpsed in a phrase like "the more, the merrier," originally meaning something like "by this (much) more, by this (much) merrier." The present-day demonstrative *that* is derived from the same. As for the indefinite article, to speakers of the language, *a* is the regular form (*a pear*), whereas *an* is the variant used before words beginning with a vowel (*an apple*). Historically, however, it is the other way around: *an* was the original form, found in Old English, of which *a* emerged as a reduced version. The numeral *one* also derives from *an*.

Classical Latin possessed three demonstrative adjective/pronouns, each of which had a different destiny. *Hic* "this" disappeared utterly. *Ille* "that," by contrast, developed multiple uses in Romance – definite article, object pronoun, third person subject pronoun – but was no longer a demonstrative. The last, *iste* "that (near the person addressed)," has continued on its own as a demonstrative in Spanish: *este* "this." The Latin intensive *ipse* "himself" (as in *rex ipse* "the king himself"), though not a demonstrative, nonetheless also got pressed into service as a Spanish demonstrative: *ese* "that."

But for the rest, the Romance languages have filled out this important class of words by combining various elements. (In what follows, the masculine singular is generally used to represent the full set of forms, masculine and feminine, singular and plural.) In Classical Latin *ecce* (sometimes *eccum*) was a particle meaning "look!, behold!," which naturally lent itself to demonstrative uses. Combined with *ille* (**eccu-illu*), it produced Italian *quello*, Spanish *aquel* "that," and Old French *icel* and *cel*, Modern French *celle* (feminine). Combined with *iste* (**eccu-istu*), it produced Italian *questo* "this" and Old French *icest*, *cest*, Modern French *cette* (feminine).

A curious thing happened to the French demonstratives. Instead of being distinguished by meaning, the *cette* and *celle* sets of forms, which at first had indicated "this" and "that," came to be distinguished by function: *cette* became used as the adjective, *celle* as the pronoun. The division of labor, once effected, created a certain difficulty. All means of distinguishing "this" from "that" were lost, and the distinction is an important one. The solution was to reinforce the demonstrative adjectives and pronouns by tacking an additional syllable on to the end, *-ci* for "this" and *-la* for "that," as in *celle-ci* "this woman (or grammatically feminine thing)" and *celle-la* "that woman." Now, the syllable *-ci* is a reduced, unaccented version of the French adverb *ici* "here," which comes from Latin **ecce-hic*, literally "look here." Thus, *celle-ci* is a boiled-down version of *eccu* + *illa* + *ecce* + *hic*! Once again we may marvel at the incessant movement in which one change in a language entails another, and a solution found often leads to a new difficulty.

ADJECTIVES

As the noun goes, so goes the adjective. The same changes – loss of the neuter gender and reduction of five cases to just one, the accusative – affected both parts of speech. Since Latin adjectives came in only two varieties, one with forms drawn from the first and second declensions (*bonus bona bonum* "good"), the other with forms from the third (*fortis forte* "brave, strong"), the disappearance of the fourth and fifth declensions had no repercussion among the adjectives. The adjective forms remaining were identical with the corresponding forms of the nouns (the chart is to be read down):

	Adjectives from First and Second Declensions				Adjectives from Third Declension	
	Masculine		Feminine		Masculine/Feminine	
	Singular	Plural	Singular	Plural	Singular	Plural
Vulgar Latin	*bonum*	*bonos*	*bonam*	*bonas*	*fortem*	*fortes*
Spanish	*bueno*	*buenos*	*buena*	*buenas*	*fuerte*	*fuertes*
Italian	*buono*	*buoni*	*buona*	*buone*	*forte*	*forti*
French	*bon*	*bons*	*bonne*	*bonnes*	*fort* (m.), *forte* (f.)	*forts* (m.), *fortes* (f.)

The adjectives from Latin's third declension did not distinguish masculine from feminine: one would refer to a *virum fortem* "brave man" in just the same way as a *mulierem fortem* "brave woman." Although Spanish and Italian have kept this, French has not. Instead, intent on distinguishing between masculine and feminine in adjectives of this type too, it has taken from the other type of adjective the ending *-e* that marks the feminine form and applied it to this one. So whereas Spanish *fuerte* and Italian *forte* are masculine as well as feminine, French has *fort* masculine and *forte* feminine. The language, then, has not only maintained Latin's general distinction between the two genders, but has extended it to where it did not exist before.

Though adjectives in Latin did not need to stand directly next to the nouns they modified (because their form indicated which one they went with), in practice they usually did. They appeared after the noun more often than before it, and this tendency grew much stronger in the Romance languages. English and the other Germanic languages, by contrast, tend to place adjectives before their nouns: contrast the title of Flaubert's novel *L'Education sentimentale* with its usual translation, *Sentimental Education*. Nonetheless, English has retained from French a number of legal phrases in which the adjective follows the noun: *attorney general*, *court martial*, *body politic*.

In the comparative and superlative degrees of the Romance adjective there is innovation, not preservation. The innovation is of the revolutionary sort familiar by now – analytic forms replacing synthetic – but nonetheless it is rooted, once again, in Classical Latin. The comparative degree of the adjective was made in Latin by adding the element *-ior-* to the stem: *altum* "tall" > *altiorem* "taller," and *grandem* "big" > *grandiorem* "bigger." This the Romance languages abandoned. Instead, they took as a model a small group of Latin adjectives that, for reasons of euphony, made their comparative by coupling *magis* "more" with the adjective: *idoneum* "suitable" > *magis idoneum* "more suitable" (not *idoneiorem*). The languages turned this into the pattern for virtually all their adjectives, with Spanish relying on *magis* to express "more" and French and Italian on the synonymous *plus*: Spanish *más alto*, French *plus haut*, Italian *più alto* "higher"; Spanish *más grande*, French *plus grand*, Italian *più grande* "bigger." The economies of the analytic form are evident here as well.

By a piquant irony, the only surviving souvenirs of Latin's synthetic comparatives come from a few common adjectives that were irregular in Latin and are irregular in the modern languages too. The irregularity is not the same, however: in Latin, the irregularity was that they were made from a stem other than that of the adjective (which remains true in the modern languages), but in the modern languages these forms appear irregular because they, and they alone, are synthetic. The comparative of Latin *bonum* "good" was not *boniorem*, but rather *meliorem* "better," which is continued in French *meilleur*, Italian *migliore*, Spanish *mejor*; similarly, *malum* "bad" > *peiorem* "worse" > French *pire*, Italian *peggiore*, Spanish *peor*. These anomalous comparatives were probably preserved by sheer frequency of use.

For the superlatives, the modern languages took the new comparatives one step further. To express "biggest," "highest," and so forth, they simply put the definite article in front of the comparative: Spanish *más grande* "bigger" > *el más grande* "biggest"; French *plus grand* > *le plus grand*; Italian *più grande* > *il più grande*. The idea was that such a phrase identified "*the* bigger one," the one bigger than any other; the definite article particularized. This was different from Latin's procedure, which had been to add the element *-issim-* to the adjective: *grandissimum* "biggest," *altissimum* "highest." Though replaced by the new superlatives made with the definite article, the old forms do survive in the Romance language with a different function. Rather than serving as the logical superlative, they now convey the idea of "very" or "highly": Latin *rarum* "rare" > *rarissimum* "rarest" > Italian *rarissimo*, Spanish *rarísimo*, French *rarissime* "very rare, very unusual." These expressive formations are not equally available to speakers of the three languages. Italian and Spanish allow them for any adjective, whereas in French their number is, if not closed, at least limited.

ADVERBS

One of the most curious transformations in the whole history of the Romance languages is that of the adverbs that are made from adjectives. An English equivalent would be *rapidly*, formed from *rapid* with the addition of the suffix *-ly*. In Classical Latin too, adverbs were made by adding a suffix to the stem of the adjective, but the two different types of adjective had each its own suffix. The adjectives of the first and second declensions added *-ē* to the stem (*rapidus* "rapid" > *rapid-ē* "rapidly"), whereas those of the third added *-ter* (*fortis* "brave" > *forti-ter* "bravely"). Our three Romance languages have discarded this in favor of a different procedure: to the feminine form of the adjective they add the suffix *-ment(e)*, which derives from Latin *mentem* "mind." So in place of Latin *rapide* "rapidly" one finds Italian *rapidamente*, Spanish *rápidamente*, French *rapidement*.

How did this come about? The origin is to be found in a particular kind of phrase, a matrix. Latin *rapida mente cogitat* meant "he, she thinks with a rapid mind," which shows a common use of the ablative case, to express manner. This was regarded as equivalent to *rapide cogitat* "he, she thinks rapidly." But once the equivalence was accepted in a context of mental activity, it got generalized, and *rapidamente* began to be used as equivalent to *rapide* in other situations, such as *rapidamente currit* "he, she runs rapidly." At this point all awareness of the original meaning was lost, and the new form was simply the adverb corresponding to the adjective.

Here again one may follow the story and still wonder what caused the old adverbial forms to be abandoned. Given the choice between the traditional *rapide* and the recently developed *rapidamente*, why did speakers ultimately prefer the latter? For one thing, each of Classical Latin's two types of adjectives employed a different adverbial suffix (*rapid-e*, *forti-ter*), whereas the new suffix was added uniformly to all adjectives. Then too the new suffix was more substantial and distinctive than one of the earlier ones (*-e*). These are the likely explanations.

Now it is evident why the feminine adjective is always used in the new adverbial formation: Latin *mentem* was feminine. Also, a certain oddity in the Spanish handling of such adverbs is explained. When two of them are linked, *-mente* is used only once: "clearly and rapidly" comes out in Spanish as *clara y rápidamente* (**claramente y rápidamente* is regarded as unacceptable). In this, we perceive a vestige of the construction's origin, with *mente* a separate word. Finally, *-ment* in French became generalized as an adverbial ending to such a point that it even got added to what was already an adverb, *comme* "as" (< Latin *quomodo* "in what way, how"), resulting in *comment* "how?"

CHAPTER THIRTEEN

THE VERB IN PROTO-ROMANCE

DESCRIPTORS OF VERB FORMS

As Latin developed into the Romance languages, the noun changed drastically. It shed nearly all its many forms, and the grammatical functions that had previously been indicated by those forms came to be indicated instead by completely different means. That was a revolution. The nouns went down a one-way street, toward reduction in number of forms, and the language, in regard to nouns at least, shifted unswervingly from synthetic to analytic. With the verbs, however, the situation is more complex. They too were simplified and regularized. Nonetheless, today they still possess a large number of forms, so, with respect to verbs, the languages remain synthetic. Many forms were altered; certain ones that had been regular in Latin became irregular, and vice versa. Moreover, the verbs, which lost many forms, also added new ones to those they had received from Latin. The picture, therefore, is not of one system overthrowing another, but rather of a system the principle of which was retained, but within which the particular forms changed. Inherited forms now exist along with innovating ones.

Here is an overview of the changes wrought in the verbs. I use the descriptors of verb forms as rubrics and point to the areas of conservatism and innovation.

In Romance verbs, person and number are still mostly marked by the verb form itself; the endings continue to indicate whether the subject is first person or second or third, singular or plural. This is quite true for Italian and Spanish, but much less so for French. In that language, where the final syllables of words were often weakened or dropped, which means the personal endings of verbs often became indistinct, it is necessary to use the subject pronouns to indicate who is performing the action of the verb: *je* for "I," *elle* for "she," and so on.

Thus, whereas Italian and Spanish *canto* means "I sing," the final *-o* declaring the subject to be first person singular, the equivalent in French is *je chante*: the pronoun is required. English resembles French in this matter.

The Romance languages retain the six tenses of Latin's indicative, but often no longer form them in the same way. The present tense of the indicative is similar to Latin, the imperfect somewhat similar. By contrast, the future, pluperfect, and future perfect are completely new. The remaining tense, Latin's perfect, has had a curious, nearly circular history. Its two uses, to express simple preterite ("they sang") and true perfect ("they have sung"), first were handed over to two different forms – one of them the inherited form, the other an innovation – but those in turn, in spoken French and Italian at least, got reduced to a single form again.

Furthermore, some Romance languages have developed progressive tenses, equivalent to "I am singing" or "they were painting," which did not exist in Latin at all. But these, again, are not uniformly available. Progressive tenses are not found in French, yet are used commonly in Spanish, less commonly in Italian. So all the languages added several tenses to those they inherited from Latin, but each possesses a somewhat different set today.

The verbs of the Romance languages still have two voices, active and passive, but Latin's synthetic passive has been eliminated in favor of new analytic forms.

The languages retain the four tenses of Latin's subjunctive, though two of them are now formed in a novel way.

The Romance verb has the same moods as the Latin – indicative, subjunctive, and imperative. To these, all the languages have added what might be considered another mood, the conditional, equivalent to "I would sing." In its origin, the conditional was actually another tense of the indicative, but with time, it has developed such novel uses that it is appropriately regarded now as a separate mood.

As for Latin's various verbal nouns and adjectives, the Romance languages have retained some (present infinitive, perfect passive participle), eliminated some (future participle, the other infinitives), and changed the function of others (present participle, gerund).

Innovations and changes of other sorts are found with the inherited forms, and the innovating forms are all based on usages already existing in Latin – so strong does its influence remain – with the result that the line drawn between inheritance and innovation is not clear-cut but blurry, and serves as a handy device rather than an absolute distinction.

The Verb in Proto-Romance

Inherited Forms

Four Conjugations

Latin possessed four conjugations – that is, four differing sets of verb forms, which were defined by their distinctive infinitives. The first conjugation, the infinitive of which ends in *-āre* (*cantāre* "to sing," for instance), has been very well preserved in the modern languages. In Latin it was well populated and extremely regular in its principal parts and in its many forms. The Romance languages all retain such verbs as a distinct group, which is even more heavily populated today than it was in Latin.

Moreover, the type of the Latin *-āre* verbs is the one type that is still productive today, the only pattern available for newly coined verbs to follow. This may be illustrated with a hypothetical example. It so happens that none of our modern languages has a simple verb to express the notion of "to tip (as a waiter)." Instead, they use phrases meaning "to give (or leave) a tip": French *donner un pourboire*, Spanish *dejar una propina*, Italian *lasciare una mancia*. Let us imagine, though, that each language, wishing to imitate English (as happens all too often), creates a new verb modeled on English "to tip." The results would be Italian **tip-are*, Spanish **tipe-ar*, French **tip-er*, each of these new creations belonging to the language's first type of verb. One may compare the infinitives of the verbs meaning "to sing": Italian *cant-are*, Spanish *cant-ar*, French *chant-er*, all derived from Latin *cantāre*. The infinitive alone is sufficient basis for producing all the remaining forms.

Latin's fourth conjugation has also survived, with infinitive ending in *-īre*, for instance, *dormire* "to sleep," which is continued in Italian *dormire*, Spanish, French *dormir*. The other two have had more checkered fortunes, Latin's second and third conjugations, with infinitives ending in *-ēre* and *-ĕre*, respectively, for instance, *debēre* "to owe" and *véndĕre* "to sell." In Latin these were distinct from one another. In Spanish, however, the two types have fallen together completely – more precisely, the third has been absorbed into the second – so the derived verbs *deber* and *vender* are conjugated entirely alike. The situation is almost identical in Italian, where the two are conjugated alike; the sole difference lies in the infinitives themselves: *dovére* and *véndere*. French in this matter has remained closest to Latin, preserving and distinguishing the two: the French verbs are *devoir* and *vendre*, and they are conjugated differently. Verbs of the *devoir* type, however, derived from

247

Latin's second conjugation, have become so few that they are perceived as irregular.

What has happened in French to the other verbs that once belonged to Latin's second conjugation? Have they disappeared from the language? No, they have switched allegiances, signed up with another conjugation. In Vulgar Latin, quite a few verbs had already changed conjugation. Some passed from the third to the second conjugation at an early date, and not only in Spanish, but across the board. Thus, Latin *sápĕre* "to be wise" (third conjugation) became Vulgar Latin *sapére* (second), as one can tell from Italian *sapére* and French *savoir*. More often, verbs passed from the second conjugation to the third: Classical Latin *respondēre* "to respond" > Vulgar Latin *respóndĕre* > Italian *rispóndere*, French *répondre*. Especially prone to change were verbs ending in *-io*, such as *fugio fúgĕre* "to flee," which joined the sturdier fourth conjugation: in Vulgar Latin it became *fugíre*, whence Italian *fuggire*, French *fuir*, Spanish *huir*.

Indicative

The present indicative of *cantare* "to sing" illustrates the relation between the Latin and the Romance verbs:

Latin *cantare*	Spanish *cantar*	Italian *cantare*	French *chanter*
canto "I sing"	*canto*	*canto*	*je chante*
cantas "you (singular) sing"	*cantas*	*canti*	*tu chantes*
cantat "he, she sings"	*canta*	*canta*	*il, elle chante*
cantamus "we sing"	*cantamos*	*cantiamo*	*nous chantons*
cantatis "you (plural) sing"	*cantáis*	*cantate*	*vous chantez*
cantant "they sing"	*cantan*	*cantano*	*ils, elles chantent*

We notice that final *-t* has nearly disappeared, and in Italian so has final *-s*; the latter change, we recall, affected the Italian nouns. Yet the continuities with Latin, especially in Spanish and Italian, are also clear. The French forms are more remote from the Latin – and indeed, far more remote than the chart conveys, because their appearance is deceptive. When written, nearly all seem to preserve Latin personal endings (Latin *cantant*: French *chantent*), and thus look distinct from one another. In speech, however, *chantent* is pronounced exactly like *chante* as well as *chantes*, so in fact four of the six forms are identical when spoken; hence the need for subject pronouns (and we observe again French's "archaeological" spelling). In the other two languages, the personal endings remain distinct, more faithfully upholding the principle of synthetic verb forms.

All three Romance languages possess many verbs with a certain mysterious quirk in the present tense: the forms of the first and second person plural differ from the other four forms in their base, that is, in the syllable(s) to which the personal endings are added. Schoolteachers sometimes call these "shoe (or boot) verbs" because of the pattern they make on the page. Samples follow (with the pronouns omitted from the French). Each of these represents many more verbs conjugated with the same peculiarity; the Spanish and Italian represent literally hundreds of others.

French *recevoir* "to receive"		Spanish *dormir* "to sleep"		Italian *capire* "to understand"	
reçois	recevons	duermo	dormimos	capisco	capiamo
reçois	recevez	duermes	dormís	capisci	capite
reçoit	reçoivent	duerme	duermen	capisce	capiscono

The bases that do not match are *recev-* (instead of *reçoi-*), *dorm-* (instead of *duerm-*), and *cap-* (instead of *capisc-*). The explanation is the same in every case, and the obstacles this irregularity creates for learners of the languages all arise from a simple, pedestrian fact – the first and second person plural personal endings in Latin consisted of two syllables, not one. This meant that for all verbs (except those of the third conjugation) the accent fell on the first of those two syllables, and therefore not on the base of the verb. You can see this readily in the present of *cantare*:

cánt-o	cant-ámus
cánt-as	cant-átis
cánt-at	cánt-ant

In the case of the other forms, the accent invariably fell on the base and, for one reason or another, altered it; in the first and second person plural, the accent did not alter the base. That the latter forms, despite being in the minority, are the original, genuine ones, is easily shown. The imperfect tense is made from the present, and in every case the first and second person plural supply the base: compare French *je reçev-ais* "I used to receive," Spanish *dorm-ía* "I used to sleep," Italian *cap-ivo* "I used to understand." The true base is also shown in the infinitives: *reçevoir, dormir, capire.*

Subjunctive

In Latin, the difference between the indicative and the subjunctive was significant. The forms were always distinct, and knowing whether to use one or the
other mood in a given syntactic situation was a basic part of mastering the
grammar. That is still the case in Spanish and Italian, but considerably less so
in French – not because the subjunctive is not used in French, but because the
present subjunctive at least is often invisible, that is to say, indistinguishable
from the indicative. (The same is true of English.) The chart suggests to what
extent the indicative and the subjunctive differ from each other in the several
languages (only two conjugations are cited as examples, and only in the third
person plural):

	cantare "to sing" (first conjugation)		*vendere* "to sell" (third conjugation)	
	Present indicative	Present subjunctive	Present indicative	Present subjunctive
Latin	cantant	cantent	vendunt	vendant
Spanish	cantan	canten	venden	vendan
Italian	cantano	cantino	vendono	vendano
French	chantent	chantent	vendent	vendent

In Spanish and Italian, the subjunctive forms differ from those of the indicative,
whereas in French they do not. A reminder of this last is contained in the
phrase *Vive le roi!* "May the king live!" (or "Long live the king!"), where *vive* is
a subjunctive expressing a wish: yet *vive* is also the indicative, as in *le roi vive*
"the king lives."

By contrast with the present, the other inherited tense of the subjunctive
is distinctive, always unmistakable in all the languages. What had been the
pluperfect subjunctive in Latin became the imperfect subjunctive in Spanish,
French, and Italian (the example is cited in the third person plural): Latin
canta(vi)ssent (even in Classical Latin, the syllable *-vi-* was often dropped) >
Spanish *cantasen*, French *chantassent*, Italian *cantassino*. We observe here too
the fidelity of the modern languages to Latin.

Participles

The two commonest participles in Latin were the present active (*cantantem*
"singing") and the perfect passive (*cantatum* "having been sung"). Both have

survived into the modern languages, but the present participle performs a different function now and has been replaced in its participial function by something else. Both the old perfect passive and the new present active participles have thrived because they do more jobs than they used to.

Many Latin present participles have survived, or been re-created, as adjectives in the Romance languages (and in English too). They are no longer truly verbal adjectives, however. The tie has been loosened between them and the verbs that originally produced them. They may no longer be perceived as derived from the verbs, and the languages are not free to produce such adjectives any more. A good example is the Latin present participle *currentem* "running," derived from *currere* "to run," and surviving in Italian *corrente,* Spanish *corriente,* French *courant.* Today, however, these are adjectives that mean, not "running," but rather "of the present time; usual, common," as in "current affairs, current practice." Despite the shift in meaning, they are still seen as related to the verbs meaning "to run." The same is scarcely true of the Romance words for "adjacent": French *adjacent,* Italian *adiacente,* Spanish *adyacente.* These go back to Latin *adjacentem* "lying near" (< *ad* "near" + *jacere* "to lie"), yet none of the modern languages possesses a verb descended from *adjacere* to which the adjectives could be attached, and in several languages even the simple, underlying verb derived from *jacere* is not easy to recognize: French *gésir* : *(ad)jacent,* Italian *giacere* : *(ad)iacente,* but Spanish *yacer* : *(ad)yacente.*

As adjectives, participles may also serve sometimes as nouns. Thus, *currentem* "running," with *aquam* "water" understood, came to be a noun in its own right. The Romance words for "current" (as of a river) are Italian *corrente,* Spanish *corriente,* French *courant.*

Such words, though historically derived from Latin present participles, no longer function as such. What then has taken their place? The ablative of the Latin gerund has, and the story of how this happened is engaging – and, in outline, familiar to us. It resembles the process by which Latin's genitive and dative cases got replaced by the prepositions *de* and *ad*: a narrow, particular near-equivalency that existed within Classical Latin was expanded beyond its proper bounds.

In a Latin sentence like *docentes discimus* "while teaching, we learn," the present participle *docentes,* strictly speaking, merely denotes that the teaching goes on at the same time as the learning. But the Romans often attributed to participles some other force beyond the temporal, such as causal (*docentes* might connote "because of teaching") or instrumental ("by teaching"). When the participle was used with instrumental force – and only then – the expression was equivalent to *docendo discimus*, in which *docendo* is the Latin verbal noun known as the gerund and is used in the ablative case to express means: "by means of teaching we learn." In time, *docendo* came to be considered equivalent to *docentem* in all usages, and then it replaced it as the present participle. The new present participle of Romance can be recognized in a pair of musical terms of direction derived from Italian: *crescendo* "increasing (in volume)" and *glissando* "sliding (the fingers or the bow)."

In the modern languages, the participle may be used freely to convey information about a person or thing referred to in the sentence: Italian *i ragazzi andavano alla scuola cantando*, Spanish *los muchachos andaban a la escuela cantando*, French *les garçons allaient à l'école chantants* "the boys used to go to school singing" (where *cantando* and *chantants* "singing" are the present participles). Though the form of the present participle is different, the employment of it in such sentences is the same as it had been in Latin.

In Italian and Spanish, the Latin present participle got converted into a pure adjective (*cantante*). That it no longer is a participle can be demonstrated in a couple of ways. Such words can no longer take objects, and verbs are no longer free to produce them. Whereas Latin *jocare* "to joke" could produce a present participle *jocantem*, the corresponding Italian and Spanish verbs (which now mean "to play") cannot: neither can Italian *giocare* produce **giocante*, nor Spanish *jugar* produce **jugante*. To replace the present participle, both languages put the Latin gerund (*cantando*) into service. The same happened in French, but the difference between the participle and the gerund is concealed from the ear and the eye because the two forms turned out identical: *cantantem* > *chantant*, and *cantando* > *chantant*. Nonetheless, the gerund is still alive in French as a verbal noun, in that the *-ant* form can be the object of a preposition, particularly (and very commonly) *en* "in": *en enseignant nous aprenons* "in teaching we learn."

Spanish and Italian were also to use the present participle to create the set of progressive tenses, as we shall see.

The perfect passive participle experienced much smaller changes than the present active. In general, its form did not alter very much. One can grasp the range of possibilities by considering the fate of a single Latin verb, *fundere* "to pour," the past participle of which is *fusus* "having been poured." The three languages exemplify three different patterns. Italian has retained the two forms of this verb almost unchanged – *fondere fuso* – which is the commonest pattern for Latin past participles in all the languages. Spanish has ignored the Latin participle and regularized the form to accord with the rest of the verb: *hundir hundido* (the usual pattern for verbs in -*ir*: *vivir vivido*, for instance); of this too there are many examples. French has also replaced the Latin participle, with a novel formation: *fondre fondu*.

That verb is interesting also from an etymological point of view, since it shows a variety of semantic developments, both within Classical Latin and between Latin and the Romance languages. Its original meaning was "to pour (as a liquid)," then, when applied to metals, "to cast, found," and, in a more general sense, "to spread" (compare *diffuse*); from the last it also came to mean "to rout (as an enemy)." In Spanish, which stressed the idea of scattering, diminishing, *hundir* now signifies "to destroy; to sink," the latter meaning probably influenced by (false) association with *hondo* "deep." Italian and French have taken the verb in a different direction, fastening on to the idea of liquifying: in those languages it means "to melt," as can be seen in French-derived *fondue*, a dish of melted cheese.

The French participle *fondu* is also an example of the most striking general change in the form of the past participles: both French and Italian created many that ended in -*utu*. Thus, from Latin *habere habitus* "to have" are derived, on the one hand, Spanish *haber habido*, faithful to Latin, and, on the other, Italian *avere avuto* and French *avoir eu*, in both of which the participle has been remodeled and the unhistorical -*u*- is evident. Such participles were based on a few Latin verbs in which the -*u*- was actually part of the stem, for instance, *tribuere tributus* "to apportion, grant." An English word that reflects this change (more distinctly to the ear than the eye) is *view*, from French *vu*, the past participle of *voir* "to see" (compare *déja vu* "already seen"). So the English words *fondue* and *view* are reminders of such altered past participles. A few other examples: *menu* < French *menu* "small, detailed" < Latin *minuere minutus* "to make smaller" (here the *u* belongs to the original stem; *minute*, adjective and noun, comes from the same source, as does *diminish*); *due* < Old French *deü* < Latin *debere debitus* "to owe"; *issue* < French *issue* < Old French *eissue* < *exuta* < Latin *exita* "outcome"; *tissue* < French *tissue* < Latin *texere textus* "to weave" (compare *texture, text, context*); *venue* < French *venu* < Latin *venire ventus* "to come," the English term having in recent years made its way from the language of lawyers into the population at large.

The perfect passive participles are used in the same ways as in Latin. But in addition to their inherited functions, they have acquired two others, which make them even commoner than they were. These participles combine with auxiliary verbs to form the Romance languages' analytic passive voice and their new set of compound past tenses.

Irregular Verbs

Two verbs irregular in all the modern languages require some attention because they are so heavily used as auxiliaries. The verb *habere* "to have" was regular in Latin, but became much less so when worn down through constant use. The verb *esse* "to be" was already anomalous in Latin.

Though many forms of the latter verb's indicative were altered, by analogy or for other reasons, many remain close to the Latin, as is particularly clear with the third person forms of the present: Latin *est* "he, she, it is" > French *est*, Spanish *es*, Italian *è*; and Latin *sunt* "they are" > French *sont*, Spanish *son*, Italian *sono*. To this verb, Spanish and Italian have added another that means "to be," derived from Latin *stare* "to stand": Italian *stare*, Spanish *estar*. One of the great difficulties for English speakers learning either of those languages is knowing when to use one of the verbs and when to use the other, for they are not interchangeable. French too has made use of *stare*, not as a separate verb, but to supplement the other forms of "to be": the infinitive *être*, for instance, < Old French *estre* (compare *raison d'être* "reason for being").

Habere "to have" has survived in all the languages, but only in drastically reduced forms. This happened because, used as an auxiliary, it regularly appeared before the main part of the verb, which received the accent; as a result, *habere* itself tended to be unaccented, and so more vulnerable. The first person singular *habeo* "I have," for instance, probably became in Vulgar Latin first /avyo/ and then /ayo/. The chart, which will be helpful later in connection with the future tense, shows the changes in this important verb.

Latin	Italian	Spanish	French
habeo "I have"	*ho*	*he*	*(j')ai*
habes "you (singular) have"	*hai*	*has*	*(tu) as*
habet "he, she, it has"	*ha*	*ha*	*(il, elle) a*
habemus "we have"	*abbiamo*	*hemos*	*(nous) avons*
habetis "you (plural) have"	*avete*	*habéis*	*(vous) avez*
habent "they have"	*hanno*	*han*	*(ils, elles) ont*

We observe again with all three languages that the first and second person plural forms, because longer, are less altered than the others, somewhat truer to the Latin.

INNOVATING FORMS

The Romance languages dropped a number of verb forms that had existed in Latin – most conspicuously the future tense and the synthetic passive voice – and so needed to fill those spaces. The languages also wanted to express things that it had not been possible to express before, such as actions still in progress, and so they created new forms for these purposes. A more accurate way to describe these changes, avoiding personification and more faithfully representing the actual course of events, would be to say that the languages developed novel means of expression, which, after rivalling, in time came to replace or supplement those already existing. The new did not follow the death of the old; rather, the appeal of the new helped the old into its grave. The various innovating forms that are found today, whether filling gaps in Latin's system or expanding it, nonetheless are themselves built of material provided by Latin, like edifices constructed of stones that have been taken from the ruins of earlier edifices on the same site.

Analytic Passive

In the tenses of the present system, Latin verbs formed the passive voice by employing personal endings that were different from those of the active. Whereas *vendi-t*, for instance, meant "he, she, it sells," *vendi-tur* meant "he, she, it is sold": the ending *-tur* marks the passive. All such synthetic forms, for the imperfect and future tenses as well as the present, were jettisoned over the years. Their place was taken by a combination of words: the verb "to be" plus the past participle. "The book is sold" comes out like this in the Romance languages: French *le livre est vendu*, Italian *il libro è venduto*, Spanish *el libro es vendido*. To change the tense of the compound, you need only to change the tense of the auxiliary "to be." The participle agrees with the subject of the verb. Thus, to express "the houses are sold" we would say, because "houses" is feminine and plural: French *les maisons sont vendues*, Italian *le case sono vendute*, Spanish *las casas son vendidas*, where *-es*, *-e*, and *-as* are the feminine plural endings.

A construction similar to this had existed in Latin, to be sure. The perfect passive participle had regularly been joined with the present of "to be," but that combination constituted the *perfect* passive tense, not the present passive: Latin *liber est venditus* meant "the book *was* sold." The Romans strongly felt the pastness of the participle, so a literal version of the phrase might be "the book is in-a-state-of-having-been-sold," which is close to "was sold." In time, the pastness of the participle grew dimmer in the consciousness of speakers, and the participle was felt to have a merely passive meaning, so combining it with the present of "to be" yielded the *present* passive; with the future of "to be," it yielded the future passive, and so on.

The new analytic passive was preferred to the old synthetic passive because it was easier to produce. All the passive personal endings, *-tur* and the others, could be ignored, as could the differences between the conjugations in the formation of the various tenses. The same familiar auxiliary "to be" was used for all verbs, together with the past participle, a single form for each verb, and requiring only modest, easy adjustments for gender and number.

Compound Perfect

Another innovation driven by ease was the creation of a different perfect system, and here too Latin's synthetic forms got replaced by analytic. Latin possessed a series of tenses built on the perfect stem: from *cantare cantavi*, for instance, *cantav-imus* "we sang, we have sung" (perfect) and *cantav-eramus* "we had sung" (pluperfect). Though these tenses were easier to handle than those of the present system because the endings were the same for all verbs, regardless of conjugation, nonetheless in time, rival forms appeared.

The new forms created in the Romance languages were compounds, combinations of the auxiliary *habere* "to have" with the past participle, combinations which, once again, grew out of constructions found in Latin. In a sentence like *bonus servus linguam domitam habet* "the good slave has (his) tongue tamed," *habet* has its usual meaning of "have," and the perfect passive participle *domitam* "tamed" acts like an adjective, modifying *linguam* "tongue." Such a phrase did not specify by whom or by what the tongue was tamed, yet the possessor was naturally understood to be the originator of the state of affairs – the slave was responsible for taming his tongue. Such a phrase, moreover, which originally described the present ("has a tongue . . ."), nevertheless, because of the reference to a past event implicit in the participle ("a tongue that has been tamed"), came to be understood as a past tense. And so *linguam domitam habet* became equivalent, or nearly equivalent, to *linguam domuit* "tamed his tongue," where *domuit* is the perfect tense. Relying on English, we could say that it was the small step from "has his tongue tamed" to "has tamed his tongue."

At first the new combination had its proper force as a true perfect – "he has tamed his tongue (and it remains so now)" – and thus represented an addition to Latin's set of tenses. A perfect form like *cantaverunt,* had represented either a simple preterite ("they sang") or a true perfect ("they have sung") – the Romans had no way to distinguish between the two. Now, however, all three Romance languages had come to possess separate forms for these two meanings: the inherited Latin form served as the preterite (Spanish *cantaron,* Italian *cantarono,* French *ils chantèrent* "they sang"), and the newly created compound form served as the perfect (Spanish *han cantado,* Italian *hanno cantato,* French *ils ont chanté* "they have sung"). This may be considered an improvement over Latin, in that it makes a helpful distinction possible.

This welcome state of affairs did not persist everywhere, however. Speakers of Spanish (more so in Europe than America) still have the two tenses available for their use, as we do in English. But in early modern times, the inherited perfect forms dropped out of use in spoken Italian and French, leaving the new compound to perform both tasks alone. As a result, those languages, at least in oral use, have regressed to the situation of Latin: the innovating, compound perfect form they created now does duty as both perfect and preterite, which therefore can no longer be distinguished from one another.

Once the new combination was accepted as a past tense, it got extended. Just as, when combined with the participle, the present of *habere* yielded a perfect tense, so the imperfect yielded a pluperfect (*habebat domitam* "he had tamed"). Similar combinations also produced other new forms: the future perfect, two tenses of the subjunctive (replacing Latin's perfect and pluperfect subjunctives), and the past conditional. The new compound verb forms obviously play a prominent role in the languages today.

The modern auxiliary verbs descended from Latin *habere* are Spanish *haber,* Italian *avere,* French *avoir.* While the Italian and French verbs also function in their own right, meaning "to have," the Spanish is now exclusively an auxiliary (except for the existential *hay* "there is, there are"), and the word for "to have" is *tener* (< Latin *tenere* "to grasp, hold"). The strong similarity of Latin *habere* to English *have,* both in sound and in auxiliary duty, might tempt you to believe they are connected. In fact, they are not. The Latin verb that is cognate with English *have* (compare German *haben*) is *capere* "to take, seize:" as for the correspondence of the initial letters, we may compare English *hide* and its Latin cognate *cutis*, or *hurry* and *currere*.

French and Italian, furthermore, possess a number of intransitive verbs – that is to say, verbs that cannot take a direct object – which form the compound past tenses, not with "to have," but with "to be" (Italian *essere*, French *être*): Italian *lei è venuta*, French *elle est venue* "she has come, she came." In these cases, the participle agrees with the subject (-*a* and -*e* are the feminine singular endings), and it retains a sense of pastness, as if to say "she is in-a-state-of-having-come." Usage in older English was similar: compare the biblical "the Savior is risen."

Future and Conditional

Perhaps the most unusual innovation among the tenses of the Romance verb was with the future. The Latin way of forming the future was completely lost. The future tense, in general, is vulnerable and by nature somewhat uncertain in its reference. It is often expressed through a periphrasis, as in English: *they will march*, where the auxiliary *will* originally expressed volition. The Latin future, moreover, presented extra difficulties, since, depending on which conjugation the verb belonged to, the future was formed according to two different patterns: we may contrast *lauda-bit* "he, she will praise" with *duc-et* "he, she will lead," where the markers of the future are -*bi*- and -*e*-. Furthermore, as the sounds of *b* and *v* converged, certain future forms became liable to confusion with the perfect: *laudabit laudabimus* "he, she will praise, we will praise" and *laudavit laudavimus* "he, she has praised, we have praised."

The Romance future arose, like the English future, from a periphrasis, of which we caught a glimpse in the *Pilgrimage to the Holy Lands*. The author wrote *traversare habebamus* "we had to cross," in which the infinitive was combined with *habere* to express obligation, just like *have* plus infinitive in English. In Vulgar Latin and then the Romance languages, this combination passed by an easy step from obligation to simple futurity, from what one needed to do to what one was going to do. The phrase cited from the *Pilgrimage* has not yet reached that stage, but an unmistakable early instance of the combination serving as a future is found in the author's contemporary, Jerome, who says "the men who will be born will not be able to know the things that are done now" (*On Ecclesiastes* 1); the phrase translated "will be born" is *nasci habent*, originally meaning "have to be born."

As Vulgar Latin became the Romance languages, the auxiliary *habere* got soldered onto the end of the infinitive instead of remaining a separate word and preceding the other part, as in the compound perfect tenses; this created a new, one-word form. Thus, the Romance words for "I will sleep" are Spanish *dormiré* (< the infinitive *dormir*), Italian *dormirò* (< *dormire*), French *je dormirai* (< *dormir*). Comparing the present tense of *habere* in the modern languages with the endings of the future shows the relationship unmistakably.

Italian		Spanish		French	
Present of *avere*	Future endings	Present of *haber*	Future endings	Present of *avoir*	Future endings
ho	-ò	he	-é	(j')ai	-ai
hai	-ai	has	-ás	(tu) as	-as
ha	-à	ha	-á	(il, elle) a	-a
abbiamo	-emo	hemos	-emos	(nous) avons	-ons
avete	-ete	habéis	-éis	(vous) avez	-ez
hanno	-anno	han	-án	(ils, elles) ont	-ont

A few traces are still to be found of the earlier stage, when *habere* had not yet been soldered to the infinitive and the two words were still independent. Old Spanish provides several instances. In the *Cid* (verse 124) we read *darvos he mis fijas*, literally "give-you I-will my daughters," or "I will give you my daughters." In Modern Spanish, nothing can separate the two parts of the verb (*dar... he*), and for "I will give" we can only say *daré*.

This novel formation of the future led in turn to a further innovation, one perhaps even more noteworthy, in that it did not replace a tense of Latin that was lacking, but added one that Latin had never possessed. The Romance languages joined the infinitive to a *past* tense of *habere* to form a future-in-the-past. A combination that at first meant "she had to sing" soon came to mean "she was going to sing, she would sing," as in "she said that she would sing": French *elle a dit qu'elle chanterait*, Italian *lei ha detto che canterebbe*, Spanish *ella dijo que cantaría*, where *chanterait*, *canterebbe*, and *cantaría* are the novel forms in question. These verb forms refer to the future as viewed from a past moment (established here by "she said"); they stand in the same relation to the past as the future does to the present: compare "she says that she will sing."

Again, it is easy to recognize the relation between the past tense of the auxiliary and the endings of the new tense, which is called the "conditional."

Italian		Spanish		French	
Preterite of *avere*	Conditional endings	Imperfect of *haber*	Conditional endings	Imperfect of *avoir*	Conditional endings
ebbi	*-ei*	*había*	*-ía*	*(j')avais*	*-ais*
avesti	*-esti*	*habías*	*-ías*	*(tu) avais*	*-ais*
ebbe	*-ebbe*	*había*	*-ía*	*(il, elle) avait*	*-ait*
avemmo	*-emmo*	*habíamos*	*-íamos*	*(nous) avions*	*-ions*
aveste	*-este*	*habíais*	*-íais*	*(vous) aviez*	*-iez*
ebbero	*-ebbero*	*habían*	*-ían*	*(ils, elles) avaient*	*-aient*

The original force of this tense was to express a future-in-the-past. Later it came to be used – and indeed used far more often – to express a conditional truth, what would happen under certain circumstances; hence the name "conditional." "With more money, I would buy a new car" is an example of this use: Italian *con più soldi comprarei una macchina nuova*, Spanish *con más dinero compraría un coche nuevo*, French *avec plus d'argent j'acheterais une voiture neuve*, where *comprarei*, *compraría*, and *acheterais* are conditional. A third, related employment of the conditional is to make less categorical statements and requests, such as "I would like to say something": Italian *vorrei dire qualcosa*, Spanish *querría decir algo*, French *je voudrais dire quelque chose*, where *vorrei*, *querría*, and *voudrais* are conditionals. The auxiliary *would*, which in origin was the past tense of *will*, performs the same three functions in English as the conditional does in the Romance languages.

Progressive Tenses

Italian and Spanish use the present participle in a novel way. They often join it with one of the verbs *to be* (Italian *stare*, Spanish *estar*) to form progressive tenses of the verb, which indicate actions in the course of occurring: Italian *stiamo provando i vini*, Spanish *estamos probando los vinos* "we're trying the wines" (*provando* and *probando* "trying"). Such a combination, though found occasionally, was irregular and unusual in Latin. In Italian and Spanish (and in English as well) it is common, and represents an innovation in the verb system, an expansion of its expressive possibilities. Progressive tenses do not exist in French.

SYNTAX OF VERBS

Despite the many alterations in the forms of verbs between Latin and the Romance languages, the uses of the verb have not changed substantially. In regard to the tenses of the indicative, the strange fate of the compound perfect has been described: today only Spanish can still distinguish in speech between the simple preterite ("I sang") and the true perfect ("I have sung"). Moreover, for different populations of Spanish speakers the perfect has developed different applications. In American Spanish *he cantado* is closely equivalent to English "I have sung," indicating continuity of a past action into a period that includes the present. In the Spanish of Spain, however, the same tense conveys simple recentness: in practice, it refers to an event that took place since the previous midnight.

Many uses of the subjunctive in Latin mentioned earlier have persisted in the modern languages, such as with clauses expressing purpose: Latin *haec dico ut sint liberi* "I say this so that they may be free" > Spanish *digo esto para que sean libres*, Italian *dico questo per che siano liberi*, French *je dis cela pour qu'ils soient libres*, where *ut, para que, per che*, and *pour que* are conjunctions introducing a purpose clause, and *sint, sean, siano*, and *soient* are subjunctives. Nonetheless, on the one hand, a number of classical uses of the subjunctive have been lost, such as in indirect questions, and, on the other, the modern languages, Italian and Spanish especially, have extended the use of the subjunctive to grammatical situations that did not require it before, such as expressions of emotion, judgment, and uncertainty.

And so the modern languages do not stand still, but continue to evolve. They have, to be sure, created new forms, for the verbs at least, and new possibilities of expression. Yet for the most part they have reduced the number of different forms required, dramatically in the case of the nouns, and they have moved away from being highly synthetic languages and towards being analytic. Which is to say that they are still participating in a process that goes back beyond Latin to Indo-European itself.

PART FOUR

EARLIEST TEXTS AND FUTURE DIRECTIONS, OR WHERE THE LANGUAGES DIVERGE

CHAPTER FOURTEEN

FRENCH

DIVERGENCE OF THE ROMANCE LANGUAGES

The final section introduces a few of the earliest texts preserved in each of the languages, and there it stops; to go beyond would be to write the separate histories of French, Italian, and Spanish. The early documents enlighten our understanding in two ways: they illustrate through concrete, textual instances the changes described in the previous section, and at the same time they reveal the individual characteristics that have already emerged in the nascent languages. They make clear, that is, both the features that the three languages share and the ways in which they were already diverging from one another.

The texts I've chosen are far from being dreary embodiments of historical changes. They are flesh-and-blood documents of human life, varied in nature and intrinsically interesting, each with its own special story and particular setting – oaths exchanged between royal brothers, a hymn to a virgin martyr, legal proceedings over land ownership, a confessional formula, a song in praise of Creation, a primitive dictionary, a stirring epic poem. One particular source of interest is the creativity displayed by several of the writers as they struggle with the problem of representing novel sounds by means of the Latin alphabet they have inherited.

Now that the similarities among the languages have been sketched, it is the turn of the differences to stand in the spotlight. Several questions force themselves upon our attention. Why didn't Latin remain the same? What caused it to diverge, to develop into such different varieties in different regions? Some pieces of the answers have been provided earlier. We may consider first those guiding dimensions of human existence, time and space. Space certainly plays a part in language change. When groups who originally spoke the same or a similar language lose contact with one another – whether because of migration, or because geographic, political, or cultural barriers keep neighbors apart – each group, feeling less bound now by their common inheritance, is likely to develop its own speech without regard for the others.

Language divergence may also be impelled by historical events. One group conquers another, which speaks a different language. Whichever language wins out in the end, the other – the substrate (of the defeated) or the superstrate (of the conquerors) – may still exert influence on it. In the realm of vocabulary, for example, we identified some of the Celtic words found in Latin and the other tongues and some of the Iberian words in Spanish. It may seem natural for the defeated to bring over into the speech of their conquerors features of their own familiar speech, but in fact, outside of the lexicon, the evidence of such influence is not strong. Pronunciation is the area in which it is most likely to be felt (which in turn may affect forms and syntax), and a persuasive instance of superstrate influence is the heaviness of the Germanic stress accent, on account of which the Franks caused French words to lose many inherited sounds. The rise of Francien and Castilian as national standards obviously has much to do with political power.

Social and cultural prestige do not always attach to those who are politically dominant, however, as the adoption of Tuscan as the basis for the Italian national standard reminds us. It was mentioned earlier that when within a community two linguistic features – two words, two forms, two sounds, and so forth – come to be regarded as equivalent, one of the factors that may affect the outcome is the prestige belonging to one of the rivals. So social life too may work to make languages different from one another.

Despite the geographic and political obstacles to contact and interchange during late antiquity and the Middle Ages – the very opposite of the current situation – the various towns, regions, and (later) countries were not completely isolated. The different groups did influence one another, and some of the similarities between languages resulted from parallel, but independent developments. Nonetheless, with the passage of time, the various factors described have tended to differentiate the languages.

The early modern period was a watershed in these stories. At the same time, as the various languages began to be associated with nationhood, differences between them came to be perceived more sharply. Soon attempts were being made to codify the individual languages, to standardize them, and these attempts, focused more on writing than speech, tended to eliminate variety and, in particular, to condemn variations that were not prestigious. This drive – toward a certain narrowness, in effect – also contributed to making the languages more different from one another.

POLITICAL HISTORY OF FRANCE

A simple outline of that segment of French history that concerns us might be pegged to the succession of royal dynasties. The Merovingian dynasty, which reigned from about 455 to 751, was responsible for establishing the Frankish people in what would become France. Under them the Romans remaining in Gaul were defeated first, then the Visigoths, and finally the Burgundians – all within a half century. After that, the borders of modern Romance speech in northern Europe were more or less settled. Among the Carolingians, the dynasty that succeeded them, the greatest ruler was Charlemagne, who during his long reign (768–814) expanded the Frankish Empire to include what are today northeastern Spain (in his day, the Frankish March), northern and central Italy, Austria, most of Germany, and the Low Countries. The kingdom did not survive intact after his death, however, but began to break apart; indeed, the subsequent struggles among his heirs are the setting for the earliest document in French. Like the other Carolingian kings, Charlemagne moved about in his realm, carrying the peripatetic court to a series of seats, his favorite being Aachen.

The succeeding dynasty, the Capetians, was the last. The monarchy under their rule began in 987 and continued under that of its related branches, the Valois and the Bourbons, until 1848. The dynasty began with the election as king of Hugh Capet, Duke of Île-de-France, which is the northern central part of the country. Capet was not more powerful than some of his nominal vassals – the Duke of Normandy, for instance. In time, however, the Capetian kings expanded their power and succeeded in making France a land governed strongly from the center. Several policies contributed to this result. The Capetian kings allied themselves with the Church and became the court of appeal in judicial cases, thus securing to themselves the forces of law and religion, and, unlike the Carolingians, they fixed their capital firmly, at Paris, the principal city of Île-de-France. The royal court and the law courts were located there, and also those schools that, in the twelfth century, would become the

University of Paris. Moreover, the spiritual heart of the kingdom, the Abbey of St. Denis, lay close by. With Paris the cultural as well as the political center of France, it was natural that the speech of that region eventually became the national standard. Although Provençal continued to thrive south of the Loire, and Franco-Provençal was still spoken to the southeast, and a Celtic language (Breton) survived on the Brittany peninsula, and the Normans developed their own distinct dialect, nonetheless the language of Paris became dominant over all. It was the language used for official purposes in law, administration, religion, and intellectual life. It was regarded as prestigious in private life too. Curiously, literature first flourished on Gallic soil in other varieties of speech – in the northern dialects and especially Provençal.

Thus, the Merovingians defined the territory of Romance speech in Gaul, the Carolingians defended it, and the Capetians determined which variety would prevail there.

THE STRASBOURG OATHS

Text and Setting

The Strasbourg Oaths, which were exchanged by two kings and their armies in the year 842, though recorded within a history written in Latin, are quoted by the author in their original languages, French and German. Whereas the German versions of the Oaths hold some slight linguistic interest on account of the early date – many other early German texts are known – the French versions are remarkable and priceless: they constitute the oldest substantial text in any Romance language. The historical moment is significant as well. The setting for the narrative is the conflict among grandsons of Charlemagne, three brothers struggling to retain the parts of their grandfather's empire they have inherited. By means of the Oaths, Louis the German, who rules the eastern, German-speaking lands, and Charles the Bald, who rules the western, French-speaking lands, reaffirm their alliance against the third brother, Lothair, located in the middle. The kings each take their oath in the language of the *other's* subjects, in order to create the most wide-spread confidence in the alliance (a similar desire probably prompted the historian to record the Oaths as precisely as he did); their followers then take an oath in their own language. The historian himself, named Nithard, is a notable figure too: he is another grandson of

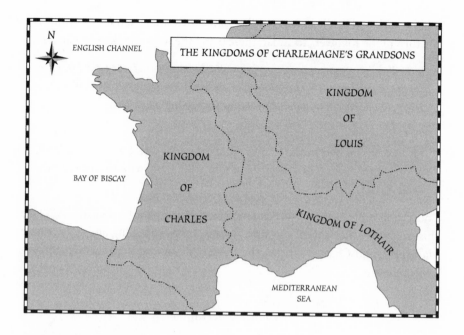

THE KINGDOMS OF CHARLEMAGNE'S GRANDSONS

Charlemagne and a cousin to the brothers, who set down his account within a year or two of the events.

Composed in Latin, the passage begins: "And when Charles had made these same declarations in Romance (*romana lingua*), Louis, because he was the elder, was the first to swear that he would observe them." It then quotes the first set of oaths:

> *Pro Deo amur et pro christian poblo et nostro commun salvament, d'ist di in avant, in quant Deus savir et podir me dunat, si salvarai eo cist meon fradre Karlo et in aiudha et in cadhuna cosa, si cum om per dreit son fradra salvar dift, in o quid il mi altresi fazet, et ab Ludher nul plaid nunquam prindrai, qui, meon vol, cist meon fradre Karle in damno sit.*

"For the love of God and for the salvation of the Christian people and our common salvation, from this day forward, so far as God gives me knowledge and power, thus will I succor this my brother Charles with aid and every thing as one ought by right to succor his brother, on condition that he do likewise to me, and never will I undertake any agreement with Lothair which, to my knowledge, may be of harm to this my brother Charles."

After Charles takes the corresponding oath in German (*teudisca lingua*), it is
the turn of the followers to swear, these being the words spoken by Charles's:

*Si Lodhuuigs sagrament que son fradre Karlo jurat conservat et Karlus, meos
sendra, de suo part lo fraint, si io returnar non l'int pois, ne io ne neuls cui eo
returnar int pois, in nulla aiudha contra Lodhuuuig nun li iu er.*

"If Louis keeps the oath that he has sworn to his brother Charles, and Charles,
my lord, for his part breaks it, if I cannot deter him therefrom, neither I nor
anyone else whom I can deter therefrom will be of any assistance to him
against Louis."

Louis's followers swear to the same effect, and the passage concludes: "Once
this was done, they set off towards Worms, Louis travelling along the Rhine
via Speyer, and Charles skirting the Vosges Mountains and passing through
Wissembourg."

Detailed Observations

Before noting general features of the text, we need to examine it phrase by
phrase, in which format, supplemented by some notes, it is surprisingly easy
to follow even if you know no French. My translations here are more literal
than in the continuous version, and I omit the asterisk that signals unattested
forms.

- *Pro Deo amur* "For of-God the-love." *Deo* "of God" comes from Latin's
  accusative case (< *Deum*), which by now has taken over the functions of
  all the cases except the nominative; here it represents the genitive. From
  this point on, it is appropriate to alter our terminology and call it the
  "oblique case" rather than the accusative.
- *et pro christian poblo et nostro commun salvament* "and for (the salvation)
  of-the-Christian people and our common salvation." *Salvament* "salvation" goes with both the noun phrase *christian poblo* and the adjective
  phrase *nostro commun*. *Poblo* "of the people" expresses the notion of
  "of," like *Deo* above; the *p* between vowels has changed to its voiced
  equivalent *b*, and, as a result of syncope, the syllable following the accent
  has been lost: *populum* > *pób(u)lo* > *poblo*.
- *d'ist di in avant* "from this day on forward." *D'* is the preposition *de*
  "of, from" elided before a following word that begins with a vowel. *Di*

"day" < *diem*; the Modern French word, *jour* is derived from the corresponding adjective, *diurnum*, originally meaning "daily." *In avant* is an adverbial phrase; *avant* "forward" < *ab* "from" + *ante* "in front"; compare *avant-garde*, literally "advance guard (of an army)," also Englished as *vanguard*.

- *in quant Deus savir et podir me dunat* "to the-extent God knowledge and power to-me gives." *In quant* "to the extent," an adverbial phrase, < *quantum* "as much, how much"; compare *quantity, quantum. Savir* and *podir* are both infinitives acting as nouns ("to know," hence "knowledge," and "to be able," hence "ability, power"); *savir* < *saber* < *sapere*, while *podir* < *poder* < *potere*, the regularized Vulgar Latin verb that replaced irregular Classical *posse*; the *b* in *saber* and the *d* in *poder*, derived from *p* and *t*, are further instances of voiced consonants that have developed from their voiceless equivalents between vowels. Both infinitives, in their modern forms, are recognizable from English: *savoir* from *savoir-faire*, literally "to know how to do," and *pouvoir* from *power. Dunat* "he gives" < *donare* "to present, endow," which in France replaced Classical *dare* "to give."
- *si salvarai eo cist meon fradre Karlo* "thus I-will-succor I this my brother Charles." *Salvarai* "I will succor": an example of the new Romance future. *Eo* "I" < *ego*; intervocalic *g* has been lost. *Cist* "this" < *(ec)ce* "look!" + *istum* "this." *Fradre* (< *fratrem* "brother"; compare *fraternal*) is, like *Karlo*, in the oblique case, here marking the direct object of the verb.
- *et in aiudha et in cadhuna cosa* "both in aid and in each thing." *Aiudha* "aid" < *adjutare*; compare *adjutant, aid(e). Cosa* "thing" < *causam* "cause, case."
- *si cum om per dreit son fradra salvar dift* "just as one by right his brother to-succor ought." *Om* "one" (impersonal) < Latin nominative *homo* "man," and accordingly still used in Modern French (*on*) as the impersonal subject of a verb. *Dift* "he ought" < *debere* (compare *debt, debit, debenture*); *f* represents the sound of *v* here.
- *in o quid il mi altresi fazet* "on condition that he to-me likewise do." *Il* "he" < *ille* "that man." *Fazet* "that he do" < *faciat*, subjunctive.
- *et ab Ludher nul plaid nunquam prindrai* "and with Lothair no agreement never I-will-undertake." *Nul ... nunquam* "none never": the double negatives do not cancel one another. *Plaid* "agreement" < *placitum*, the sound of *c* between vowels having been lost; the word, used in the specific sense of "lawsuit," is the source of *plead* and *plea* (but not *plaid*).

- *qui, meon vol, cist meon fradre Karle in damno sit* "(no agreement) which, to-my knowledge, to-this my brother Charles of harm may-be." *Vol* "with consent, knowledge" and *fradre Karle* "to brother Charles" are both nouns in the jack-of-all-trades oblique case; since they are employed here without prepositions, their syntactic function needs to be inferred from the context, the former indicating means (in Latin, it would be the ablative case), the latter the indirect object (the dative).

Here is the second oath, as taken by Charles's army.

- *Si Lodhuuuigs sagrament que son fradre Karlo jurat conservat* "If Louis the-oath that to-his brother Charles he-has-sworn he-keeps," that is, if Louis keeps the oath he has sworn to his brother Charles. *Lodhuuuigs* is shown to be nominative, thus the subject, by the *-s* ending (compare even now *Louis* and *Charles*). *Fradre Karlo* is the oblique case, here designating the indirect object, "to brother Charles."
- *et Karlus, meos sendra, de suo part lo fraint* "and Charles, my lord, for his part it breaks." *Sendra* "lord, master" < *sen(jo)rem* "elder, superior"; compare Spanish *señor*, Italian *signore* "sir, mister." An unetymological *d* is added between *n* and *r* to ease the pronunciation (it is called a "glide consonant"); French also inserted a *d* into Latin *cin(e)rem* "ash" (compare *incinerate*) and came up with *cendre* "cinder"; similarly, Vulgar Latin *gen(e)rem* "race; kind; gender" > French *gendre* (> *gender*); and, this time with a different glide consonant, Greco-Latin *cam(e)ra* "room" > French *chambre* (> *chamber*). *Fraint* "he breaks" < *frangere fractus*; compare *fragile, fraction*.
- *si io returnar non l'int pois* "if I to-deter not him therefrom am-able." *Returnar* "to deter" < *retornare* "to turn back" < *tornare* "to turn on a lathe; turn" < Greek *tornos* "lathe." The simple negative *non* "not" found here is no longer in use today; in Modern French it has been replaced by *ne... pas* (as in *vous ne parlez pas* "you do not speak"), which, however plain now, was originally colorful – it meant "not a step." *L'*: the elided form of the pronoun *le* "him."
- *ne io ne neuls cui eo returnar int pois* "neither I nor no-one whom I to-deter therefrom am-able." *Neuls* "no one" < *nullus*; compare *null, nullify*.
- *in nulla aiudha contra Lodhuuuig nun li iu er* "of no assistance against Louis not to-him there I-will-be." *Iu* < *ivi* < Latin *ibi* "there"; here the meaning must be something like "in that matter." *Er* "I will be" < *ero*.

The Big Picture

The Strasbourg Oaths reveal with brilliant clarity a language in a state of transition. They display abundant signs of the new, very different language that was emerging, yet also include many relics of the past.

Though written unmistakably in a Romance language, the Oaths still retain conspicuous traces of Latin forms and words, which perhaps do not consort harmoniously with the rest. These might be due to slips made by the transcribing author, the rest of whose narrative is written in Latin (or perhaps made by the scribe, for our sole manuscript is not Nithard's original, but a later copy), or they may be explained by the legal nature of the language, for which Latin forms and phrases would be both apt and familiar. *Deus* "God" and *Kar(o)lus* "Charles" are Classical forms of the nominative, *jurat* "he has sworn" and *conservat* "he keeps" Classical forms of the indicative, and both *nunquam* "never" and *in damno sit* "may be of harm" are pure Latin. Also a likely Latinism is the marked tendency to place the verb at the end of its clause: of the twelve clauses found in the Oaths, all but one conclude with the verb, the sole exception being *salvarai*. Because the other version of the oaths positions verbs at the end, this may be due to German influence also – unless the German is itself influenced by Latin.

Nithard clearly signals his consciousness that the language is not Latin when he identifies it as *lingua Romana* "Romance language."

The feature that most clearly stamps the Oaths as French, and no longer Latin, and not Italian or Spanish either, is the fate of the final syllables: most unstressed final vowels are lost. This is probably due to Frankish influence. The Germanic language stressed the accented syllable so heavily that the one following was weakened, even to the point of disappearance. Thus, in the Oaths we find Vulgar Latin *salvaméntum* > *salvament* "salvation," *quómo* > *cum* "as," *retornáre* > *returnar* "to deter," *índe* > *int* "therefrom," *íbi* > *iu* "there; in that matter," etc. Right here, in this extremely early text, we witness the emergence of a feature of French that is very distinctive, the tendency for words to end with a consonant, or at least not with a clear vowel. Italian words, in sharp contrast to French, nearly always end with a clear vowel – when it is asserted that Italian is a very "musical" language, that is what is meant. Many Spanish words end in a clear vowel as well. The differences between the languages are easily illustrated with a few further, representative words from the Oaths:

Vulgar Latin	Italian	Spanish	Oaths	Modern French
amore "love"	*amore*	*amor*	*amur*	*amour*
quantu "how much"	*cuanto*	*cuanto*	*quant*	*quant*
sapere "to know"	*sapere*	*saber*	*savir*	*savoir*
directu "right"	*diritto*	*derecho*	*dreit*	*droit*

All the Italian words end in a vowel, two of the four Spanish do, but none of the French.

The unstressed final vowel is preserved, however, in two situations: when it is *a* (*dunat, aiudha, cosa* – contrast, in successive clauses of the second Oath, *neuls* < *nullus* but *nulla* < *nulla*); and when it is needed to make a cluster of consonants pronounceable (*poblo, nostro, fradre, Karle*). In the former situation, the *a* later came to be pronounced as a schwa, that is, the colorless sound of *e* in *the*, and to be written uniformly with *e* – the modern words are *donne, aide, chose*. In the latter situation, the weak vowel, though represented here through a variety of letters (*fradra, Karle, nostro*), was also pronounced as a schwa. Soon, it too came to be written uniformly as *e* – the modern words are *frère, Charles, nôtre*. Then later, the schwa sound of the final *e*, from whichever source, although still indicated in writing, ceased to be pronounced at all (except in song: think of *Frè-re Jac-ques*). As a result, many French words, despite being written with final *e*, end with the sound of a consonant, as is also true for English. (And by the same token, many words that are written with a final consonant in fact end with some vowel sound, because the consonant is not pronounced: thus *droit* is pronounced /dwa/ and *quant* finishes with a nasalized *a* – neither *t* is sounded.)

The loss of some final vowels and the weakening of others had dramatic effects on the syntax of the language, as well as the sound, and they explain several of the conspicuous differences between French and the other two languages. French does not enjoy that neat pattern by which words ending in *-o* are masculine, those in *-a* feminine: Vulgar Latin *amicum, amicam* "friend" > Italian *amico, amica*, Spanish *amigo, amiga*, but French *ami, amie*, which are spoken identically. Similarly, many of the personal endings on the French verb are not distinct: Latin *canto, cantas, cantat* "I sing, you (singular) sing, he, she sings" > Spanish *canto, cantas, canta* and Italian *canto, canti, canta*, but French *chante, chantes, chante* (Old French *chantet*), all of which are pronounced alike, despite the spelling; hence the need for personal pronouns (*je* "I," or *tu*

274

"you"). Moreover, as we saw in Chapter Twelve, the loss of final vowels helped deal a death blow to the two-case system that Old French maintained for a while.

Two of the most dramatic and widespread Romance sound changes, described in Chapter Eleven, are exemplified in the Oaths, and for each one the writer, attempting to represent sounds that did not exist in Latin, has deployed the Latin alphabet in a creative way. As a result of palatalization, Latin *faciat*, originally pronounced /fa-ki-at/, became /fa-kyat/, we saw. The /ky/ sound continued to evolve: /ky/ > /ty/ > /tsh/ > /ts/ > /s/. Nithard here employs *z* (*fazet*) to represent the penultimate stage, /ts/. Then, in *aiudha*, which comes from *ajuta*, the letters *dh* represent the penultimate stage of another process. Intervocalic *t* had changed to its voiced equivalent, *d*, which in turn came to be sounded like the *th* in *then*; this pronunciation is ingeniously signaled here by *dh*. Eventually, the sound would disappear completely: Latin *vitam* "life" > Modern French *vie*.

A Merovingian king, Chilperic, so we are told, attempted to reform the Latin alphabet by adding several letters that represented new sounds that had entered the language. Unfortunately, we do not know the details, yet his experiment clearly came to naught. Nithard and other early authors strove to make do with the inherited Latin alphabet.

The above observations about the Oaths are not altered by the fact that the author is sometimes inconsistent in his spelling: *fradre* and *fradra* are found, *Karlo* and *Karle*, *io* and *eo*, *non* and *nun*. For French, and for our other languages as well, including English, spelling would not begin to become standardized until modern times. For Latin, this had been carried out, unofficially but authoritatively, by the classicizers of the first century B.C.E.

The Latin system of five cases has fallen away to such an extent that in the Oaths only nominative and oblique are found. Nonetheless, the language here has not yet reached the stage at which two of the most important jobs formerly done by the cases have been regularly handed over to specific prepositions. Prepositions are employed (*pro, de, in*), but *de* + oblique case has not yet acquired the functions of the old genitive case (expressing possession, for instance), nor has *a(d)* + oblique acquired those of the old dative (the indirect object). Instead, these relations are conveyed by the oblique case alone: *poblo* "of the people," *fradre* "to a brother"; in Modern French these would be *du peuple* and *à son frère*. The earlier grammar of cases has nearly disappeared, but the new one is not yet in service. With personal pronouns, however, the situation is different. They continue to have a variety of forms: *il* "he," *le* "him," *li* "to him"; the same is true of the pronouns in the other languages.

Articles definite or indefinite, later a conspicuous feature in the language, are not found here at all: *sagrament* "the oath."

As with the nouns, so with the verbs: the Oaths reveal the language at a moment of transition. Though the ending of *salvar-ai* "I will succor" marks it clearly as first person singular (like *prindrai* "I will take"), nonetheless it is still accompanied by the personal pronoun *eo* "I," which from a logical point of view could have been dispensed with; likewise, *io...pois* "I am able." And, although *salvarai* and *prindrai* are instances of the new Romance future, the soldiers still say *er* "I will be," which is a survival of the inherited (irregular) Latin future *ero*; the form that corresponds to *salvarai* for the verb "to be" would be (*je*) *serai*. So the new future has not yet utterly ousted the old.

The lexicon of the Oaths is 100 percent Latin. Every one of the 115 words originates in Latin. The only element that might be considered an exception is the *cadh-* in *cadhuna* "each," which derives from the Greek preposition *kata*, but which must already have become naturalized in Late Latin: we may compare Spanish *cada* "each." Not a single Germanic word is to be found.

THE SEQUENCE OF ST. EULALIA

Text and Setting

The only other text preserved from the ninth century presents a piquant contrast to the Strasbourg Oaths. Known as the *Sequence of St. Eulalia,* it is an anonymous religious poem and the earliest literary work written in French. This hymn to Eulalia, its content based on a Latin poem by the fourth-century author Prudentius, was composed to be inserted into the mass celebrated on her saint's day, December 10. The time, place, and occasion of its composition are known. Eulalia was a Spanish saint, martyred in 304, whose cult had been revived in 878, when what were said to be her bones were discovered in Barcelona and then translated to a convent near the Benedictine monastery of Saint-Amand-les-Eaux, in Picardy, northern France. Other contents of the manuscript that preserves the poem prove that it was written close to the year 880. Since the manuscript came from that monastery, which was a center of scholarship, the poem was probably composed there, and it seems to bear some traces of northern dialects.

Partly because it is constrained by meter and rhyme, and partly perhaps because it is so early a composition, the *Sequence* contains a few awkward phrases in its twenty-nine verses.

> *Buona pulcella fut Eulalia,*
> *Bel auret corps, bellezour anima.*
> *Voldrent la veintre li Deo inimi,*
> *Voldrent la faire diaule servir.*
> *Elle no'nt eskoltet les mals conselliers,*　　　　　5
> *Qu'elle Deo raneiet, chi maent sus en ciel,*
> *Ne por or ned argent ne paramenz,*
> *Por manatce regiel ne preiement;*
> *Niule cose non la pouret omque pleier*
> *La polle sempre non amast lo Deo menestier.*　　10
> *E por o fut presentede Maximiien,*
> *Chi rex eret a cels dis soure pagiens.*
> *Il li enortet, dont lei nonque chielt,*
> *Qued elle fuiet lo nom christiien.*
> *Ell'ent adunet lo suon element;*　　　　　　15
> *Melz sostendreiet les empedementz*
> *Qu'elle perdesse sa virginitét;*
> *Por os furet morte a grand honestét.*
> *Enz enl fou la getterent com arde tost;*
> *Elle colpes non auret, por o nos coist.*　　　　20
> *A czo nos voldret concreidre li rex pagiens;*
> *Ad une spede li roveret tolir lo chieef.*
> *La domnizelle celle kose non contredist:*
> *Volt lo seule lazsier, si ruovet Krist;*
> *In figure de colomb volat a ciel.*　　　　　25
> *Tuit oram que por nos degnet preier,*
> *Qued auuisset de nos Christus mercit*
> *Post la mort et a lui nos laist venir*
> > *Par souue clementia.*

"A virtuous girl was Eulalia; she had a fair body, but a fairer soul. The enemies of God wanted to vanquish her; they wanted to make her serve the Devil.

Although those wicked men advised her to renounce God, who dwells in heaven above, she paid them no heed, not for gold or silver or finery, not for royal threats or pleas. Nothing could ever prevent the girl from constantly loving the service of God. So, she was brought before Maximian, who at that time was king of the pagans. He urged her to flee the name of Christian – but in that she had no interest at all. Then she gathered up her strength: she would rather endure torture than lose her virgin purity. Because of this, she died with great honor. They threw her into a fire so that she might quickly be burned to death, but, because she had no faults, she was not burned by the fire. The king of the pagans would not tolerate this. He ordered her head to be cut off with a sword, and the maiden did not resist. Because she wanted to leave this world, she called upon Christ. And so, in the likeness of a dove she flew up to heaven. Let us all ask that she deign to pray for us, and that Christ have mercy on us after our death and, by his grace, allow us to come to him."

Detailed Observations

Except for the poem's conclusion, the sense is invariably completed at the end of a single verse or a couplet.

- *Buona pulcella fut Eulalia* (1) "a-good girl was Eulalia." *Buona* "good": compare *bonny, bounty, bonanza*. *Pulcella* "girl" < *pullicellam*, a diminutive of *pulla* (see verse 10).
- *Bel auret corps, bellezour anima* (2) "beautiful she-had a-body, more-beautiful a-soul." *Bellezour* "more beautiful" < *bellatiorem*, the comparative of *bellata* ("beautifulled," as it were), used in place of the common *bellam* "beautiful" (source of the names *Bella* and *Belle*). *Anima* "soul": compare *animal, animate*.
- *Voldrent la veintre li Deo inimi* (3) "they-wanted her to-vanquish, the of-God enemies," that is, the enemies of God wanted to vanquish her. *La* "her," direct object pronoun < *illam* "that woman," demonstrative. *Veintre* "to conquer" < *vincere victus*; compare *vanquish, Vincent, victory*. *Li Deo inimi* "the enemies of God": *Deo* is the oblique case, functioning as the genitive; the phrase, although it follows the verb, is clearly marked as the subject by being in the nominative.

- *Voldrent la faire diaule servir* (4) "they-wanted her to-make the-Devil to-serve," that is, they wanted to make her serve the Devil. *Faire* "to make" < *facere factus*; compare *manufacture, factory*; the intervocalic *c* has disappeared. *Diaule* "devil" < *diabolum* < Greek *diabolos* "slanderer, accuser."

- *Elle no'nt eskoltet les mals conselliers* (5) / *Qu'elle Deo raneiet, chi maent sus en ciel* "she not in-this heeded the wicked advisers, (advising) that she God renounce, who dwells above in the-sky." *Elle* "she" < *illa* "that woman." *Eskoltet* "she heeded" < *auscultare* "to listen to"; compare *auscultation*, a particular kind of attentive listening, with a stethoscope. *Conselliers* "advisers" awkwardly introduces the clause following, as if it were a verb instead of a noun. *Qu'* "that": the elided form of the all-purpose conjunction *que*. *Raneiet* "that she renounce," subjunctive < *renegare* "to deny"; compare *renege* and, from Spanish, *renegade*; the intervocalic *g* has been lost. *Maent* "he dwells": compare *mansion, remain*. *Ciel* "heaven": compare *celestial, Celeste*.

- *Ne por or ned argent ne paramenz,* (7) / *Por manatce regiel ne preiement* "not for gold nor silver nor finery, for threat royal nor entreaty." *Or* "gold" < *aurum. Argent* "silver" < *argentum*, as in *Argentina*, a remarkable country that takes its name from the Río de la Plata "River of Silver." *Au* and *Ar* are the chemical symbols for gold and silver. *Manatce* "threat" < *minaciam*; compare *menace. Regiel* "royal" < *regalem*; compare *regal, regalia, royal*.

- *Niule cose non la pouret omque pleier* (9) "no thing not her was-able ever to-prevent." *Pleier* "to divert; prevent" < *plicare* "to fold, bend."

- *La polle sempre non amast lo Deo menestier* (10) "(to prevent that) the girl always not love the of-God service." *Polle* "girl" < Latin *pullam*, originally "the female young of an animal," but applied most often specifically to domestic fowl (compare *poultry*), "young hen," hence "girl"; the development of *chick* is closely parallel. *Amast* "that she love," subjunctive < *ama(vi)sset. Menestier* "service" < *ministerium*; compare *ministry, minister, minstrel* (originally "servant").

- *E por o fut presentede Maximiien* (11) "and for this she-was presented to-Maximian." *Maximiien* "to Maximian": the oblique case, here indicating the indirect object. Maximian was co-emperor of Rome from 285 to 308 and is known to have persecuted Christians in Spain at precisely this time, 304.

- *Chi rex eret a cels dis soure pagiens* (12) "who the-king was in those days over the-pagans." *Cels* "those" < *(ec)ce* "look!" + *illos* "those." *Soure* "over" < *supra*; compare *supranational.*

- *Il li enortet, dont lei nonque chielt,* (13) / *Qued elle fuiet lo nom christiien* "he her exhorts – (a thing) which to-her never matters – that she flee the name of-Christian." *Fuiet* "that she flee," subjunctive < *fugere*; compare *fugitive, fugue.*

- *Ell'ent adunet lo suon element* (15) "she thereupon gathers the her strength." *Adunet* "she gathers" < Late Latin *adunare* "to unite" < *unum* "one." The combination of article with possessive adjective in *lo suon element* "the her strength," though foreign to Modern French and English, is regular in Italian, for instance, *il mio libro* "the my book."

- *Melz sostendreiet les empedementz* (16) / *Qu'elle perdesse sa virginitét* "rather she-would-endure the tortures than (that) she lose her virgin-purity." *Melz* "rather" < *melius* "better" (adverb); compare *ameliorate. Sostendreiet* "she would endure" is the conditional, the innovating Romance verb form; for the meaning, compare *sustain. Perdesse* "that she lose," subjunctive < *per(di)disset*; compare *perdition. Empedementz* < *impedimentos*, literally "obstacles" (compare *impediment*), here a euphemism for "tortures."

- *Por os furet morte a grand honestét* (18) "for this she-died with great honor." *Os = o* "this" (< *hoc*) + *se* "herself," a reflexive pronoun that goes with the verb, *se furet morte* "she died."

- *Enz enl fou la getterent com arde tost* (19) "inside into the fire her they-threw so-that she-would-burn quickly." *Enl* "into the" = *en* + *le. Fou* "fire" < *focum* "hearth," which replaced Classical *ignem* in the Romance languages. *Getterent* "they threw" < *jectare*; compare *jet. Arde* "she would burn," subjunctive < *ardere*; compare *ardent, arson. Tost* "quickly," if one attends to its etymology, forms a striking collocation with *arde: tostum* "heated; roasted; burned" (compare *toast*), because often applied to food, came to mean "promptly, quickly, soon," since, in the matrix of the kitchen, serving food quickly was the equivalent of serving it hot.

- *Elle colpes non auret, por o nos coist* (20) "she faults not had; for that not she-got-burned." *Colpes* "faults": compare *culpable, exculpate. Nos = no* "not" + *se*, the reflexive pronoun. *Se coist* "she got burned" < *coxit* < *coquere* "to cook," the English word being of Germanic origin yet akin to the Latin.

- *A czo nos voldret concreidre li rex pagiens* (21) "to this not himself he-wanted to-yield, the king of-the-pagans." *Nos* = *no* "not" + *se* "himself." *Pagiens* "of the pagans": oblique plural.

- *Ad une spede li roveret tolir lo chieef*(22) "with a sword he asked to-remove the head." *Roveret* "he asked" < *rogare*; compare *interrogate*.

- *La domnizelle celle kose non contredist* (23) "the maiden those things not opposed." *Domnizelle* "maiden," source of English *damsel*, comes from a diminutive of *dominam* "lady."

- *Volt lo seule lazsier, si ruovet Krist* (24) "she-wanted the world to-leave; thus she-asked-for Christ." *Seule* "the world" (as opposed to heaven) < *saeculum* "age, generation"; compare *secular*.

- *In figure de colomb volat a ciel* (25) "in the-likeness of-a-dove she-flies to heaven." *Volat* "she flies": compare *volatile*.

- *Tuit oram que por nos degnet preier* (26) "all let-us-pray that for us she-deign to-pray." *Tuit* < *toti* "entire; all" (compare *total*); the adjective replaced Classical *omnes* in all three languages. *Oram* "let us pray" < *orare*; compare *oratorio, oratory* "place for prayer." *Degnet* "that she deign," subjunctive < *dignare* "to consider worthy" < *dignum* "worthy." *Preier* "to pray" < *precare* (compare *imprecation, precarious*; also *preiement*, line 8, above), from which the intervocalic *c* has been lost. *Deign* and *pray* come into English from the French.

- *Qued auuisset de nos Christus mercit*(27) / *Post la mort* "(pray) that he-have for us, Christ, mercy after the death," that is, that Christ have mercy on us after our death. *Auuisset* "that he have": subjunctive. *Mercit* "mercy" < *mercedem* "wage, payment, reward"; this is also the source of *merci* "thanks." *Mort* "death": compare *mortal*.

- *et a lui nos laist venir* (28) / *Par souue clementia* "and to him us that-he-allow to-come, by his grace," that is, and that, by his grace, he allow us to come to him. *Laist* "that he allow," subjunctive < *laxare* "to slacken"; the sense developed so because to slacken the reins of an animal was to allow it to go where it wanted, and out of this matrix emerged the general meaning "to allow"; the same verb is used in verse 24 with the meaning "to leave."

The Big Picture

Broadly speaking, the picture is the same as for the Oaths: while some traces of Latin remain, marks of the vernacular that has emerged are many and unmistakable. The Latinisms in the *Sequence* are fewer, and this text brings us closer to Modern French in several other regards as well.

As the Oaths had a somewhat legal character, so the *Sequence* is, obviously, religious, and in a text composed for inclusion in the liturgy, it is not surprising that most of the Latinisms, or near-Latinisms, are connected with theology: *Christus* (verse 27), *virginitét* (17), *clementia* (29). Content and context have shaped the forms of the words. *Rex* "king" (12, 21) and *post* "after" (28), however, are ordinary words used here in their Latin form. As in the Oaths, most unstressed final vowels here have disappeared: Vulgar Latin *manet* > *maent* "he dwells" (6), *consiliarios* > *conselliers* "advisers" (5), *argentum* > *argent* "silver" (7). And here too the weak schwa sound at the end of words is still represented variously, by *a* in *anima* (2; Modern French *âme*), by *e* in *cose* (9; Modern *chose*).

Other spellings, however, differ from those of the Oaths in two important ways and point to basic features of pronunciation still characteristic of French today. Stressed *a*, if it is free (that is, not followed by a consonant in the same syllable), closes to *e*: Vulgar Latin *spá-tam* > *spede* "sword" (22; the final *e* is a separate matter); Vulgar Latin *presentá-tam* > *presentede* "presented" (11). For this to happen, the *a* must be stressed; contrast the fates of the two *a*s in *pagános* > *pagiens* "pagans" (12, 21), where the first, unstressed *a* remains unaltered. The *a* must also be free in order to change. This is illustrated in the second syllable of *a-más-set* > *amast* "that she love" (10).

I pointed out in Chapter Eleven that in all three languages stressed vowels tended to become diphthongs. Now here in the *Sequence* we meet the earliest instances: Classical Latin *caelum* "heaven" > Vulgar Latin *célu* > *ciel* (6); Classical Latin *vincere* "to vanquish" > Vulgar Latin *vénc(e)re* > *veintre* (3); Vulgar Latin *bónam* "good" > *buona* (1); Classical Latin *súpra* "above" > Vulgar Latin *sóra* > *soure* (12). In the Oaths, a couple of diphthongs were found, but they were of a different type: they resulted from the loss of a consonant, which brought two vowels into contact with each other, as with *pla(c)itum* > *plaid*. The diphthongs in the *Sequence*, by contrast, arose in a spontaneous fashion, as described earlier.

The anonymous author, like Nithard, wrestles with the problem of adapting the Latin alphabet to novel sounds. Before the sound of *e* or *i*, he uses the grapheme *ch* to represent /k/: *chi* "who" (12), *chieef* "head" (22), *chielt* "it matters" (13). The letter *c* by itself ran the risk of being pronounced /ts/ at this time, so *h*, now available because it no longer served any other purpose, was employed; Italian would do the same. To represent the sound /ts/, the author relies on no fewer than four combinations: *domnizelle* "maiden" (23) < *domnicella, czo* "this" (21) < *(ec)ce hoc, manatce* "threat" (8) < *minacia, lazsier* "to allow" (24) < *laxare*. The different spellings for the same sound are partly influenced by awareness of the words' etymologies.

Alone among the three languages, French retained Vulgar Latin's two-case system of nouns and adjectives long enough for it to be registered in writing. The *Sequence* contains instances of distinct nominative and oblique forms. Nouns of the first class reveal nothing in this regard since they never showed any difference between the two cases: for example, *capre* nominative and oblique singular, *capres* nominative and oblique plural. Those of the second and third classes, however, do distinguish the oblique plural with -*s*: thus, *inimi* "enemies" (3), *tuit* "all" (26), nominative, but *conselliers* "advisers" (5), *pagiens* "pagans" (12, 21), oblique. Within a few centuries, the distinction between the two cases would be effaced for these classes of words too, and -*s* would become the general sign of the plural.

As in the Oaths, the oblique case by itself can still perform the duties of the Latin genitive and dative cases: *rex pagiens* "king of the pagans" (21), *Maximiien* "to Maximian" (11). Yet at the same time the *Sequence* illustrates how prepositions were beginning to take on those tasks: *figure de colomb* "likeness of a dove" (25). The poem, in this regard, occupies an intermediate position, between the Latin past and the French future.

Persistence of the inherited is seen again in *bellezour* "more beautiful" (2; < *bellatiorem*), which represents Latin's synthetic forming of comparative adjectives (compare *latiorem* "broader") rather than the analytic formation that would come to replace it (for instance, *plus belle* "more beautiful"). And, as in Latin and the other Romance languages, object pronouns precede the verb: *la veintre* "to vanquish her" (3), *li enortet* "urged her" (13); similarly, *me dunat* "gives to me" in the first Strasbourg Oath. By contrast, an important innovation is found in the use of articles for the first time, both definite (*les empedementz* "the tortures," 14) and indefinite (*una spede* "a sword," 22), such as were unknown to the composers of the Oaths.

The *Sequence*, with its many verbs, provides the earliest instances in a vernacular text of several significant Romance innovations. Instead of Latin's mostly synthetic passive, the author uses the new analytic passive, combining the verb "to be" with the past participle: *fut presentede* "she was presented" (11). For the first time, a conditional form of a verb is found: *sostendreiet* "she would

Latin Alive

endure" (16). Like the new Romance future, of which the Oaths presented a couple of examples, the conditional is built on the infinitive. And for the first time, reflexive verbs are seen. Nowadays these are often and more appropriately called "pronominal verbs," because the pronouns used with the verb, though they are the reflexive pronouns, are not used reflexively. *Se coist* (20) cannot mean "she burned herself," but rather "she got burned," and in *se furet morte* "she died" (18) the pronoun can hardly be said to indicate the subject acting for or upon herself. Pronominal verbs were to have a long, complicated, confusing history in our Romance languages, and it begins here.

In contrast to the forms, the syntax of the verb remains faithful to Latin. All eight subjunctives in the *Sequence* are employed where Classical Latin syntax would also require that mood: *amast* (10) in a clause of preventing, *arde* (19) in a purpose clause, the remainder in noun clauses dependent on verbs of exhorting (14), preferring (17), requesting (26), etc. In Modern French too the subjunctive would be used in every instance.

The *Sequence*, like the Oaths, relies on a lexicon that is 100 percent Latin; not a single word of the 192 is Frankish. Because it is closer to what would become standard French, it presents a number of words familiar to us, since English later acquired them from French. *Inimi* "enemies" (3) is recognizable at once. So too are *corps* "body" (2) and *chieef* "head" (22), although in English they have surrendered their literal meanings for transferred: *corps* is used as in "diplomatic corps," *chieef* as in *chief* and *chef*, without reference to body parts. *Fou* "fire" (19) is also found in English, concealed inside *curfew*, which, derived from Old French *covrefeu* "cover fire," at first indicated a signal given in the evening by municipal authorities, and then was applied to a different official command that kept residents off the streets at certain hours.

Literary Appreciation

The poetic form of the *Sequence* doubtless influenced its language, and for that reason, and also because it is the first piece of Romance literature, it is worthwhile briefly noting some of its literary features.

The poem consists of fourteen couplets followed by a single verse; in the manuscript, in fact, each couplet is written as one long verse. The couplets rhyme. The rhyme is sometimes assonant, that is, the final one or two vowels correspond (*inimi... servir, mercit... venir*); sometimes it is consonant rhyme, with correspondence between consonants as well as vowels (*contredist...*

ruovet Krist). Since each line seems to consist of ten syllables, length also is a constituent element of the verse. These requirements must have affected the choice and position of words, and so a pleasant variety of word orders is found, with the verb, for instance, placed now at the end of the clause (*Elle colpes non auret* "she had no faults," 20), now first (*Voldrent la veintre li Deo inimi* "the enemies of God wanted to vanquish her," 3), now somewhere in the middle (*Elle no'nt eskoltet les mals conselliers* "she did not heed the wicked advisers in this," 5). For the number of syllables in the verse to come out right, the author sometimes accepts elision (*Qu'elle* for *que elle* "that she," 6, 17), but sometimes, in order to add a syllable, he inserts a consonant that prevents elision (*Qued elle*, 14; *ad une spede* "with a sword," 22 – contrast the usual form of the preposition in *a ciel* "to heaven," 25). The choice of the consonant *d* to block elision is not arbitrary: it arises from the author's awareness that the Latin words from which the French are derived ended in *d* (*quod, ad*).

The author marks the end of the poem by varying the rhythm of his verses. The sense is monotonously complete, with either a pause or a full stop at the end of every verse – until the twenty-seventh, which runs over into the one following (this is called "enjambment"): *Qued auuisset de nos Christus mercit / Post la mort* "that Christ have mercy on us after our death." The poem then ends with a half-verse (*Par souue clementia* "by his grace") that is not part of a couplet, but stands on its own, receiving thereby a strong emphasis. The jolt in rhythm the reader experiences here corresponds to an abrupt shift of focus. At its end, the *Sequence*, like other hymns, turns outwards to those who speak or who hear it – the two groups become one in *Tuit oram* "let us all pray." From a starkly moving but impersonal narrative, the poem becomes a gesture that reaches out and embraces its audience.

ROMANCE SPEECH REACHES BRITAIN

Norman French

The Normans, who had settled on the lower Seine in the early tenth century, quickly developed a political and cultural life inferior to none in Europe. Having given up their Scandinavian traditions of paganism and piracy, they had become assimilated to their new home. The tradition of adventurousness, however, did not desert them, and in 1066, William, the Duke of Normandy, invaded England, defeated an Anglo-Saxon army in the battle of Hastings, and soon conquered the rest of the country. For several centuries thereafter England was ruled by a nobility that continued to speak French. French was the language of their ancestors and peers; the administrative and judicial systems operated in French; and the nobility kept up relations with France, where many still owned estates. The eventual amalgamation of the conquerors' French with the Anglo-Saxon of their subjects produced the remarkable hybrid that is Modern English. In no other European tongue have two language stocks been blended so fully and in such nearly equal measure. Arabic words are found in Spanish, to be sure, and Rumanian contains many items of Slavic origin, while English crops up in everybody else's language nowadays, but none of these situations approaches that of English itself, which is characterized by the thorough interpenetration of Germanic and Latin elements.

The French that the Normans acquired was of the Langue d'Oïl (northern) type, yet it was not identical with the Francien spoken in Paris. Two differences of pronunciation in particular are exceptionally interesting to us because they have led to a series of curious doublets in English.

Many Frankish words began with *w-*. This sound Norman French maintained, but Francien altered to *gu-*, pronounced /gw/ at first, later simply /g/. As a consequence of this split, English possesses a number of pairs of words that in origin were the same, but of which one entered the language with Norman French whereas the other was introduced later from Francien. A clear instance is the pair *warranty* (arriving via Norman French) and *guarantee* (via Francien). The words that came from Francien, like *guarantee*, typically entered the language about two hundred years after the Conquest, when England's contacts with Paris grew stronger. Some other examples of such doublets are *wile* and *guile*, *ward* (along with *warden*) and *guard*, *wise* (as in *likewise, otherwise*) and *guise*, and, to return to the man responsible for joining the two languages, William, whose name in French is Guillaume. From a Germanic verb meaning "to protect, take care of" derive both *garage* (originally a sheltered place for storing a car) and *ware* (as in *warehouse*) along with *wary* and *aware*. And similarly, from a Germanic noun *wadi* "payment of money" come both *wage, wager* and *gage* (meaning "pledge, security"), *engage*. From *wadi* in the transferred sense of "pledge" English has also gotten *wed* – which leads to the astonishing realization that, from an etymological point of view, and despite appearances, an engagement and a wedding are the same thing! Tell that to the bride left waiting at the altar!

Norman French was more conservative than the ancestor of the modern language in another regard as well. Before the sound of *a*, it retained *c* and *g* with their hard pronunciations, whereas Francien first palatalized them and then, in stages, altered them to /tsh/ and /dj/, respectively. These changes too have provided English with a number of doublets, one set beginning with *ca*- and *ga*-, the other with *cha*- and *ja*-: Vulgar Latin *captiare "to try to capture" > both *catch* (arriving via Norman French) and *chase* (via Francien); Latin *carum* "dear" > both *caress* and *charity, cherish*; Celtic-Latin *carrum* "wagon" > both *car, cart* and *chariot*; Late Latin *capitale* "possession" > both *cattle* (at certain times, the possession par excellence) and *chattel*; Late Latin *gambam* "leg" > both *gams, gambrel* and *jamb* (the "leg" of a door), *enjambment* (a phrase that straddles two verses).

The presence of such pairs has undeniably enriched the language. Little is gained by the co-existence of the synonyms *warranty* and *guarantee*. But *chase* and *catch* usefully distinguish the stages of a pursuit. While *wage* has stayed close to its earliest meaning, *engage* has greatly expanded its sphere of reference: it is found not only in phrases like "to engage the services of a tutor," but also with a general meaning, as in "to engage in horseplay." Neither *cattle* nor *chattel* has retained its original meaning of "possession"; instead, one has become concrete and specific, while the other has moved towards abstraction and defines a type of possession.

A Few Further Inheritances from French

What French has contributed to English is vast – not just vocabulary items, but also pronunciation (the *-ti-* in *nation* pronounced /sh/, for instance), morphology (plurals marked by *-s*), and syntax (the word order in "attorney general"). Some of these I have already touched upon. A few others, exampled in the two earliest texts and each affecting the shape and sound of a whole series of English words, may serve as final reminders of how rootedly French – which is to say, Latin also – persists in English.

The Oaths include the word *savir* "knowledge," derived from Latin *sapere* "to be wise, to know." The *p* became *f* (thus, Vulgar Latin *capu* "head" > *chef*), and then *f* regularly turned into *v*. The result of this sound change, glimpsed in Chapter Eleven, is another series of English doublets, one word with *p*, the other with *v*. (The changes are easy, natural. *P* and *f* represent similar sounds in that they are made with both lips, and then *v* is the voiced equivalent of *f*.)

English includes, on the one hand, *pauper*, taken directly from Latin *pauperem* "poor," and on the other, *poverty*, received from French. The number of French words showing the change of intervocalic *p* to *v* is large, and often, as with *pauperem*, English prepares us to recognize both the before and after states. The links between Latin *ripam* "bank, shore" (> *riparian*) and French *rive* (> *river*) and between Latin *sapere* (> *sapient*) and French *savoir* (> *savant, savoir-faire*) were noted earlier. Some fresh examples: Latin *recipere* "to receive" > both *receipt, recipe* and *receive* (similarly, the other compounds of *capere: conceive, deceive, perceive*); *separare* > both *separate* and *sever*; *cupere* "to desire" > both *Cupid, cupidity, concupiscent* and *covet*; *rapere* "to seize" > both *rape, rapid* and *ravish*; *capillum* "(individual) hair" > both *capillary* "a hair-thin blood vessel" and *disheveled* "with the hair disarranged."

Several familiar words or phrases connected with food are further instances of the same change: *capram* "goat" > both the zodiacal constellation *Capricorn* "Goat's Horn," along with *to caper*, originally "to frolic like a goat," and French *chèvre*, which we might recognize at the cheese store in *fromage de chèvre* "goat cheese," also (by an obscure path) *chevron* and *Chevrolet*; *piperem* "pepper" > both *pepper* and French *poivre*, which we might read on a menu in *steak au poivre* "steak with pepper sauce"; *operam* "work" > both *operate, opera* and French *oeuvre* "work," as in *hors d'oeuvre*, literally "outside the work," thus "inessential part (of a meal)," also *maneuver*, originally "to work with the hands," and *chef d'oeuvre* "masterwork, masterpiece."

The story of how Latin *tropare, passing through French, became English *trove* is an etymological saga. From Greek, Latin acquired the word *tropus* "trope, figure of speech," two examples of which would be metaphor and synecdoche. In late antiquity the same term, applied to music, referred to a melodic ornament added to a chant. The derived verb *tropare* meant "to compose a melody," next "to compose, create (in general)," then "to invent, discover," and finally "to find," which is the meaning of French *trouver* today. The familiar phrase "treasure trove," literally "treasure found," got shortened in usage to *trove*, as in "a valuable trove of ancient manuscripts." In medieval France, *tropare* was often employed of literary composition, so in Provençal, where the *p* turned into a *b* (rather than a *v*), one who wrote or performed poetry was called a *troubadour*. Because Provençal was the language of Europe's earliest body of vernacular poetry, it is not surprising that *troubadour* became fixed in both French and English. The Italian equivalent is *trovatore*, as in the name of the Verdi opera.

(An alternative etymology for *trovare* derives it from *turbare* "to disturb." In that account, fishing was the matrix, and the sequence of senses would be "to stir up (the water)," next "to seek," and then "to find.")

A final pair of words showing the change of intervocalic Latin *p* to French (and English) *v*: Vulgar Latin *prepós(i)tum* "one placed in front, in charge," with assimilation of the first vowel to the second, > Old French variant *provost* > English *provost*, nowadays most often a high-ranking academic officer; and Latin *papilionem* "butterfly" > French, English *pavilion*, originally a capacious tent, so called because of its similarity to a butterfly with wings outstretched.

In the Oaths appears the verb *salvar* "to save"; the English word in fact comes from the French. The noteworthy change here, which was to take place only after the time of the earliest texts, is that *l* when occurring before another consonant became the vowel *u*: Old French *salvar* > French *sauver* > English *save*. This is regular and characteristic of French, and would in time affect several other words found in the Oaths and the *Sequence*. The adjective *altre* "other" (< Vulgar Latin *altrum* < Classical *álterum*) would become in Modern French *autre*, and *eskolter* "to listen, heed" (< Latin *auscultare*) would become *écouter*.

The change of *l* from a consonant sound to a vowel affects many other words, including a number we have already met: Latin *calvum* "bald" > French *chauve*, as in *chauve souris* "bat," literally "bald mouse"; Classical Latin *collocare* "to put in place" > Vulgar Latin *colcare* > French *coucher* "to lay down, put to bed" > English *couch*; Vulgar Latin *colpum* "blow, stroke" > French *coup* as in *coup d'état* and *coup de grace*; Latin *galbinum* "yellow" > French *jaun* > English *jaundice*; Latin *saltare* "to jump" > French *sauter* > English *sauté*.

The change has also influenced a number of additional words we recognize in English, but their origins are concealed by the change in sound: Latin *salsam* "salted, seasoned" > French, English *sauce*; Latin *silvaticum* "of the forest" (< *silva* "forest"), with assimilation of the first vowel to the second, > Vulgar Latin *salvaticum* > French *sauvage* "wild" > English *savage*; Latin *falsum* "false" > French *faux*, as in *faux pas* (literally, "false step"); Latin *album* "white" (compare *album*, *albumen*) > *alburnum* "whitish" > French, English *auburn*; Latin *altum* "high" > French *haut* (where the unetymological *h-* was introduced early under the influence of Germanic **hoh* "high"), as in *haute cuisine*, literally "high cooking."

The *Sequence* documented what happened in French to certain /a/ sounds. It is worthwhile, and easy, to pursue this a little further, since it reveals the unsuspected origin of a host of English words. The development of Latin *presentátam* into *presentede* "presented" illustrated, with the first *a*, the closing of stressed *a* to *e*. This change affected a large number of words, including the past participles of the numerous -*are* verbs (French -*er*), which originally all ended with -*átum* (*cantátum* "sung"). Today, after the –*m* was dropped (early) and the final vowel was lost, and after the *t* changed to *d* and then was lost also, such words end uniformly in -*é* (*chanté*). In short, Latin -*átum* > French -*é*; also, Latin -*átam* > French -*ée*. The result is reflected in English words such as *émigré*, from *emigrátum*; the corresponding form for a woman is *émigrée*.

Similar to *émigré(e)* is *protégé(e)*, which, since it refers to persons, also has both masculine and feminine written forms (although they are pronounced alike). Other former French participles in -*é* – some are now nouns, some adjectives – have entered our language as well, directly from French and unchanged: *attaché, cliché, communiqué, divorcée, exposé, résumé, risqué, soignée,* et al., all introduced into English within the last two centuries or so.

So far-reaching for English have been the consequences of that one sound change that had already taken place in the very earliest French texts!

CHAPTER FIFTEEN

ITALIAN

Political History of Italy

Although it would be an unusually complex task to summarize the history of Italy, one of the chief features of that history is readily identified – the persistent lack of political unity. This is explained partly by the geography of the peninsula, divided into discrete regions by the chain of the Apennine Mountains, and partly by the political situation that obtained as the Roman Empire broke apart. Like other tribes before them, such as the Ostrogoths under Theoderic, the Lombards invaded Italy in the mid-sixth century, and they succeeded in conquering most of it; the only lands remaining in the hands of the Eastern (or Byzantine) Empire were Venice, the territory between Rome and Ravenna, Naples, and the far south. Even those lands under Lombard rule were far from constituting a political unit; rather, they were a series of independent duchies. Then, in the second half of the eighth century, the Pope, by now a temporal no less than a spiritual lord, summoned the Franks to aid against the Lombards, and so the Franks for a short while controlled most of the peninsula.

For more than a millennium afterwards, Italy continued to be a shifting patchwork of small political units. A crude but perhaps helpful picture of the fragmented situation can be formed by surveying the different groups.

In the central-northern area were the papal lands, extending from Rome north towards Bologna and southeast across the plain of Latium.

During much of this period, certain cities in the north maintained their independence. These tended to be either tyrannies exercised by powerful families, such as the Este in Ferrara and the Visconti in Milan, or oligarchic republics, such as Sienna and Florence; sometimes the latter too came into the hands of a powerful family, as happened with Florence and the Medici.

As a result of further invasion, the lower part of the peninsula long formed part of some other empire. In the early eleventh century, southern Italy and then Sicily began to be occupied by Normans. As in France a century earlier, this Scandinavian people quickly developed a refined culture, material remains of which are still to be seen in the splendid architectural monuments in and around Palermo. The Norman kingdom later became part of the Holy Roman Empire, and then, in the mid-thirteenth century, passed to the ruling house of Aragon.

Italy's lengthy coasts were dotted with a number of prosperous, independent maritime cities: Genoa, Pisa, Amalfi, Bari, Venice.

In the mid-nineteenth century the peninsula, together with Sicily and Sardinia, was at last united, piece by piece, under the King of Sardinia, Victor Emmanuel II, who thus became the first King of Italy. The final piece of present-day Italy to be cemented into place was the Papacy's penultimate possession: in 1870 the city of Rome, except for the Vatican, was joined to the Kingdom.

One of the consequences of this tale of prolonged disunity is the relatively greater linguistic fragmentation of modern Italy, in which the number and diversity of different dialects, and indeed of different languages, exceed those of France and Spain; some dialects are mutually unintelligible. The question of a national standard, seriously debated during the nineteenth century, was made urgent by the success of political unification and the consequent creation of a national educational system. In the end the dialect of Tuscany was accepted in this role. The chief reason was not the political power of one region, as in France, but rather the prestige attached to that version of the language that had been nobly employed by Dante, Petrarch, Boccaccio, and others.

JUDICIAL RECORDS FROM MONTE CASSINO

The Benedictine monastery of Monte Cassino, situated towards the southeastern end of the plain of Latium, yet closer to Capua and Naples than to Rome, was an immeasurably influential center of Christian learning throughout the Middle Ages. Established by Benedict early in the sixth century, it served as the principal model for medieval monasticism. It also came to contain a vast library of manuscripts and a scriptorium in which manuscripts could be copied. Like other religious foundations, it possessed lands with which to maintain itself. The archives of Monte Cassino contain records of several judicial proceedings, conducted in the mid-tenth century, in which the monastery itself or one of its dependencies is a party to a case involving land ownership. The records of the cases are in Latin, naturally, but on a few occasions when witnesses are introduced, their testimony in behalf of the monastery is quoted in the vernacular, and these brief, formulaic statements are our earliest indisputably Italian texts. Of the four such formulas recorded, one, the oldest, provides sufficient material for our purposes.

This proceeding, held at Capua in March of 960, ends by confirming that certain lands do belong to Monte Cassino and thus rejecting the claim of a certain Rodelgrimo, who asserted he had inherited them from his father. For lack of documentary evidence, witnesses are called, who identify the lands in question by reference to a map and then state that those lands have been in the possession of the monastery for thirty years. (Under Roman law, the actual use of a property for a certain period secured ownership to the user.) The four witnesses, clerics all, each utter precisely the same legal formula, which must have been drafted by notaries:

> *Sao ko kelle terre, per kelle fini que ki contene, trenta anni le possette parte sancti Benedicti.*

> "I know that those lands, within those boundaries that are found here, for thirty years the party of St. Benedict possessed them."

The vernacular is used, presumably, not for the benefit of the judge and others involved in the trial, who would have known Latin, but so that some wider audience as well could be certain of the statements made; thus, the testimony given could not be denied later. In this regard the value of the vernacular here reminds us of the situation with the Strasbourg Oaths.

- *Sao ko kelle terre* "I-know that those lands." *Sao* "I know" < Latin *sapio. Kelle* "those" < *(ec)ce* "look!" + *ille* "those." *Terre* "lands": compare *terrestrial, terrain, territory.*
- *per kelle fini que ki contene* "within those boundaries that here it-contains." *Fini* "boundaries; ends": compare *final, finite. Ki* "here" < *(ec)ce*

"look!" + *hic* "here," meaning the map he had just referred to; out of *ki*, a subject like "this map" needs to be understood for *contene.*

- *trente anni le possette parte sancti Benedicti* "thirty years them it-possessed, the-party of-St. Benedict." *Anni* "years": compare *annual, anniversary, perennial. Le* "them," direct object pronoun, feminine plural < *ille* "those," demonstrative. *Possette* "it possessed," a shortened form of *possedette,* < *possidere possessus*; compare *possess.*

A bit of Latin still clings to this text: *sancti Benedicti* "of St. Benedict" is pure Latin, the genitive case. For the rest, it is unmistakably Italian, and so close to the modern language that it could be understood today by a child.

Of the seventeen words, all but one (*per*) end in a vowel, a feature that distinguishes this language from the others. A characteristic sound change is seen in *trenta* "thirty" < Latin *triginta.* Intervocalic *g* had changed to yod (/y/) in Vulgar Latin and, in Italian, that sound, when followed by an accented *i* or *e,* disappeared: thus, from Latin *magistrum* "teacher, master" (compare *magisterial, magistrate, master*) comes Italian *maestro,* which we recognize in English, and from *quadragésima* "fortieth" (that is, the fortieth day before Easter) comes *quaresima* "Lent." *Sao* < *sapio* and *possette* < *possedette* both show loss of intervocalic plosive consonants, which, though seen in all three modern languages, is less common in Italian. The characteristic Italian plurals, derived from Latin nominatives (not accusatives), are all found here: nouns of the first class (*terra,* for instance) make their plural in *-e* (*terre* "lands"); nouns of the second (*anno*), in *-i* (*anni* "years"); nouns of the third (*fine*), also in *-i* (*fini* "boundaries").

It is noteworthy that a pair of words that today in standard Italian begin with *qu-* and are pronounced /kw/ (*quelle* "those" and *qui* "here") in this text are written with *k-* (*kelle, ki*) – an early instance of what is still, more than a millennium later, a feature of the Neapolitan dialect!

UMBRIAN FORMULA OF CONFESSION

Text and Setting

From some time in the second half of the eleventh century, two hundred years or more after the proceedings at Capua, a manuscript has preserved a formula for confession that is also unmistakably Italian. Since the manuscript comes from the Abbey of St. Eutizio, near Norcia, in Umbria, it is not surprising that the dialect is Umbrian. Found among other sacramental formulas for penance, the one containing vernacular passages consists of two parts, the confession of the penitent and the reply of the confessor. Of all the instances of improper behavior listed in the formula, the penitent, presumably, admitted only to those of which he was guilty. I present two excerpts:

> *Me accuso de lu corpus Domini, k'io indignamente lu accepi. Me accuso de li mei adpatrini et de quelle penitentie k'illi me puseru e nnoll'observai. Me accuso de lu genitore meu et de la genitrice mia et de li proximi mei, ke ce non abbi quella dilectione ke mesenior Dominideu commandao. Me accuso de li mei sanctuli et de lu sanctu baptismu, ke promiseru pro me et noll'observai. . . . Me accuso de la sancta treva, k'io noll'observai siccomo promisi.*

"I accuse myself of having received the body of the Lord in an unworthy manner. I accuse myself of not having kept the penances that my confessors imposed on me. I accuse myself of not having had, towards my father and my mother and my relatives, the love that the Lord God commanded. I accuse myself of not having kept the promises made in my behalf by my god-parents at my holy baptism. . . . I accuse myself of not having kept the holy truce as I promised."

After other similar statements, the penitent concludes thus:

> *De istis et his similia sì me nde metto en colpa, com'ipsu Dominideu lo sa, k'io menesprisu nde sono. Prego nde la sua sancta misericordia et la intercessione de li soi sancti ke me nd'aia indulgentia. Et prego nde te, sacerdote, ke nd'ore pro me, miseru peccatore, ad dominum nostrum Iesum Christum, et dieme nde penitentia, ke lu diabolu non me nde poza adcusare, k'io iudecatu nde non sia de tutte le peccata mie.*

"I blame myself for these and similar things, since God himself knows that I have fallen into sin. I beg for his holy pity upon them and for the intercession of his saints, that I may have indulgence for them. And I ask you, priest, to pray to our Lord Jesus Christ for me, a miserable sinner, and to grant me penance, so that the devil cannot accuse me of not having been judged for all my sins."

Detailed Observations

- *Me accuso de lu corpus Domini, k'io indignamente lu accepi* "Myself I-accuse of the body of-the-Lord, that I unworthily it received." *Lu corpus Domini* "the body of the Lord": the eucharist is meant. *Lu* "the," definite article < *illu* "that," demonstrative. *K'* "that": the elided form of the all-purpose conjunction and relative pronoun *ke. Io* "I" < *ego*, the intervocalic *g* having dropped out. *Indignamente* "unworthily" < *dignum* "worthy"; the standard Romance way of forming an adverb from an adjective is to add the suffix *-ment(e)* to the feminine form of the adjective – the origin of this procedure was narrated in Chapter Twelve. The second *lu* "it" (< *illu*) is the direct object pronoun, masculine singular.
- *Me accuso de li mei adpatrini et de quelle penitentie k'illi me puseru e nnoll' observai* "Myself I-accuse of the my confessors and of those penances that they on-me imposed and not them I-kept." *Li mei adpatrini* "the my confessors" shows the Italian idiom by which possessive adjectives are accompanied by the definite article. *Puseru* "they imposed" < *posuerunt. Nnoll'* = *non* "not" + *le* "them."
- *Me accuso de lu genitore meu et de la genitrice mia et de li proximi mei* "Myself I-accuse of the father mine and of the mother mine and of the relatives mine." *Proximi* "relatives" < *proximi* "those near by"; compare *proximity, approximate*.
- *ke ce non abbi quella dilectione ke mesenior Dominideu commandao* "that for-them not I-had that love that master Lord-God commanded." *Dilectione* "love": compare *predilection, dilettante. Mesenior* is an honorific term, originally meaning "my lord," and thus comparable to French *monsieur*; the second element (< *seniorem* "elder") is present also in English *sir, sire. Dominideu* "Lord-God" < *dominum* "master" (compare *dominate, dominion, dominatrix*) + *deum* "god" (compare *deity, deify*). *Commandao* "he commanded" < *commandaut* < *commandavit*; the *-t* had been dropped from *commandavit*, and the *v* turned from a consonant sound into a vowel, the resulting diphthong pronounced like *how*.
- *Me accuso de li mei sanctuli et de lu sanctu baptismu, ke promiseru pro me et noll'observai* "Myself I-accuse of the my god-parents and of the holy baptism, that they-promised for me, and not them I-kept." *Sanctuli*

"god-parents": a diminutive of *sancti* "holy ones; saints"; compare *sanctify, saint.*

- *Me accuso de la sancta treva, k'io noll'observai siccomo promisi* "Myself I-accuse of the holy truce, that I not it kept as I-promised." *La sancta treva* "the holy truce," also known as "the truce of God," refers to the periods of Lent and Advent, when men were enjoined, for instance, to refrain from attacking their enemies.

These comments refer to the second excerpt.

- *De istis et his similia sì me nde metto en colpa* "Concerning these-things and to-them similar-things, thus myself of-them I-put at fault." *Nde* "of them," a pronoun < *inde* "thence," an adverb. *Metto* "I place" < *mittere missus* "to send" (compare *admit, remit, submit, mission*), which in all three languages has come to mean "to put, place." *Colpa* "fault": compare *culpable, exculpate* (also *colpes* in the *Sequence of St. Eulalia*).
- *com'ipsu Dominideu lo sa, k'io menesprisu-nde sono* "since himself Lord-God it knows, that I fallen-into-sin have." *Menesprisu sono* is the new analytic Romance perfect, with the verb "to be" as the auxiliary rather than "to have," as happens commonly with intransitive verbs in Italian and French.
- *Prego nde la sua sancta misericordia et la intercessione de li soi sancti* "I-beg for-them (that is, my sins) the his holy pity and the intercession of the his saints." *Prego* "I beg" < *precare* "to beg, pray," which is the source, via French (compare *preier* in the *Sequence*), of *pray*, and also of *precarious*, taken over directly from Latin in the seventeenth century, which meant at first "obtained by begging," then "dependent on the sufferance of another," and finally "chancy, uncertain."
- *ke me nd'aia indulgentia* "that for-me of-them (that is, my sins) there-be indulgence." *Aia* "that there be" < *habere* "to have," often used to express existence; *aia* is subjunctive, in a clause expressing purpose.
- *Et prego nde te, sacerdote, ke nd'ore pro me, miseru peccatore, ad dominum nostrum Iesum Christum et die-me-nde penitentia* "and I-beg for-these-things you, priest, that henceforth you-pray for me, miserable sinner, to lord our Jesus Christ, and that-he-give me for-them penance." *Ore* "that you pray": compare *oratorio, oratory* "place for prayer" (also *oram* in the

Sequence); *ore*, like *die*, is the subjunctive, in a noun clause that is the object of "I beg."

- *ke lu diabolu non me nde poza adcusare, k'io iudecatu-nde non sia de tutte le peccata mie* "that the devil not me of-them be-able to-accuse, that I judged of-them not be of all the sins mine." *Poza* "that he be able" < *poteat* < *potere*, the Vulgar Latin verb that had replaced the irregular Classical *posse*; the form, pronounced /potza/, shows the effect of palatalization (compare *fazet* < *faciat* in the Oaths); *poza* is subjunctive in a clause expressing purpose. *Iudecatu sia* "that I be judged": the new Romance analytic passive, here subjunctive in a noun clause dependent on "to accuse"; *iudecatu* < *iudicare* "to judge"; compare *adjudicate, judicial, judge. Peccata* "sins": compare *peccadillo*, from a Spanish diminutive, and *impeccable* "without sin; flawless."

The Big Picture

In this text also, with its somewhat formulaic religious language, the influence of Latin is still evident, not only in the faithful reproduction of Latin phrases like *dominum nostrum Iesum Christum* "our lord, Jesus Christ" and *de istis et his similia* "concerning these and similar things," but also in the retention of Latinate spellings for words that had changed their pronunciation, as in *dilectione* "love" (contrast modern *dilezione*).

Nonetheless, the Formula reveals several outstanding sound characteristics of Italian: spoken aloud, it would be recognized unmistakably as Italian and could in no way be confused with French. Most conspicuous is the tendency to end words with a vowel. Of the 168 words, only 16 end in a consonant, of which seven are *et* "and" and seven are Latin words, like *corpus* "body." Another distinctive feature of the language is the occasional "irrational" doubling of consonants: *tutte* (< *tote*) and the double *n* in *nnoll'* (< *non* + *le*). (The other doubled consonants are etymological: *accuso* < Latin *accuso*.) Examples of this abound in the modern language: *pubblico* "public" < Latin *publicum, malattia* "illness" < Italian *malato* "ill."

So many Italian words finish in a vowel because so many Latin verb forms that finished in a consonant had lost their distinctive personal endings. Thus, the Formula includes *puseru* "they imposed" < *posuerunt* and *commandao* < *commandavit*. One consequence of so many words ending in a vowel is that elision is frequent. In these excerpts from the Formula, ten instances are found (*k'io* for *ke io, nd'ore* for *nde ore*). In our early French texts, by contrast, elision is much less common: there are only two instances in the Oaths and three in the *Sequence.*

Word order, not inflection, determines meaning. As in all three modern languages, the subject precedes the verb and the object follows it, except for object pronouns (as in *me accuso* "I accuse myself," *lo sa* "he knows it"). Other relations are conveyed through prepositions: *la intercessione de li soi sancti* "the intercession of his saints," *pro me* "for me." The definite article is used freely. Both the new analytic perfect (*menesprisu sono* "I have fallen into sin," where the auxiliary verb is "to be" rather than "to have") and the new analytic passive (*iudecatu sia* "that I be found guilty") are exampled here. In other regards, however, grammar remains unchanged. Several subjunctives are found, employed in the same situations as in Latin: to express purpose (*ke lu diabolu non me poza accusare* "so that the devil not be able to accuse me") and in noun clauses (*prego ke ore pro me* "I beg that you pray for me").

The structure of the sentences in the first excerpt may appear awkward to us. "I accuse myself of the body of the Lord, that I received it unworthily," for instance, sounds almost childish. It could be rendered more smoothly as "I accuse myself of having received the body of the Lord unworthily," but the original shape of the sentence has an appealing directness. It consists of two short, simple clauses rather than one long, complex one. It is concrete and does not involve an abstract verbal noun phrase like "of having received." It announces all its essential elements in the first, main clause – me, the body of the Lord, confession – leaving it to the following, subordinate clause to detail the relations among them.

The vocabulary of the Formula includes the first example we have met so far in these early texts of a word that is not Latin in origin. Whereas all other items here are inherited from Latin, *treva* "truce" is Germanic, from **treuwa.* The word's history is extensive – it reaches English – and exceptionally interesting. Originally, **treuwa* meant "faith; pledge, covenant," whence both *treva* here and English *truce* refer to a specific form of covenant, an armistice. From the same source is derived *true* (and along with it *trust, troth,* and *betrothe*), the earliest sense of which is still seen in a phrase like "she remained true (that is, faithful) to her upbringing." *True* as the opposite of *false,* although the commonest current meaning, is a later development.

ST. FRANCIS OF ASSISI: *SONG OF BROTHER SUN*

Text and Setting

Though earlier verse texts exist in Italian, the *Song of Brother Sun* is commonly regarded as the first distinguished poem of Italian literature. It was composed by one of the most famous and enduringly popular of saints, Francis of Assisi, who lived from around 1182 to 1226. The *Song* (in Latin, *Canticum Fratris Solis*) was composed shortly before Francis's death, and the traditional story about its origin is touching. Feeling himself especially ill and in pain, and close to death, Francis awoke one morning, summoned several of his closest associates, and sang to them this hymn. The language is simple, direct, transparent:

> I. *Altissimu, onnipotente, bon Signore,*
> *tue so le laude, la gloria e l'honore et onne benedictione.*
> *Ad te solo, Altissimo, se konfano;*
> *et nullu homo ene dignu te mentovare.*
>
> II. *Laudato sie, mi Signore, cun tucte le tue creature,*   5
> *spetialmente messor lo frate Sole,*
> *lo qual è iorno, et allumini noi per loi.*
> *Et ellu è bellu e radiante cun grande splendore.*
> *De te, Altissimo, porta significatione.*
>
> III. *Laudato si', mi Signore, per sora Luna e le Stelle;*   10
> *in celu l'ai formate clarite et pretiose et belle.*
>
> IV. *Laudato si', mi Signore, per frate Vento*
> *et per Aere et nubilo et sereno et onne tempo,*
> *per lo quale a le tue creature dai sustentamento.*
>
> V. *Laudato si', mi Signore, per sor' Aqua,*   15
> *la quale è multo utile et humile et pretiosa et casta.*
>
> VI. *Laudato si', mi Signore, per frate Focu,*
> *per lo quale ennallumini la nocte,*
> *ed ello è bello et iocundo et robustoso et forte.*
>
> VII. *Laudato si', mi Signore, per sora nostra matre Terra,*   20
> *la quale ne sustenta et governa*
> *et produce diversi fructi con coloriti fiori et herba.*
>
> VIII. *Laudato si', mi Signore, per quelli ke perdonano per lo tuo amore*

et sostengo infirmitate et tribulatione.
Beati quelli kel sosterrano in pace,   25
ka da te, Altissimo, sirano incoronati.
    IX. Laudato si', mi Signore, per sora nostra Morte Corporale
da la quale nullu homo vivente po skappare.
Guai a cquelli ke morrano ne le peccata mortali;
beati quelli ke trovarà ne le tue sanctissime voluntati,   30
ka la morte secunda nol farrà male.
    X. Laudate et benedicete mi Signore et rengratiate
et serviateli cun grande humilitate.

I. "Lofty, almighty, kindly Lord, yours is the praise, yours the glory and
   honor, yours every blessing; to you alone, lofty one, do they belong, and
   no man is worthy to mention you.

II. Praise be to you, my Lord, along with all your creatures, especially
   brother Sun, who is daylight, and through whom you shed light upon us.
   He is comely and radiant, with great splendor. He represents you, lofty
   one.

III. Praise be to you, my Lord, for sister Moon and the Stars; in heaven you
   have made them, clear and precious and beautiful.

IV. Praise be to you, my Lord, for brother Wind and for the Air, cloudy or
   clear, in every weather, through whom you give sustenance to your
   creatures.

V. Praise be to you, my Lord, for sister Water, who is very useful and
   humble, valuable and pure.

VI. Praise be to you, my Lord, for brother Fire, through whom you brighten
   the night. He is handsome and playful, sturdy and strong.

VII. Praise be to you, my Lord, for our sister, mother Earth, who sustains
   and nourishes us, and brings forth varied fruits along with grass and
   colorful flowers.

VIII. Praise be to you, my Lord, for those who, because of their love for
   you, forgive others and endure illness and tribulation. Blessed are those
   who will endure them in peace, for by you, lofty one, they shall be
   crowned.

IX. Praise be to you, my Lord, for our sister, the Death of the Body, from
   whom no living man can escape. Woe to those who will die in mortal
   sin; but blessed are those whom death will come upon living in accord

Latin Alive

with your holy wishes, for the second death will do them no
harm.
X. Praise and bless my Lord, and give thanks, and serve him with great
humility."

Detailed Observations

The sense of each line is complete in itself.

- *Altissimu, onnipotente, bon Signore* (1) "very-lofty, almighty, kindly Lord."
  Altissimu continues Latin's synthetic superlative *altissimum* "highest, very
  high" < Latin *altum* "high"; compare *altitude*. *Bon* "kindly, good" <
  bonum; compare *bonny, boon, bonbon, bounty, bonanza*, the last having entered American English from Spanish. *Signore* "lord" < *seniorem*
  "elder."
- *tue so le laude, la gloria e l'honore et onne benedictione* (2) "yours are the
  praises, the glory and the honor and every blessing." *So* "they are" <
  sunt. *Laude* "praises": compare *laud, laudable. Onne* "every" < *omnem*,
  with assimilation of *m* to *n*, as in *onnipotente* in the previous line; *omni-*
  appears in many compounds, such as *omnivorous* "all-devouring," *omni-*
  scient "all-knowing." *Benedictione* "blessing" < *bene* "well" + *dictionem*
  "a speaking"; compare *benediction*.
- *Ad te solo, Altissimo, se konfano* (3) "to you alone, very-lofty-one, they-
  belong." *Ad te* "to you": this represents what in Latin would have been
  the dative case. *Se konfano* "they belong" is a pronominal verb.
- *et nullu homo ene dignu te mentovare* (4) "and no man is worthy you
  to-mention." *Nullu* "no, none": compare *null, nullify. Homo* is unusual in
  that it derives from Latin's nominative case, not the accusative (*hominem*).
  Mentovare "to mention" < French *mentevoir* < Latin *mente habere* "to
  have in mind"; even at this early date the Romance languages are borrowing from one another.
- *Laudato sie, mi Signore, cun tucte le tue creature* (5) "praised be-you, my
  Lord, with all the your creatures." *Laudato sie* "praised be you" is the analytic Romance passive; *sie* is the subjunctive, here expressing an indirect
  command. *Tucte* "all" < *totte* < Latin *totae* "entire"; the etymologically
  unjustified *-ct-* may be an attempt to restore an assumed Latin spelling,
  motivated by awareness that other Italian words with *-tt-* were derived
  from Latin words with *-ct-*, for instance, *fatto* "made" < *factum*.

302

- *spetialmente messor lo frate Sole* (6) "especially master the brother Sun." *Messor* "master": of the same origin as *mesenior* in the confessional formula, but showing loss of an interior syllable. *Frate* "brother": compare *fraternal, fraternity* (also *fradre* in the Strasbourg Oaths).
- *lo qual è iorno, et allumini noi per loi* (7) "the which is day(light), and you-shed-light on-us through him." *Iorno* "day" < *diurnum*. *Allumini* "you shed light" < Late Latin *alluminare* < *lumen* "light"; compare *luminous, illuminate*.
- *Et ellu è bellu e radiante cun grande splendore* (8) "and he is handsome and radiant, with great splendor." *Ellu* "he," pronoun < *illum* "that one," a demonstrative. *Bellu* "handsome" < *bellum* "pretty," a colloquial word in Latin, which became so popular that it drove out other comparable terms (*pulcher, formosus*) and produced many cognates in the Romance languages and English; compare *belle, beau, beauty*.
- *De te, Altissimo, porta significatione* (9) "of you, very-lofty-one, it-brings representation." *Porta* "it brings" < *portare*, a thoroughly regular verb that ousted the common but irregular *ferre*.
- *Laudato si', mi Signore, per sora Luna e le Stelle* (10) "praised be-you, my Lord, for sister Moon and the Stars." *Sora* "sister" < *sorora* < *sororem*; compare *sorority*. *Luna* "moon": compare *lunar, lunatic*. *Stelle* "stars": compare *stellar, constellation*.
- *in celu l'ai formate clarite et pretiose et belle* (11) "in heaven them you-have formed clear and valuable and beautiful." *Celu* "heaven": compare *celestial*. *L'* is an elided *le* "them" (< *ille*), the feminine plural object pronoun. *Pretiose* "valuable" < *pretium* "price, value"; compare *precious, price*.
- *Laudato si', mi Signore, per frate Vento* (12) "praised be-you, my Lord, for brother Wind." *Vento* "wind": compare *ventilate* (*wind* is a Germanic word cognate with *ventum*).
- *et per Aere et nubilo et sereno et onne tempo* (13) "and for Air, both cloudy and calm and (in) every weather." *Nubilo* "cloudy" < *nubem* "cloud" (also "veil," in particular "bridal veil," whence *nubile, nuptial*). *Tempo* "weather" (compare *tempest*) < *tempus* "time"; compare *temporal, temporary*.
- *per lo quale a le tue creature dai sustentamento* (14) "through the which to the your creatures you-give sustenance."

- *Laudato si', mi Signore, per sor' Aqua* (15) "praised be-you, my Lord, for sister Water." *Aqua* "water": compare *aqueous, aquarium, aquatic.*
- *la quale è multo utile et humile et pretiosa et casta* (16) "the which is very useful and humble and valuable and pure." *Multo* "very" < *multum* "much"; compare *multitude, multiple, multi-*. *Humile* "humble" < *humilem* "close to the ground; humble" < *humum* "ground."
- *Laudato si', mi Signore, per frate Focu* (17) "praised be-you, my Lord, for brother Fire." *Focu* "fire" < *focum* "hearth."
- *per lo quale ennallumini la nocte* (18) "through the which you-brighten the night." *Nocte* "night": compare *nocturnal.*
- *ed ello è bello et iocundo et robustoso et forte* (19) "and he is handsome and playful and sturdy and strong." *Iocundo* "playful": compare *jocund* and the title of the opera by Ponchielli, *La Gioconda* "The Joyful Girl." *Robustoso* "sturdy": compare *robust. Forte* "strong": compare *fortitude, fortify, fort, force.*
- *Laudato si', mi Signore, per sora nostra matre Terra* (20) "praised be-you, my Lord, for sister our mother Earth." *Matre* "mother": compare *(alma) mater, maternal, matron.*
- *la quale ne sustenta et governa* (21) "the which us sustains and nourishes." *Ne* "us" < *nos*, whereas the *ne* in lines 29 and 30 comes from *in* "in." *Governa* "she nourishes, guides" < *gubernare* "to steer (a ship)" (compare *govern, gubernatorial*) < Greek *kybernan* (compare *cybernetic*).
- *et produce diversi fructi con coloriti fiori et herba* (22) "and produces varied fruits with colorful flowers and grass." *Fiori* "flowers" < *florem*; compare *floral, florid.*
- *Laudato si', mi Signore, per quelli ke perdonano per lo tuo amore* (23) "praised be-you, my Lord, for those who forgive for the your love." *Perdonano* "they forgive" < *perdonare* "to give wholeheartedly" < *donare* "to give."
- *et sostegno infirmitate et tribulatione* (24) "and they-endure illness and tribulation." *Sostengo*: shortened from *sosténgano*, the syllable following the stress having been lost. *Infirmitate* "illness" < *infirmum* "weak" (compare *infirm, infirmary*) < *in-* "not" + *firmum* "strong" (compare *firm*).
- *Beati quelli kel sosterrano in pace* (25) "blessed (are) those who them will-endure in peace." *Beati* "blessed": compare *beatify, beatitude. Kel* = *ke* "who" + *le* "them." *Sosterrano* "they will endure" is the Romance

future, like *sirano, morrano, trovarà,* and *farrà* in the verses following. *Pace* "peace": compare *pacific, peace.*

- *ka da te, Altissimo, sirano incoronati* (26) "for by you, very-lofty-one, they-shall-be crowned." *Sirano incoronati* "they shall be crowned" is the Romance analytic passive. *Incoronati* < *coronam* "crown"; compare *corona, coronation.*
- *Laudato si', mi Signore, per sora nostra Morte Corporale* (27) "praised be-you, my Lord, for sister our Death Bodily." *Corporale* "bodily": compare *corpus, corps, corpuscle, corporal.*
- *da la quale nullu homo vivente po skappare* (28) "from the which no man living can escape." *Vivente* "living": compare *vivid. Skappare* has the same colorful origin as *escape*: both derive from Late Latin *excappare* "to take off one's cloak (when fleeing)" < *ex* "off" + *cappam* "cape, cloak."
- *Guai a cquelli ke morrano ne le peccata mortali* (29) "woe to those who will-die in the sins mortal."
- *beati quelli ke trovarà ne le tue sanctissime voluntati* (30) "blessed (are) those whom it-will-find in the your very-holy wills." *Trovarà* "it will find": the understood subject is "death"; the unusual etymology of this verb is recounted in the previous chapter. *Voluntati* "wills": compare *voluntary, volunteer, volition* (also *vol* in the Oaths.)
- *ka la morte secunda nol farrà male* (31) "for the death second not to-them will-do harm." In "the second death" Francis refers to Judgment Day, when sinners will be damned forever. *Nol* = *non* "not" + *li* "to them."
- *Laudate et benedicete mi Signore et rengratiate* (32) "praise and bless my Lord and give-thanks." *Rengratiate* "thank," imperative plural < *gratiam* "thanks; favor"; compare *grateful, gratitude, grace.*
- *et serviateli cun grande humilitate* (33) "and may-you-serve him with great humility." *Serviateli* = *serviate* "may you (plural) serve" (present subjunctive, here expressing an indirect command or a wish) + *li* "to him."

The Big Picture

Many of the words in the poem are very close to Latin: *benedictione* (2) and *voluntati* (30), for instance, for which the modern language uses *benedizione* and *voluntà*. The *h*, though silent for centuries, appears written here in *humilitate* (33) and *herba* (22); contrast modern *umiltà* and *erba*. These features result from Francis's conscious attempt to write in a Latinate manner rather than from the long persistence of Classical norms.

Nonetheless, the language is unmistakably Italian. Its most characteristic feature of sound, once again, is the powerful tendency for words to end in vowels. Of the 261 words here, only 34 end with a consonant, and of those, all but two are grammatical words, like *per* "for, on account of" and *et* "and." The combination of initial *s* followed by a consonant is tolerated: *spetialmente* (6), *skappare* (28), *splendore* (8) – with the last, contrast Spanish *esplendor*. The characteristic occasional doubling of consonants is found here too: *ennallumini* (18, the double *n*), *farrà* (31). (Other double consonants in the text, some resulting from assimilation, are etymological: *allumini* (7), < *ad* + *luminare*.)

At this early stage, and possibly due also to the interference of Classical Latin, spelling appears inconsistent: for "and" Francis writes not only the Latinate *et* (2) but also *ed* (19) and *e* (8). (The vagaries of the manuscript tradition may well be a cause too.) Certain clusters of consonants are retained intact: *nocte* "night" (18) and *sanctissime* "very holy" (30), which may be contrasted with modern *notte* and *santissime*. No diphthongs are found: "he can" is *po* (28, < *potet*), not yet *può*, and "fire" is *focu* (17), not yet *fuoco*.

A number of words occurring in Francis's poem give an opportunity to point out two sounds that are very distinctively Italian. Similar to one another – they are both called "affricates" – neither found in French and only one in Spanish, the sounds are /tsh/, as in *church*, and /dj/, as in *judge*; the latter is the voiced version of the former. The *t* in *spetialmente* "especially" (6) and the *c* in *benedicete* "bless" (32) and *produce* "produces" (22) were probably already pronounced /tsh/ in Francis's day, and the opening sounds of *iorno* "day" (7) and *iocundo* "playful" (19), which today are written *giorno* and *giocondo*, if not then, soon after came to be pronounced /dj/. These characteristic sounds are found in many Italian words.

The final -*t* that marks the third person singular verb forms has been lost. Francis writes *sustenta* "she sustains" and *produce* "she produces," the Latin forms corresponding to which were *sustentat* and *producit*. These may be contrasted with *dunat* "he gives" in the Oaths. Only a few sounds have been lost within words: *sor(a)* "sister" (10, 15) is shortened from *sorora*, *sostengo* "they endure" (24) from *sostengano*. The contrast between Italian and French in this point is striking, and the word for "price" is a handy further illustration. Latin *pretium* presumably would have remained *pretiu* here (compare *pretiose*, 11), whereas Old French *prix* (> *price*) has already lost the plosive *t* and the entire middle syllable. Because he remains close to Latin, Francis feels no need to experiment with novel letter combinations to represent novel sounds.

No traces of the case system remain in the poem. Word order alone indicates the subject and the object of the verb. Other relations are expressed through prepositions: *a le tue creature* "to your creatures" (14), for example, an indirect object, which in the Oaths would have been conveyed by the oblique case (and in Latin by the dative). The distinctive Italian plural markers are found here too: *-e* for nouns ending in *-a* (*stelle* "stars," 10), *-i* for those ending both in *-o* (*fructi* "fruits," 22) and in other letters (*voluntati* "wills," 30). The definite article is common. The text includes instances of all three of the big Romance innovations in the verb: the future built on the infinitive (*farrà* "it will do," 30), the analytic passive made with the verb "to be" (*sirano incoronati* "they will be crowned," 26), and the analytic perfect made with "to have" (*ai formate* "you have formed," 11). In the last two examples, in accord with the origins of the constructions, the participle shows agreement: in the passive, agreement with the subject of the verb ("they," masculine plural); in the perfect, with the object (the stars, feminine plural).

The vocabulary of the poem is pure Latin; not one word is of Celtic, Germanic, or Arabic origin. And yet it is remarkable how many words appear which, though always of Latin provenance, have become the Romance replacements for standard Classical terms. Thus, we read *signore* (1) and *messor* (6) "lord, master" in place of Classical *dominum*; *tucte* "all" (5) for *omnes* (though the latter is also used here); *iorno* "day" (7) for *diem*; *bellu* "beautiful" (8) for *formosum*; *grande* "big" (8) for *magnum*; *portare* "to carry" (9) for *ferre*; *focu* "fire" (17) for *ignem*, *perdonare* "to pardon" (23) for *ignoscere*; *skappare* "to escape" (28) for *fugere*; and *trovare* "to find" (30) for *invenire*.

Literary Appreciation

The *Song of Brother Sun*, though poetic, is not a poem in strict form. With its parallel phrasings and its groupings of short phrases by twos and threes, it resembles more than anything the Psalms of the Bible, and since it is modeled on them, that is hardly surprising. At the same time, it shows the influence of rhythmic, rhymed prose, which was becoming prominent in Francis's day. Assonant rhyme is common in the poem, sometimes consisting of two vowels, sometimes of just one. The first stanza illustrates the possibilities: *signore*...

Latin Alive

benedictione... konfano... mentovare. Consonant rhyme is also heard, for instance in the third stanza: *stelle... belle.*

Within the governing pattern by which nearly every stanza begins with *laudato si', mi Signore* "praise be to you, my Lord," Francis varies stanzas two through seven by praising brothers and sisters in strict alternation: *frate Sole... sora Luna,* and so on. The poem has a clear structure, moving towards its conclusion in marked stages. The first stanza is a general glorification of the Lord himself, ending with a reminder of the distance between the Lord and mankind: "no man is worthy to mention you." The second stanza, introducing the poem's central section, which glorifies the Lord through aspects of his Creation, contains three significant phrases. The Lord is praised not alone, but "along with all [his] creatures" – that union defines the unfolding poem. Then, the Lord is said to shed light upon us by means of the Sun, the first aspect of the Creation. At the end, Francis adds "[the Sun] represents you" – literally, "brings [to us] the significance of you" – which applies equally to all the following aspects as well. The entire universe, the Lord's creation, is inseparable from him, we are told; it is the agency of his helping us; it is a reflection and reminder of him.

The enumeration of the various aspects continues. After the heavenly bodies, which are remote from us but close to the Lord (*Altissimo* he is thrice called), Francis moves on to the four elements that, according to a medieval notion, constitute our material world: air, water, fire, and earth. All is seen in its relation to mankind: the Sun provides us with light and the Earth nourishes us.

The poem comes to a climax in stanzas eight and nine, where the focus shifts from the inanimate natural world to mankind – it is noteworthy that in this poem Francis makes no mention of birds or other animals – and mankind is now viewed in relation to the Lord, a contrast to the opening stanza. In the eighth stanza, the Lord is praised on account of those who, through love for him, pardon others and calmly endure sufferings; forgiveness and forbearance are prominent features of human life as Francis conceives of it. The ninth stanza, which deals with death, nearly reproduces the structure of the previous one. The Lord is praised on account of something – here, the death of the body – and this stanza also ends with a statement of who shall be blessed and why ("blessed are those who..." and "for..." get repeated). But in this stanza the blessed are contrasted with the damned, those who will die in mortal sin and not be resurrected on Judgment Day; that will be their "second death." In the end, the Lord is *praised* for the death of the body – a striking, perhaps disturbing, paradox, which can be justified on the grounds that death reveals and rewards, ineluctably and eternally, the quality of a person's moral life; the death of the body, for some, is the start of the true life. In Francis's eyes, this is the noblest feature of Creation.

Yet the oneness he feels with even the inanimate features of Creation he movingly conveys by presenting them as our siblings: he refers to them as "brother Wind," "sister Water," and so forth. Furthermore, he attributes human features to them through the adjectives he applies, which are typically ones suitable for people and at the same time suggestive of their own intrinsic qualities: in calling Water "chaste" and "humble," he points to its purity and its tendency to seek the lowest level; in calling Fire "playful," he reminds us of the unpredictable leaping about of flames.

My understanding of the poem, though shared by many, is controversial, because it rests on taking the repeated *per* in *laudato si', mi Signore, per* ("may you be praised, my Lord") as meaning "on account of, because of." Many other interpreters have taken *per* to mean "by," a sense the preposition can unquestionably also have. This leads to a completely different reading of the poem. On that view, the Lord is to be glorified *by* Creation, not on account of it; all features of the universe are to join in singing his praises. This yields splendid significance and is supported by Psalm 148, the most direct inspiration for Francis's poem, which bids all Creation praise the Lord. The arguments on both sides of the question are strong, and the intense and significant controversy, though it cannot be settled here, must at least be registered.

CHAPTER SIXTEEN

SPANISH

POLITICAL HISTORY OF THE IBERIAN PENINSULA

Three centuries after the Visigoths, who had entered from France, the Arabs crossed the Strait of Gibraltar and invaded the Iberian peninsula. After a swift, decisive victory over the Christians at Jerez de la Frontera in 711, they needed only seven more years to overrun the peninsula. They did not, however, succeed in conquering the whole of it, for the northernmost regions remained beyond their grasp. That the north stayed free is not surprising because by invading from the south the Arabs pushed their surviving opponents into territory more mountainous and therefore more resistant. The next eight centuries in Iberia were dominated by the Reconquest, the gradual success of the Christian kings in retaking what had been lost to the Arabs. The linguistic–political history of the peninsula can be conveniently, if crudely, envisioned as the unrolling of three vertical stripes: three northern regions that each extended its political power and linguistic influence southwards. The western stripe represents the Galician and Portuguese languages; the eastern, Catalan; the broad central stripe, Castilian.

Galicia is the northwestern region of Spain. As the Reconquest, starting from the Kingdom of Asturias, advanced slowly southwards, the local version of Romance speech spread with it. After the capture of Toledo, in 1085, a signal event in the story, the King of Castile, Alfonso VI, gave two of his daughters in marriage to two Burgundian brothers, presenting each son-in-law with a broad strip of territory along the western edge of the peninsula, with the River Minho set as the border between them. The northern of those two dowry territories, Galicia, stayed close to Castile and today forms part of Spain. The dynasty that ruled the southern territory was more independent, and in 1143 was recognized

as ruling the Kingdom of Portugal. In continuing the Reconquest, it pushed its southern border all the way down to the Mediterranean, its present boundary; the Minho remains the country's northern frontier. The speech in the two territories was closely similar for several centuries, and even today Galician resembles Portuguese more than it does Spanish.

Catalonia, in the northeast of the peninsula, was once the Spanish March of the Franks, established as a buffer against Arab invasion. In the early twelfth century, the various counties composing the March were united under the sway of Barcelona. The ruling dynasty, in the course of the next century, expanded its domains steadily southwards, past Valencia to Alicante, and also captured the islands of Majorca and Minorca. By a marriage, the County of Barcelona was joined in 1137 to the Kingdom of Aragon, which in turn was later joined to Castile. Links between Catalonia and southern France have always been close, and, like the land itself, the Catalan language occupies an intermediate position between Spanish and French.

A couple of the terms I just used to describe Catalonia's political status are etymologically intriguing. *March* is of Germanic origin, deriving from Frankish *marka*, which at first meant "boundary" and then "border district." In Britain, *the Marches* refers to those parts of England adjoining Wales and Scotland; the man governing such a border area was known as a *marquis.* A Latin cognate of *marka* is *marginem* "edge," which we recognize in English. *Marka* also appears in English as *mark,* in which the sense of "boundary" has developed through "track, trace" to "imprint." *County,* by contrast, comes from Latin. In the late Roman Empire *comitem* "companion" became a formal title bestowed by the emperor; via French *comte,* it entered English as *count.* A *county* was, originally, the territory governed by a count. (*March* in the sense of "walk" and *count* in the sense of "number" are unrelated.)

Castile, located in the northern central region of the peninsula, was, in alliance with León, most responsible for conducting the Reconquest. Its successful push towards the south can be traced in the recapture of Toledo (1085), Córdoba (1236), and Seville (1248). Finally, in the epoch-making year of 1492, the Kingdom of Granada, the last relic of Moorish presence in the peninsula, was destroyed, and the Arabs were utterly expelled from Europe. By virtue of its leadership during the Reconquest, and through a series of well-executed marriages and other alliances, Castile became the dominant power, the locus of Spanish rule, with its capital established first at Burgos and then, from 1561, in Madrid. As a consequence, the Castilian version of Romance speech became the standard national language. The explanation for Castilian's primacy therefore resembles that for Francien's.

THE GLOSAS EMILIANENSES AND GLOSAS SILENSES

Two manuscripts from the tenth century preserve priceless documents of early Romance speech in Spain, in the form of glosses. These two sets of glosses, written into the margins or between the lines of Latin texts, form a fascinating treasury of Spanish, giving us insights into the state of the language at that time and place. They differ from the *Reichenau Glossary* in that they are preserved together with the continuous texts they gloss, with the result that the juxtaposed Latin original can often help us understand the meaning or use of the Romance words. One particularly remarkable feature is the variety of languages other than Latin that are the sources of the glossing vocabulary.

The glosses are named for the monasteries in which the manuscripts containing them were compiled, San Millán de la Cogolla (the Glosas Emilianenses) and Santo Domingo de Silos (the Glosas Silenses), both located in far northern central Spain and therefore in territory that had not fallen into Arab hands. The former lies in what was then the Kingdom of Navarre, and a few of its features correspond to the local dialect. The latter, although it lies in Castile, the kingdom adjoining Navarre to the west, also shares Navarrese features. The two sets of glosses are united, nonetheless, in revealing to us a version of the language close to Castilian.

The two manuscripts are made up of varied religious texts – sermons, epistles, homilies, edifying episodes from the lives of early Christians, and a penitential that lays down the penance to be performed for specific sins. The manuscript from San Millán was written in the late ninth or early tenth century, but the glosses were added by other hands later, around the middle of the tenth century. The texts and glosses in the manuscript from Silos were both written by the same person and at the same time, in the second half of the tenth century, which implies they were copied from an earlier manuscript that already contained the glosses. (If these dates are right, the glosses are roughly contemporary with the judicial proceedings from Monte Cassino; a few scholars, however, put them a century later.) Certain similarities, including some shared errors, suggest that both sets may have drawn from a common source, presumably a lost Latin-Romance glossary. Since they originate at the same time and place, for our purposes they can be treated together.

The entries reveal much through not only the glossing items but also the glossed. On the one hand, the words selected for glossing inform us about the state of Latin comprehension at that period. The very presence of a gloss indicates that a Latin word or phrase was unclear. From *bellum : pugna* "fight" (Glosas Emilianenses 4) we deduce that Classical Latin *bellum* was not understood by a reader or a potential reader. On the other hand, the explanatory glosses reveal many features of the vernacular, the language that had already changed a great deal from Classical Latin, and it is with them that our interest lies.

The Earliest Spanish Prose

The glosses consist of single words usually, sometimes short phrases – with one exception. In the manuscript from San Millán, at the end of a sermon by

Augustine, a brief, continuous vernacular passage is found, which constitutes
the earliest known instance of Spanish prose (Emil. 89):

> *Cono ajutorio de nuestro dueno, dueno Christo, dueno Salbatore, qual dueno*
> *get ena honore, e qual duenno tienet ela mandatjone cono Patre, cono Spiritu*
> *Sancto, enos sieculos de los sieculos. Faca nos Deus omnipotes tal serbitjo fere*
> *ke denante ela sua face gaudioso segamus. Amem.*

"With the help of Christ, our Lord and Savior, who is honored and holds the
power together with the Father and the Holy Ghost, for ever and ever. May
almighty God make us perform such service that we may be blessed in his
eyes. Amen."

- *Cono ajutorio de nuestro dueno, dueno Christo, dueno Salbatore* "With
  the help of our Lord, Lord Christ, Lord Savior." *Cono = con* "with" +
  o "the" (< *lo*), masculine singular article. *Ajutorio* "help" < Classical
  Latin *adjutare* "to help"; compare *adjutant, aid(e)*, also *aiudha* in the first
  Strasbourg Oath. *Dueno* "lord" < *dominum* "master"; compare *dominate*,
  also *domnizelle* in the *Sequence of St. Eulalia. Salbatore* "savior" < *salvare*
  "to save"; compare *salvation, save, safe*, also *salvar* and *salvament* in the
  first Oath.
- *qual dueno get ena honore* "which Lord is in the honor." *Ena = en* "in" +
  a "the" (< *la*), feminine singular article.
- *e qual duenno tienet ela mandatjone* "and which Lord has the power."
  Tienet "he has" < *tenere* "to hold, have"; compare *tenet, tenant, tenacious.*
  Mandatjone "power" < *mandare* "to entrust; order"; compare *mandate,
  command, demand.*
- *cono Patre, cono Spiritu Sancto, enos sieculos de los sieculos* "with the Father,
  with the Spirit Holy, for the centuries of the centuries." *Enos = en* "in" +
  os "the" (< *los*), masculine plural article. *Sieculos* "centuries" < *seculum*
  "age, generation, century"; compare *secular.*
- *Faca nos Deus omnipotes tal serbitjo fere* "May-he-make us, God almighty,
  such service to-do," that is, may God almighty make us do such service.
  Faca "may he make," subjunctive expressing a wish, < *facere* "to do, make"
  (compare *manufacture, factory*); from the same verb comes *fere* "to do"
  (compare *faire* in the *Sequence*). *Serbitjo* "service" < *servire* "to serve";
  compare *serve, service, servitude*, also *servir* in the *Sequence.*

- *ke denante ela sua face gaudioso segamus* "that before the his face joyous we-may-be." *Denante* "before" < *de* "from" + *in* "in" + *ante* "before," a typical compound Romance preposition. *Gaudioso* "joyous" < *gaudium* "joy"; compare *joy*. *Segamus* "we may be," subjunctive in a purpose clause, < *sedeamus*; the *g* here represents the sound of yod /y/, the sequence of pronunciations running /sed-e-a-mus/, with palatalization, > /sed-ya-mus/ > /se-ya-mus/.

We observe here the preservation of voiceless intervocalic plosives (*ajutorio, faca*). This is a feature of the Navarrese dialect, while in Castilian the *t* and *c* would turn into their voiced equivalents, *d* and *g* (*ayuda, haga*). In regard to sound, the most distinctive trait of the text – and a characteristic of the Spanish language generally – is the large number of diphthongs: *tienet* (< *tenet*), *sieculos* (< *seculum*), *nuestro* (< *nostrum*), *dueno* (< *dominum*). Stressed vowels in Spanish, we recall, became diphthongs in more situations than in the other two languages.

Grammatical function of nouns is indicated by word order or by preposition, not by inflection. The plural is marked by *-s* (*sieculos* "ages"). *Honore* "honor," though a masculine noun in Latin (and masculine too in Modern Spanish), is feminine here – a reminder that the genders of nouns, especially those of the third declension, like *honorem*, were somewhat liable to vary. *Seculum* "age," neuter in Latin, has been converted, typically, to masculine. The definite article is common, and its forms in this text are surprisingly varied. The feminine singular is *ela* or *la* (< *illa*), the masculine plural *los* (< *illos*), but, when combined with certain prepositions, they lose the *l* sound: *en* + *la* > *ena*, *en* + *los* > *enos*.

The verbs also present some interesting forms. The third person singular ending *-t*, soon to be lost, is still preserved here: *get* "he is," *tienet* "he has." Noteworthy in particular is *segamus* "that we may be," the subjunctive of *esse* "to be." This fundamental verb, already irregular in Latin, underwent many changes in its passage to the various Romance languages. Among other things, several of its forms got replaced by others derived from a different verb. The verb *sedere sessus*, originally meaning "to sit" (compare *seat, sedentary, session*), became employed in Spanish for the present infinitive (*ser*) and the subjunctive (*segamus*).

315

Sounds and Writing

The individual glosses, which make up the rest of the two sets, give further evidence of the changes in sound that already characterized Spanish Romance. The confusion of *b* and *v*: *culpauiles* "guilty" (Sil. 106, < *culpabilis*); *beces* "times, opportunities" (Emil. 73, < *vices*; compare *vice versa*). Palatalization: *fazen* /fatsen/ "they do" (Emil. 72, < *faciunt*); *zerte* /tserte/ "certainly" (Emil. 137, < *certe*). Diphthongization of accented vowels, especially *e* and *o*: *bientos* "winds" (Sil. 276, < *ventos*; compare *ventilate*); *conbienet* "it is right" (Sil. 228, < *convenit*; compare *convenient*); *cuempetet* "let him calculate" (Emil. 70, < *computet*; compare *compute, count*); *muerte* "death" (Sil. 57, < *mortem*; compare *mortal*). The letter *g* used to represent yod: *punga* /pu-nya/ "fight" (Sil. 48, < *pugnam*; compare *pugnacious, repugnant*).

It is worth mentioning several of the changes that have *not* taken place. The Royal Spanish Academy of the Language has not yet imposed etymological spellings, so the silent letter *h* sometimes is written, but sometimes not: we read both *honore* "honor" (Sil. 89, < *honorem*) and *uamne* "man" (Emil. 70, < *hominem*). The prothetic *e-* is not found on *spiritu* "spirit" (Emil. 89 – contrast modern *espíritu*), which, to be sure, may be due to this word's being familiar from the Latin of religious usage. Many words, infinitives particularly, end with an *-e* that would soon be lost: *cantare* "to sing" (Sil. 250), *flore* "flower" (Emil. 133). *Fartare* "to suffice" (Sil. 336) and *famne* "hunger" (Sil. 340) show us that, in this time and place, initial *f-* has remained and not been changed to *h-*, nor indeed ought anything else to be expected in these Navarrese documents, since that puzzling sound change was in fact one of the peculiarities of the Castilian dialect: in Modern Spanish the words are *hartar* and *hambre*.

Forms and Syntax

The plurals of nouns are invariably formed with *-s*, whether the singular ends with *-a* (*penas* "tortures," Emil. 104, singular *pena*), or *-o* (*paganos* "pagans," Sil. 51, singular *pagano*), or another letter (*partes* "parts," Emil. 24, singular *parte*). Latin neuters have regularly become Spanish masculines, their plurals now ending in *-s* rather than *-a*: *cuerpos* "bodies" (Sil. 327, instead of Latin *corpora*), *agueros* "auguries" (Sil. 111, instead of *auguria*). The other common fate of Latin neuters is also exampled here, conversion of the plural, ending in *-a*, into a feminine singular, for which then a new plural in -*as* is created: *las votas* "marriage" (Sil. 248, < *votum* "vow," plural *vota*).

Prepositions have taken over the function of Latin's oblique cases: the genitive is replaced by *de* (*rurium* [genitive plural]: *de las tierras* "of the lands," Sil. 360), the dative by *a* (*voluptatibus* [dative plural]: *a las voluntates malas* "for pleasures : for evil desires," Sil. 195 – notice the equation!), the ablative by some preposition (*sponte* [ablative singular] : *de voluntate* "by one's own will," Sil. 94).

The new Romance way of forming adverbs from adjectives can be glimpsed among the glosses: *caste : munda mientre* "purely" (Sil. 20 – *mientre* is often found in early Spanish for *miente* or *mente*); *buena mientre* "well, carefully" (Emil. 58). Similarly, the comparative forms are analytic now rather than synthetic: *asperius: plus aspero, mas* "more harshly" (Emil. 105). The gloss offers *mas (aspero)* as an alternative translation to *plus aspero*: both adverbs were evidently in use, although ultimately *mas* won out in Spanish, as *plus* did in French and Italian.

The verb too, of course, has changed much from Latin: many old forms have been discarded, and new ones take their place. The third person singular ending -*t* is still retained (*venot* "he came," Emil. 9, < *venit*), but the -*nt* of Latin's third person plural, though sometimes written (*fuerent* "they were," Sil. 101, < *fuerunt*), is decidedly more often shortened to -*n* (*sierben* "they serve," Sil, 49, < *serviunt*), which soon became the standard ending.

The innovating Romance future is frequent: *tornaras* "you will turn" (Emil. 143), where -*as* (from the auxiliary *habere* "to have") is added to the infinitive *tornar(e)*; *faras* "you will do" (Emil. 140). It is fascinating to observe that, at the time the glosses were created, the two elements of the new form had not yet been welded together. They were still independent enough that it was possible to insert a pronoun between them: *tardarsan* "they will delay" (Emil. 70, = *tardar-se-an*, modern *se tardarán*); *enplirnosamus* "we will be filled" (Emil. 124, = *enplir-nos-amus*, modern *nos henchiremos*).

The combination of the verb "to be" with the past participle has taken the place of Latin's synthetic passive: *tradantur : donatu siegan* "let them be handed over" (Sil. 172); *comburatur: kematu siegat* "let it be burnt" (Sil. 9 – with Latin *comburere* "to burn," compare *combustion*, also *bust* < Latin *ambustum*). The construction is common to the Romance languages, but Spanish shows a certain peculiarity in regard to the passive: more freely than the other languages, it can express the notion of the passive by using a verb reflexively (that is to say, with a reflexive pronoun). This also is found in these early documents. A fine, probative instance, in which the intended meaning is put beyond doubt by the Latin, is *abitationes antiquas desolabuntur : nafregarsan* "the old houses will be destroyed" (Emil. 20 – and note that in the Latin the subject of the verb is in the accusative case), where *nafregarsan = nafregar-se-an*. Since the subject is inanimate, the verb cannot be a genuine reflexive here, for it makes no sense to say literally "the houses will destroy themselves." (*Nafregare* originally had the more specific, more colorful meaning "to suffer shipwreck," < *navem* "ship" + *frangere* "to break.") Another example of the passive reflexive is *dum mazerentur : ata ke se monden* "until they (pigs) are purified" (Sil. 328); despite the reflexive pronoun, this cannot mean "until the pigs purify themselves."

Latin's present participle had already fallen out of use by the time the glosses were composed. Occasionally it is translated into the vernacular with a relative clause: *euntes : qui ban* "going (ones): those who go" (Sil. 152), where *ban < vadunt.* More often, it is rendered with the Romance languages' replacement for the present participle, the ablative of the Latin gerund: *revertente : retornando* "returning" (Sil. 160), *ignorans : non sapiendo* "not knowing" (Sil. 339).

In these early documents the subjunctive occurs often – even in the past tense: *naisceset* "(before) he had been born" (Sil. 271, < *nasci(vi)sset*, the pluperfect subjunctive) – and in the same grammatical situations as in Latin. For indirect commands: *labatu siegat* "let it be washed" (Sil. 11; *labatu < lavare* "to wash" – compare *lave, lavabo, lavatory, laundry*). To express purpose (or result): *ke . . . gaudioso segamus* "so that we may be joyous" (Emil. 89). In clauses referring to a future event: *ata que mueran* "until they die" (Sil. 210).

Vocabulary

The more than five hundred glosses found in the two manuscripts yield an exceptionally interesting crop of vocabulary items. Most of those types of alteration to the inherited Latin words that we surveyed earlier are exampled here, as are, remarkably, all the significant non-Latin sources of the Romance lexicon.

The glosses register the fact that certain common Latin words had gone out of use, to be replaced by other Latin words that were somehow more distinctive. The third person pronoun gives way to what had been a forceful demonstrative: *eos : akelos* "them" (Sil. 300), < *eccu* "behold!" + *illos* "those." One of the Latin demonstratives disappears in favor of another, which was more substantial and more distinctive: *hii : estos* "these (men)" (Sil. 87), < *istos* "those" (compare *ist* in the first Strasbourg Oath.) The word for "every, all," which must once have been on everyone's lips, gets changed too: *omnia : totas cosas* "all things" (Sil. 121 – *omnia* is neuter, a notion that the modern languages can only capture with a separate word). The suppletion of the verb "to be" we have already come across: *esse : sedere* "to be" (Sil. 72). Another common irregular verb, *ferre*, has completely disappeared from the lexicon, as can be seen from *fere : levare* "to carry, lift" (Sil. 351; modern *llevar*).

It is also easy to discover verbs used in the glosses that, because they were particular or otherwise vivid, took the place of others less colorful. For *invenire* "to find" the vernacular substitutes *afflare*, originally "to blow towards" (modern *hallar*): *jnveniebit : aflarat* "he will find" (Emil. 29 – the story, which involves hunting, is narrated in Chapter Seven, as is the story of the next word). Instead of the plain *accedere* "to draw near," the language turns to a term that at first referred specifically to sailing: *accedant : aplekan* "they approach, arrive" (Sil. 127), < *applicare* "to put in." We also read among the glosses *interficiat : matare* "kill" (Sil. 93); the literary *interficere* is replaced by a word once associated with ritual sacrifice. It is curious to find in a Spanish text *ederit : manducaret* "he will eat" (Sil. 338), since, although all the modern languages abandoned Classical *edere*, French and Italian eventually replaced it with this verb (*manger, mangiare*) meaning "to chomp, chew," whereas Spanish replaced it with *comer* (< *comedere*).

Other changes to the lexicon are less easy to characterize, if not less intriguing. *Catare* (< *captare*, frequentative of *capere* "to capture") was a common verb in early Spanish, with a variety of meanings; in *adtendat : katet* (Emil. 65) the sense is "let him pay attention." From the language of veterinarians *gamba* had passed into general usage, and is now found among our glosses: *femora : campas* "legs" (Sil. 139). In the entry *respuit : geitat* "he rejects" (Emil. 45), the modern verb *echar* makes an early appearance; it derives from *iectare* "to toss out, toss away," which is also the basis for those many English compounds with *-ject*, such as *reject, project*, etc.

Despite their early date, the glosses illustrate the full panorama of languages other than Latin that added to the Romance vocabulary. From Late Greek come a pair of kinship terms: *abunculi : tio* "uncle" (Sil. 223) and *matertere : tia* "aunt" (Sil. 224). Celtic contributes a word that was central in feudal society: *militatores : basallos* "soldiers, vassals" (Sil. 247); the base of the word, Latinized as *vassus*, is cognate with Old Irish *foss* "servant," wherein lies the origin of the familiar surname. The gloss *galea : bruina* "helmet" (Emil. 89) presents several problems. For one thing, it is wrong: a *byrnie*, as it is called in English, is armor for the body, not the head. And in any event its origin is unclear, since, although it is found in Old English, and is presumably Germanic, it may derive in turn from a Celtic word.

Indisputably Germanic, however, are these two glosses: *galea : gelemo* "helmet" (Emil. 112 – compare *helmet*), a correct translation; and *pecuniam : ganato* "money; cattle" (Emil. 84). An interesting tale, and a precious souvenir of early societies, lies embedded in the latter. Latin *pecunia* at first meant "cattle" (< *pecus* "herd") and then, within the Classical period, because cattle were a conspicuous form of wealth and a useful standard of valuation, "money." The Spanish term (modern *ganado*) traveled in precisely the opposite direction, signifying originally "earnings; goods" (English *gain* is related) and later, more specifically, "cattle," the current meaning. After the German tribes came the Arab invaders, and they too made a contribution that can be caught in these texts: *donec : ata cuando* "until" (Emil. 110), where *ata* (modern *hasta*) is of Arabic origin. Finally, these tenth-century glosses reveal that one Romance language was already borrowing from another. In *consobrina : cusina* "(female) cousin" (Sil. 222), the vernacular translation has certainly entered Spanish, not directly from Latin, but from French (compare French *cousine*).

THE CID

Text and Setting

One of the foundational poems of Spanish literature is the anonymous early epic, the *Cid*, which recounts the exploits of the warrior, Rodrigo (Ruy) Díaz de Bivar, nicknamed the Cid. Despite his military successes in behalf of the King of Castile, Alfonso VI, the Cid becomes suspect in his eyes, and the king banishes him. This occurs at the start of the poem, in the course of which the Cid battles in behalf of both Moors and Christians and undergoes other trials as well. The figure of the Cid, a historical personage, who we know died in 1099, soon after became shrouded in legendary episodes, which have continued their popularity until today. The nearly complete poem that survives, written in the late twelfth or early thirteenth century, at least a hundred years after the events it narrates, is the chief source for the story, but by no means the only one. Composed early and in the Castilian dialect, which would become the national standard, it is scarcely less valuable as a linguistic document than as a historical or literary one.

Like other anonymous medieval epics – *Beowulf* or the *Song of Roland* – the *Cid* has been preserved by an extremely slender thread, a single manuscript, which in fact is defective, lacking the beginning, the end, and a passage in the middle. The manuscript is not the author's original, but a copy made in the mid-fourteenth century. What we do have of the poem, some 3,700 verses, is enough, nevertheless, to create a rounded, persuasive, memorable image of early Spain, a society in which honor is of paramount importance. Our excerpt, drawn from the beginning of the poem, tells of the exiled Cid's departure from his home and his reception in Burgos.

> *De los sos ojos tan fuertemientre llorando,*
> *Tornava la cabeça i estáva-los catando.*
> *Vío puertas abiertas e uços sin cañados,*
> *Alcándaras vázias sin pielles e sin mantos*
> *E sin falcones e sin adtores mudados.* 5
> *Sospiró mio Çid, ca mucho avie grandes cuidados.*
> *Fabló mio Çid bien e tan mesurado:*
> *"Grado a tí, señor padre, que estás en alto!*
> *Esto me han buolto mios enemigos malos."*
> *Allí pienssan de aguijar, allí sueltan las riendas.* 10
> *A la exida de Bivar ovieron la corneja diestra,*
> *E entrando a Burgos oviéron-la siniestra.*
> *Meçió mio Çid los ombros y engrameó la tiesta:*
> *"Albricia, Álbar Fáñez, ca echados somos de tierra!*
> *Mas a grand ondra tornaremos a Castiella."* 14b
> *Mio Çid Ruy Díaz por Burgos entróve,* 15
> *En sue conpaña sessaenta pendones;*
> *Exien lo ver mugieres e varones,* 16b
> *Burgeses e burgesas por las finiestras sone,*
> *Plorando de los ojos, tanto avien el dolore.*
> *De las sus bocas todos dizían una razone:*
> *"Dios, qué buen vassallo, si oviesse buen señore!"* 20
> *Conbidar le ien de grado, mas ninguno non osava:*
> *El rey don Alfonsso tanto avie la grand saña.*

Antes de la noche en Burgos dél entró su carta,
Con grand recabdo e fuertemientre sellada:
Que a mio Çid Ruy Díaz, que nadi nol diessen posada,   25
E aquel que gela diesse sopiesse vera palabra,
Que perderie los averes e más los ojos de la cara,
E aun demás los cuerpos e las almas.
Grande duelo avien las yentes cristianas;
Ascónden-se de mio Çid, ca nol osan dezir nada.   30

"With his eyes weeping so copiously, he turned his head and looked back at his palaces. He saw the gates thrown open, the doors without their padlocks, empty pegs, without their furs and mantles, perches without their molted falcons and hawks. The Cid sighed, because he was very troubled. The Cid spoke, well and with moderation: "Thanks be to you, Father, who is in heaven! My wicked enemies have brought this upon me." Then they thought of spurring on the horses and gave them their head. When departing from Bivar, they had had a crow on the right. Entering Burgos now, they had one on the left. The Cid shrugged his shoulders and shook his head. "Good news!, Álvar Fáñez, for we have been exiled from the land. But we will return to Castile with great honor." The Cid Ruy Díaz entered Burgos with sixty banners in his entourage. Men and women came out to see him; all the townspeople were at the windows. Their eyes weeping, they were deeply grieved. Everyone's mouth expressed but a single opinion: "O God, what a good vassal, if only he had a good master!" They would gladly have invited him, but nobody dared. The King, don Alfonso, was furiously angry. Before nightfall a letter from him had reached Burgos, boldly sealed and conveying his strong injunction: let nobody give lodging to the Cid Ruy Díaz; let any who should give it to him know for certain that he would lose his possessions and the eyes in his head, even his body and soul. The Christian folks were sorely grieved. They hid themselves from the Cid, for they dared not say anything to him."

Detailed Observations

- *De los sos ojos tan fuertemientre llorando* (1) "from the their eyes so powerfully weeping." *Ojos* "eyes" < *oculum*; compare *ocular, oculist. Llorando* "weeping" < Latin *plorare*; compare *implore.*

- *Tornava la cabeça i estáva-los catando* (2) "he-turned the head and he-was them looking-at." *Tornava* "he turned" < *tornare* "to turn on a lathe; turn" < Greek *tornos* "lathe." *Cabeça* "head" < *capittiam*, a diminutive of *caput*; compare *capital*. *Estava* "he was" < *stare* "to stand."
- *Vío puertas abiertas e uços sin cañados* (3) "he-saw gates open and doors without padlocks." *Vío* "he saw" < *videre visus* "to see"; compare *video, visual, vision*. *Puertas* "gates": compare *portal*. *Abiertas* "open" < *aperire apertus*; compare *apéritif, aperture*. *Uços* "doors" < Late Latin *ustium* < *ostium*; from *ustiarius*, originally "doorkeeper," comes, via French, *usher*, now one who shows people to their seats.
- *Alcándaras vázias sin pielles e sin mantos* (4) "pegs empty, without furs and without mantles." *Alcándaras*, an Arabic word, refers to wooden rods used for various purposes; it is rendered as "pegs" here and "perches" in the next verse.
- *E sin falcones e sin adtores mudados* (5) "and (perches) without falcons and without hawks molted." *Falcones* "falcons" < Late Latin *falconem*, perhaps < *falcem* "sickle," on account of the shape of the bird's hooked claws; from *falconem* derives the surname Faulkner. *Adtores* "hawks" (modern *azores*) is the origin of *Azores*, the Atlantic archipelago that once abounded in these birds. *Mudados* "molted" < *mutare* "to change" (compare *mutate*), also the source of *molt*. The point of this detail is that they are strong and healthy, having already passed through the period of molting their feathers, during which they are particularly vulnerable.
- *Sospiró mio Çid, ca mucho avie grandes cuidados* (6) "sighed my Cid because much he-had great worries." *Çid*: for his prowess, the hero Ruy Díaz was called "the Cid," which in Arabic means "lord." *Avie* "he had" < *habebat*.
- *Fabló mio Çid bien e tan mesurado* (7) "spoke my Cid well and so measured." *Fabló* "he spoke" (modern *habló*) < *fabulare* "to tell a tale."
- *"Grado a tí, señor padre, que estás en alto!"* (8) "'thanks to you, lord father, who are on high!'" *Grado* "thanks!" < *gratum* "pleasing"; compare *gratify, grateful* (also *de grado* "gladly," verse 21).
- *Esto me han buolto mios enemigos malos"* (9) "'this for-me they-have stirred-up, my enemies wicked.'" *Han buolto* "they have stirred up" < *volvere* "to turn; disturb"; compare *revolve, revolution*. *Enemigos* "enemies" < *inimicum*; compare *inimical, enemy*.

- *Allí pienssan de aguijar, allí sueltan las riendas* (10) "then they-think of spurring-on (their horses), then they-slacken the reins." *Pienssan* "they think" < *pensare* "to weigh; consider" < *pendere pensus* "to weigh"; compare *pendant, pending, dependent, pensive. Riendas* "reins" < Vulgar Latin *retinam* "bond, check" < *retinere* "to hold back"; compare *retain, retinue, rein* (English *retina* has a different source). The full sequence of changes in sound was: *retinam*, with voicing of the intervocalic *t*, > *rédina*, with loss of the post-tonic vowel, > *redna*, with interchange of the consonants, > *renda*, with diphthongization, > *rienda*.
- *A la exida de Bivar ovieron la corneja diestra* (11) "at the departure from Bivar they-had the crow on-the-right." *Exida* "departure": compare *exit.* Bivar was the city where the Cid lived. *Corneja* "crow": from the French cognate derives the surname of the French dramatist Pierre Corneille (1606–1684), one of whose most famous tragedies is, by a curious coincidence, *Le Cid. Diestra* "on the right": compare *dexterous.* A bird appearing on the right was regarded as a favorable omen, one on the left as unfavorable.
- *E entrando a Burgos oviéron-la siniestra* (12) "and, entering into Burgos, they-had it on-the-left." *Siniestra* "on the left": compare *sinister*; in the Romance languages the words indicating "right" and "left" are feminine because the noun understood with them is the feminine *manus* "hand." The Modern Spanish word for "left," *izquierda*, is not Latin at all, but a native Iberian word.
- *Meçió mio Çid los ombros y engrameó la tiesta* (13) "shrugged my Cid the shoulders and shook the head." *Ombros* "shoulders": compare *humerus.* *Tiesta* "head" < *testam* "(ceramic) pot; cranium"; *tiesta*, though used here (and in Italian *testa*, French *tête*), has in the modern language been replaced as the ordinary word by *cabeza* (see verse 2).
- *"Albricia, Álbar Fáñez, ca echados somos de tierra!"* (14) " 'Good-news!, Álvar Fáñez, for thrown-out we-are from the-land!' " *Echados* "thrown out" < *iectare.* Álvar Fáñez is the Cid's right-hand man.
- *Mas a grand ondra tornaremos a Castiella* "but with great honor we-will-return to Castile'"(14b). *Ondra* "honor" < *hon'ra* < *honorem*, with the glide consonant *d* inserted to ease pronunciation; compare *sendra* (< *sen'ra* < *seniorem*) in the second Strasbourg Oath. *Tornaremos* "we will return": the new Romance future. This verse, although not found in

the manuscript, is supplied by editors to satisfy the sense of the passage; it is based on the words of another account.

- *Mio Çid Ruy Diaz por Burgos entróve* (15) "my Cid, Ruy Díaz, through Burgos entered."

- *En sue conpaña sessaenta pendones; exien lo ver mugieres e varones* (16a and b) "in his company (were) sixty banners; they-came-out him to-see, women and men." *Conpaña* "company" is the collective noun from Late Latin *companionem* "one with whom one takes bread, companion" < *cum* "with" + *panem* "bread"; the word did not exist in Classical Latin, but was formed later by translating into Latin the elements of Germanic *gahlaiba* "mess mate," < *ga-* "with" + *hlaifs* "loaf" (compare *loaf*) – a word so created is called a "semantic calque." *Varones* "men" is also ultimately a word of Germanic origin, < *baronem* "warrior, man" (compare *baron*).

- *Burgeses e burgesas por la finiestras sone* (17) "male-town-folk and female-town-folk among the windows are." *Burgeses, burgesas* "townspeople" < Germanic *burg* "fortress, citadel; city"; compare *burgher, burgess, borough, bourgeois,* and city names like *Freiburg* and *Pittsburgh*.

- *Plorando de los ojos, tanto avien el dolore* (18) "weeping from the eyes, so-much they-had the grief." *Dolore* "grief": compare *doleful, Dolores.*

- *De las sus bocas todos dizían una razone* (19) "from the their mouths all said one opinion." *Bocas* "mouths" < *buccam* "chaps, jaw." *Razone* "opinion" < *rationem* "reason; discourse."

- *"Dios, qué buen vassallo, si oviesse buen señore!"* (20) "'God, what a-good vassal, if he-had a-good master!'" *Oviesse* < *habuisset*, pluperfect subjunctive.

- *Conbidar le ien de grado, mas ninguno non osava* (21) "invite him they-would, with pleasure, but no-one not dared." *Conbidar-ien* "they would invite": the innovating Romance conditional, composed of the infinitive plus the imperfect of the auxiliary verb *habere* "to have." With *-ien*, originating as *habebant* but with loss of the first syllable, compare *avien* "they had" (18). *Mas* "but" < *magis* "more; rather." *Ninguno non* "no one not": in Spanish, added negatives do not cancel one another, but reinforce (other instances are found in verses 25 and 30). *Osava* "he dared" < *ausare*, frequentative of *audere ausus*; compare *audacious.*

- *El rey don Alfonsso tanto avie la grand saña* (22) "the King, lord Alfonso, so-much he-had the great rage." *Don* "lord," an honorific title, < *dominum* "master"; compare *Don Quixote* and *don* (the Oxford noun). *Saña* "rage" < *insaniam* "madness"; compare *insanity*.

- *Antes de la noche en Burgos dél entró su carta* (23) "earlier than the night(fall) into Burgos of him entered his letter." *Noche* "night" < *noctem*; compare *nocturnal*. *Dél* = *de* "of" + *él* "him." *Carta* "letter, epistle" < *chartam* "(roll of) paper"; compare *chart, charter, card*.

- *Con grand recabdo e fuertemientre sellada* (24) "with strong injunction and firmly sealed." The latter detail emphasizes the authoritativeness of the King's order.

- *Que a mio Çid Ruy Díaz, que nadi nol diessen posada* (25) "that to my Cid, Ruy Díaz, that nobody not to-him they-give lodging." *Nadi* "nobody" has a remarkable etymology. It comes from *nati* "born" (compare *natal, native, nature*) as used in the phrase *homines nati* "men born," which was an emphatic, colorful way of saying "absolutely everybody," rather like "every mother's son among them." The phrase was often employed with a negative: *non homines nati* "no men born," that is, "nobody." In time, *homines* was dropped, and *nadi* (< *nati*) came to be understood, even without the negative, as "nobody." *Nol* = *no* "not" + *le* "to him." *Diessen*: past subjunctive in an indirect command. *Posada* "lodging" < Late Latin *pausare* "to stop, stay" < Greek *pauein*; compare *pause, menopause*.

- *E aquel que gela diesse sopiesse vera palabra* (26) "and that-one who to-him it should-give, that-he-know (this) true word," that is, that he know for certain. *Gela* = *ge* "to him" + *la* "it" (lodging). *Sopiesse* < *sapere* "to know." *Vera* "true": compare *verity, verify, very, Vera*. *Palabra* "word," with interchange of the consonants, < Greek *parabola* "comparison; parable; phrase"; compare Italian *parola*, French *parole* "word."

- *Que perderie los averes e más los ojos de la cara* (27) "that he-would-lose the possessions and, more, the eyes of the face." *Perderie* "he would lose," conditional, < *perdere* "to destroy, lose"; compare *perdition*. *Averes* "possessions" < *habere* "to have," the infinitive used as a noun. *Cara* "face" < Greek *kara* "head."

- *E aun demás los cuerpos e las almas* (28) "and even in-addition the bodies and the souls." *Almas* "souls," with dissimilation and loss of the post-tonic vowel, < *ánimam*; compare *animate, animal*.

- *Grande duelo avien las yentes cristianas* (29) "great grief they-had, the folks Christian." *Yentes* "folks" < *gentem* "tribe, people"; compare *gentile, gentle*.

- *Ascónden-se de mio Çid, ca nol osan dezir nada* (30) "they-hide themselves from my Cid, for not to-him they-dare to-say nothing." *Nol* = *no* "not" + *le* "to him." The etymology of *nada* "nothing" is parallel to that of *nadi* "nobody" (verse 25). *Rem natam,* literally "the thing born," meaning "the matter in question," also got used often in negative sentences; the noun *rem* dropped out; and *nada* (< *natam*), standing on its own and without the negative, became understood as "nothing." In other words, Latin *(rem) natam non fecerunt* "they did not do the matter in question" > Spanish *nada no hicieron* "they did nothing" > *nada hicieron.*

The Big Picture

Two orthographic novelties that strike the eye in reading this passage are the *n* with the swung mark, called tilde, over it (*ñ*) and the *c* with the hook, called cedilla, beneath it (*ç*). The first, as in *señor* "lord," indicates the sound of *n* followed by yod, /ny/, and is still used in Spanish. The other, as in *Çid* and *uços* "doors," shows that the *c* is to be pronounced /s/; it is no longer used in Spanish, but is in French (for instance, in *français* "French").

A number of the phonological features in which the language of this text has diverged from Latin are familiar. Palatalization: *dezir* "to say" (30) < *dicere,* in which the /k/ sound of Classical Latin has become /ts/. Interchanges of consonants: *riendas* "reins" (10) < *rednas; palabra* "word" (26) < *parabolam.* Intervocalic voiceless plosives that have turned into their voiced equivalents: *mudados* "molted" (5) < *mutatum; enemigos* "enemies" (9) < *inimicum; cabeça* "head" (2) < *capittiam.* In this late-twelfth or early-thirteenth century Castilian text, initial *f-* has not yet changed to *h-: falcones* "falcons" (5) and *fabló* "he spoke" (7), which may be contrasted with modern *halcones* and *habló.*

Mudados "molted" (5) < *mutatum* offered a double example of intervocalic *t* becoming *d*. It turns out that a number of familiar English words originating in Spanish contain the same change: *armada* < Spanish *armada* < Latin *armata* "armed" (*army,* entering English through French, is akin, and *armadillo* is a diminutive of *armado* "an armed man"), *desperado* (still preserving the Spanish ending), *renegade, esplanade* (via French), the geographic names *Colorado* "red," *Nevada* "snowy," and *El Dorado* "the gilded (country)," and the western American *hoosegow* "jail" (< *juzga'o* < *juzgado* "panel of judges, court" < Latin *iudicatum* – the loss of *d* in *juzga'o* reflects some speakers' tendency to drop intervocalic *d*, as happened regularly in French).

One feature that marks the language here as different from Latin and, to some extent, different also from French and Italian, is the prominence of diphthongs. In a mere six verses, 9–14, eight instances occur: *buolto* "stirred up" < *voltum*; *pienssan* "they think" < *pensan*; *sueltan* "they slacken" < *soltan*; *riendas* "reins" < *rendas*; *diestra* "right" < *dextra*; *siniestra* "left" < *sinestra*; *tiesta* "head" < *testa*; *tierra* "earth" < *terra*.

In regard to verb forms, this passage of the *Cid*, unlike the Glosas, no longer shows signs of Latin's third person singular ending *-t*: *tornava* "he was turning" (2), *vío* "he saw" (3) – contrast *venot* "he came" (Emil. 9). The third person plural always ends in *-n*, never in *-nt* (*pienssan* "they think," 10). We find examples here of all the great Romance innovations: the compound perfect (*han buolto* "they have stirred up," 9); the analytic passive (*echados somos* "we are exiled," 14); the future built on the infinitive (*tornaremos* "we will return," 14b); the conditional, likewise (*perderie* "he would lose," 27, and *conbidar le yen* "they would invite him," 21); and – one we have not met an instance of before – the progressive tense, made by combining the verb "to be" with the present participle (*estava catando* "he was looking at," 2).

The subjunctive is still used as it had been in Latin, to express contrary-to-fact conditions (*si oviesse buen señor* "if only he had a good master," 20), in noun clauses conveying an indirect command (*que nadi nol diessen posada* "that nobody give him lodging," 25, dependent on *recabdo* "injunction"), in generalizing clauses (*aquel que gela diesse* "whoever should give it to him," 26).

Like the Glosas, the passage well illustrates the variety of languages other than Latin that fed vocabulary into Romance: Celtic (*vassallo* "vassal," 20), Germanic (*varones* "men," 16, and *burgeses, burgesas* "townspeople," 17, with influence also exerted on the Latinate *conpaña* "company," 16), and Arabic (*alcándaras* "pegs, perches," 4, and *albricia* "good news!," 14, not to mention *Çid* itself).

Literary Appreciation

The poetic form of this epic narrative is defined by two features, the structure of the individual verse and the presence of rhyme. Each verse is constituted of two half-lines. Each half-line is about seven syllables long, although the actual number can range between five and ten; the second half is most often longer than the first. Each verse tends to be syntactically complete in itself, with no enjambment, as you can verify by running your eye down the right-hand margin and noting that every verse save one finishes with some mark of punctuation. Each half-line, moreover, tends to be a discrete syntactic unit (subject, predicate, object, prepositional or participial phrase, etc.). These features impart a rather monotonous rhythm to the narrative, since all units of sense are nearly the same length. Verses 17–20 may serve for example:

- *Burgeses e burgesas / por las finiestras sone* "townspeople, men and women / were at the windows": 7 syllables + 7; subject / verb with modifier.
- *Plorando de los ojos, / tanto avien el dolore*: "weeping from their eyes / they had great grief": 7 + 8; participial phrase / verb with object.
- *De las sus bocas / todos dizían una razone* "from their mouths / all said one opinion": 5 + 10; prepositional phrase / verb with subject and object.
- *"Dios, qué buen vassallo, / si oviesse buen señore!"* "'God, what a good vassal / if he had a good master'": 7 + 8; main clause / dependent clause.

The rhyme in the *Cid* is assonant, with the last two vowels matching throughout a sequence of verses. In the first nine lines of our selection, for instance, each final word ends with the vowels *a* and *o*: *llorando, catando, cañados, mantos*, etc. In the lines just quoted, the vowels are *o* and *e*: *sone, dolore, razone, señore*. Each such rhymed sequence acts like a stanza.

The boundedness of the individual verses gives to the poem its characteristic texture. It can create a stark and forceful brevity, as when the journey from Bivar to Burgos is condensed into a single line: "then they thought of spurring on the horses, then they gave them their head" (10). That line is also an example of the poet's saying in effect the same thing twice, though in different language. He does that again with "open gates and doors without padlocks" (3) and "women and men, male and female townspeople" (16–17). At the same time, successive half-lines and lines are linked – and the forward movement of the poem promoted – by the simple rhetoric of opposite or contrasting terms: "spurs ... reins" (10), "on the right ... on the left" (11–12), "entered ... came out" (15–16), "women and men" (16), "eyes ... mouths" (18–19), "vassal ... lord" (20), "bodies and souls" (28). And, like any great narrator, the poet has an eye for the telling detail, such as the empty perches in the Cid's palace, which bring to mind the recent past, when the hero could enjoy the leisurely, aristocratic, and, in a sense, warlike sport of falconry.

As long as the *Cid* is studied, so long will it be associated with the name of an extraordinary Spanish scholar, Ramón Menéndez Pidal (1869–1968). His combination of philological, literary, and historical erudition has been a model and an inspiration to countless others, including the renowned Peruvian scholar (and centenarian), Estuardo Núñez. While in his twenties, Menéndez Pidal prepared a magisterial edition of the *Cid*, eventually published in three volumes, which was awarded a prize from the Royal Spanish Academy of the Language and is still consulted, still valued today. (Later, he served as president of the Academy during several turbulent decades.) For the rest of his long life he continued to publish studies of the poem and of many related literary and historical problems. Running the risk of limiting his polymathy, I might say that his principal drive as a scholar was to search out documents that illuminated the origins of the Spanish nation, and so his chief interest naturally lay in the Middle Ages.

Yet Menéndez Pidal's connection to the *Cid* had a personal side as well: the sole manuscript that preserves the epic, now in the National Library, in Madrid, formerly belonged to his family!

Working in a more purely philological vein, Menéndez Pidal also elucidated our other early Spanish documents, the Glosas Emilianenses and Silenses. In a ground-breaking study, he was the first to publish those texts accurately, and the first to mine them thoroughly for nuggets of knowledge about the earliest stages of the language. His researches, publications, and teaching in the field of history were no less vast and influential. In America, he had close ties to Columbia University: a series of lectures he gave there was the basis for a book on Spanish romances; he helped create an institute devoted to Spanish studies at the university; and while taking refuge from the Spanish Civil War, he taught for a while at Columbia and there composed his history of the Spanish language.

Well beyond the particular contributions he made to our understanding of the Glosas and the *Cid*, Menéndez Pidal exemplifies the ideal scholar of Romance.

Epilogue: Latin – the River and the Well

The Latin language is like a great river. Small in its beginnings, hardly more than a brook, it saw its waters swell immeasurably over the course of the years. It gradually branched into a number of streams, some of which became in turn great rivers themselves. One of those streams, French, at a certain point overflowed its banks, so to speak, and poured into the stream of English, which had arisen in an altogether different watershed, that of the Germanic languages. This simile, which is intended to bring out the unbroken continuity between successive stages of the language, could aptly be applied to many other languages.

In another regard, however, Latin is markedly different from other languages, for it also resembles a well. In its Classical form, it has remained unchanging, ever pure and fresh, always available as a source of sustenance or inspiration. At virtually every stage of its later history, speakers and writers availed themselves of this inexhaustible resource. Whether they were seeking a word for something new or attempting to reform grammar or spelling, they continued to draw water from the well. (In a similar fashion, and linked to the language, Latin literature and Roman history were also nearly always present as models for later generations.) This is the feature that makes the evolution of Latin into the Romance languages – and its entry into English – a unique story: the constant presence and employment of Classical Latin alongside the vernacular.

Many European languages have splendid, fascinating histories. Nevertheless, no other shares this feature with Latin. Whatever the turns that English, Slavic, Celtic, and the others took in the course of the centuries, they lacked an equivalent to Classical Latin; they never had an idealized form to look back to as a model and source of innovation. For Edmund Spenser, speaking personally, Chaucer was the "well of English undefiled." Classical Latin, for all later western civilization, was no less precious a well.

And here we come upon a final likeness between the Romance languages and English: each one is a hybrid, with a hybrid's typical sturdiness. English is blended from two stocks, the Germanic and the Romance, whose kinship with each other is remote. The Romance languages also are a blend, but a blend of the vernacular with the classical, of the derivative with the source, two versions of one self, which is the Latin language.

Latin, then, perhaps because of its double existence as both river and well, has come to occupy the conspicuous and important place it does in our world. As I reflect on this, I'm put in mind of a comment made back at the beginning of my teaching career by a student of elementary Latin, who wrote: "Latin has engulfed me all my life, and I'm amazed that only now have I come to realize it!" Perhaps that will have proven to be true for you as well.

SUGGESTIONS FOR FURTHER READING

All the following are accessible to the reader of this book.

Histories of the Latin language, from ancient times to the present: Tore Janson, *A Natural History of Latin*, transl. Merethe Damsgard Sorensen and Nigel Vincent (Oxford, 2004); Nicholas Ostler, *Ad Infinitum: A Biography of Latin* (New York, 2007).

On Indo-European: Calvert Watkins, ed., *The American Heritage Dictionary of Indo-European Roots*, 2nd ed., (Boston and New York, 2000), also found as an appendix to that dictionary.

On Vulgar Latin: József Herman, *Vulgar Latin*, transl. Roger Wright (University Park, 2000).

On the Romance languages: Rebecca Posner, *The Romance Languages: A Linguistic Introduction* (Garden City, 1966); Peter Boyd-Bowman, *From Latin to Romance in Sound Charts* (Washington, 1954); Mario Pei, *The Story of Latin and the Romance Languages* (New York, 1976).

English etymological dictionaries: Robert K. Barnhart, ed., *The Barnhart Dictionary of Etymology* (New York, 1988); Ernest Klein, *A Comprehensive Etymological Dictionary of the English Language* (Amsterdam, 1971); C. T. Onions, ed., *The Oxford Dictionary of English Etymology* (New York, 1966).

On the histories of English words: [Frederick C. Mish, ed.] *Webster's Dictionary of Word Origins* (Springfield, MA, 1989); James Bradstreet Greenough and George Lyman Kittredge, *Words and Their Ways in English Speech* (Boston, 1900; reprinted); Louis Heller, Alexander Humez, and Malcah Dror, *The Private Lives of English Words* (London, 1984); Geoffrey Hughes, *Words in Time: A Social History of the English Vocabulary* (Oxford, 1988), and *A History of English Words* (Oxford, 2000); Owen Barfield, *History in English Words*, rev. ed. (Grand Rapids, 1967).

GENERAL INDEX

inherited forms in Romance languages,
247–54
innovating forms in Romance languages,
255–60
irregular, 160, 254–55, 319
moods, 85–86, 102–5, 246, 250
number, 76–77, 84
participles, 87–88, 94–96, 97, 98, 250–54,
318
personal endings, 89–90, 91, 298
progressive forms, 260
pronominal (reflexive), 280, 284, 317–18
"shoe" verbs, 249
syntax, 101–5, 261, 284
tenses, 84, 101–2, 246
voices, 85, 246, 255–56
See also ablative absolute
Visigoths, 40–42, 189

vowels, 63, 80, 207–9, 211
Vulgate, 164, 173

Welsh, 10, 50
word histories, 20–21, 44–45, 131–33, 156–57,
158–59, 171, Chapters 7–10
commonness, 167–71
convenience, 159–61
distinctiveness, 161–63
doublets, 25–26, 171, 176–80, 220–21,
286–87
folk etymology, 162–63, 171, 216
intensity, color, 165–67, 319
matrix, 140–42, 280
monosyllables avoided, 163–65
redundancy, 156
semantic shift, 133–43
word order, 58, 238, 241, 273, 285, 287, 299

INDEX OF ENGLISH WORDS

This index includes not only English words (*bus*, *corn*, and *precarious*, for example), but also elements of English words (*mis-*, *-ify*, *-wick*), proper nouns (*Audi*, *Herbert*, *Manchester*), words and phrases from both Latin (*vice versa*, *habeas corpus*), and other foreign languages (*trompe l'oeil*, *fortissimo*) that are likely to be familiar to many English speakers, abbreviations (*lb.*, *etc.*), and, in italics, the names of works of art (*Rio Bravo*, *Déjeuner sur l'herbe*, *Trovatore*) – always provided that the text conveys something of interest about such items, most often, their origin.

judicial, 298
junior, 73

kennel, 19
kirk, 183
Kryptonite, 179

Lancaster, 33
lance, 223
Langue d'Oc, 45
Langue d'Oïl, 45
lapsus, 69
lapsus calami, 65
lapsus linguae, 63
lariat, 193
Las Vegas, 185
laud(able), 302
laundry, 101, 318
lavabo, 90, 318
lavatory, 318
lave, 318
lb., 79
league, 220
lectern, 88
lecture, 88
leg, 131
legal, 179
legend, 88, 100
legible, 88
lemon, 191
leniency, 95
lethal, 131
leveret, 218
levitate, 160
levity, 160
liaison, 220
libretto, 150
lick, 11
lien, 220
lieu(tenant), 220
ligature, 220
linguine, 150

llama, 195, 205
local, 220
locate, 220
loquacious, 166
Louis, 272
love, 131
low, 131
loyal, 179
luminous, 303
lunar, 303
lunatic, 303
luncheonette, 150

madame, 76
madonna, 76
maestro, 294
magazine, 191
magnificent, 168
magnitude, 168
maize, 195
major, 75
majority, 75
Manchester, 33
mandamus, 89
mandate, 314
mandible, 168
maneuver, 288
manor, 136
manse, 136
mansion, 136, 279
manufacture, 279, 314
marble, 117
march, 311–12
mare, 170
margin, 312
mark, 312
marshal, 170
martyr, 183
marvel, 116
Mary, 217
mass, 182
mater, alma, 304